Now, let's go!!

You—Me Purchase—in—Force Model

Full Armor Fuuko

The season I love the most is autumn. It's an easy season to be in, the scenery can be both peaceful and melancholy, and dishes with matsutake mushrooms are delicious.

What seasons do you all love? Fun fact: the old Fuuko loved winter. It allowed her to escape suspicion since she normally dresses in layers, meaning she would have a slightly easier time going outside. Apparently, she is a fan of summer now.

Yoshifumi Tozuka made his manga debut with the one-shot *Uchuu Kankou C-Arc* (Cosmic Arc Travel), which was published in *Jump Next!* in May 2014. *Undead Unluck*, his first series, began serialization in *Weekly Shonen Jump* in January 2020.

UNDEAD UNLUCK

Volume 6
Shonen Jump Edition

STORY AND ART BY
Yoshifumi Tozuka

Translation: **David Evelyn**
Touch-Up Art & Lettering: **Michelle Pang**
Design: **Kam Li**
Shonen Jump Series Editor: **Karla Clark**
Graphic Novel Editors: **Amy Yu**, **Karla Clark**

UNDEAD UNLUCK © 2020 by Yoshifumi Tozuka
All rights reserved.
First published in Japan in 2020 by SHUEISHA Inc., Tokyo.
English translation rights arranged by SHUEISHA Inc.

The stories, characters, and incidents mentioned in this
publication are entirely fictional.

Printed in Canada

Published by VIZ Media, LLC
P.O. Box 77010
San Francisco, CA 94107

10 9 8 7 6 5 4 3 2 1
First printing, March 2022

PARENTAL ADVISORY
UNDEAD UNLUCK is rated T+ for Older Teen
and is recommended for ages 16 and up. This
volume contains suggestive themes, crude
humor, and violence.

viz.com

UNDEAD UNLUCK

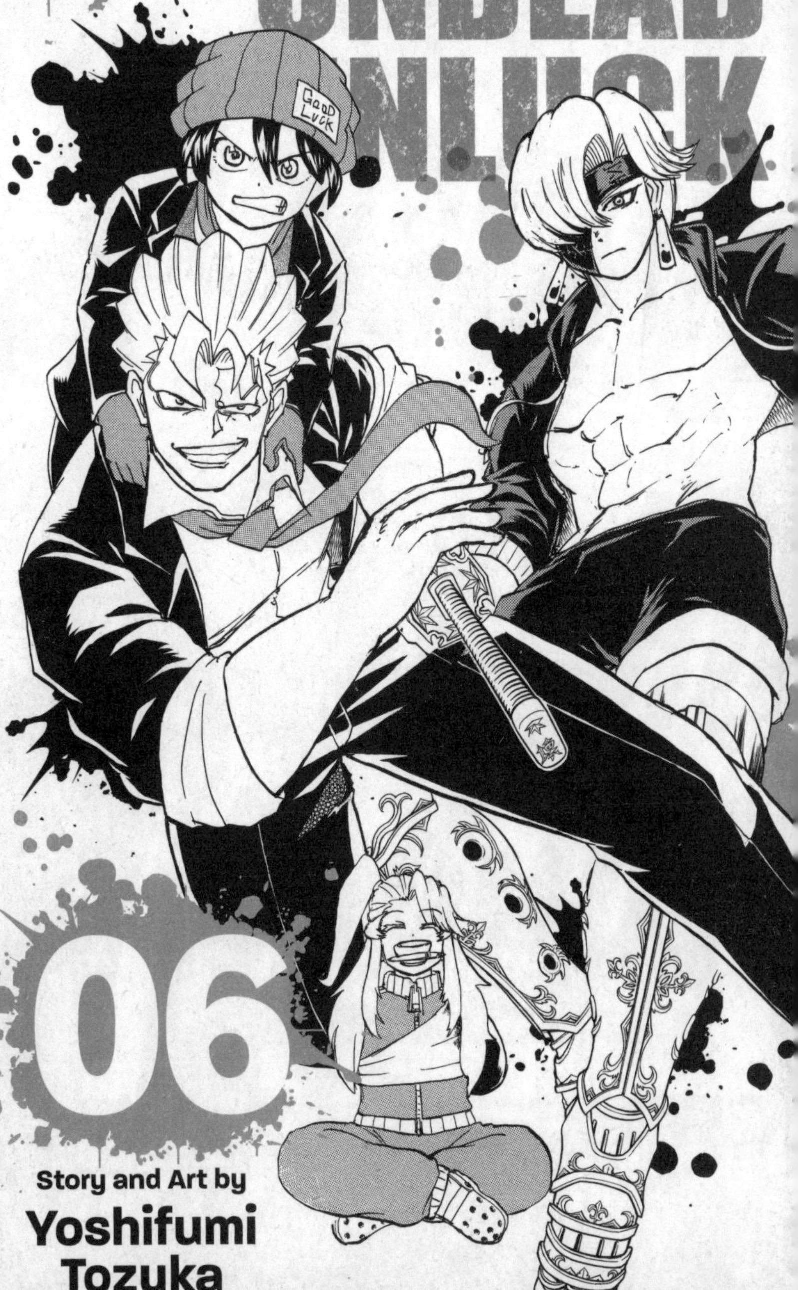
GOOD LUCK

06

Story and Art by
Yoshifumi Tozuka

CHARACTER

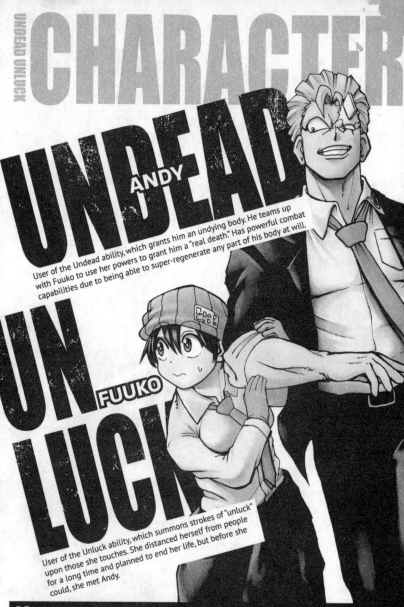

UNDEAD
ANDY

User of the Undead ability, which grants him an undying body. He teams up with Fuuko to use her powers to grant him a "real death." Has powerful combat capabilities due to being able to super-regenerate any part of his body at will.

UNLUCK
FUUKO

User of the Unluck ability, which summons strokes of "unluck" upon those she touches. She distanced herself from people for a long time and planned to end her life, but before she could, she met Andy.

STORY

Fuuko consigned herself to death due to her body's ability to inadvertently bring misfortune—called "unluck"—to those she touches. However, after meeting Andy, a mysterious man with an undying body, she gained the will to live. During their journey, they learn about the Union, an organization that polices UMA (unidentified mysterious animals) and unexplainable phenomena. After defeating enough of the Union's members to join their ranks, Andy and Fuuko discover the true purpose for the organization's existence—to rebel against God and overcome his quests. Andy and Fuuko visit the author of a book of prophecy, Anno Un. There, they run into the UMA Autumn and are defeated, realizing they are woefully unprepared to take it on. To strengthen Fuuko, Anno Un sends her into Andy's past, but that's where Fuuko's life is targeted—by Andy's alter ego, Victor!

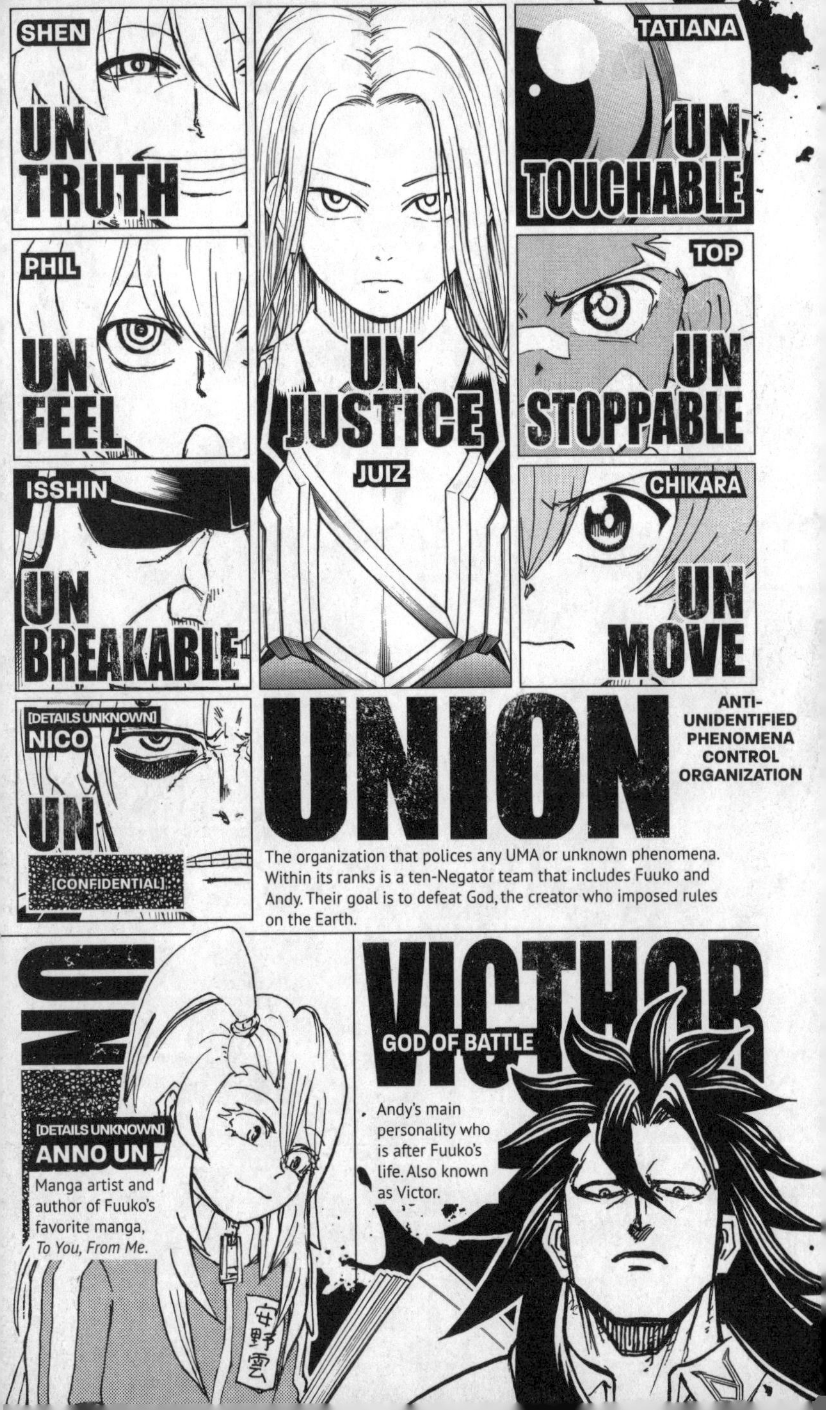
TATIANA
UN TOUCHABLE
TOP
UN STOPPABLE
CHIKARA
UN MOVE
UN JUSTICE
JUIZ
SHEN
UN TRUTH
PHIL
UN FEEL
ISSHIN
UN BREAKABLE
UNION
ANTI-UNIDENTIFIED PHENOMENA CONTROL ORGANIZATION
The organization that polices any UMA or unknown phenomena. Within its ranks is a ten-Negator team that includes Fuuko and Andy. Their goal is to defeat God, the creator who imposed rules on the Earth.
[DETAILS UNKNOWN]
NICO
UN
[CONFIDENTIAL]
VICTOR
GOD OF BATTLE
Andy's main personality who is after Fuuko's life. Also known as Victor.
UN
[DETAILS UNKNOWN]
ANNO UN
Manga artist and author of Fuuko's favorite manga, *To You, From Me*.
安野雲

UNDEAD UNLUCK

06

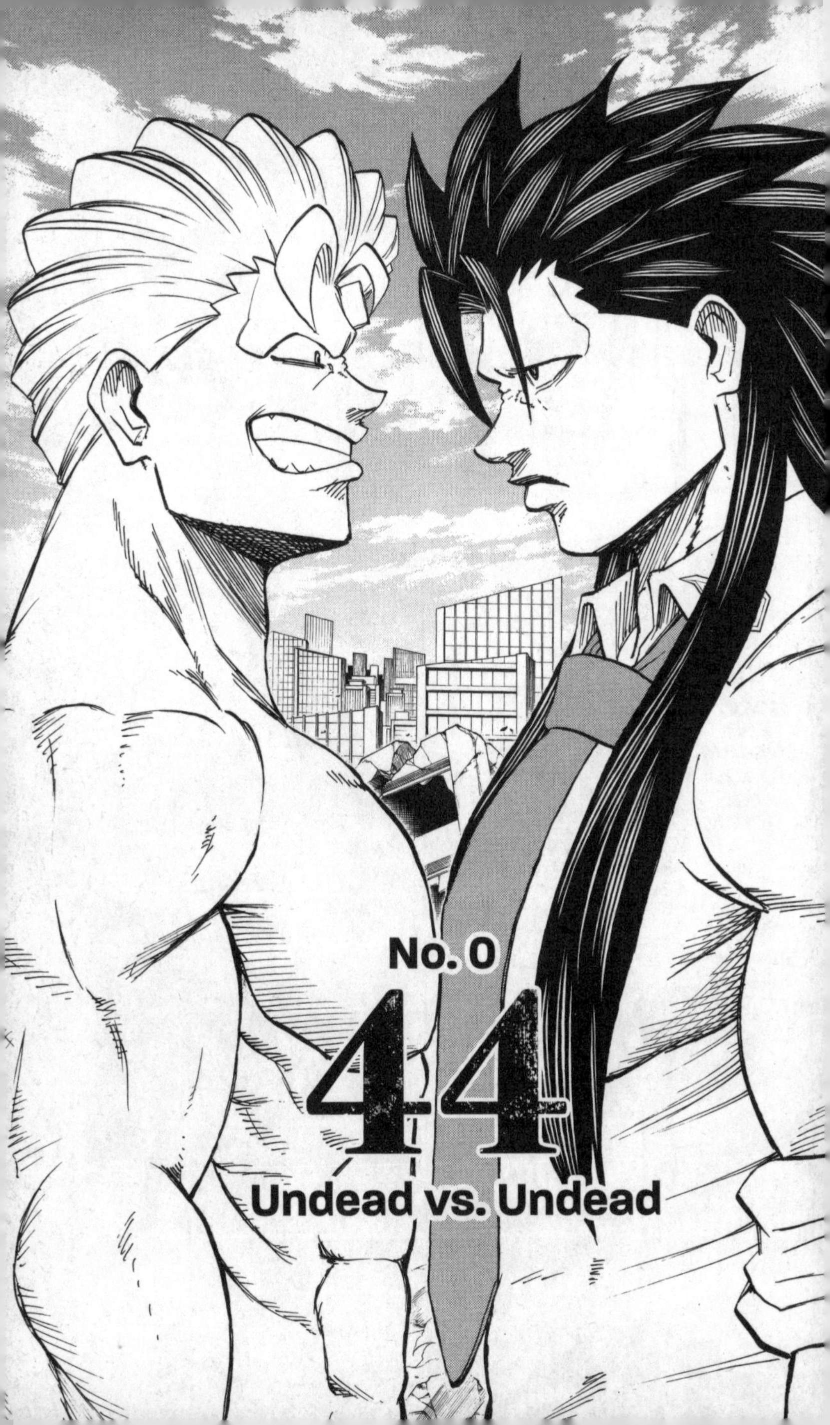
No. 044
Undead vs. Undead

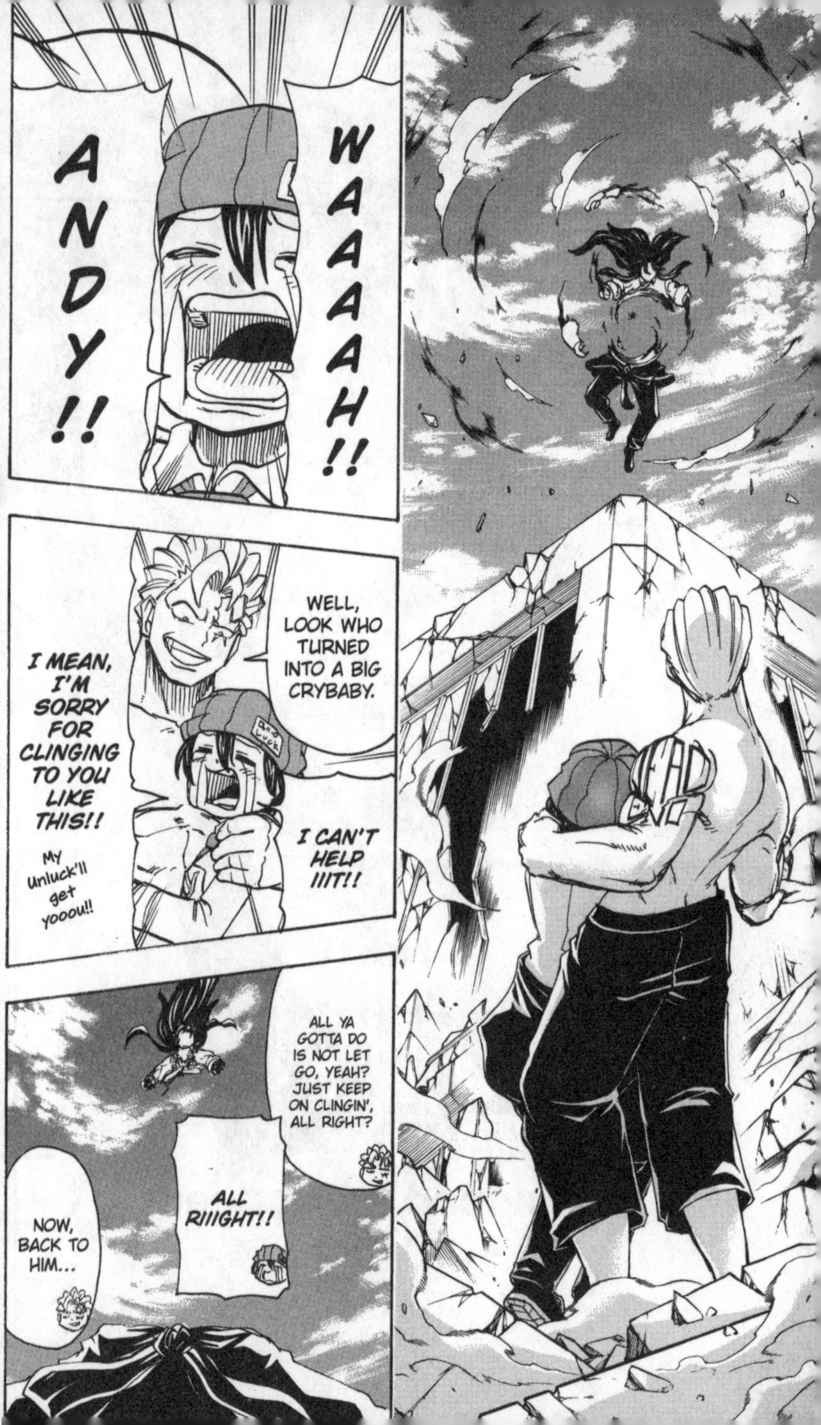
WAAAAAH!!
ANDY!!
WELL, LOOK WHO TURNED INTO A BIG CRYBABY.
I CAN'T HELP IIIT!!
I MEAN, I'M SORRY FOR CLINGING TO YOU LIKE THIS!!
My Unluck'll get yooou!!
ALL YA GOTTA DO IS NOT LET GO, YEAH? JUST KEEP ON CLINGIN', ALL RIGHT?
ALL RIIIGHT!!
NOW, BACK TO HIM...

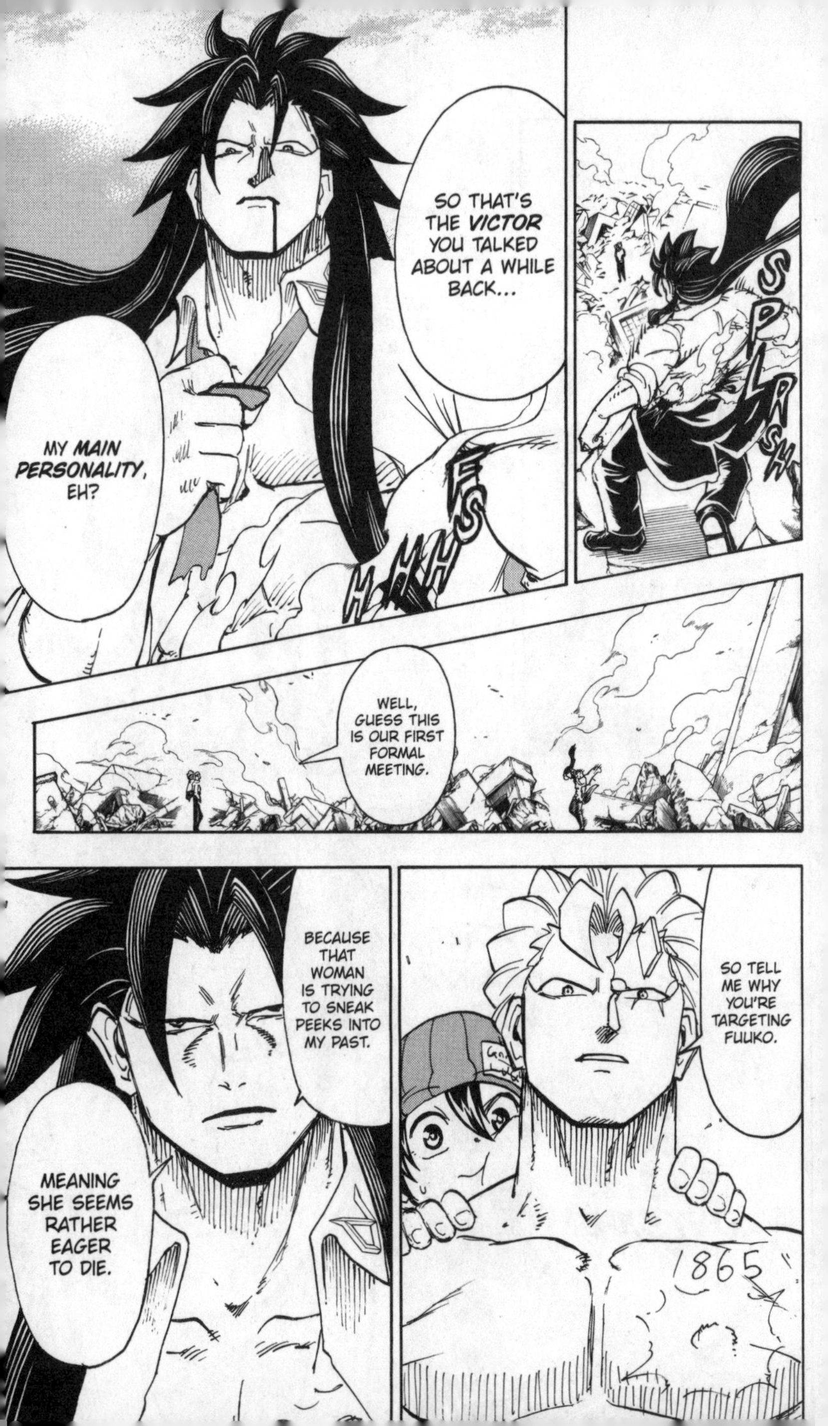
SPLRSH
SO THAT'S THE *VICTOR* YOU TALKED ABOUT A WHILE BACK...
MY *MAIN PERSONALITY*, EH?
FSHHHH
WELL, GUESS THIS IS OUR FIRST FORMAL MEETING.
SO TELL ME WHY YOU'RE TARGETING FUUKO.
BECAUSE THAT WOMAN IS TRYING TO SNEAK PEEKS INTO MY PAST.
MEANING SHE SEEMS RATHER EAGER TO DIE.

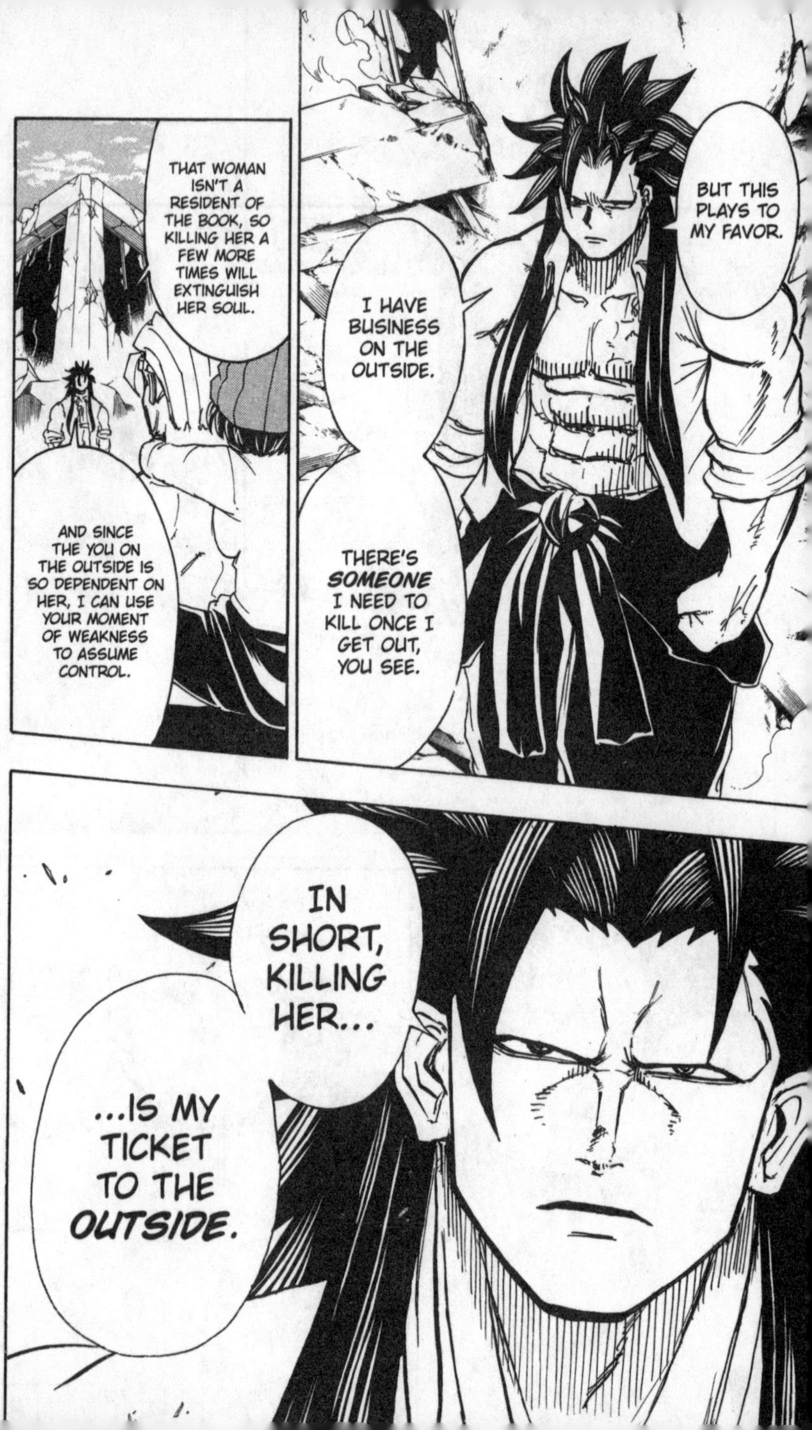
BUT THIS PLAYS TO MY FAVOR.
I HAVE BUSINESS ON THE OUTSIDE.
THERE'S *SOMEONE* I NEED TO KILL ONCE I GET OUT, YOU SEE.
THAT WOMAN ISN'T A RESIDENT OF THE BOOK, SO KILLING HER A FEW MORE TIMES WILL EXTINGUISH HER SOUL.
AND SINCE THE YOU ON THE OUTSIDE IS SO DEPENDENT ON HER, I CAN USE YOUR MOMENT OF WEAKNESS TO ASSUME CONTROL.
IN SHORT, KILLING HER...
...IS MY TICKET TO THE *OUTSIDE*.

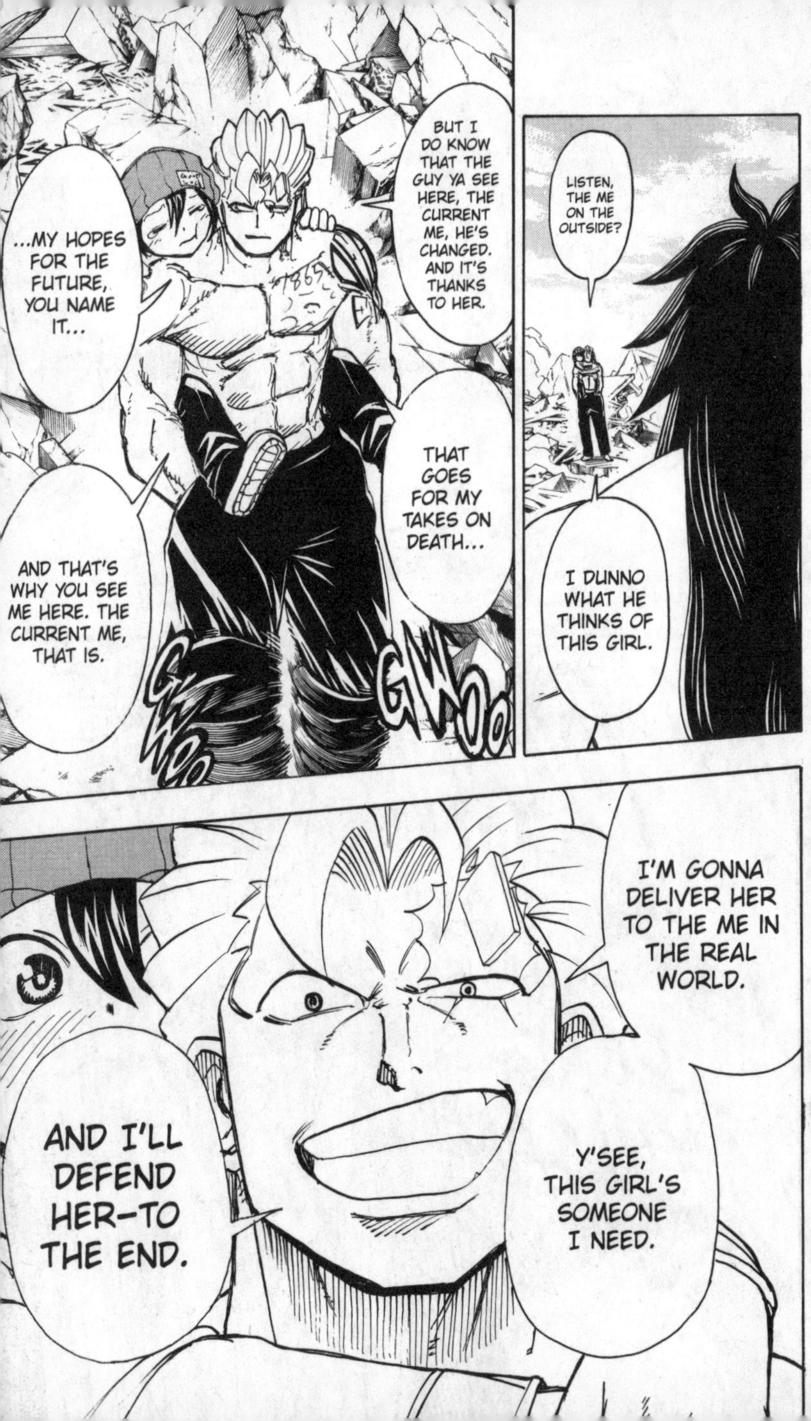
LISTEN, THE ME ON THE OUTSIDE?
I DUNNO WHAT HE THINKS OF THIS GIRL.
BUT I DO KNOW THAT THE GUY YA SEE HERE, THE CURRENT ME, HE'S CHANGED. AND IT'S THANKS TO HER.
...MY HOPES FOR THE FUTURE, YOU NAME IT...
THAT GOES FOR MY TAKES ON DEATH...
AND THAT'S WHY YOU SEE ME HERE. THE CURRENT ME, THAT IS.
GWOO
GWOO
I'M GONNA DELIVER HER TO THE ME IN THE REAL WORLD.
Y'SEE, THIS GIRL'S SOMEONE I NEED.
AND I'LL DEFEND HER—TO THE END.

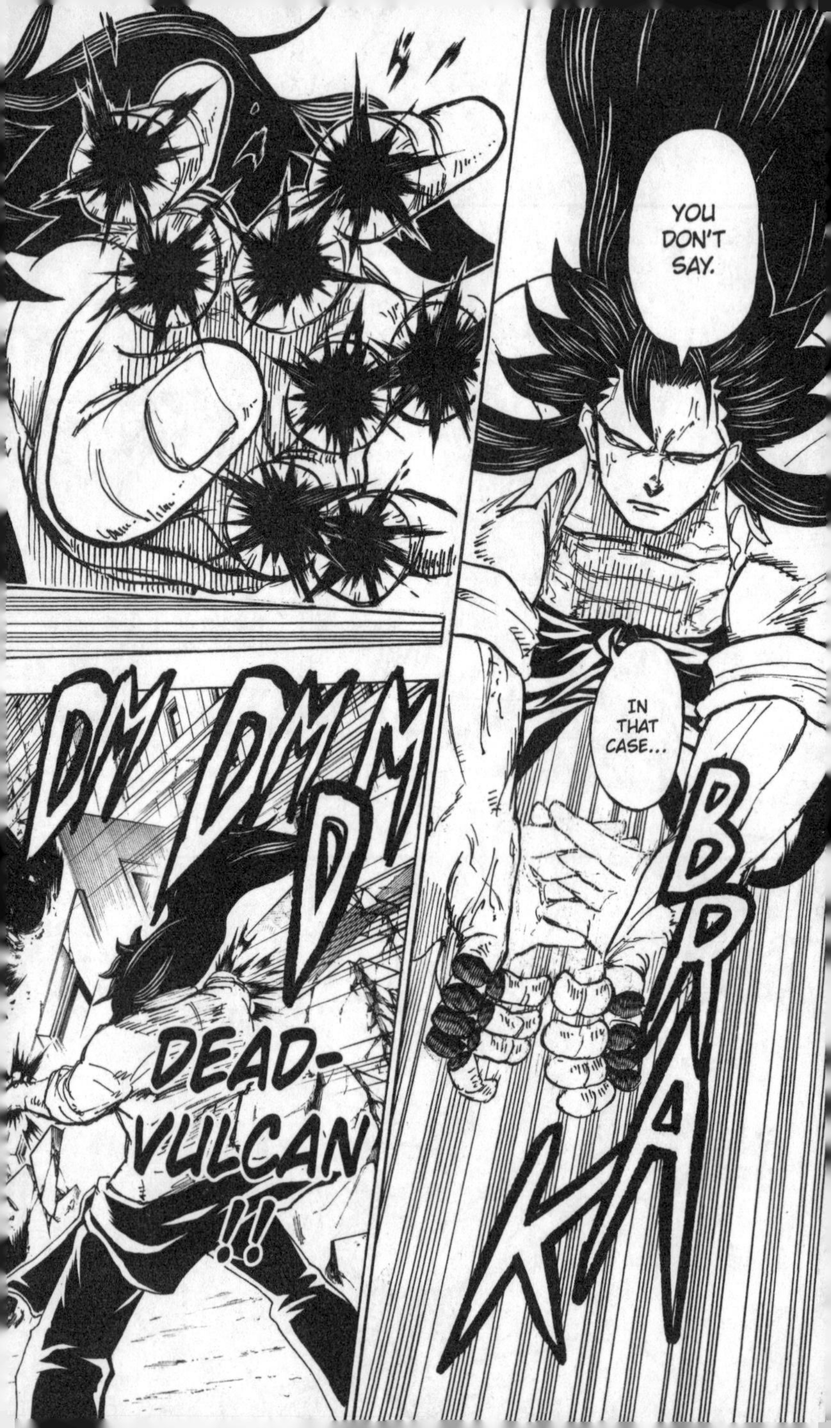
YOU DON'T SAY.
IN THAT CASE...
BRAKA
DM DMM DM
DEAD-VULCAN!!

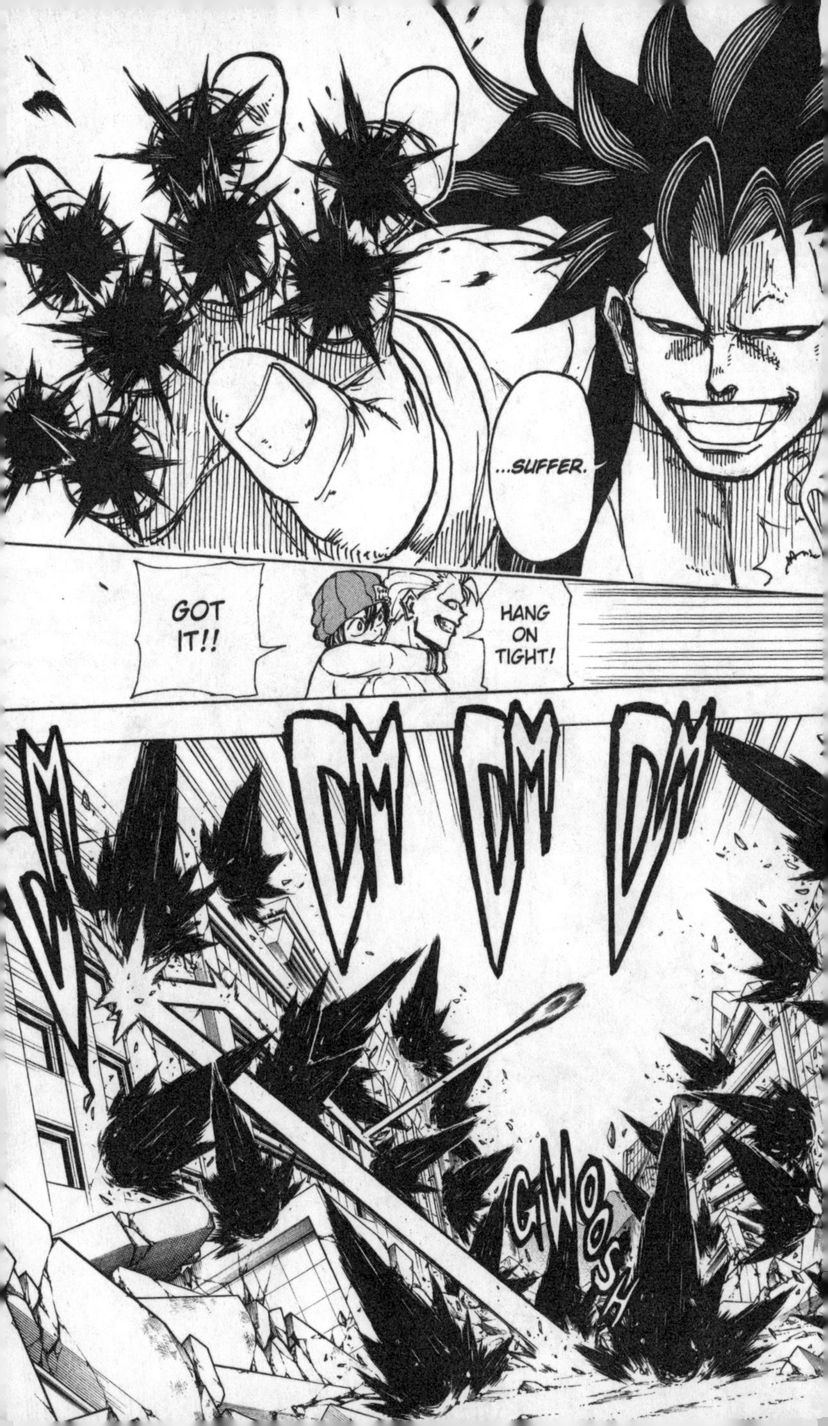

...SUFFER.
HANG ON TIGHT!
GOT IT!!
DM DM DM DM
GWOOSH

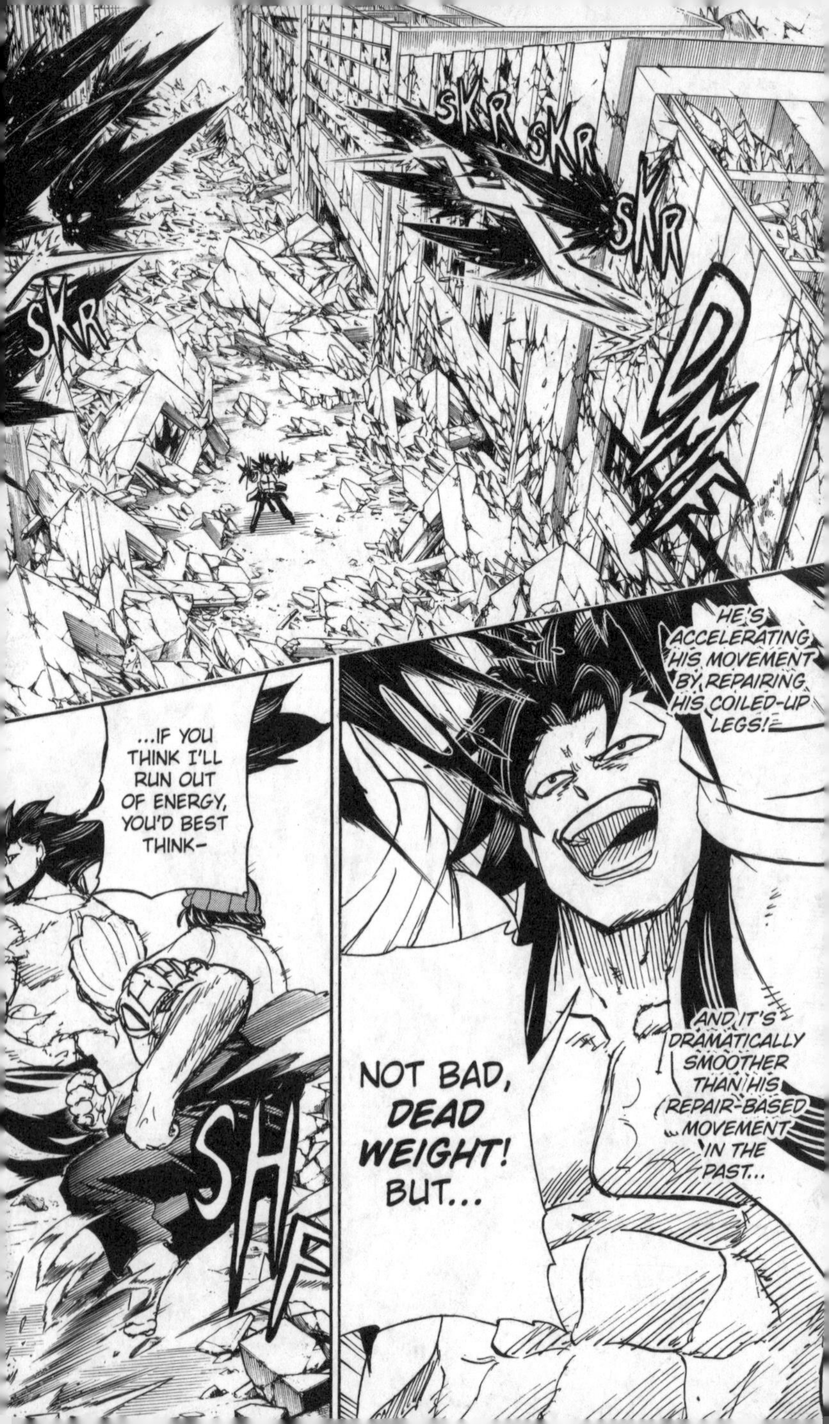
SKR SKR SKR
SKR
HE'S ACCELERATING HIS MOVEMENT BY REPAIRING HIS COILED-UP LEGS!
AND IT'S DRAMATICALLY SMOOTHER THAN HIS REPAIR-BASED MOVEMENT IN THE PAST...
NOT BAD, *DEAD WEIGHT!* BUT...
...IF YOU THINK I'LL RUN OUT OF ENERGY, YOU'D BEST THINK–
SHF

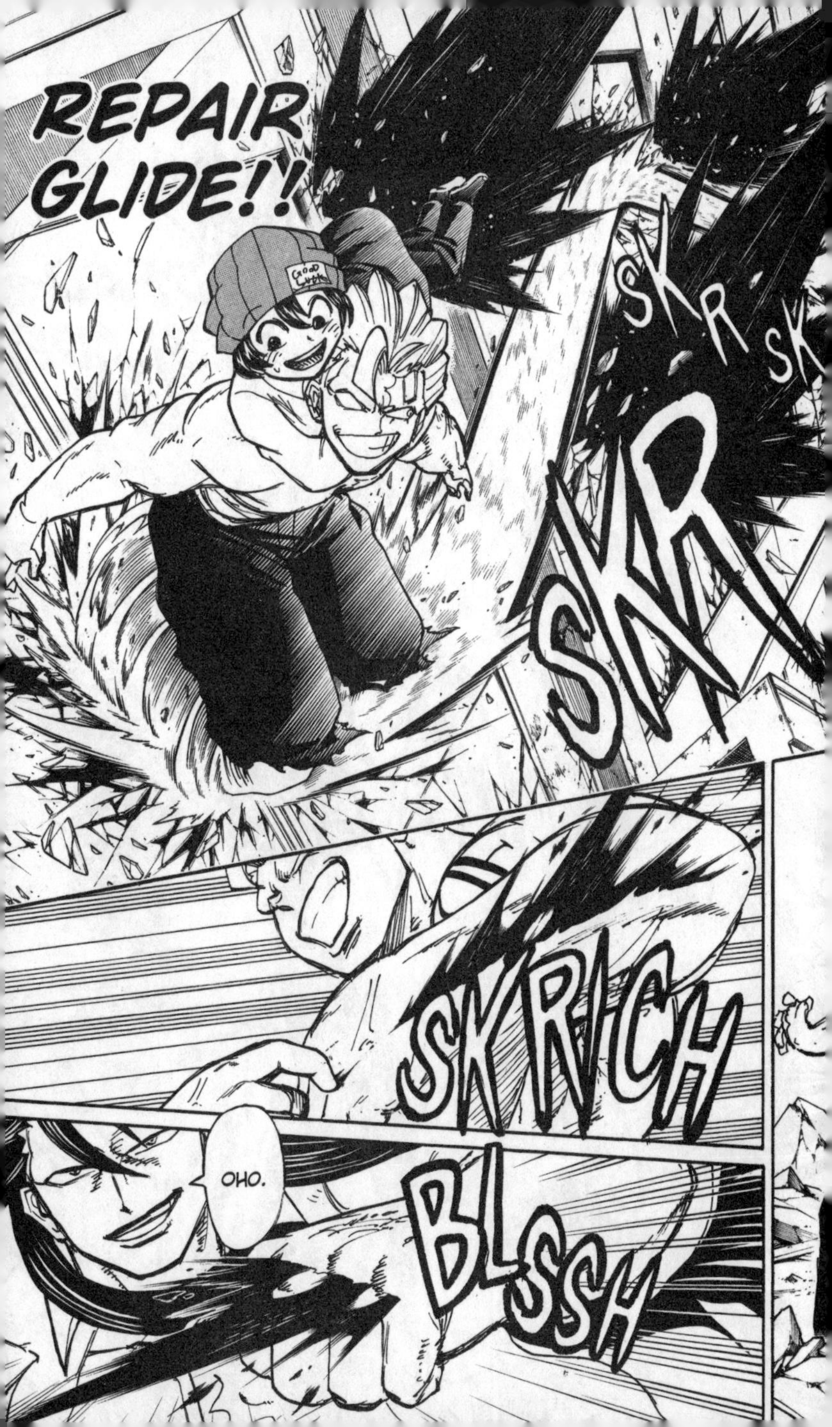

SK R SK
SKR
REPAIR GLIDE!!
SKRICH
OHO.
BLSSH

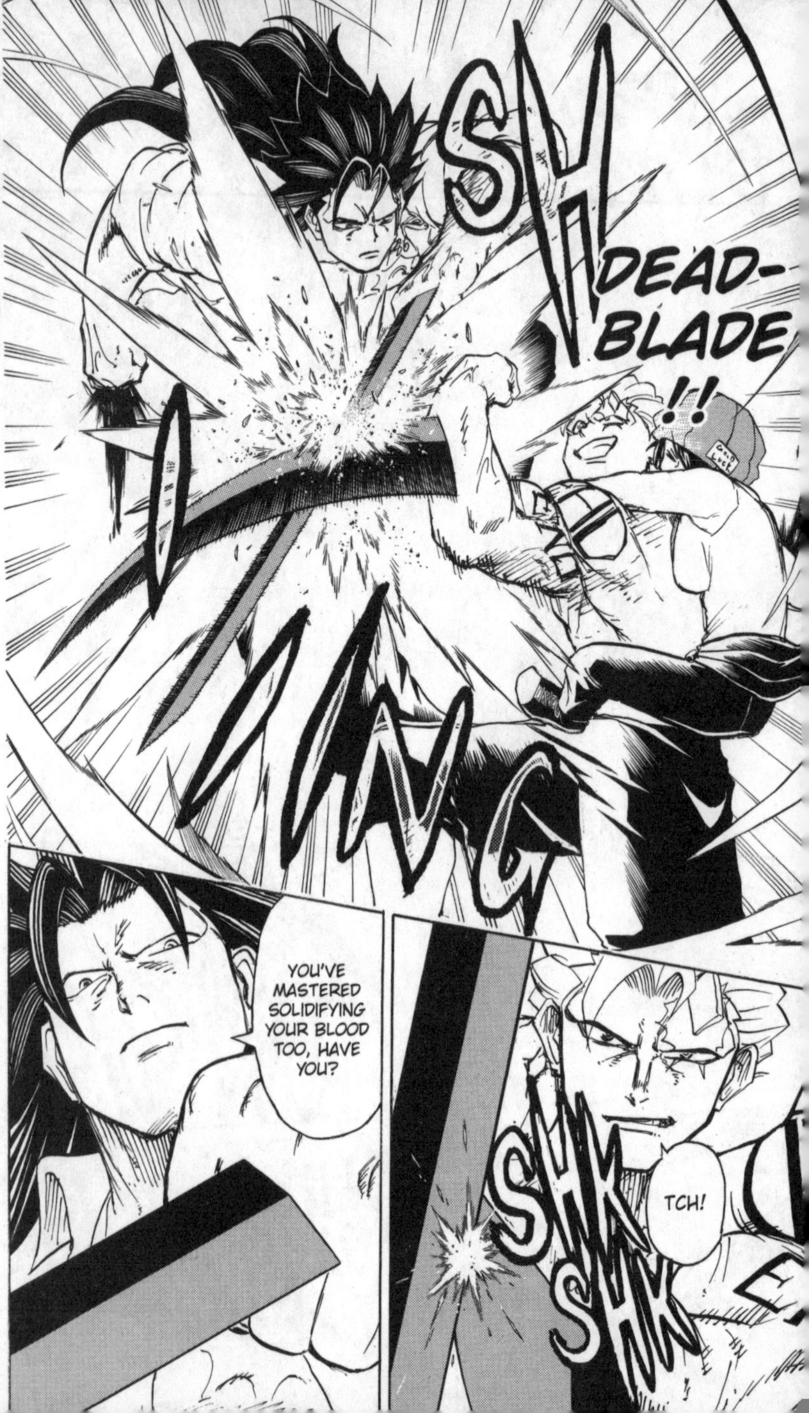
SH
DEAD-BLADE!!
ZING
SHK SHK
TCH!
YOU'VE MASTERED SOLIDIFYING YOUR BLOOD TOO, HAVE YOU?

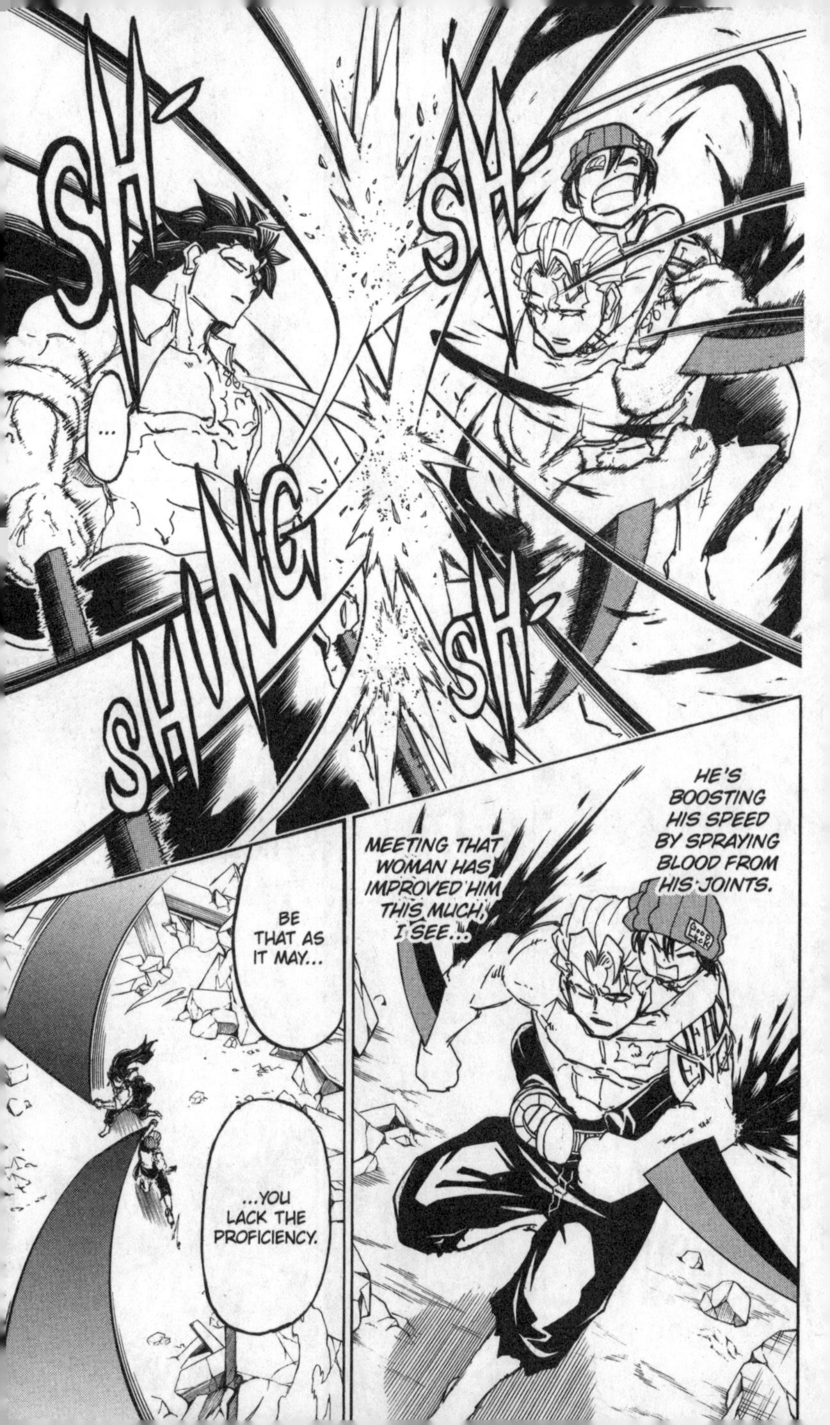
SH
SH
...
SH
SHING
HE'S BOOSTING HIS SPEED BY SPRAYING BLOOD FROM HIS JOINTS.
MEETING THAT WOMAN HAS IMPROVED HIM THIS MUCH, I SEE...
BE THAT AS IT MAY...
...YOU LACK THE PROFICIENCY.

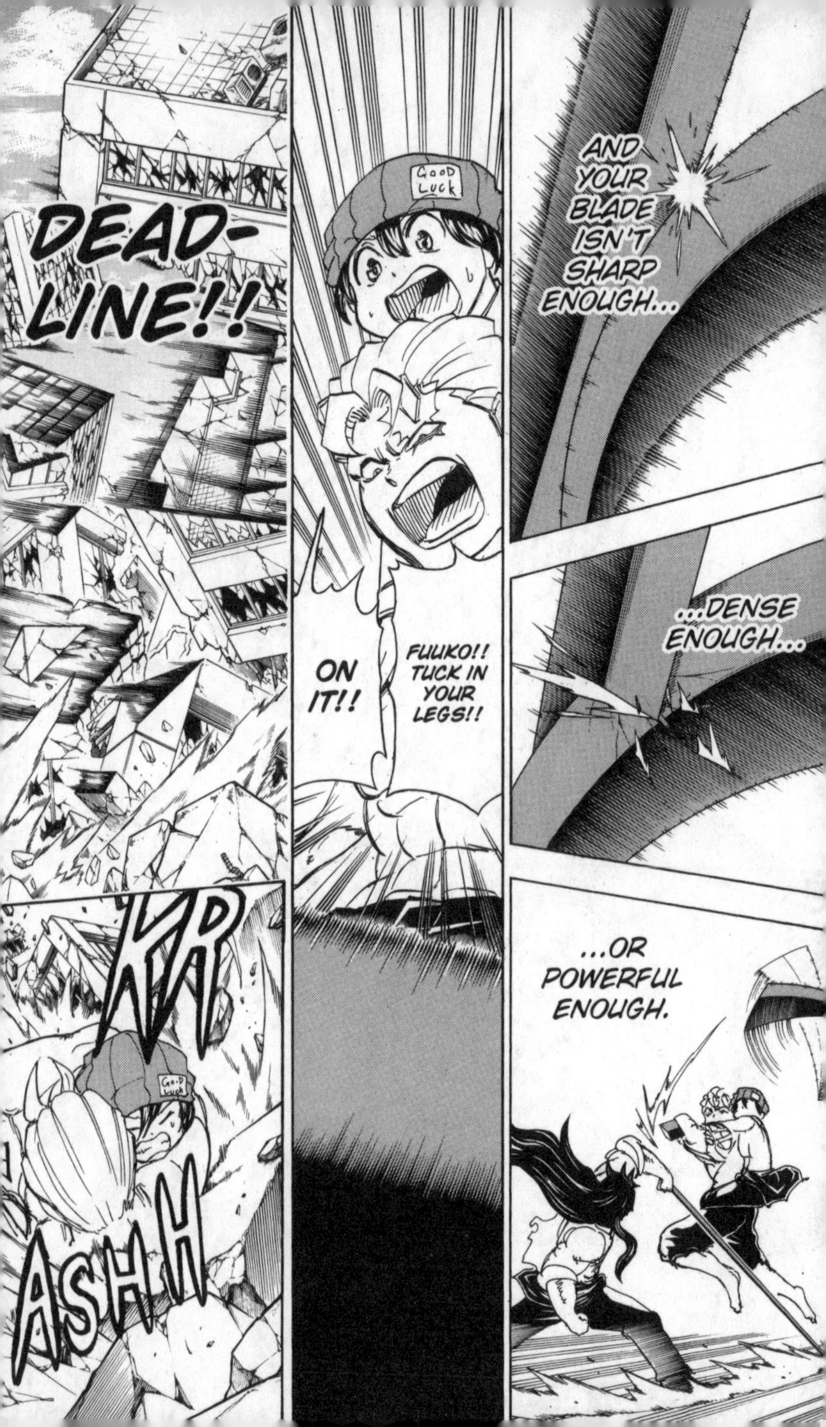
AND YOUR BLADE ISN'T SHARP ENOUGH...
...DENSE ENOUGH...
...OR POWERFUL ENOUGH.
GOOD LUCK
FUUKO!! TUCK IN YOUR LEGS!!
ON IT!!
DEAD-LINE!!
KR
ASHH
GOOD LUCK

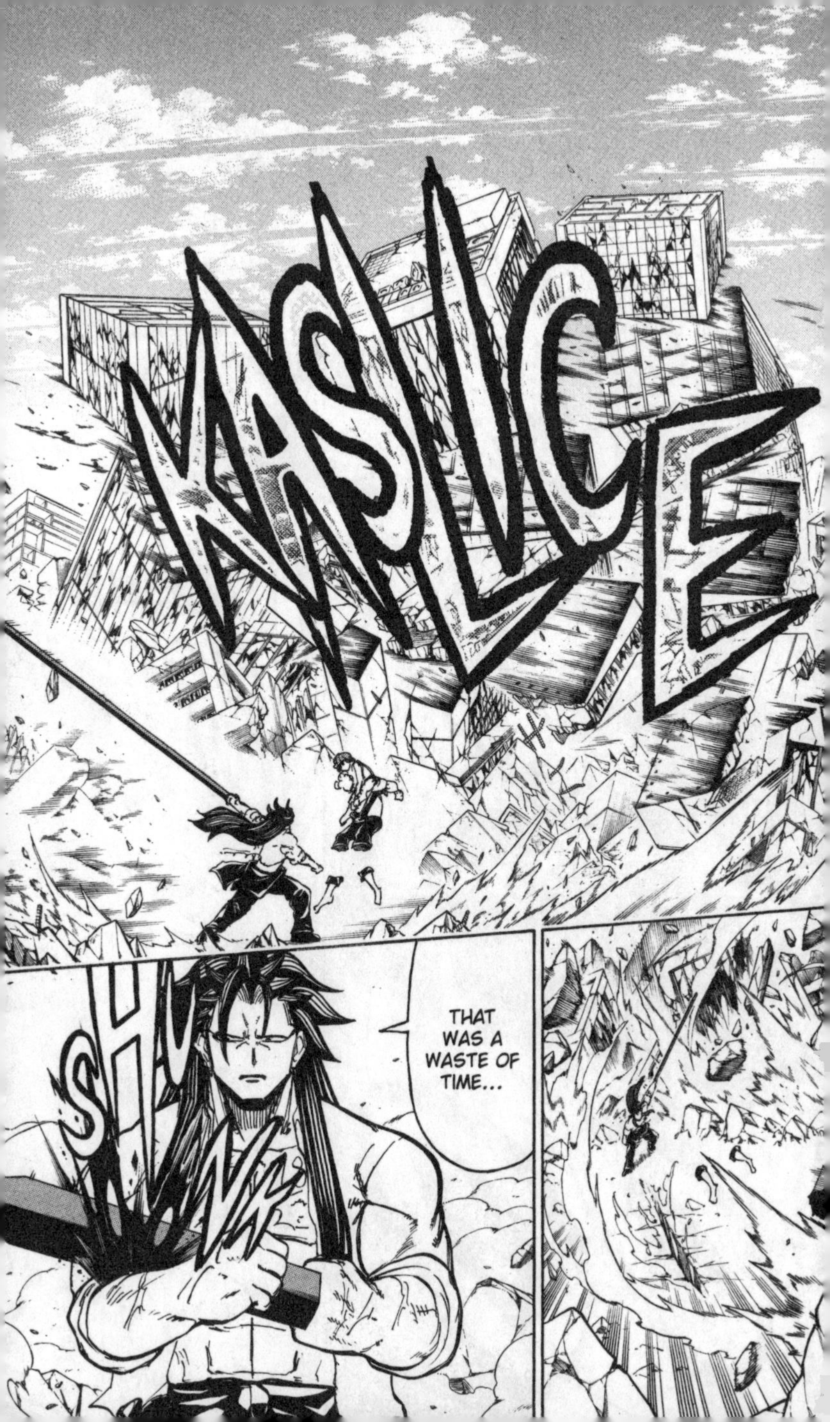
THAT WAS A WASTE OF TIME...

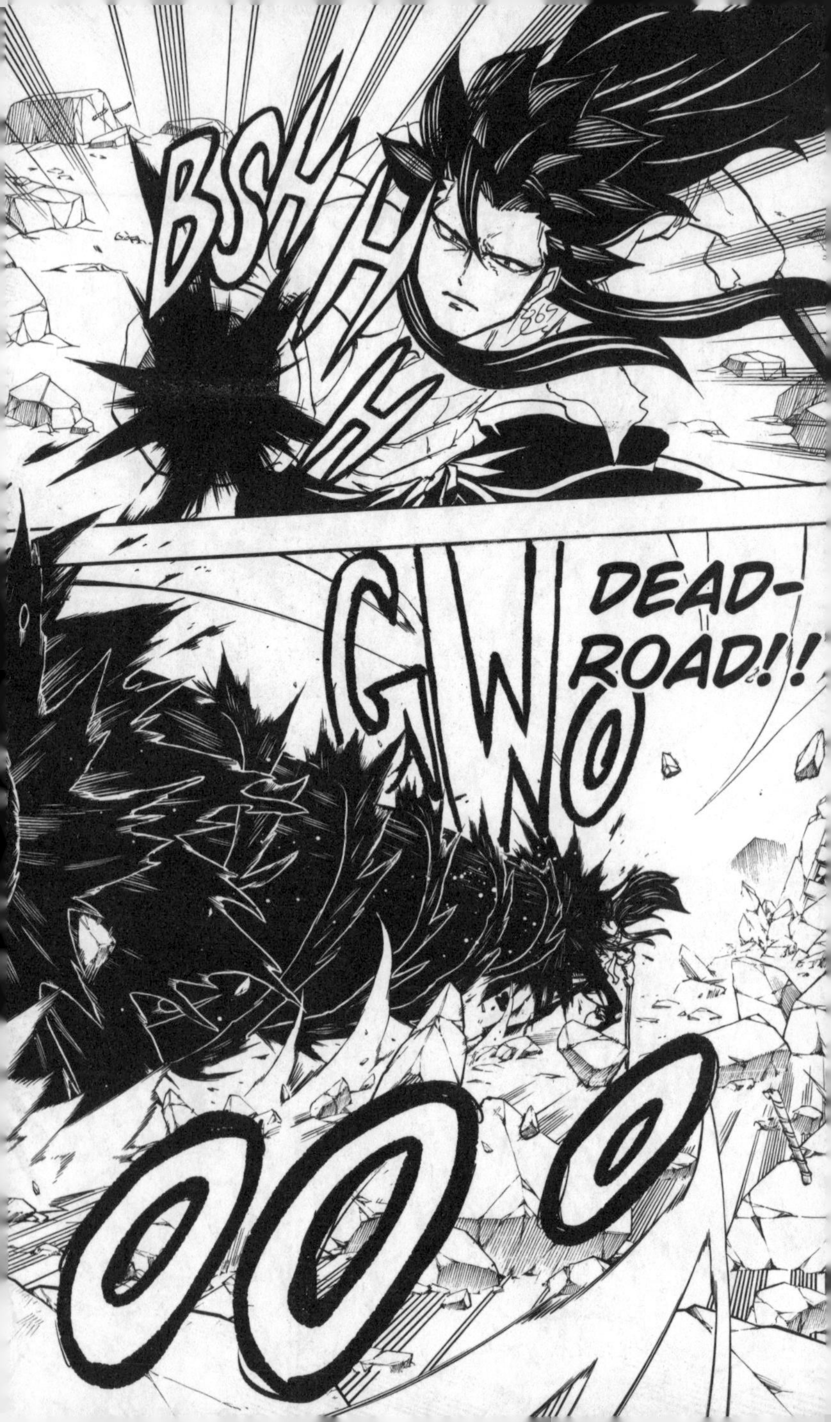
BSHHH
GWOOOO
DEAD-ROAD!!

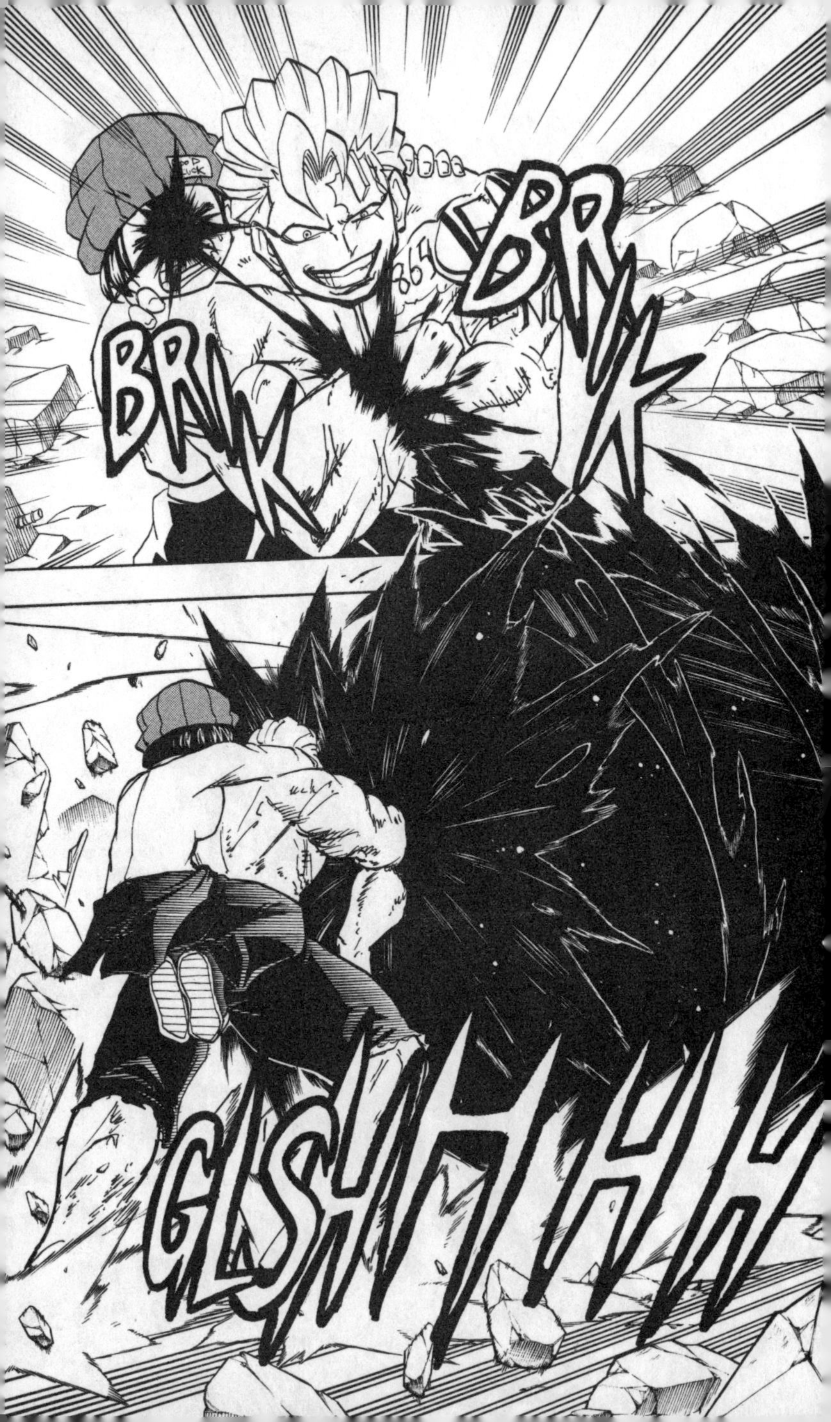
GOOD LUCK
864
BRK
BRK
GLSHHHH

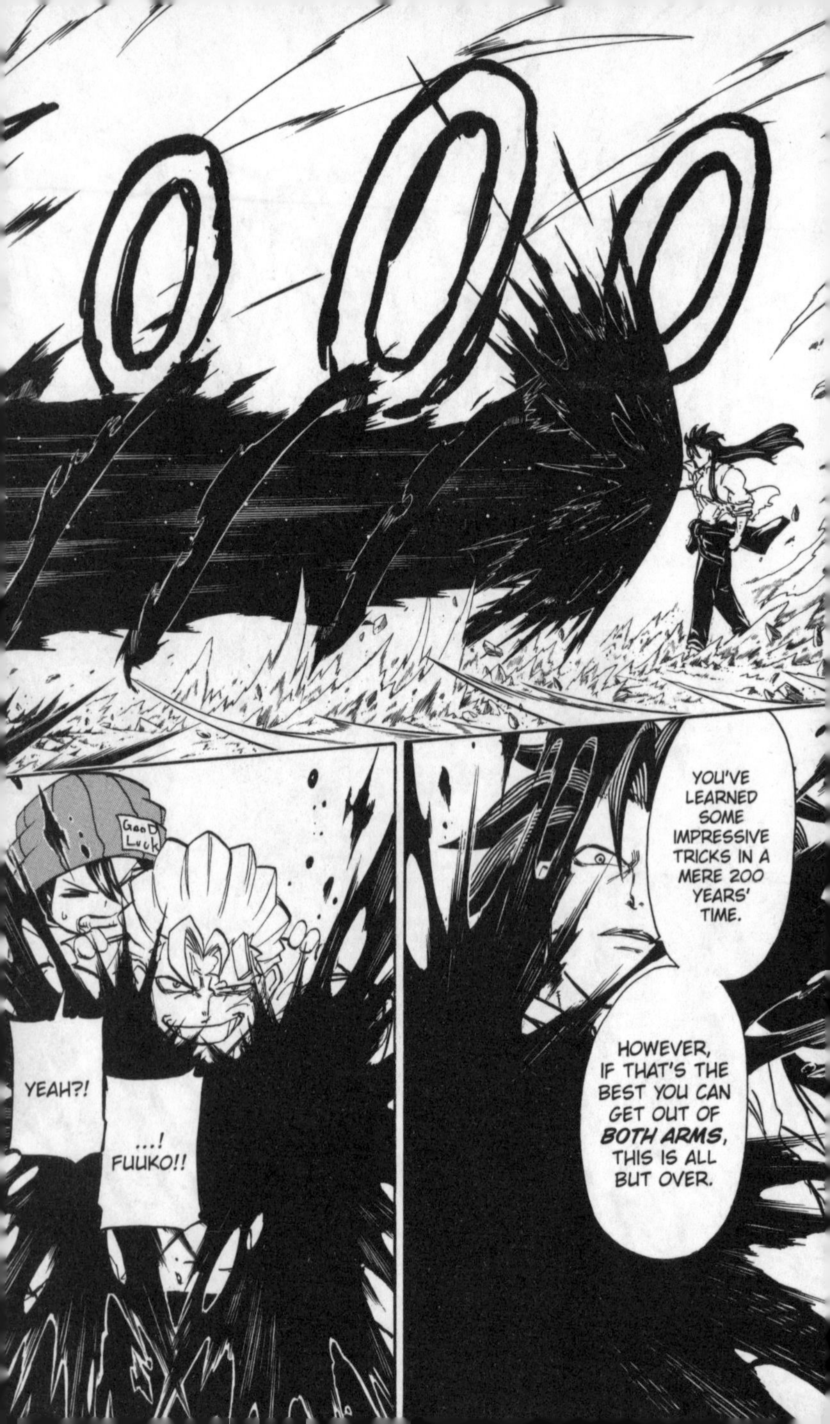
YOU'VE LEARNED SOME IMPRESSIVE TRICKS IN A MERE 200 YEARS' TIME.
HOWEVER, IF THAT'S THE BEST YOU CAN GET OUT OF ***BOTH ARMS***, THIS IS ALL BUT OVER.
GooD Luck
...! FUUKO!!
YEAH?!

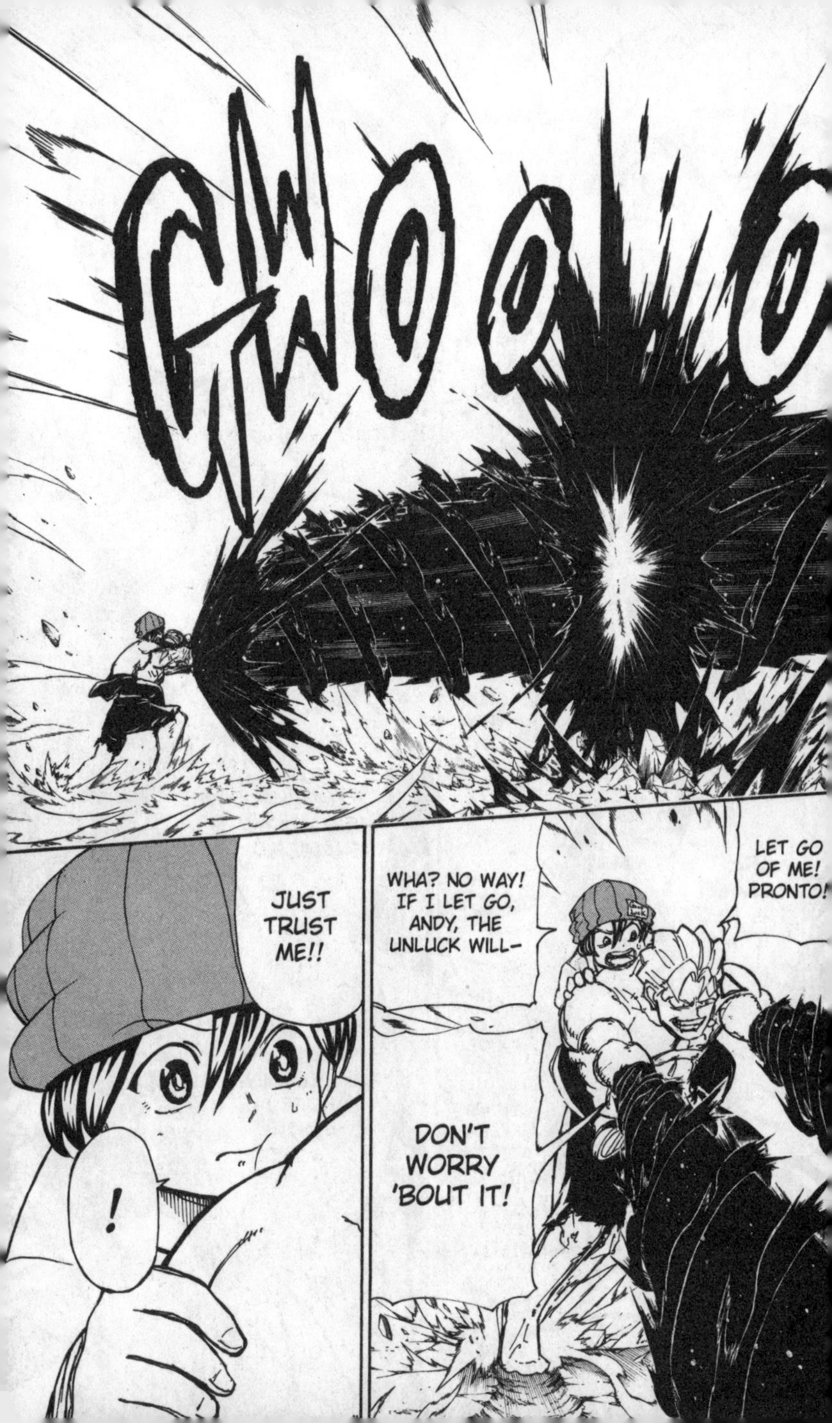
LET GO OF ME! PRONTO!
WHA? NO WAY! IF I LET GO, ANDY, THE UNLUCK WILL-
DON'T WORRY 'BOUT IT!
JUST TRUST ME!!
!

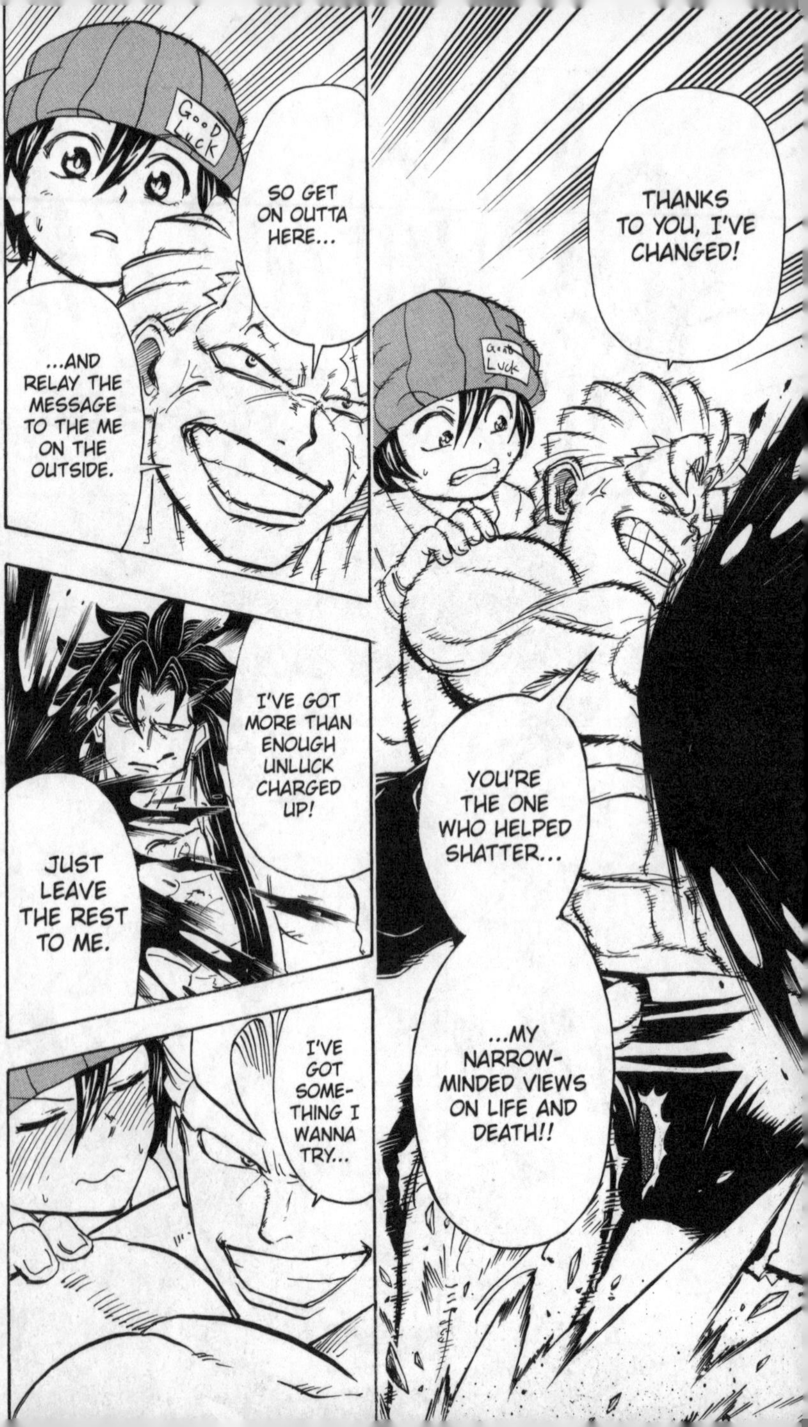
THANKS TO YOU, I'VE CHANGED!
Good Luck
YOU'RE THE ONE WHO HELPED SHATTER...
...MY NARROW-MINDED VIEWS ON LIFE AND DEATH!!
GooD Luck
SO GET ON OUTTA HERE...
...AND RELAY THE MESSAGE TO THE ME ON THE OUTSIDE.
I'VE GOT MORE THAN ENOUGH UNLUCK CHARGED UP!
JUST LEAVE THE REST TO ME.
I'VE GOT SOME-THING I WANNA TRY...

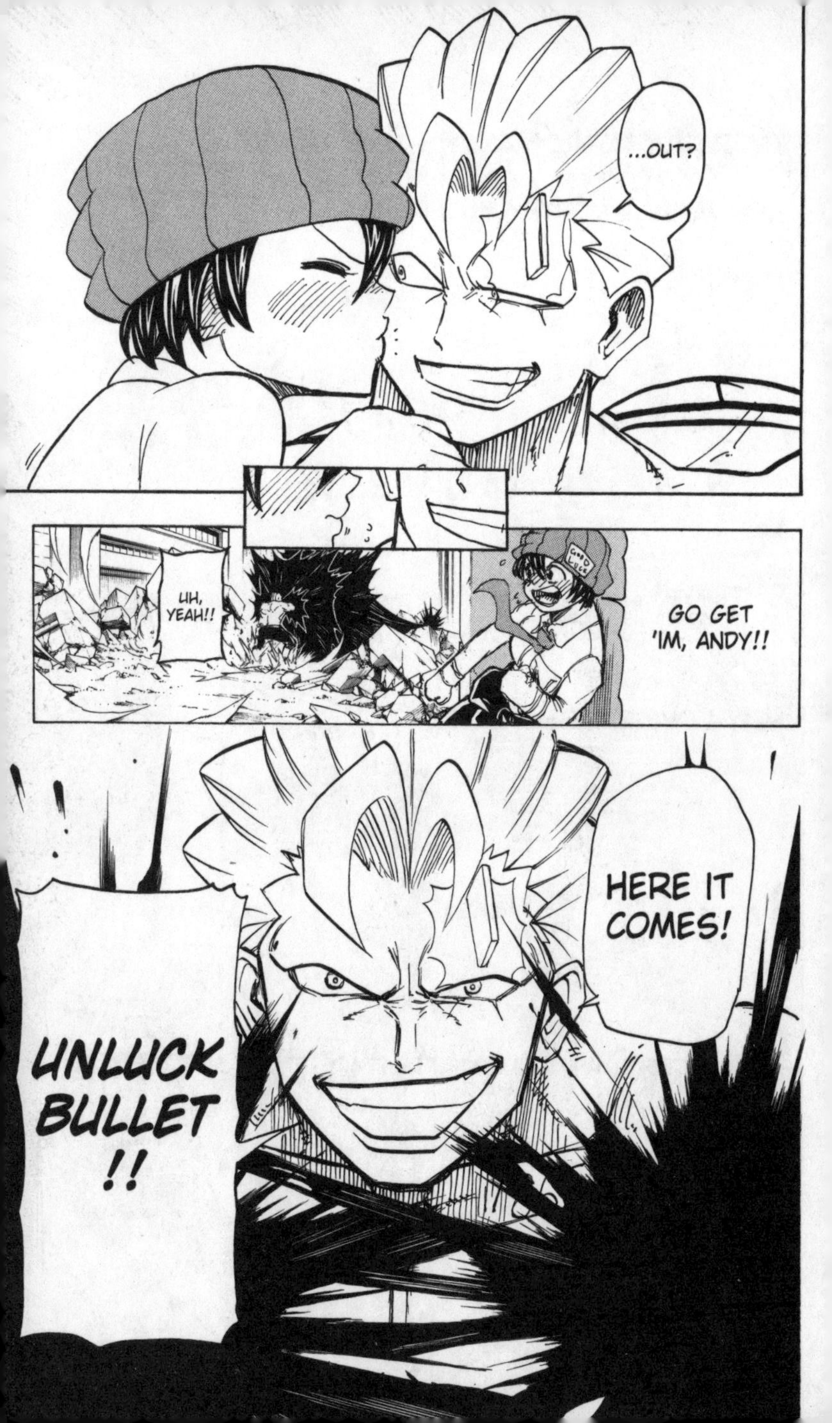
...OUT?
GO GET 'IM, ANDY!!
UH, YEAH!!
HERE IT COMES!
UNLUCK BULLET !!

INTRODUCTION OF ANDY'S NEW MOVES ①

NEW MOVE 1: VORTEX BULLET

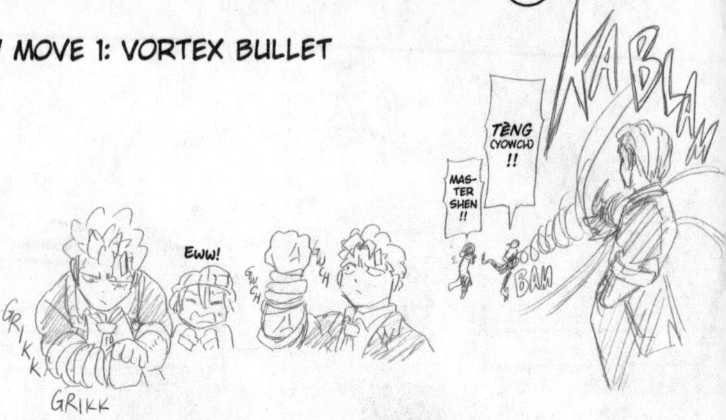
GRIKK
GRIKK
Eww!
GWCH
GWCH
TÈNG
(YOWCH)
!!
MASTER SHEN !!
BAM
KABLAM

① HE TWISTS HIS ARM AS HARD AS HE CAN.

② USES MUSCLE STRENGTH TO FORCE IT IN PLACE AS IT TRIES TO RETURN TO NORMAL WITH HIS REGENERATION.

③ PUSHES IT OUT WITH BLOOD AND LETS IT RIP.

NEW MOVE 2: REPAIR GLIDE

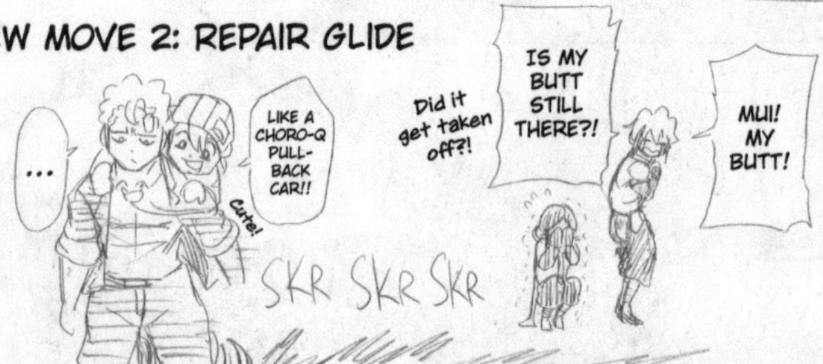
MUI! MY BUTT!
IS MY BUTT STILL THERE?!
Did it get taken off?!
LIKE A CHORO-Q PULL-BACK CAR!!
Cute!
...
SKR SKR SKR

UTILIZES ① AND ②. TOOK TEN YEARS TO USE SUCCESSFULLY.

NEW MOVE 3: DEADROAD

CONTINUOUSLY REGENERATES BLOOD IN HIS BODY AT HIGH SPEEDS AND FIRES IT.

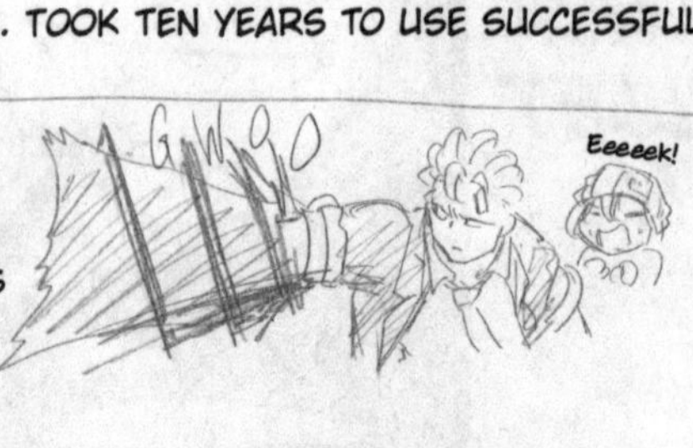
Eeeeek!

No. 045
Unluck Bullet

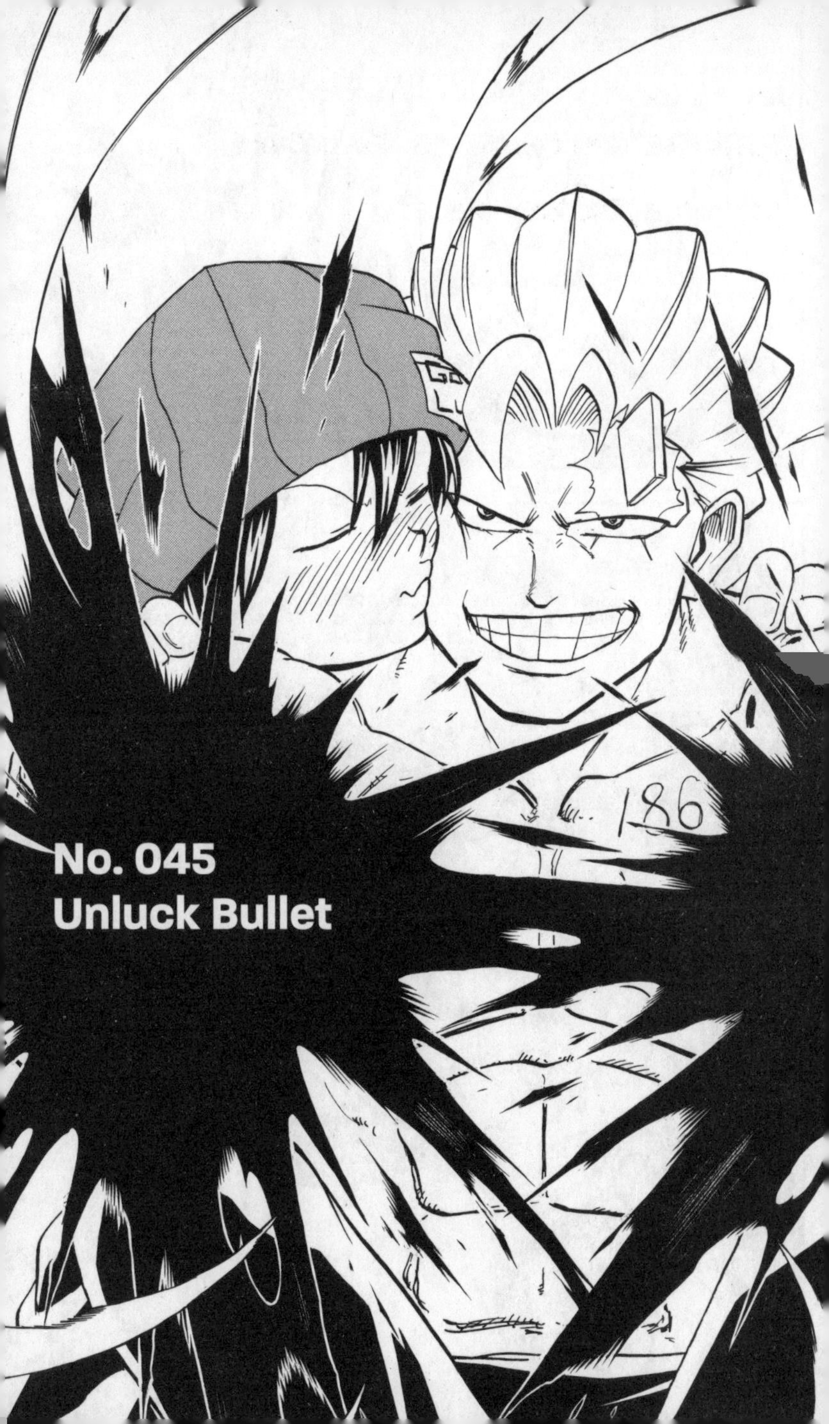
186

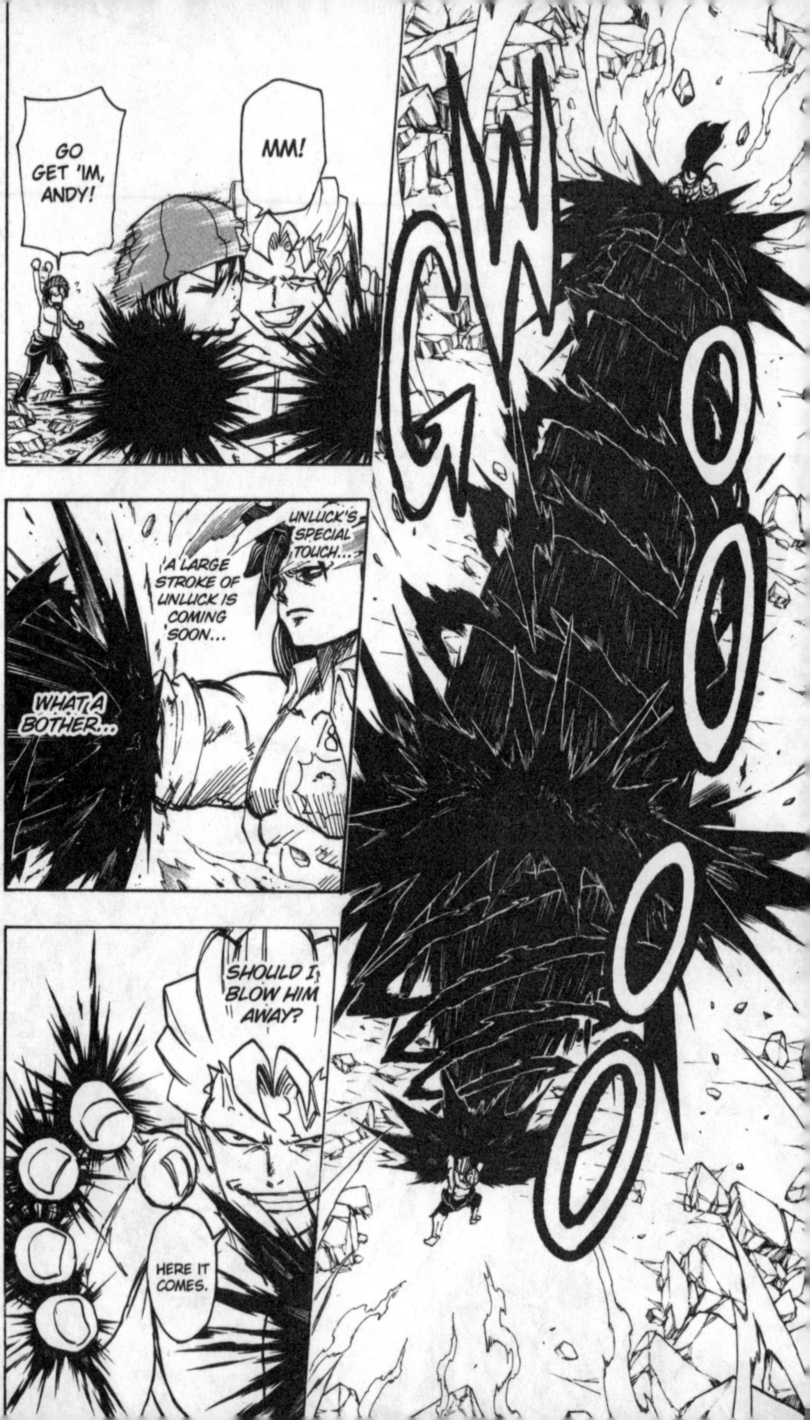
GWOOOOO
MM!
GO GET 'IM, ANDY!
UNLUCK'S SPECIAL TOUCH...
A LARGE STROKE OF UNLUCK IS COMING SOON...
WHAT A BOTHER...
SHOULD I BLOW HIM AWAY?
HERE IT COMES.

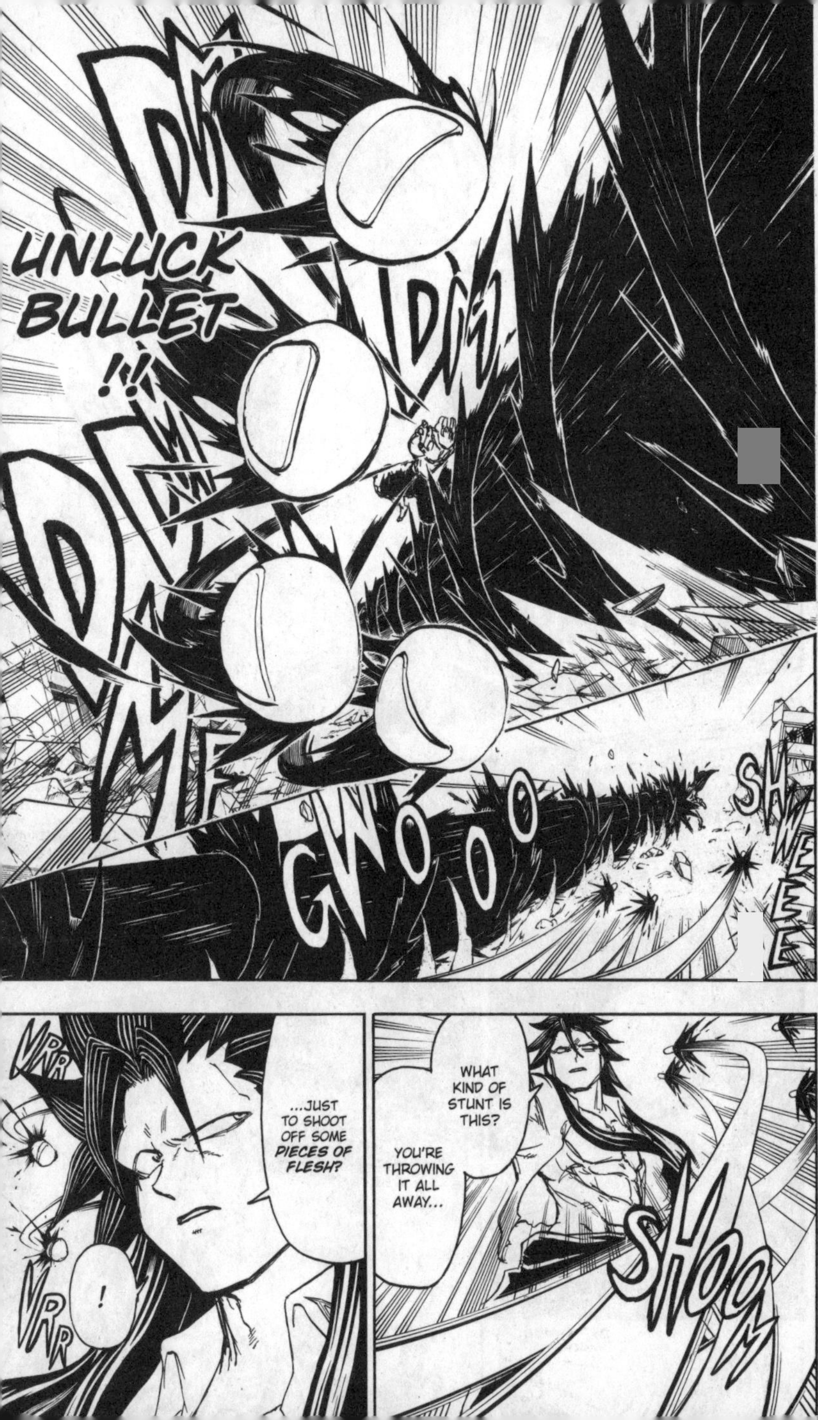
UNLUCK BULLET!!
GWOOOO
SHWEEE
WHAT KIND OF STUNT IS THIS?
YOU'RE THROWING IT ALL AWAY...
SHOOM
...JUST TO SHOOT OFF SOME *PIECES OF FLESH?*
VRRR
!
VRRR

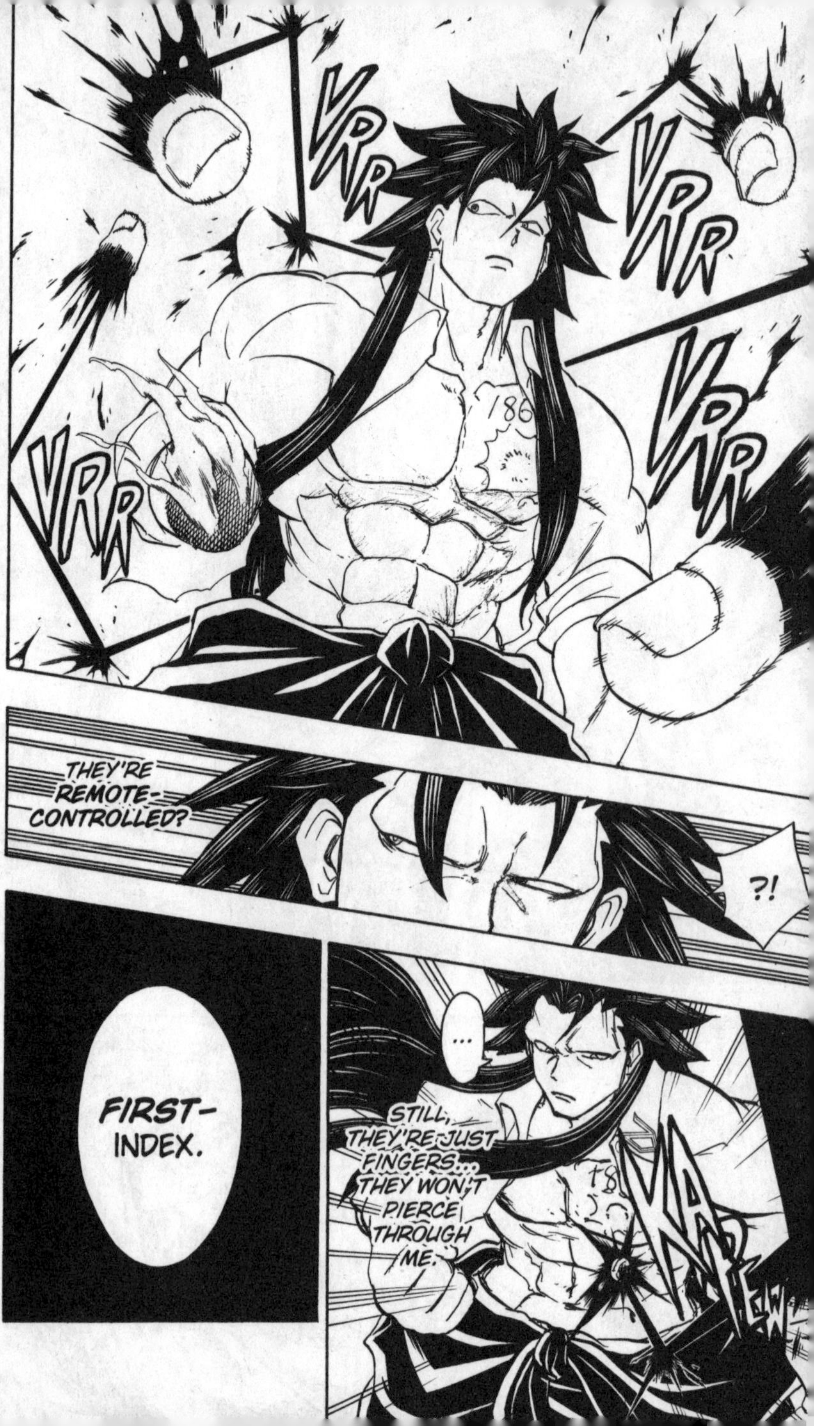

VRR
VRR
VRR
VRR
THEY'RE REMOTE-CONTROLLED?
?!
...
STILL, THEY'RE JUST FINGERS... THEY WON'T PIERCE THROUGH ME.
FIRST-INDEX.

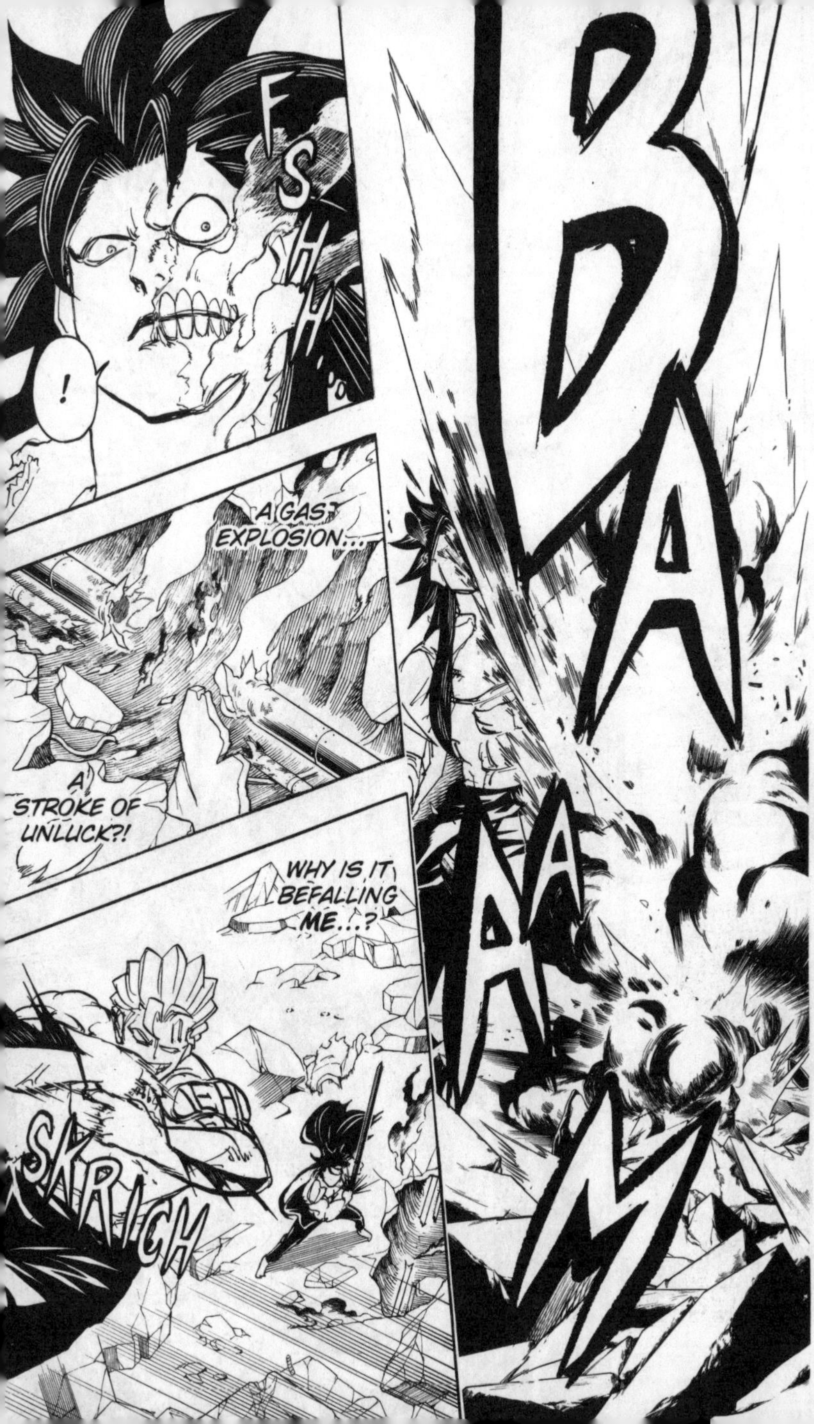
DDAAAM
FSHH
!
A GAS EXPLOSION...
A STROKE OF UNLUCK?!
WHY IS IT BEFALLING ME...?
SKRICH

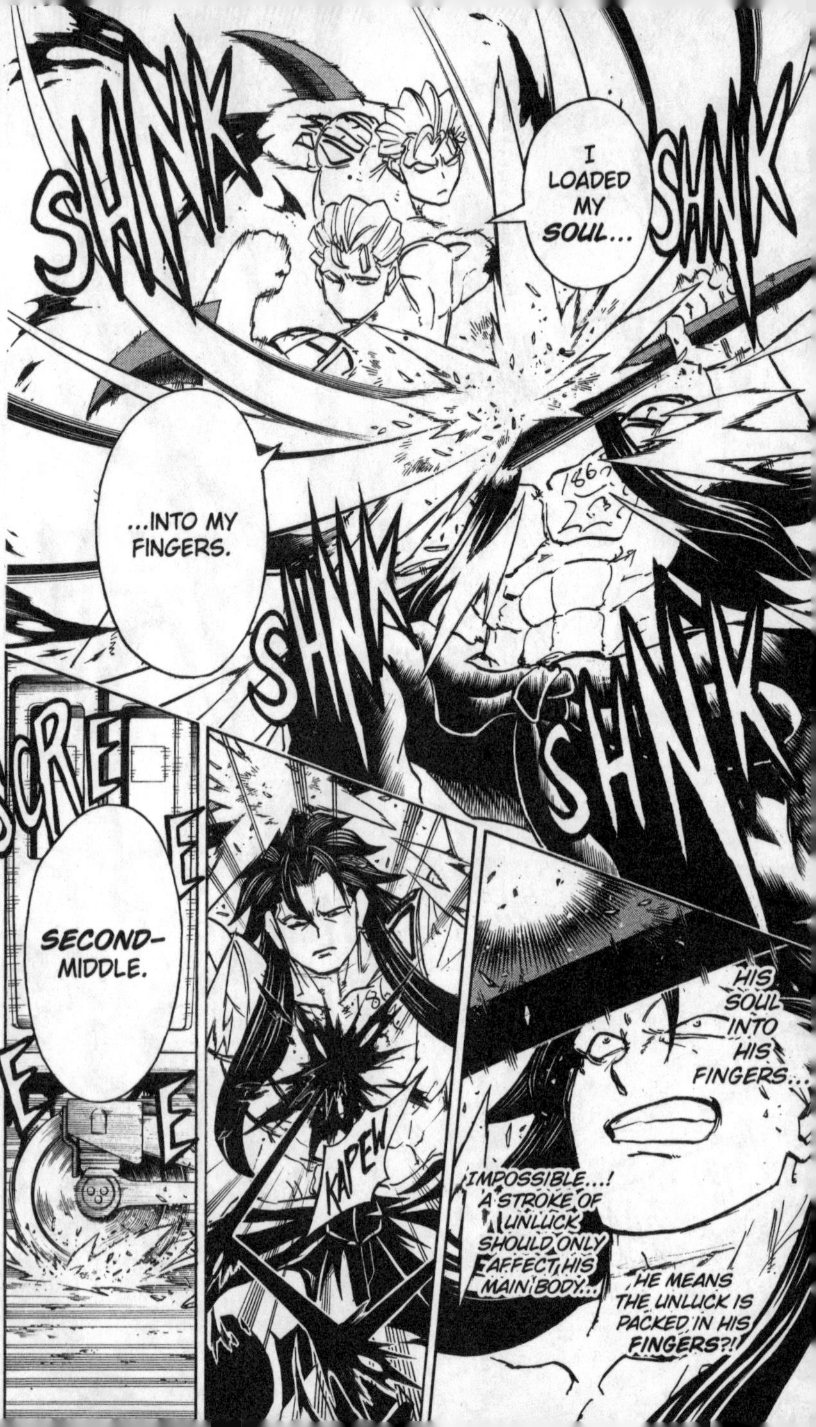
SHNK
I LOADED MY SOUL...
SHNK
...INTO MY FINGERS.
SHNK
SHNK
HIS SOUL INTO HIS FINGERS...
IMPOSSIBLE...! A STROKE OF UNLUCK SHOULD ONLY AFFECT HIS MAIN BODY...
HE MEANS THE UNLUCK IS PACKED IN HIS FINGERS?!
KAPEW
SCREEEE
SECOND-MIDDLE.

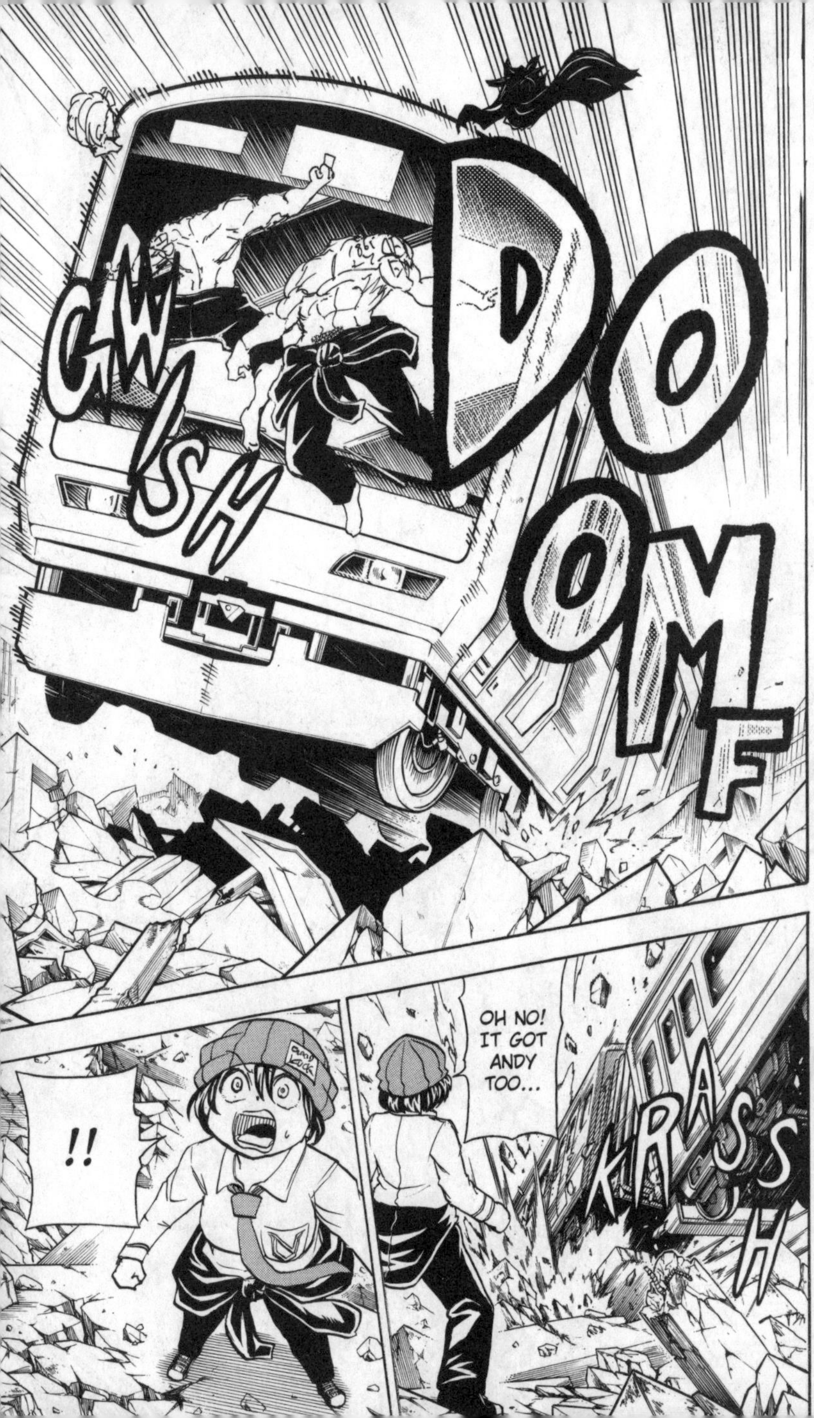
DOOMF
CWISH
OH NO! IT GOT ANDY TOO...
KRASSH
!!

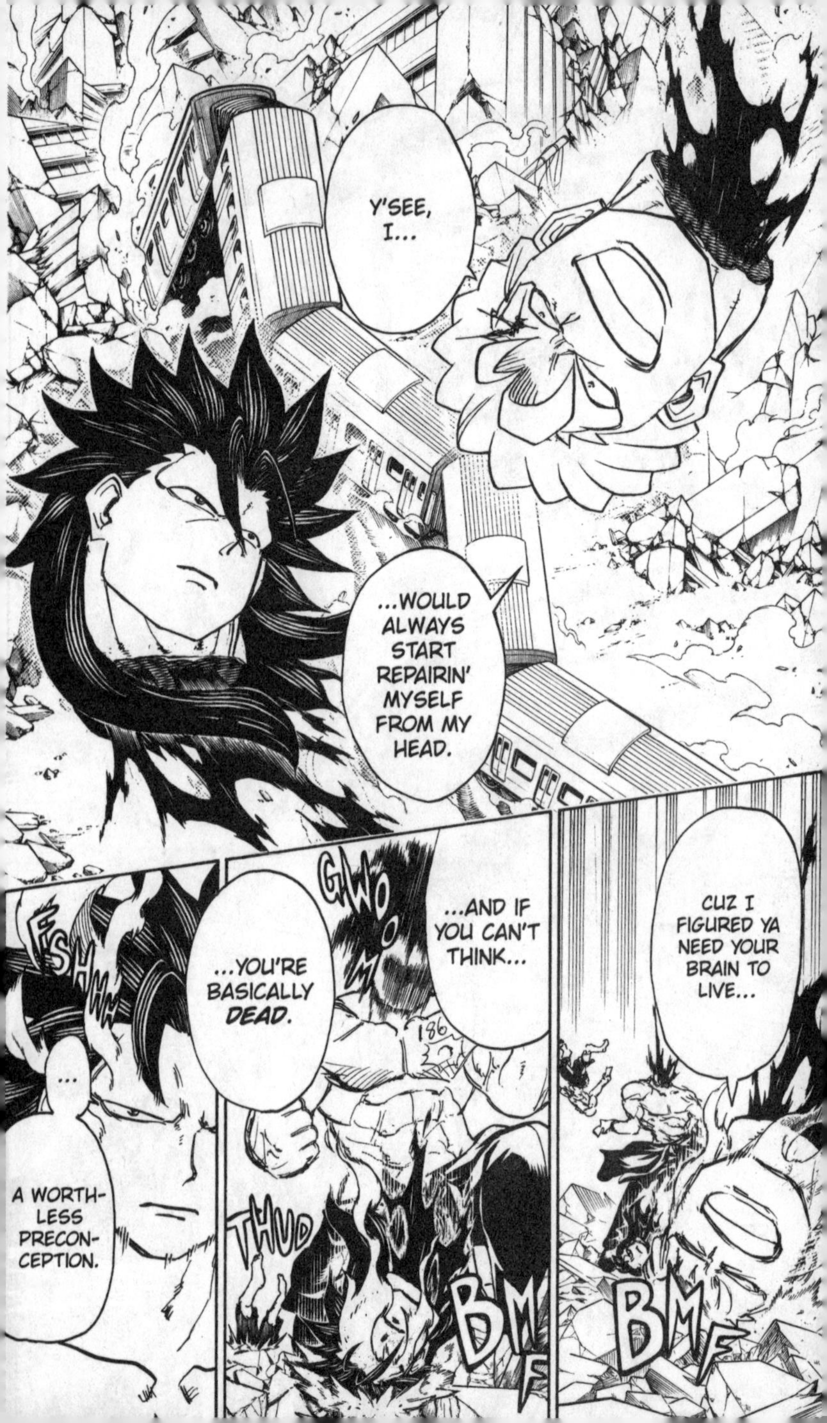
Y'SEE, I...
...WOULD ALWAYS START REPAIRIN' MYSELF FROM MY HEAD.
CUZ I FIGURED YA NEED YOUR BRAIN TO LIVE...
BMF
...AND IF YOU CAN'T THINK...
GWOOM
...YOU'RE BASICALLY DEAD.
THUD
BMF
FSHHH
...
A WORTH-LESS PRECON-CEPTION.

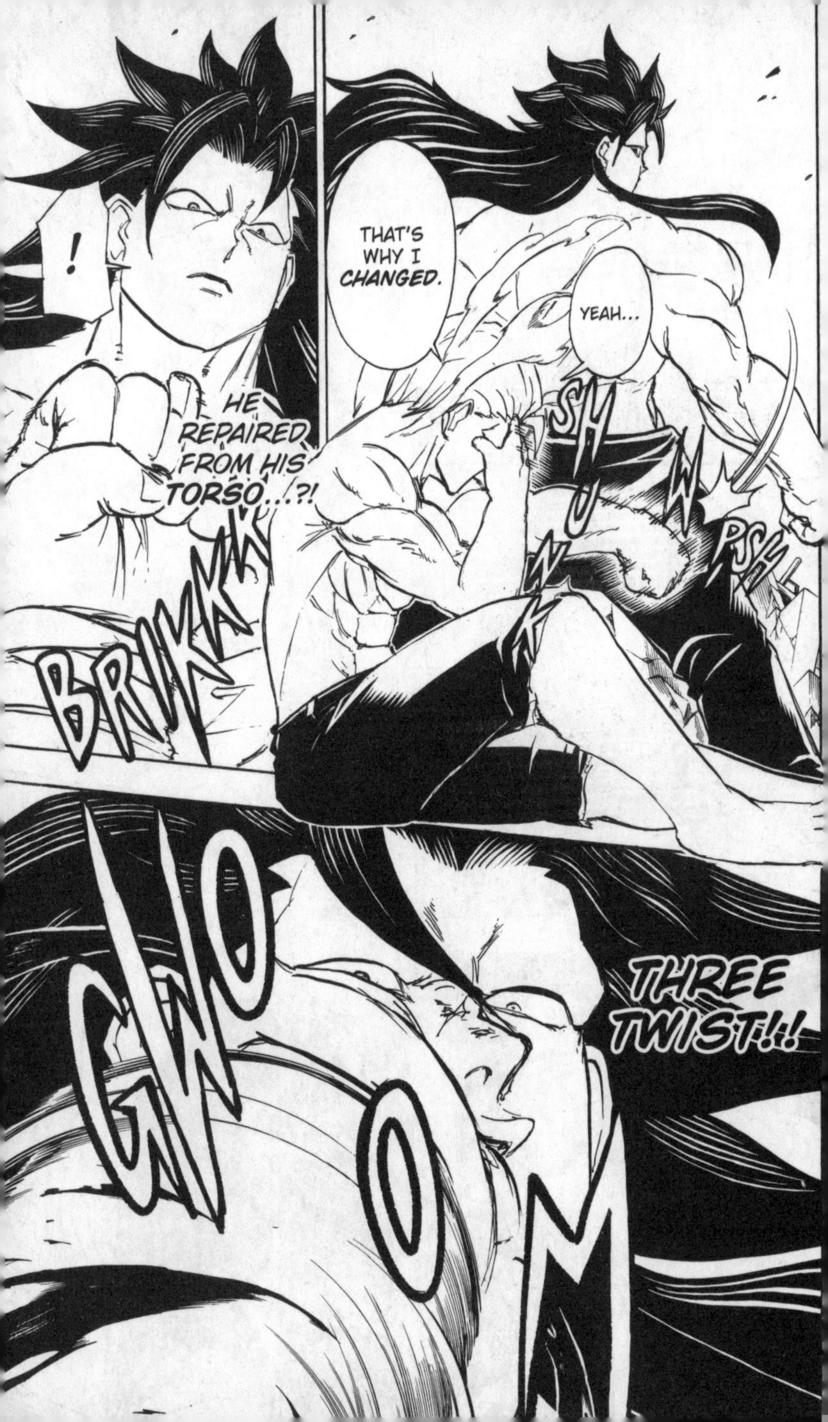
YEAH...
THAT'S WHY I *CHANGED.*
SHUNK
PSH
!
HE REPAIRED FROM HIS TORSO...?!
BRIKK
THREE TWIST!!
GHOOM

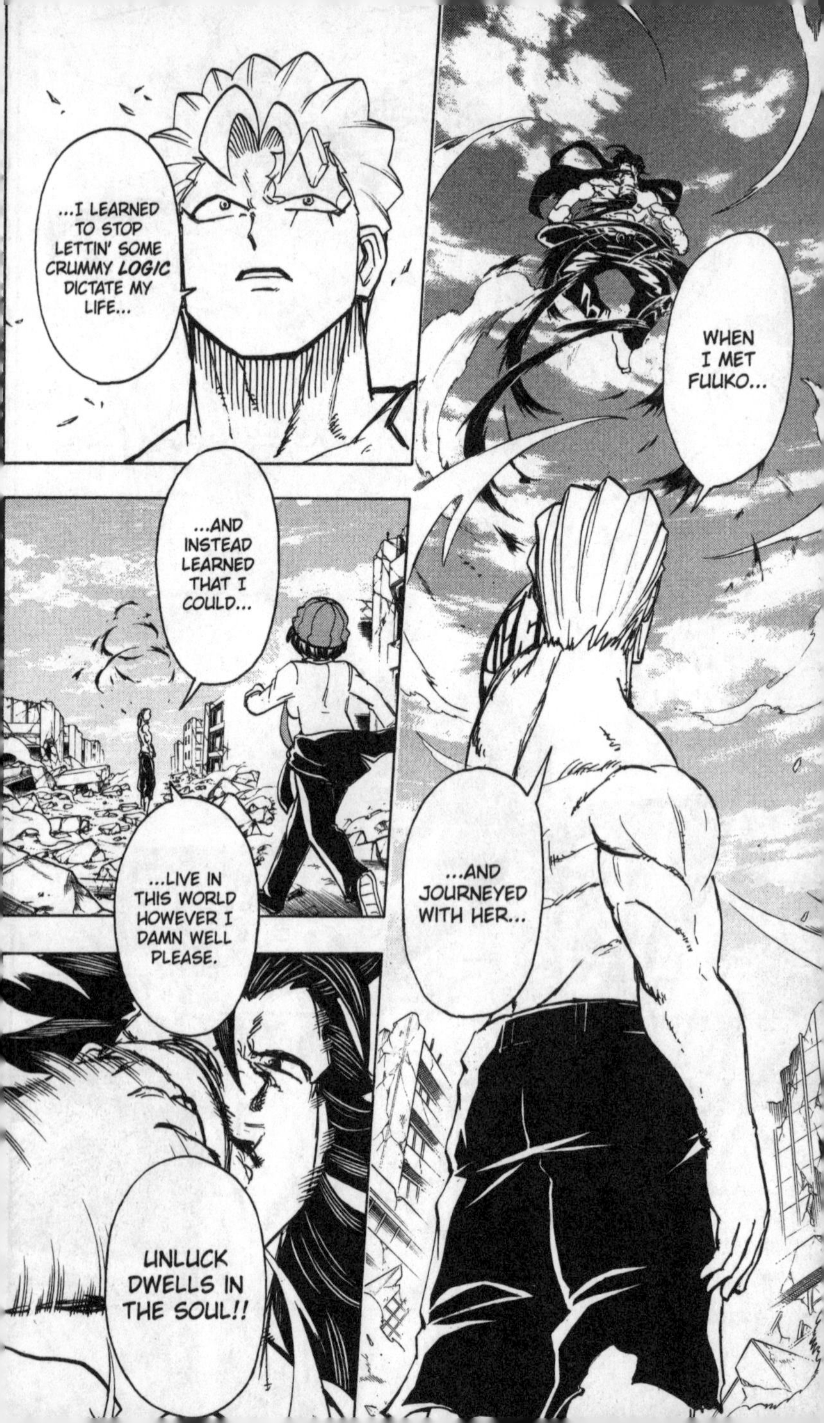
WHEN I MET FUUKO...
...AND JOURNEYED WITH HER...
...I LEARNED TO STOP LETTIN' SOME CRUMMY *LOGIC* DICTATE MY LIFE...
...AND INSTEAD LEARNED THAT I COULD...
...LIVE IN THIS WORLD HOWEVER I DAMN WELL PLEASE.
UNLUCK DWELLS IN THE SOUL!!

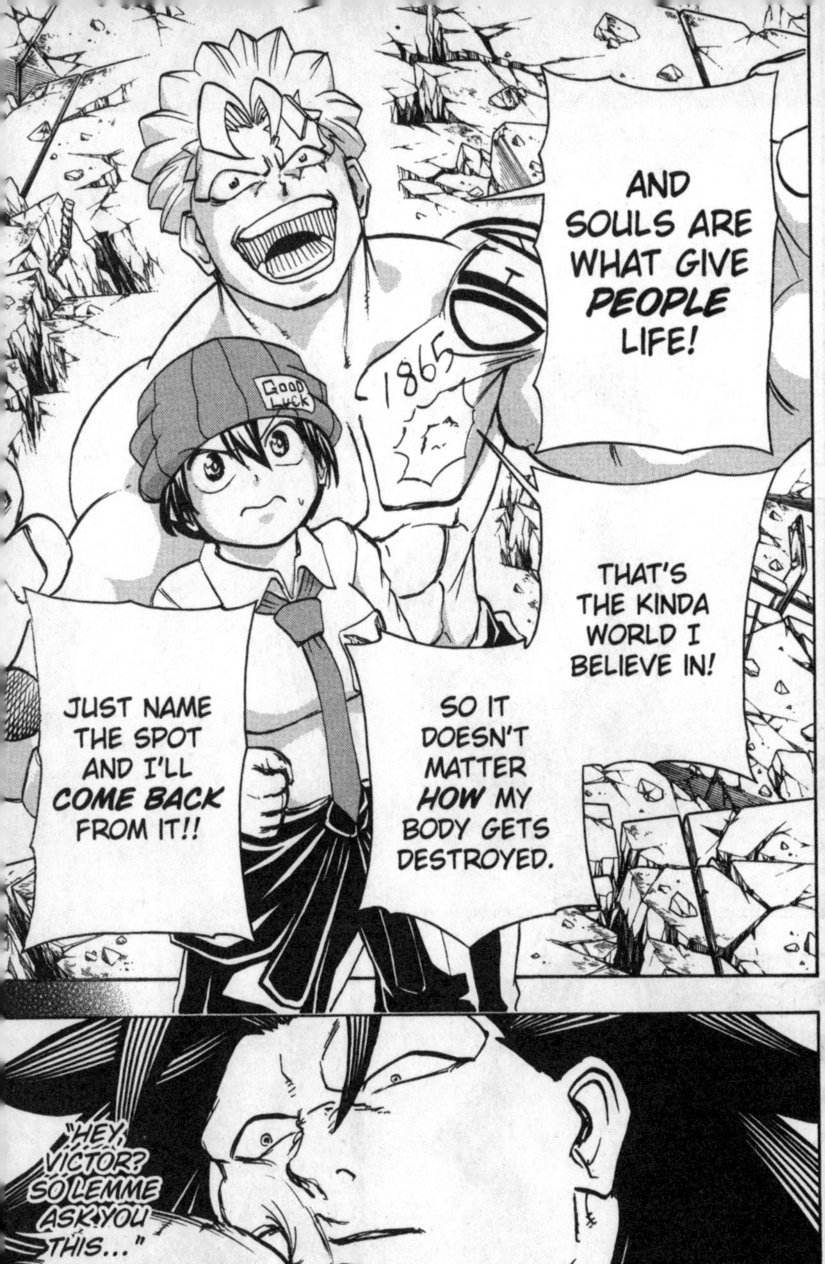
AND SOULS ARE WHAT GIVE *PEOPLE* LIFE!
1865
THAT'S THE KINDA WORLD I BELIEVE IN!
SO IT DOESN'T MATTER *HOW* MY BODY GETS DESTROYED.
GOOD LUCK
JUST NAME THE SPOT AND I'LL *COME BACK* FROM IT!!
"HEY, VICTOR? SO LEMME ASK YOU THIS..."

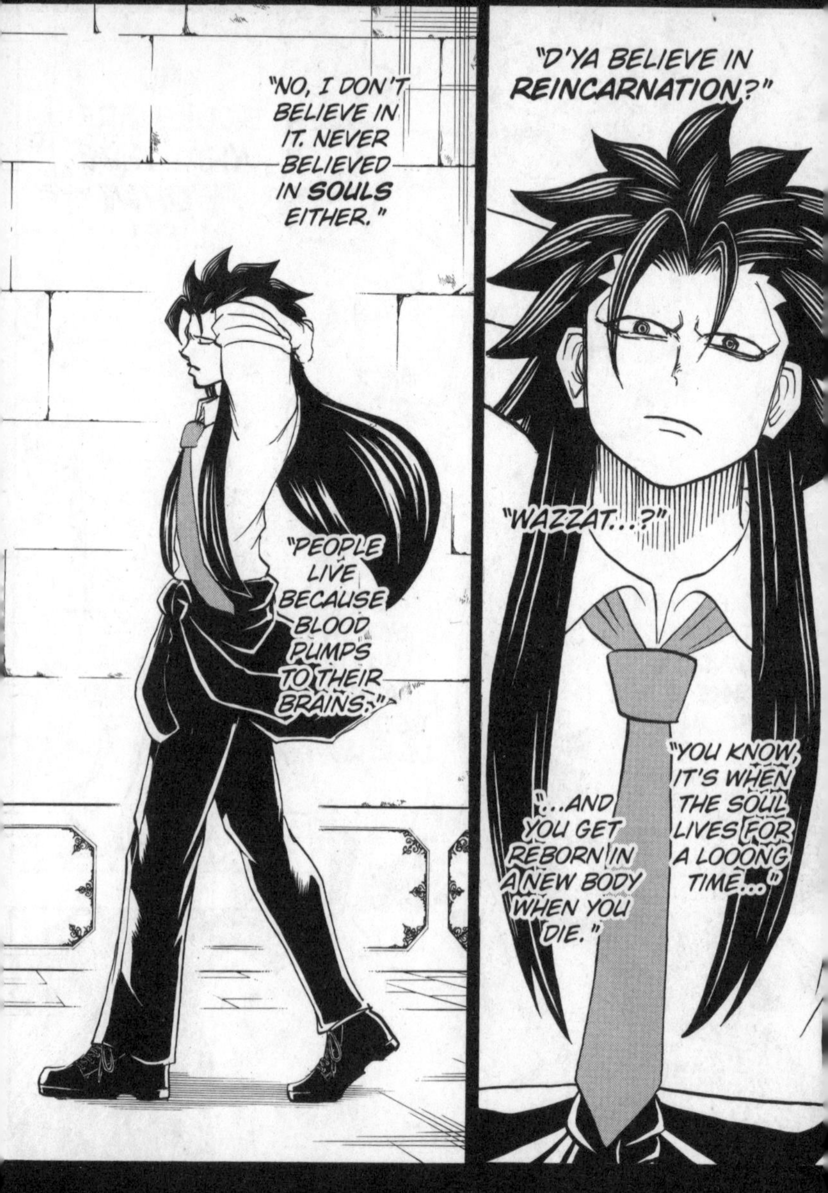
"D'YA BELIEVE IN REINCARNATION?"
"WAZZAT...?"
"YOU KNOW, IT'S WHEN THE SOUL LIVES FOR A LOOONG TIME..."
"...AND YOU GET REBORN IN A NEW BODY WHEN YOU DIE."
"NO, I DON'T BELIEVE IN IT. NEVER BELIEVED IN SOULS EITHER."
"PEOPLE LIVE BECAUSE BLOOD PUMPS TO THEIR BRAINS."

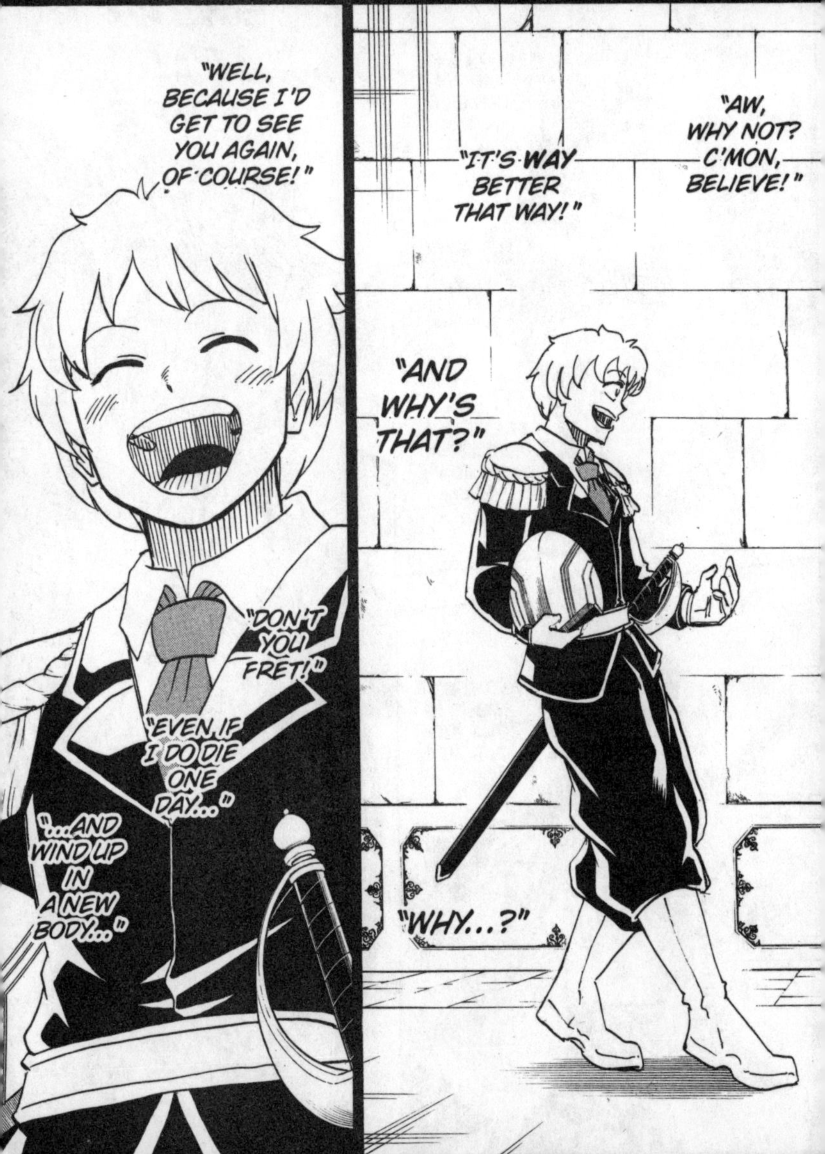
"AW, WHY NOT? C'MON, BELIEVE!"
"IT'S WAY BETTER THAT WAY!"
"AND WHY'S THAT?"
"WHY...?"
"WELL, BECAUSE I'D GET TO SEE YOU AGAIN, OF COURSE!"
"DON'T YOU FRET!"
"EVEN IF I DO DIE ONE DAY..."
"...AND WIND UP IN A NEW BODY..."

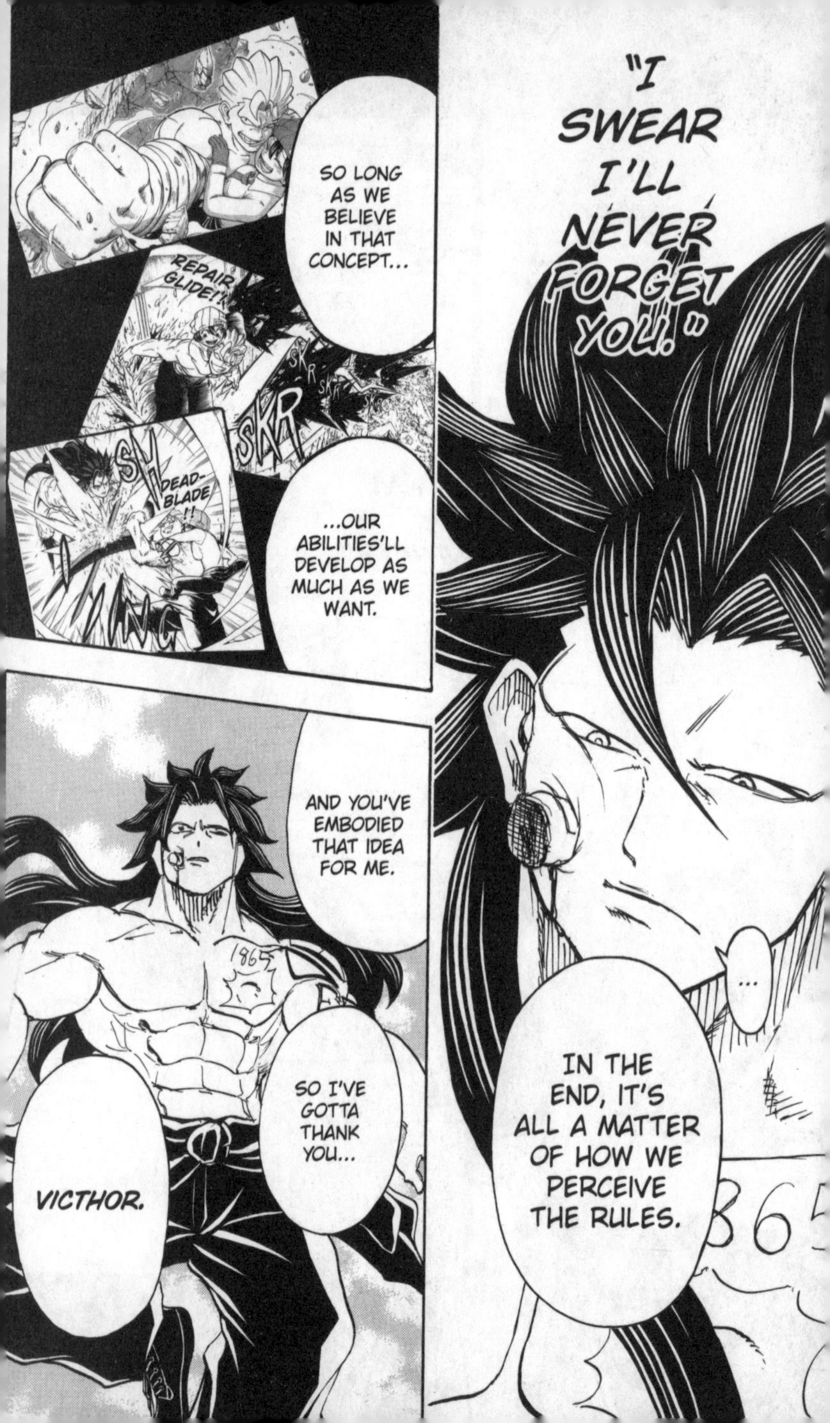

"I SWEAR I'LL NEVER FORGET YOU."
...
IN THE END, IT'S ALL A MATTER OF HOW WE PERCEIVE THE RULES.
SO LONG AS WE BELIEVE IN THAT CONCEPT...
REPAIR GLIDE!!
SKR
SKR
...OUR ABILITIES'LL DEVELOP AS MUCH AS WE WANT.
SH
DEAD-BLADE!!
AND YOU'VE EMBODIED THAT IDEA FOR ME.
1865
SO I'VE GOTTA THANK YOU...
VICTHOR.

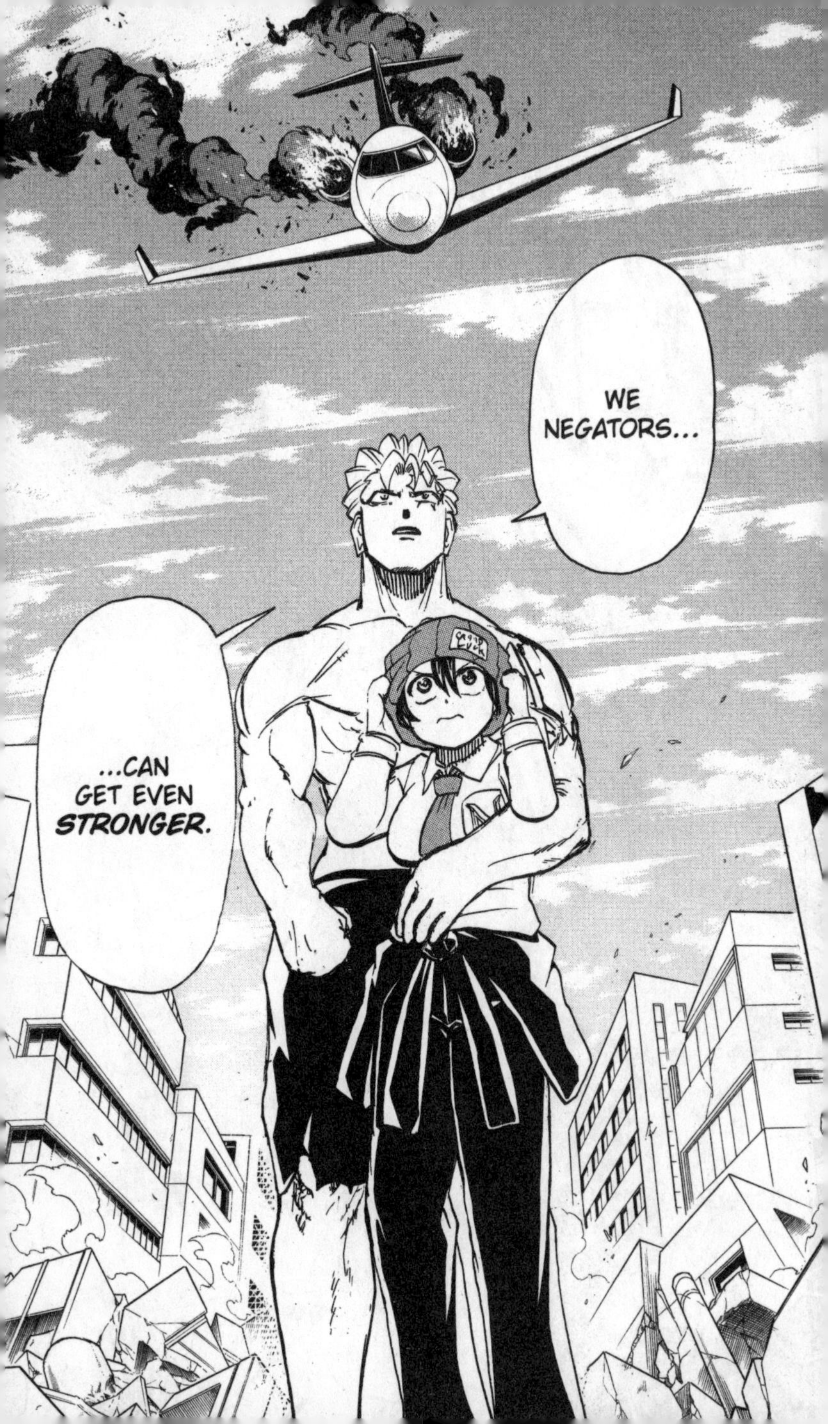
WE NEGATORS...
...CAN GET EVEN STRONGER.

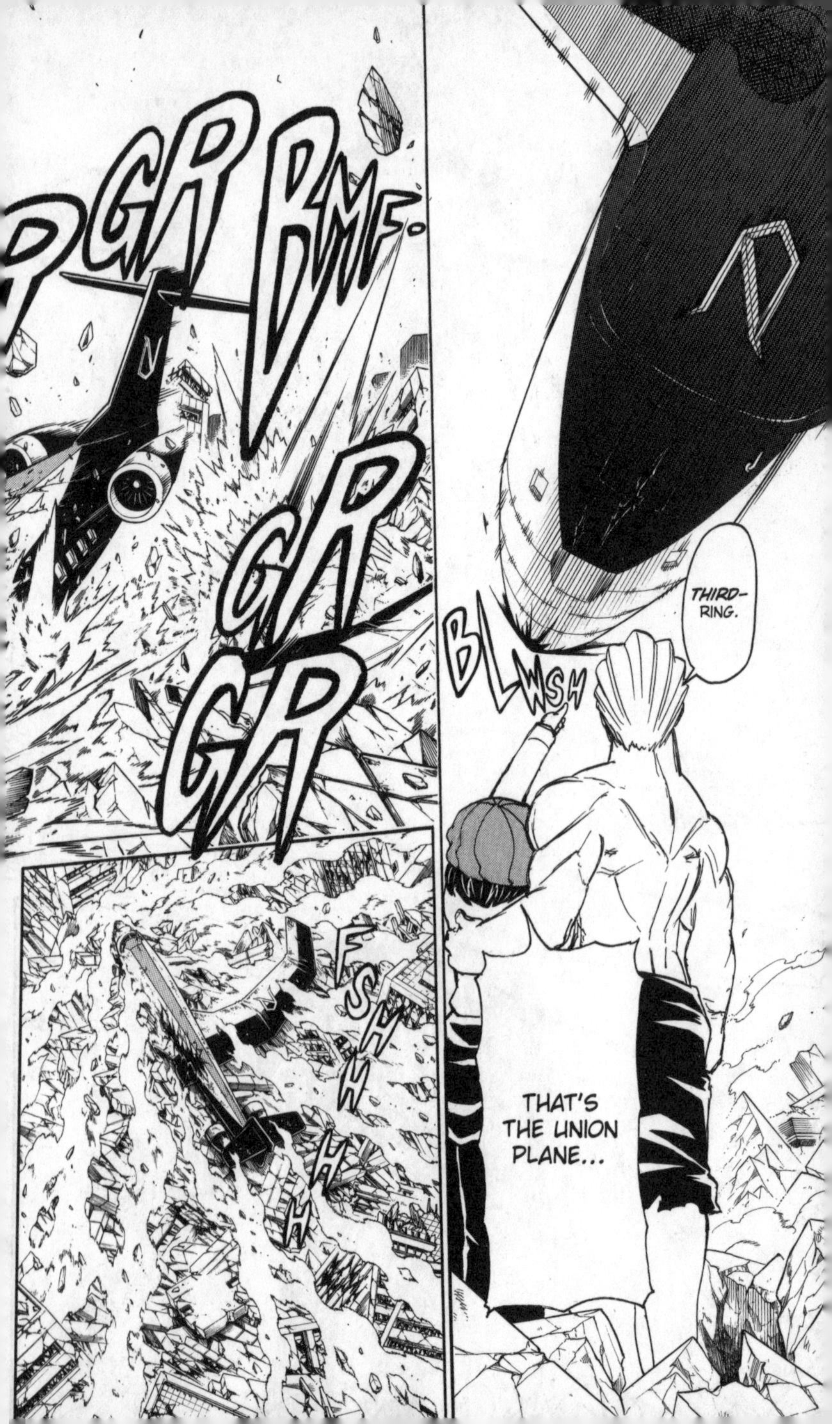
THIRD-RING.
BLWSH
THAT'S THE UNION PLANE...
GR
GR

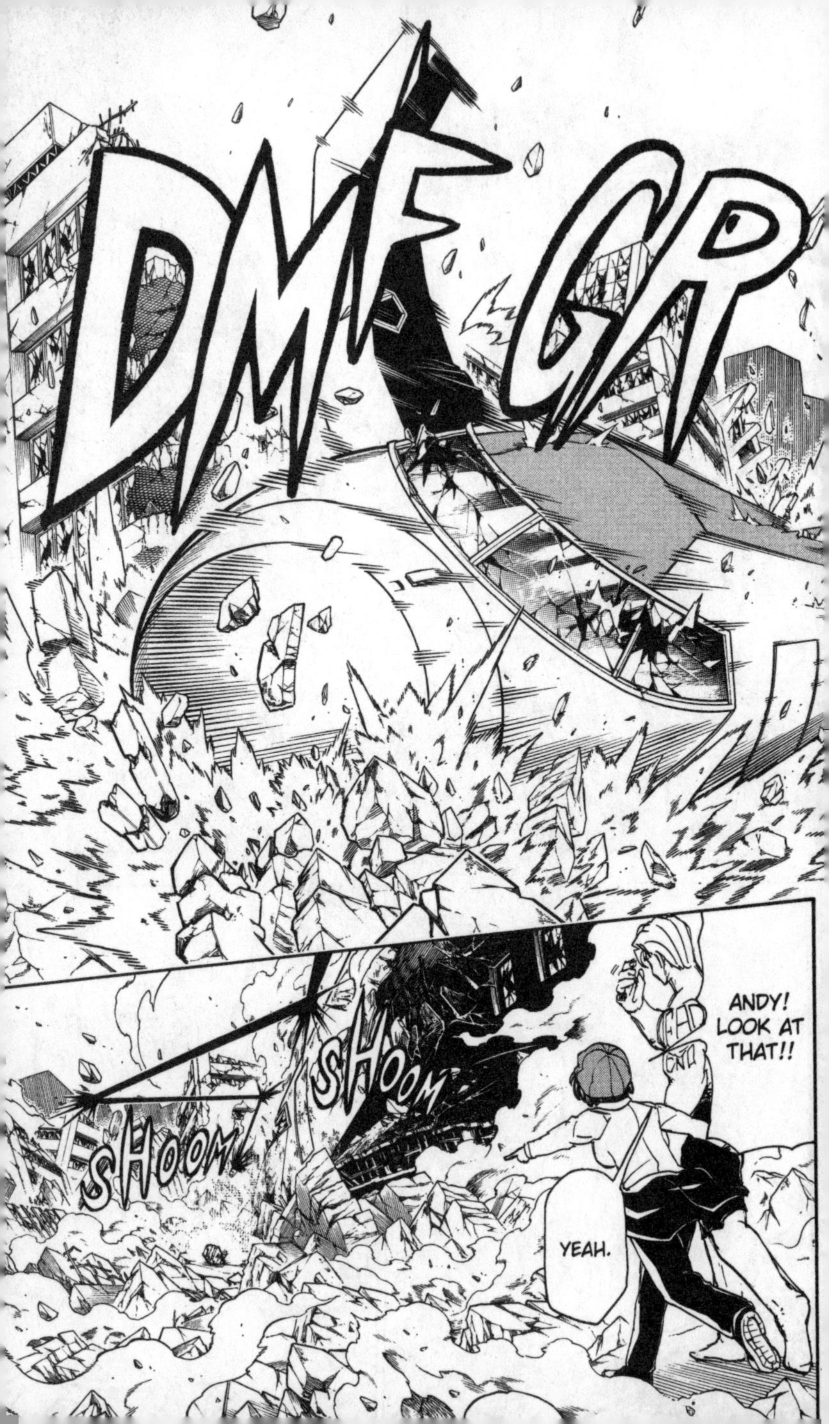
DMFGP
ANDY! LOOK AT THAT!!
SHOOM
SHOOM
YEAH.

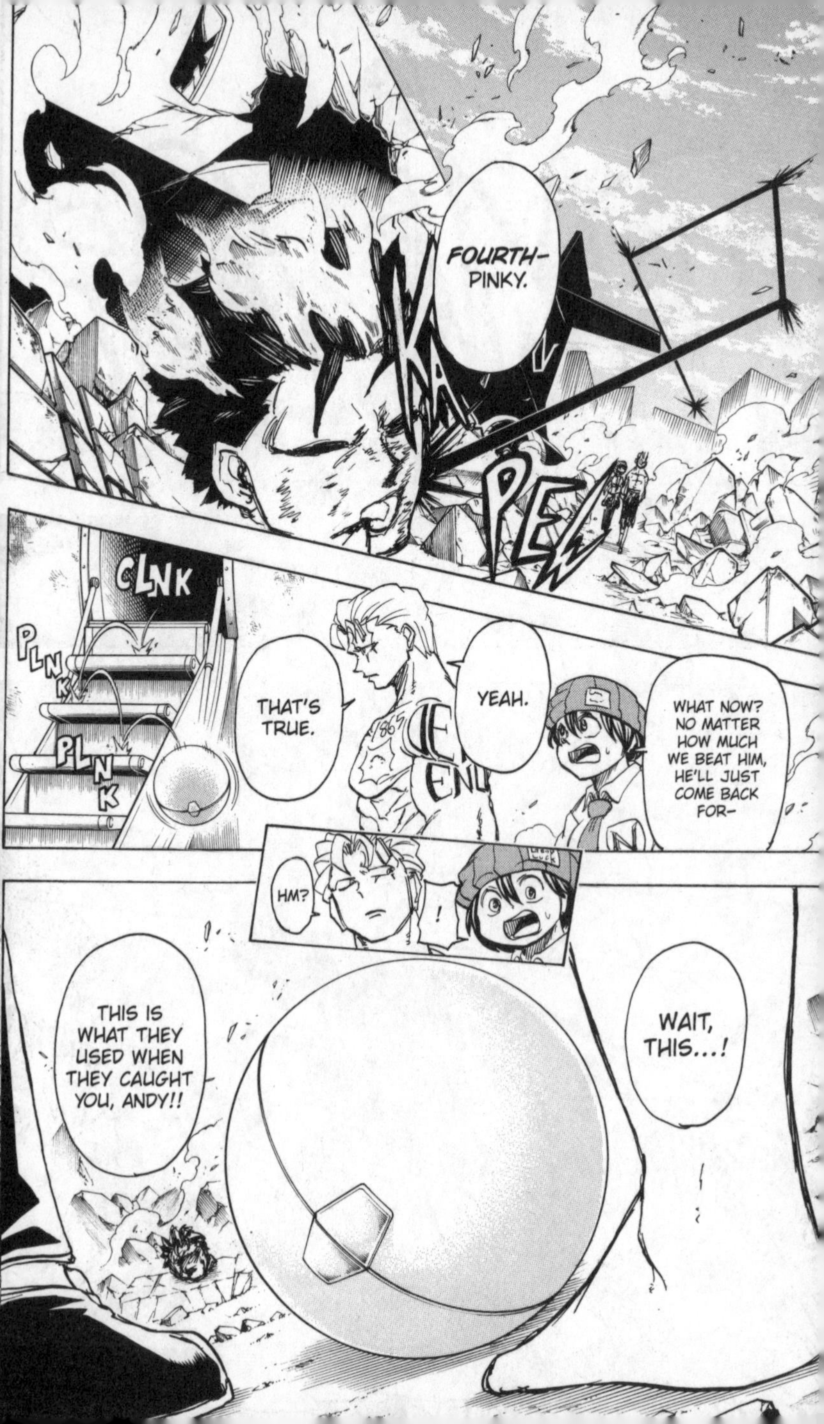
FOURTH-PINKY.
KA
PEW
WHAT NOW? NO MATTER HOW MUCH WE BEAT HIM, HE'LL JUST COME BACK FOR-
YEAH.
THAT'S TRUE.
CLNK
PLNK
PLNK
!
HM?
WAIT, THIS...!
THIS IS WHAT THEY USED WHEN THEY CAUGHT YOU, ANDY!!

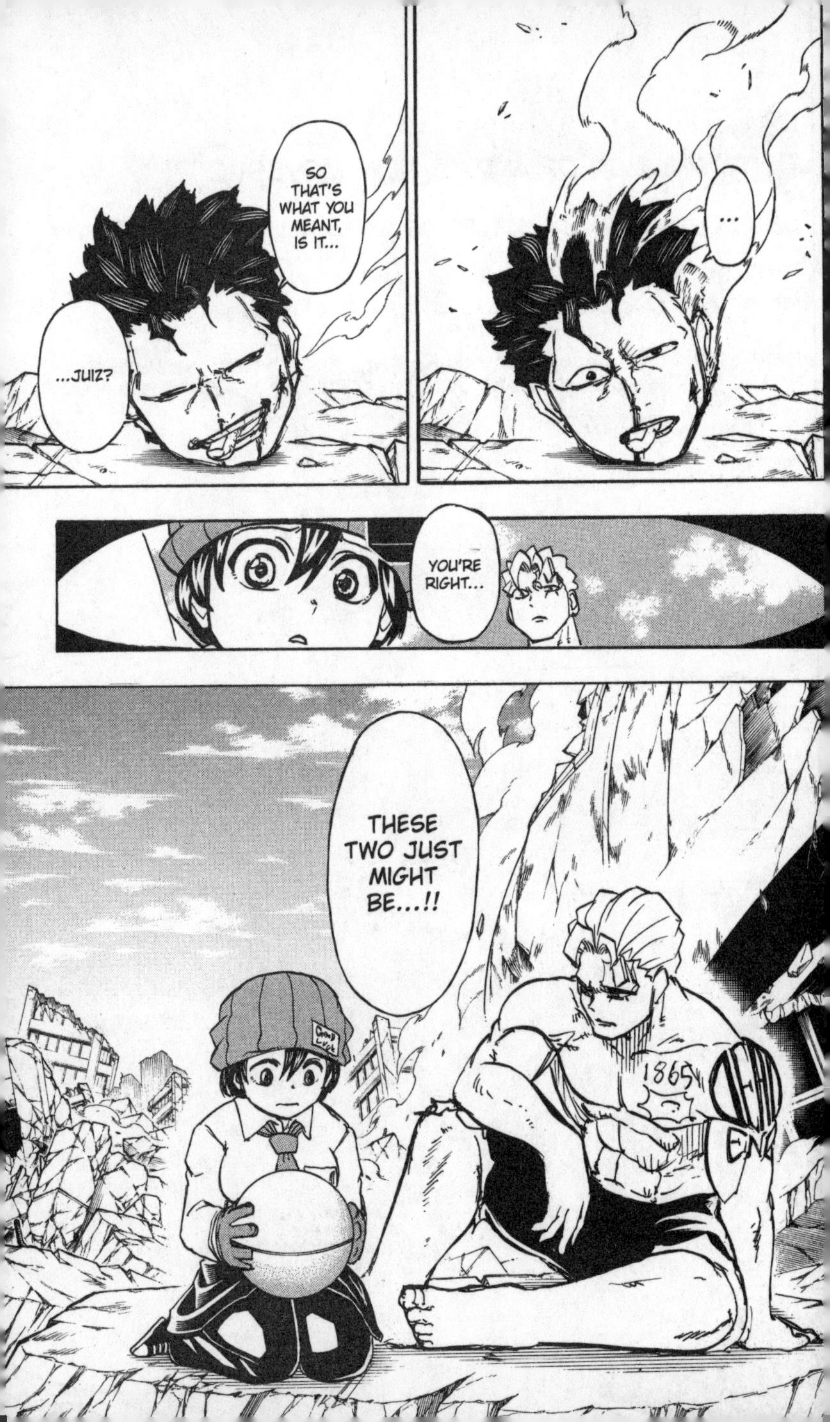
...
SO THAT'S WHAT YOU MEANT, IS IT...
...JUIZ?
YOU'RE RIGHT...
THESE TWO JUST MIGHT BE...!!
1865

INTRODUCTION OF ANDY'S NEW MOVES ②

NEW MOVE 4: UNLUCK BULLET AS EXPLAINED BY CURRENT ANDY

PREREQUISITE ①: ASSUME THINGS LIKE SOULS ACTUALLY EXIST.

PREREQUISITE ②: ASSUME FUUKO'S UNLUCK DWELLS IN THE SOUL OF WHO SHE TOUCHES.

PREREQUISITE ③: ASSUME THAT THIS INDEFINITE "THING" THAT I'VE MORE OR LESS IDENTIFIED OVER THE COURSE OF 140 YEARS IS A SOUL.

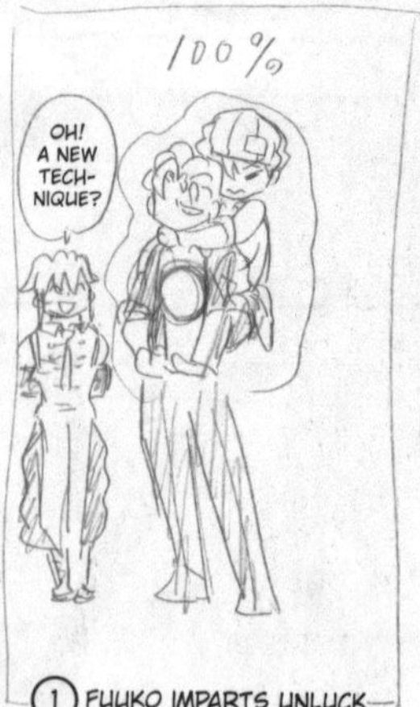
100%
OH! A NEW TECH-NIQUE?

① FUUKO IMPARTS UNLUCK ONTO MY SOUL.

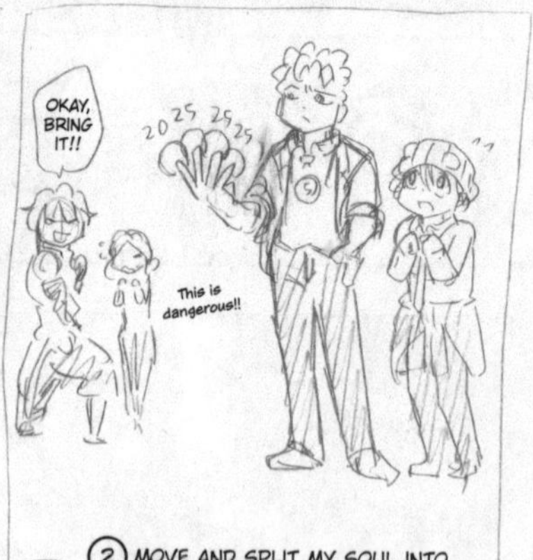
20 25 25 25
OKAY, BRING IT!!
This is dangerous!!

② MOVE AND SPLIT MY SOUL INTO MY FINGERTIPS. I LEAVE A BIT OF MY SOUL IN MY BODY. (OTHERWISE, MY BODY WOULDN'T BE ABLE TO ACT AGAIN AFTER FIRING.)

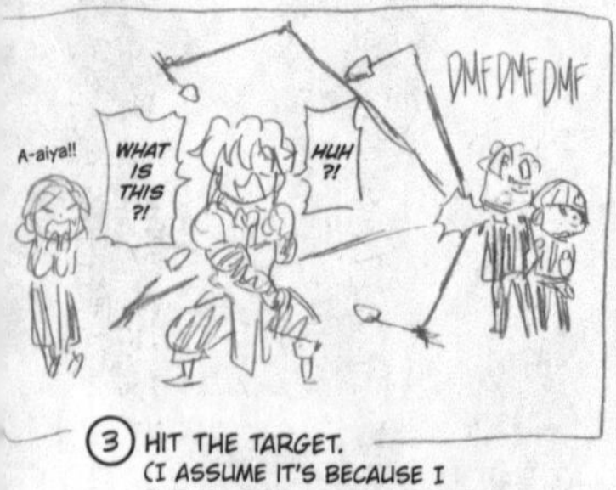
DMF DMF DMF
HUH ?!
WHAT IS THIS ?!
A-aiya!!

③ HIT THE TARGET. (I ASSUME IT'S BECAUSE I PUT MY SOUL IN THEM, BUT EACH FINGER MOVES AUTOMATICALLY TO HIT ITS TARGET.)

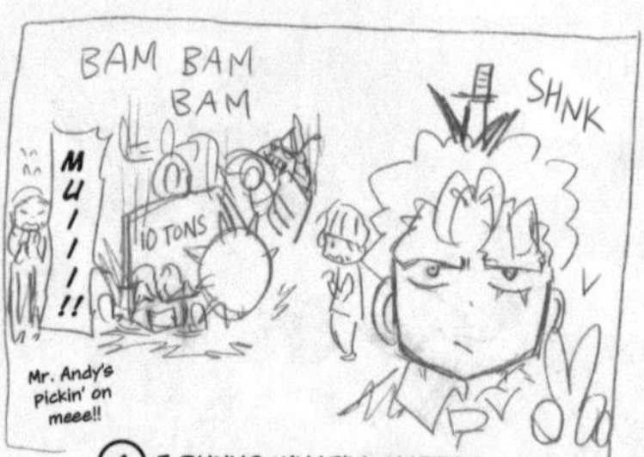
SHNK
BAM BAM BAM
10 TONS
MU/////!!
Mr. Andy's pickin' on meee!!

④ I DUNNO WHAT'LL HAPPEN AFTER THAT. MY BODY WILL TAKE 5 PERCENT DAMAGE.

No. 046
See You in the Here and Now

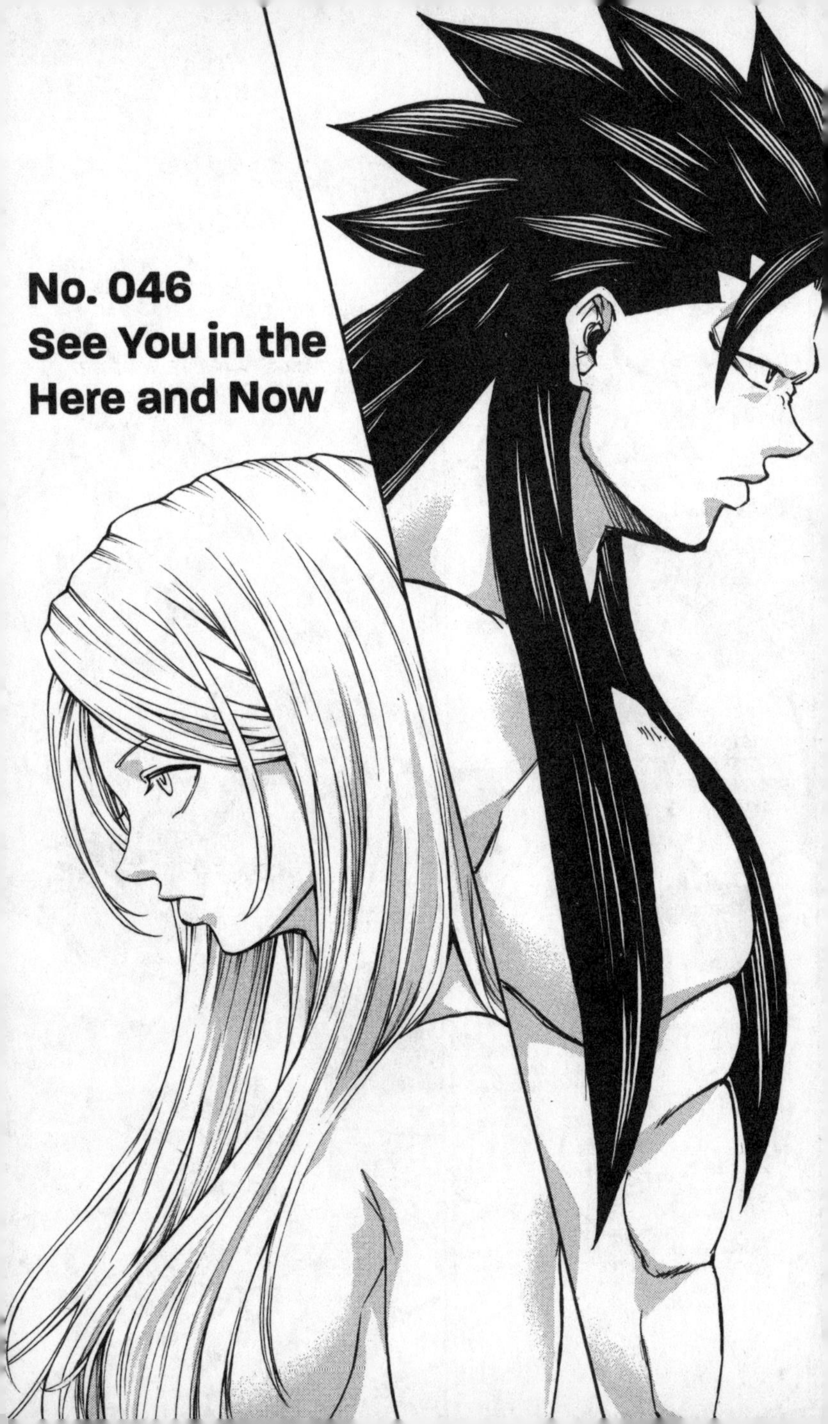

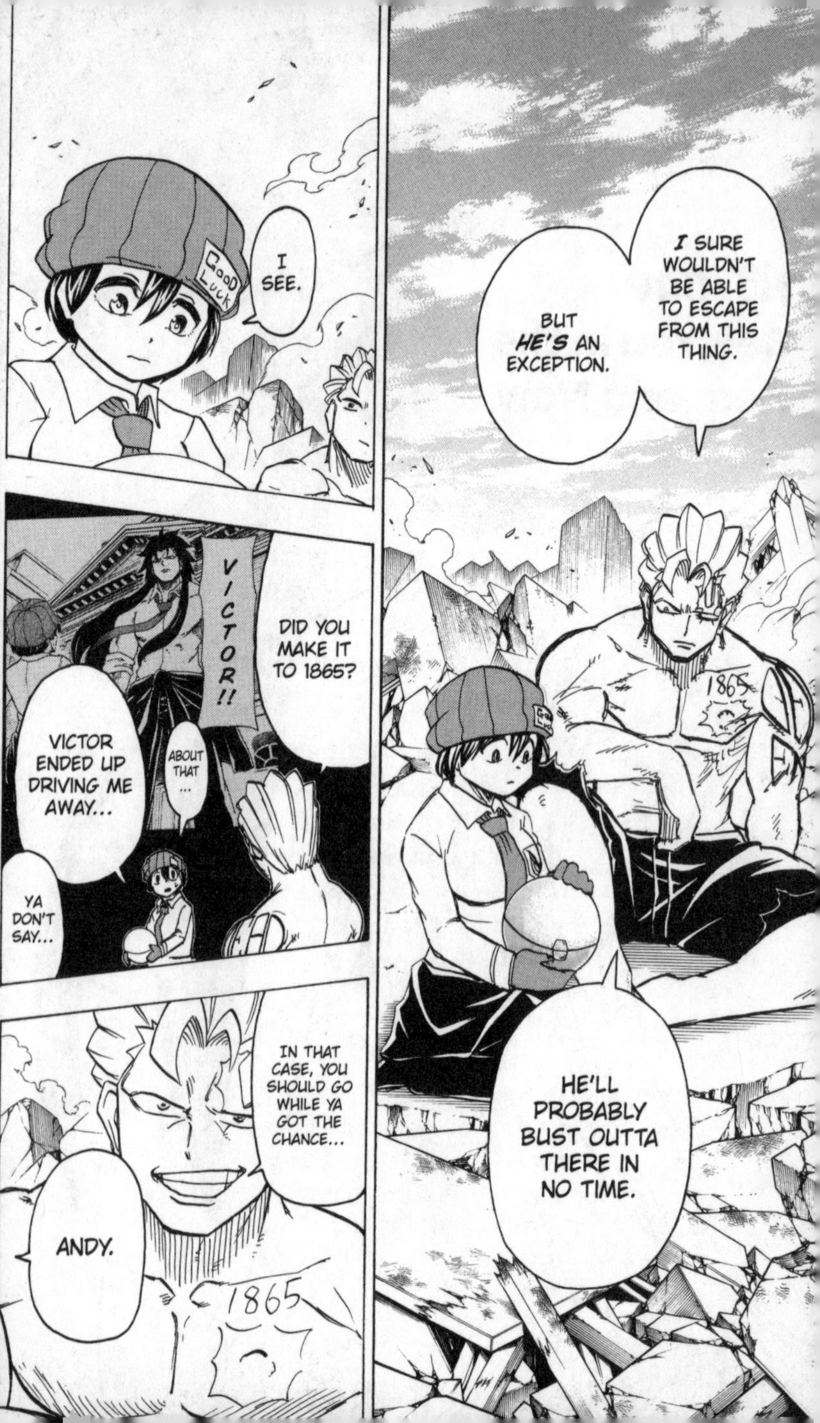
I SURE WOULDN'T BE ABLE TO ESCAPE FROM THIS THING.
BUT HE'S AN EXCEPTION.
1865
HE'LL PROBABLY BUST OUTTA THERE IN NO TIME.
GOOD LUCK
I SEE.
DID YOU MAKE IT TO 1865?
VICTOR!!
ABOUT THAT ...
VICTOR ENDED UP DRIVING ME AWAY...
YA DON'T SAY...
IN THAT CASE, YOU SHOULD GO WHILE YA GOT THE CHANCE...
ANDY.
1865

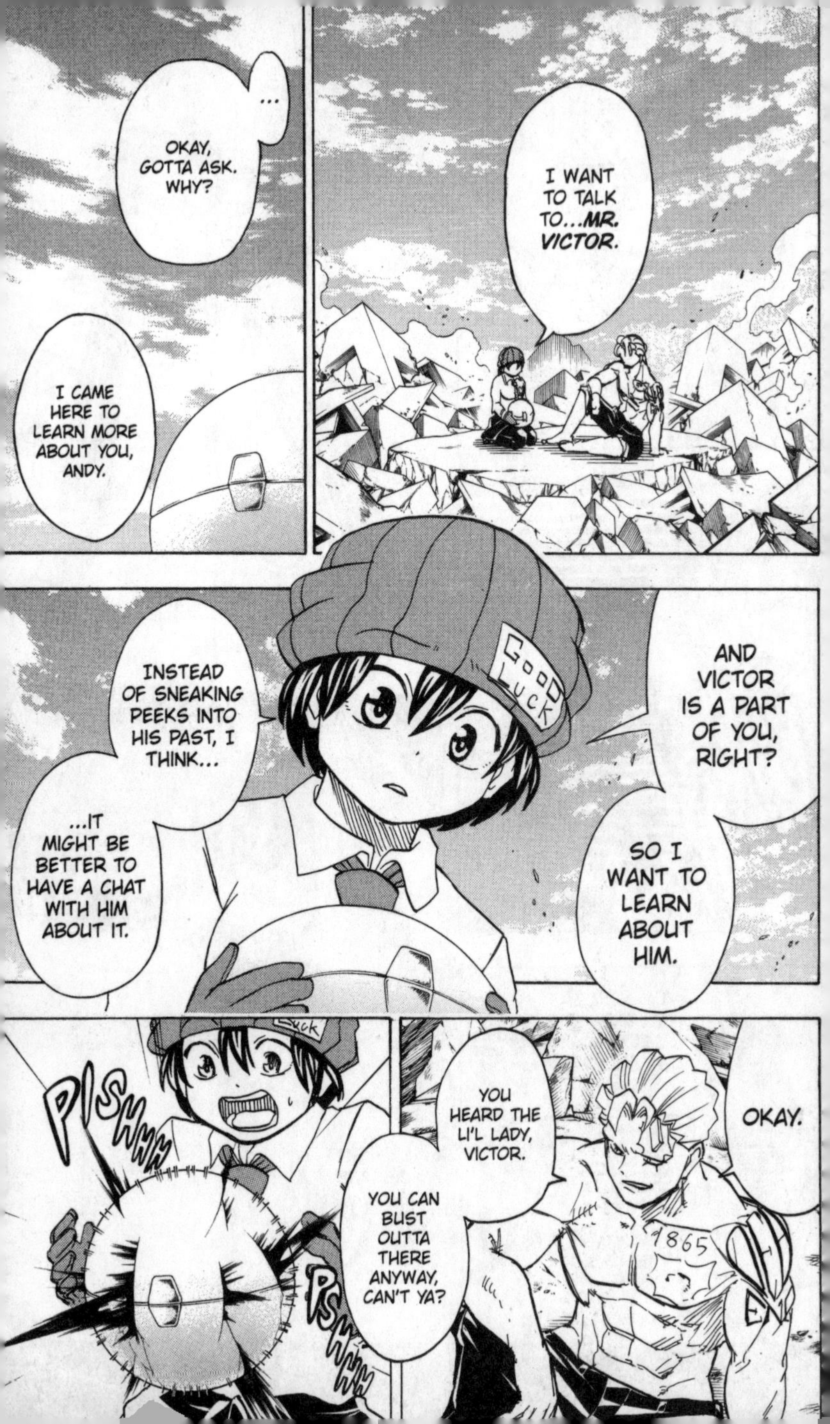
I WANT TO TALK TO...**MR. VICTOR**.
...
OKAY, GOTTA ASK. WHY?
I CAME HERE TO LEARN MORE ABOUT YOU, ANDY.
AND VICTOR IS A PART OF YOU, RIGHT?
SO I WANT TO LEARN ABOUT HIM.
GOOD LUCK
INSTEAD OF SNEAKING PEEKS INTO HIS PAST, I THINK...
...IT MIGHT BE BETTER TO HAVE A CHAT WITH HIM ABOUT IT.
OKAY.
YOU HEARD THE LI'L LADY, VICTOR.
YOU CAN BUST OUTTA THERE ANYWAY, CAN'T YA?
1865
PISHHH
PSHHH

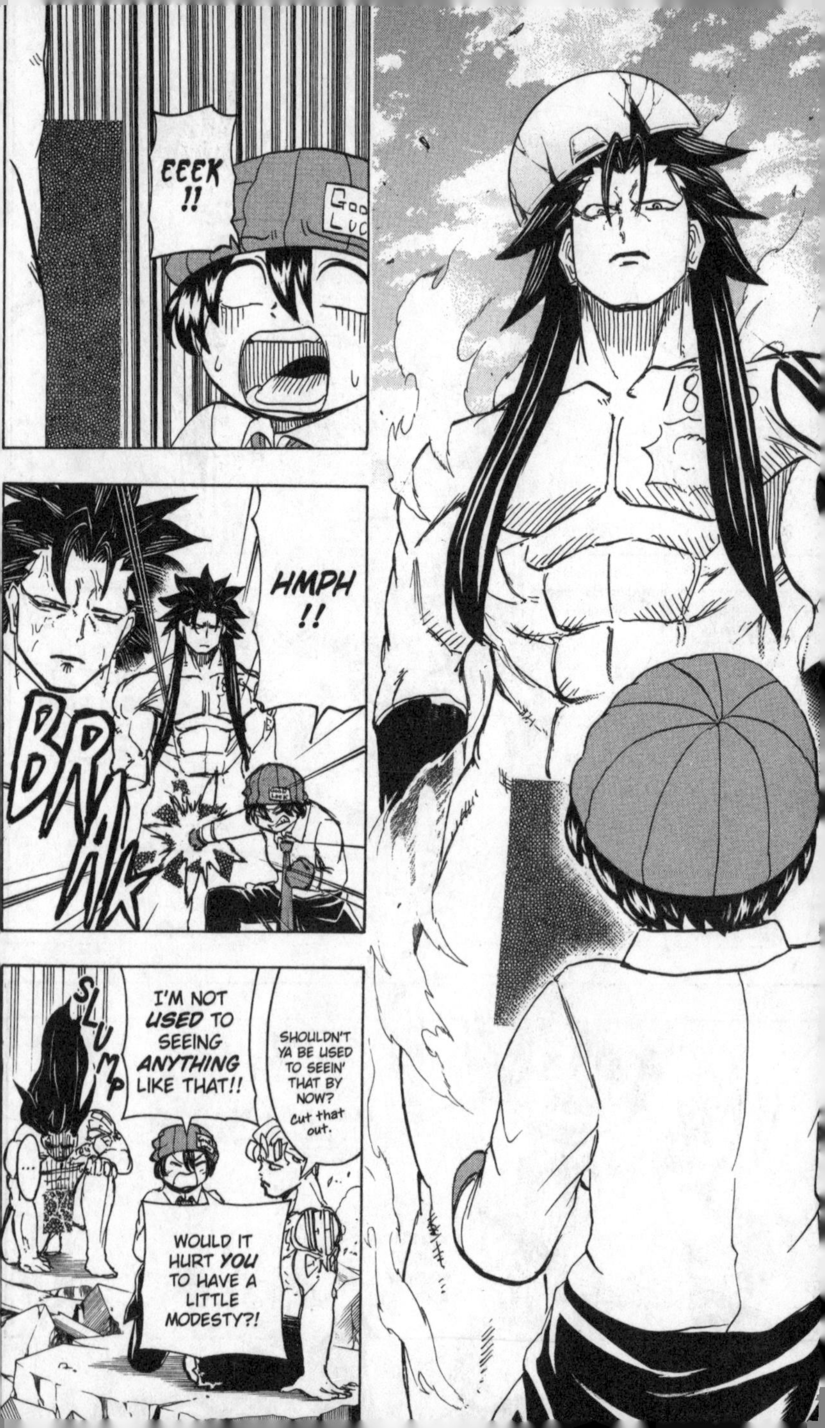
18
EEEK !!
HMPH !!
BRAAK
SHOULDN'T YA BE USED TO SEEIN' THAT BY NOW?
Cut that out.
I'M NOT *USED* TO SEEING *ANYTHING* LIKE THAT!!
SLUMP
...
WOULD IT HURT *YOU* TO HAVE A LITTLE MODESTY?!

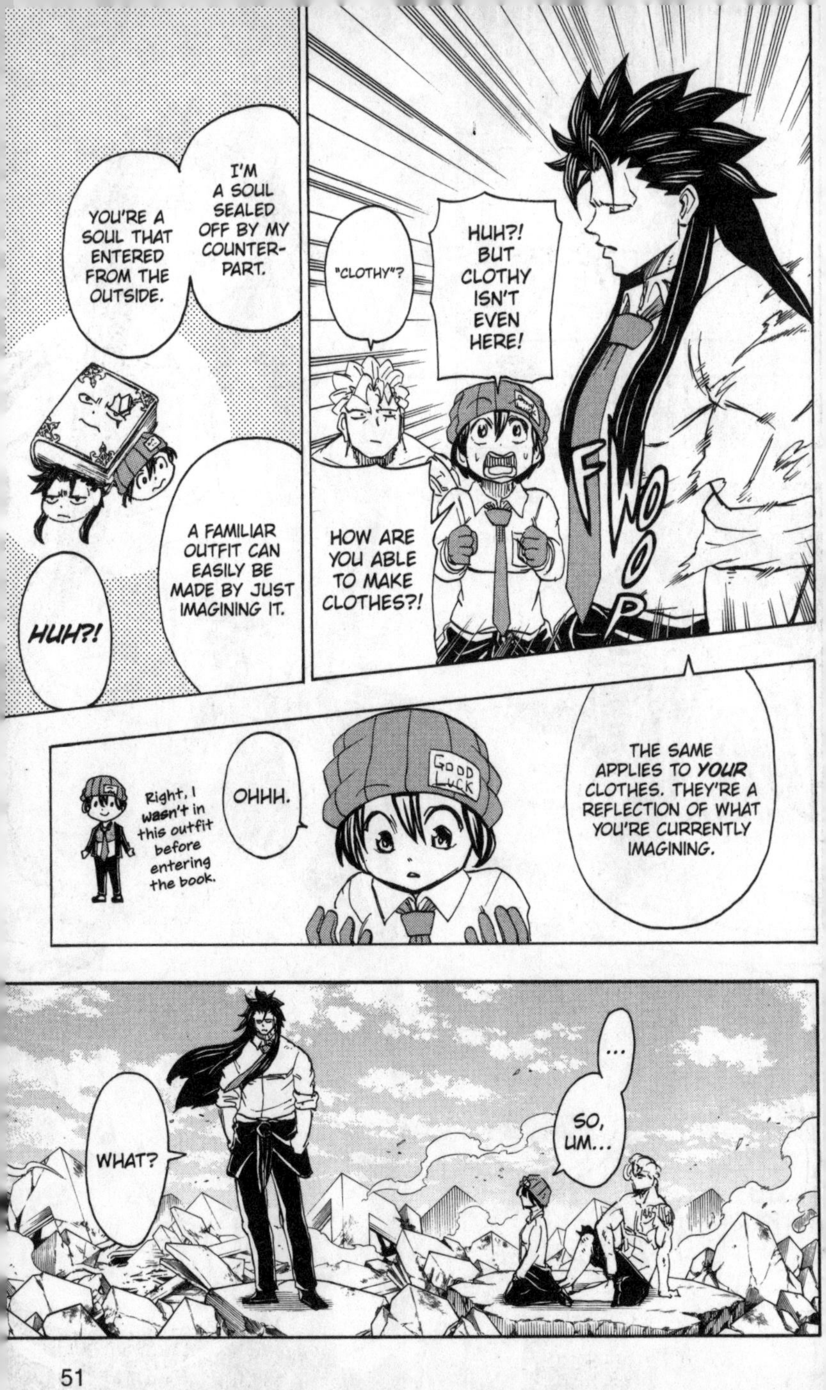
HUH?! BUT CLOTHY ISN'T EVEN HERE!
"CLOTHY"?
HOW ARE YOU ABLE TO MAKE CLOTHES?!
FWOOP
I'M A SOUL SEALED OFF BY MY COUNTER-PART.
YOU'RE A SOUL THAT ENTERED FROM THE OUTSIDE.
A FAMILIAR OUTFIT CAN EASILY BE MADE BY JUST IMAGINING IT.
HUH?!
THE SAME APPLIES TO YOUR CLOTHES. THEY'RE A REFLECTION OF WHAT YOU'RE CURRENTLY IMAGINING.
OHHH.
Right, I wasn't in this outfit before entering the book.
...
SO, UM...
WHAT?

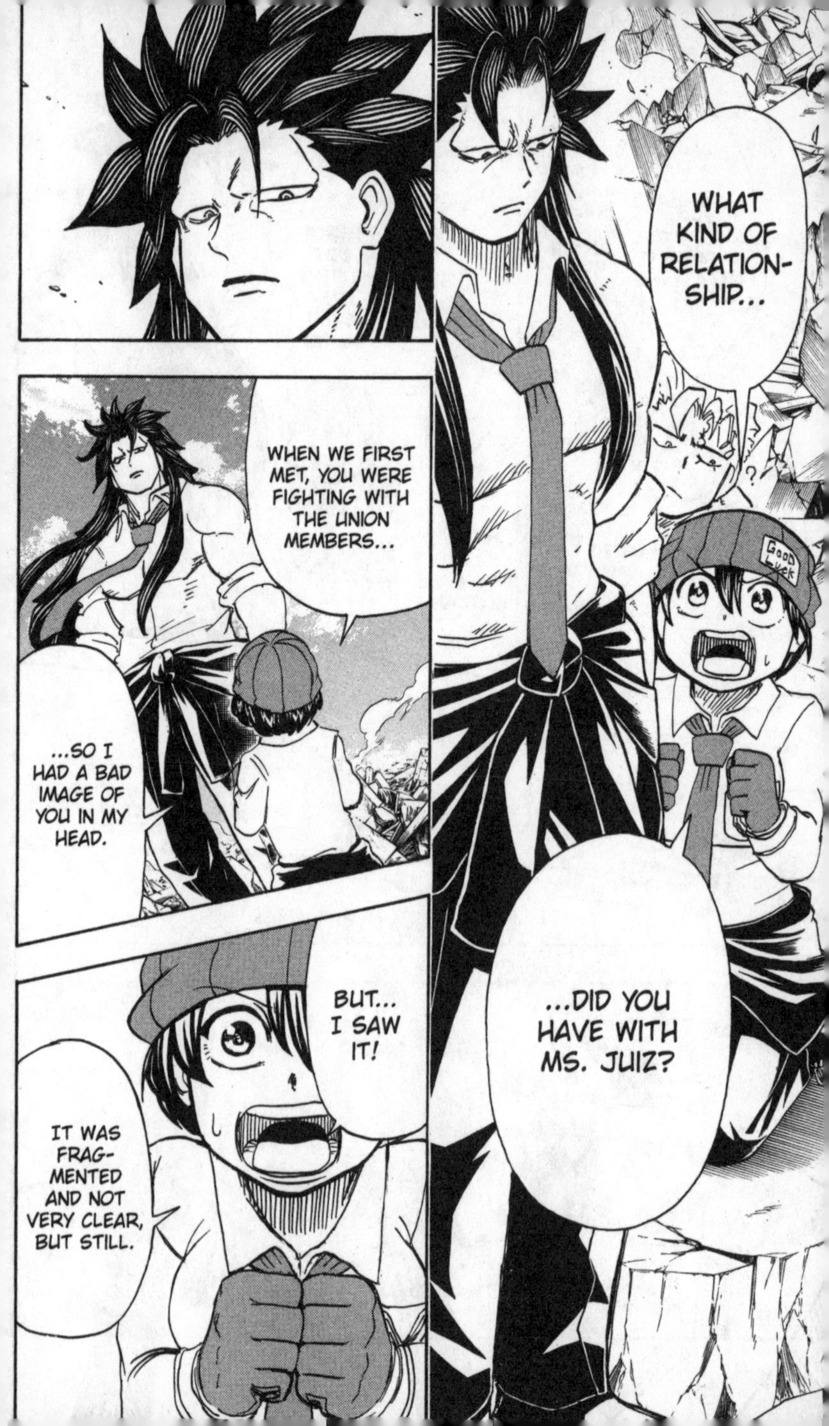

WHAT KIND OF RELATIONSHIP...
GOOD LUCK
...DID YOU HAVE WITH MS. JUIZ?
WHEN WE FIRST MET, YOU WERE FIGHTING WITH THE UNION MEMBERS...
...SO I HAD A BAD IMAGE OF YOU IN MY HEAD.
BUT... I SAW IT!
IT WAS FRAGMENTED AND NOT VERY CLEAR, BUT STILL.

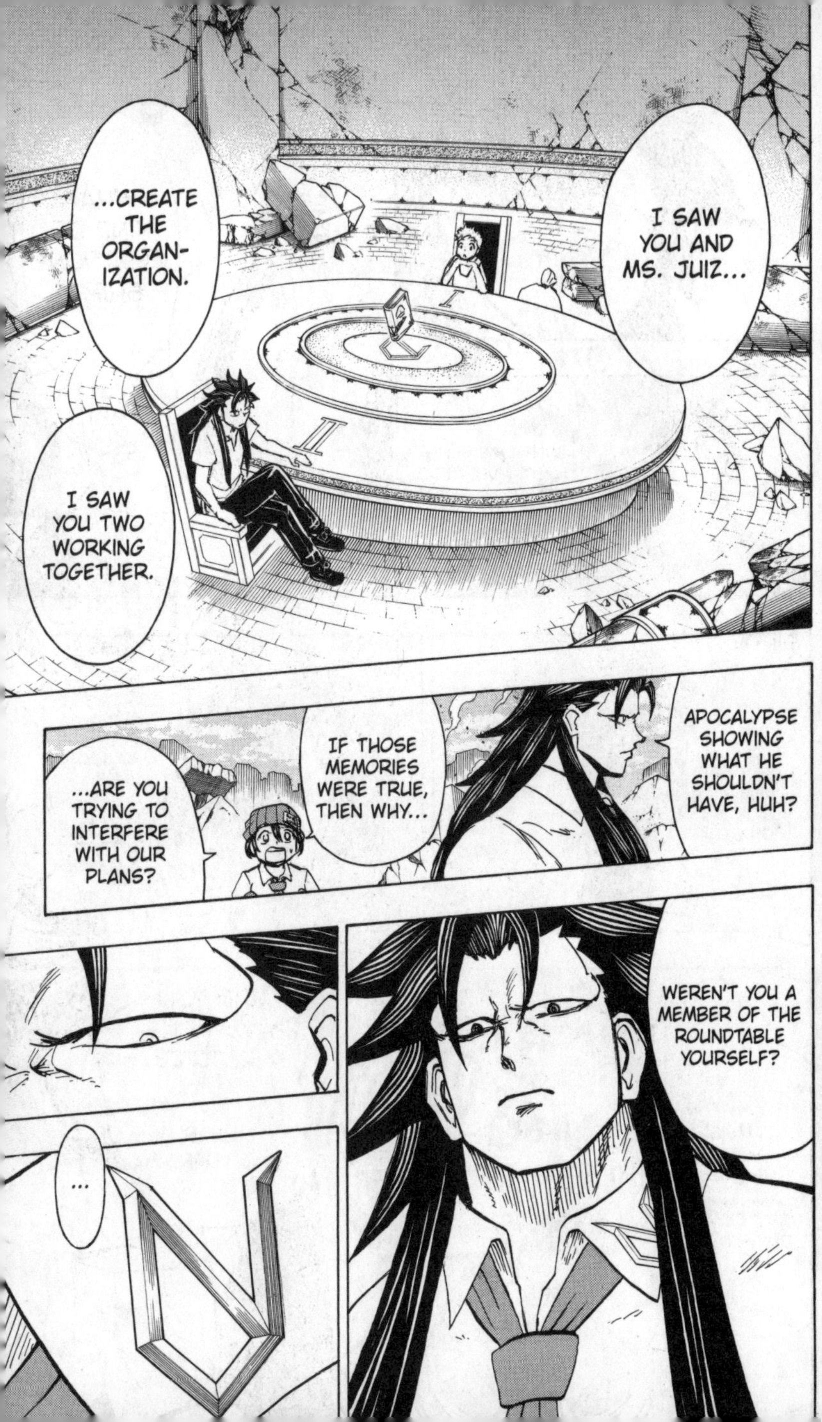
I SAW YOU AND MS. JUIZ...
...CREATE THE ORGANIZATION.
I SAW YOU TWO WORKING TOGETHER.
APOCALYPSE SHOWING WHAT HE SHOULDN'T HAVE, HUH?
IF THOSE MEMORIES WERE TRUE, THEN WHY...
...ARE YOU TRYING TO INTERFERE WITH OUR PLANS?
WEREN'T YOU A MEMBER OF THE ROUNDTABLE YOURSELF?
...

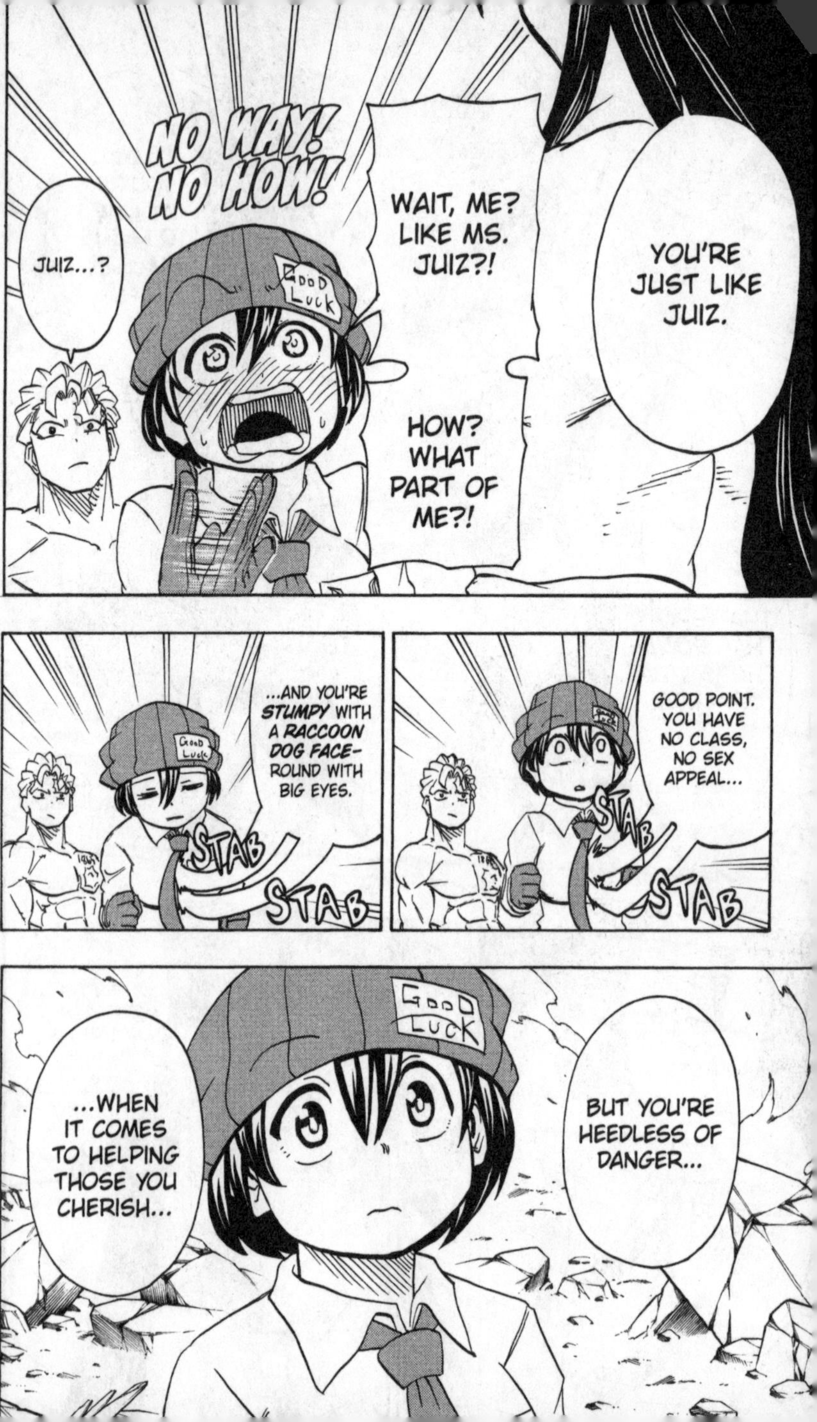
YOU'RE JUST LIKE JUIZ.
WAIT, ME? LIKE MS. JUIZ?!
HOW? WHAT PART OF ME?!
NO WAY! NO HOW!
JUIZ...?
GOOD POINT. YOU HAVE NO CLASS, NO SEX APPEAL...
STAB
STAB
...AND YOU'RE *STUMPY* WITH A *RACCOON DOG FACE*-ROUND WITH BIG EYES.
STAB
STAB
BUT YOU'RE HEEDLESS OF DANGER...
...WHEN IT COMES TO HELPING THOSE YOU CHERISH...

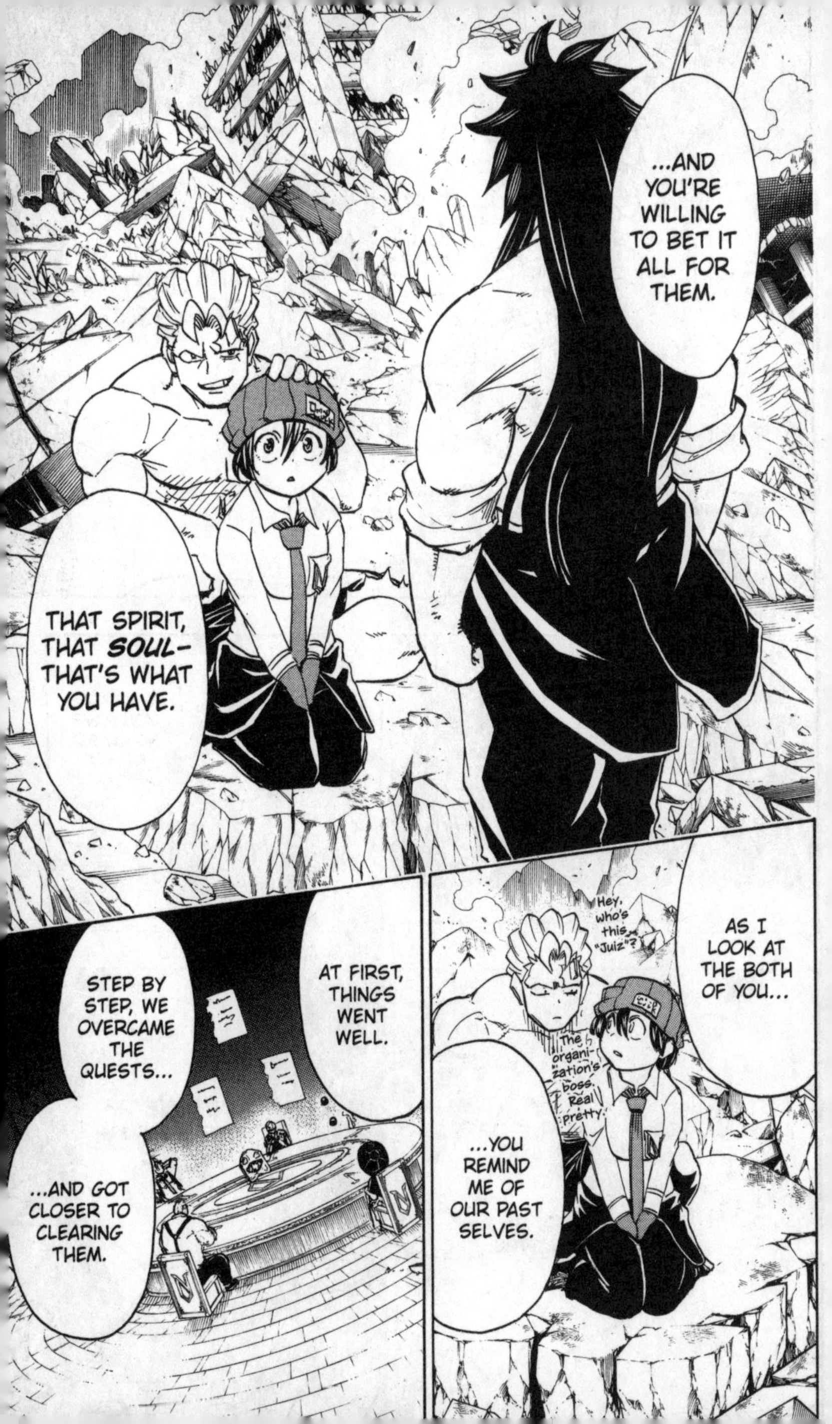
...AND YOU'RE WILLING TO BET IT ALL FOR THEM.
THAT SPIRIT, THAT **SOUL**—THAT'S WHAT YOU HAVE.
AS I LOOK AT THE BOTH OF YOU...
Hey, who's this "Juiz"?
The organization's boss. Real pretty.
...YOU REMIND ME OF OUR PAST SELVES.
AT FIRST, THINGS WENT WELL.
STEP BY STEP, WE OVERCAME THE QUESTS...
...AND GOT CLOSER TO CLEARING THEM.

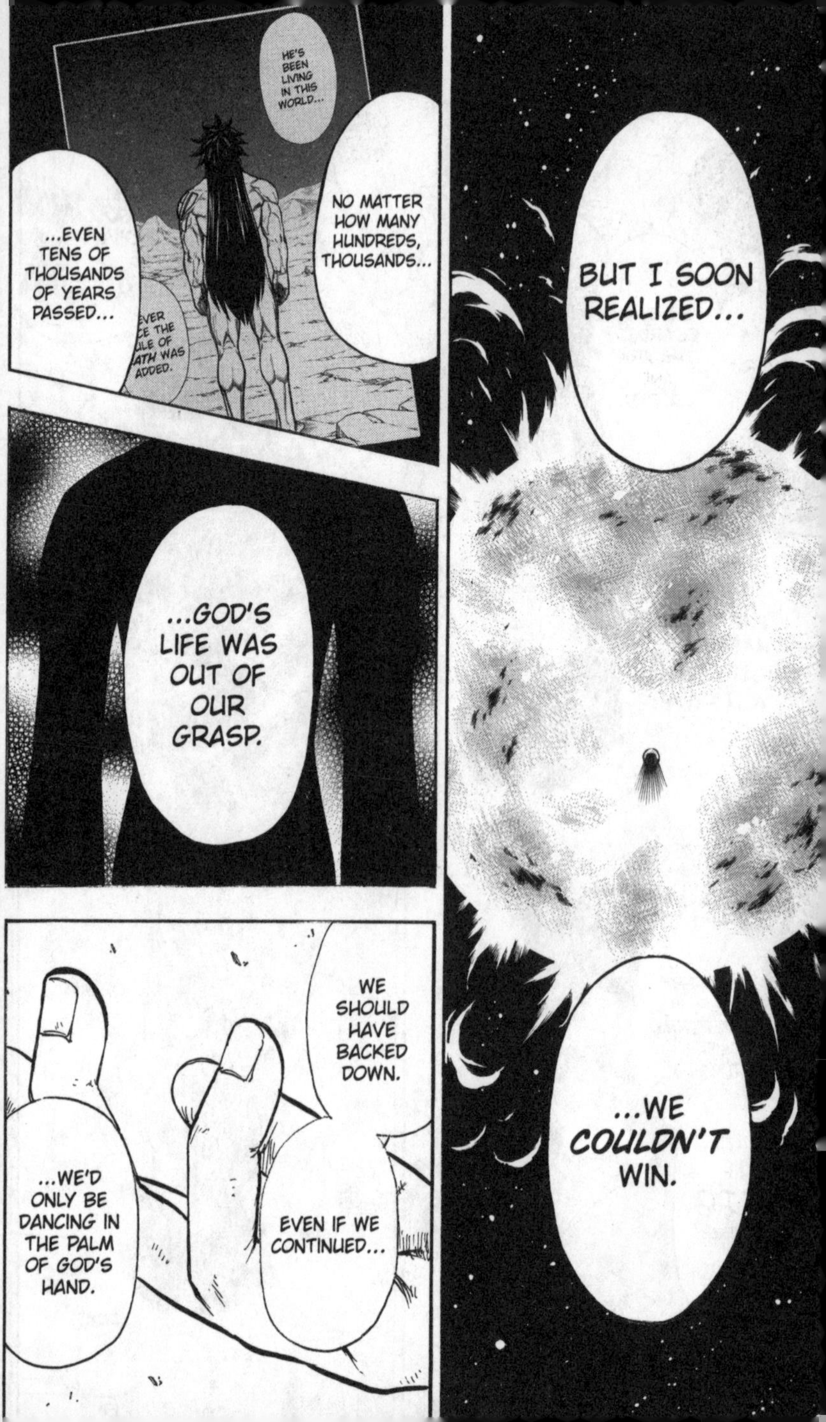
BUT I SOON REALIZED...
...WE COULDN'T WIN.
HE'S BEEN LIVING IN THIS WORLD...
NO MATTER HOW MANY HUNDREDS, THOUSANDS...
...EVEN TENS OF THOUSANDS OF YEARS PASSED...
EVER CE THE ULE OF ATH WAS ADDED.
...GOD'S LIFE WAS OUT OF OUR GRASP.
WE SHOULD HAVE BACKED DOWN.
EVEN IF WE CONTINUED...
...WE'D ONLY BE DANCING IN THE PALM OF GOD'S HAND.

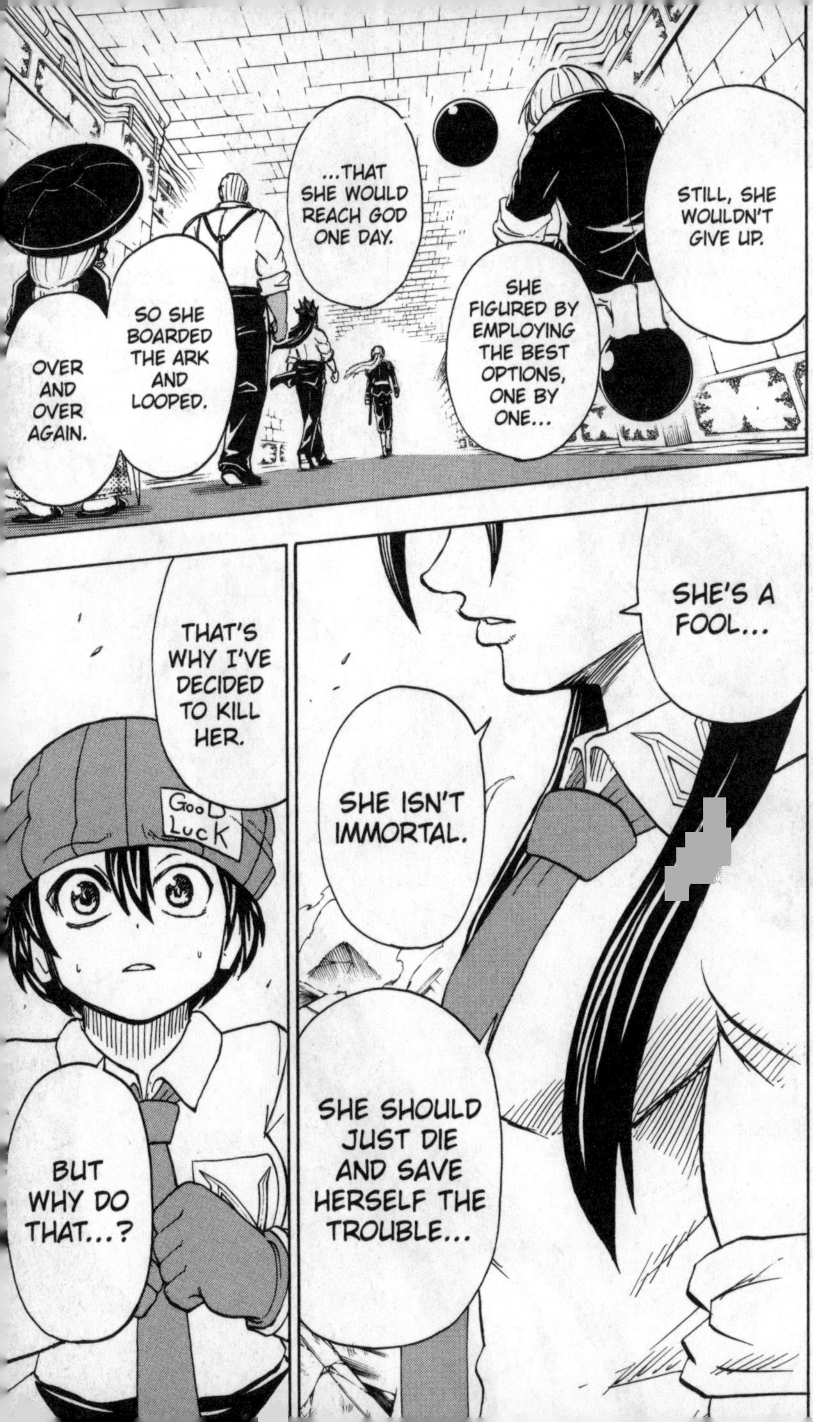
STILL, SHE WOULDN'T GIVE UP.
SHE FIGURED BY EMPLOYING THE BEST OPTIONS, ONE BY ONE...
...THAT SHE WOULD REACH GOD ONE DAY.
SO SHE BOARDED THE ARK AND LOOPED.
OVER AND OVER AGAIN.
SHE'S A FOOL...
SHE ISN'T IMMORTAL.
SHE SHOULD JUST DIE AND SAVE HERSELF THE TROUBLE...
THAT'S WHY I'VE DECIDED TO KILL HER.
GooD LucK
BUT WHY DO THAT...?

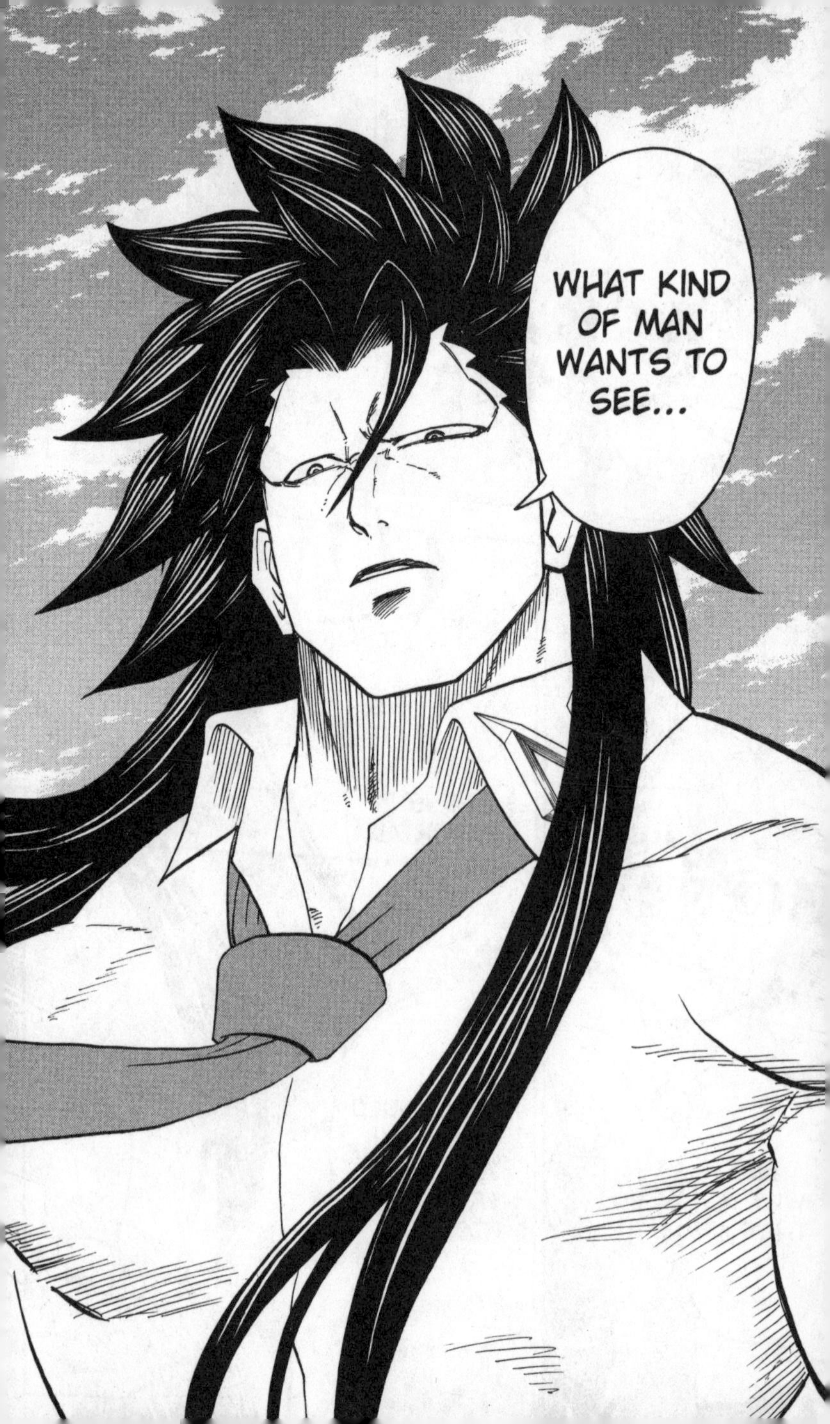
WHAT KIND OF MAN WANTS TO SEE...

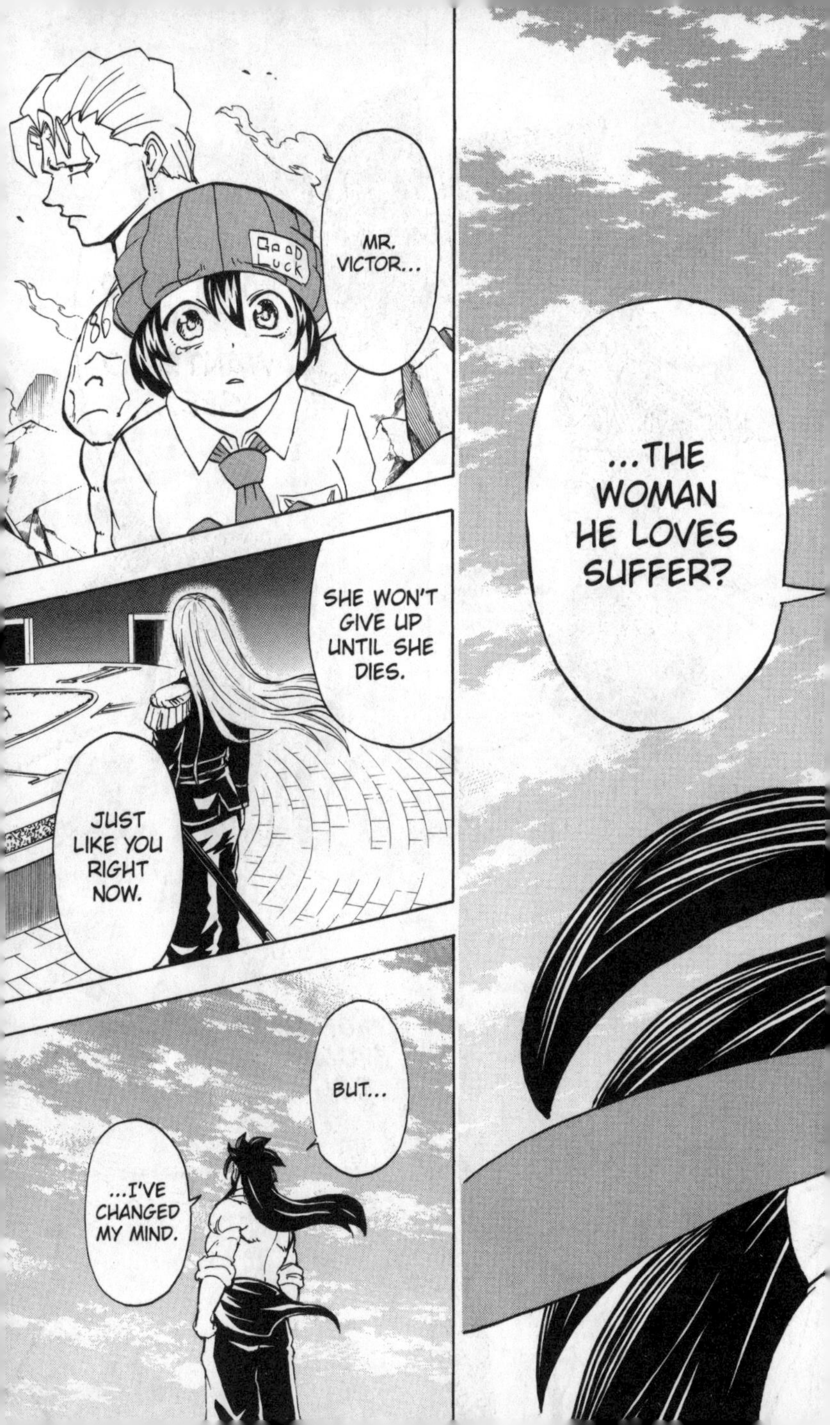
...THE WOMAN HE LOVES SUFFER?
MR. VICTOR...
SHE WON'T GIVE UP UNTIL SHE DIES.
JUST LIKE YOU RIGHT NOW.
BUT...
...I'VE CHANGED MY MIND.

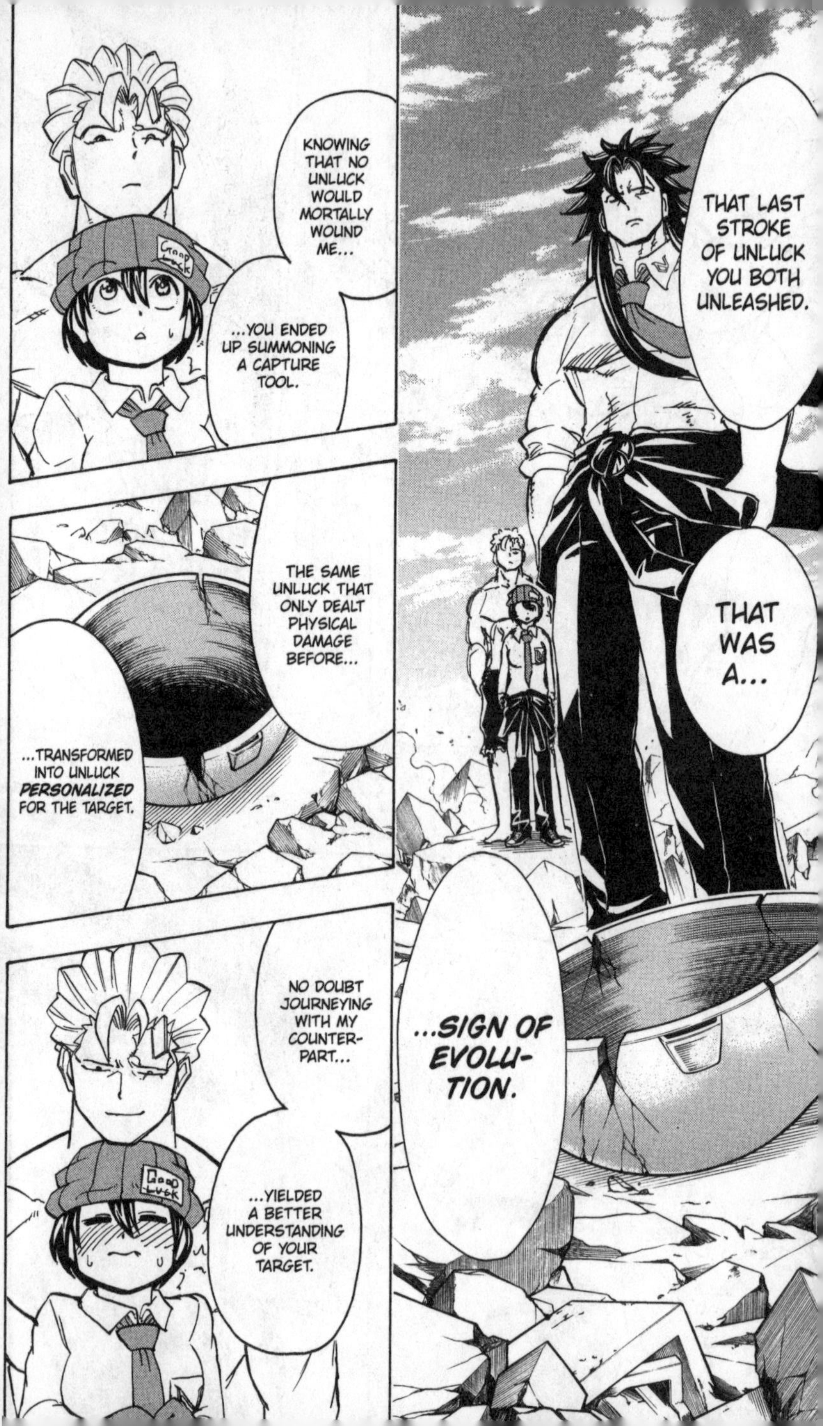
THAT LAST STROKE OF UNLUCK YOU BOTH UNLEASHED.
THAT WAS A...
...*SIGN OF EVOLU-TION.*
KNOWING THAT NO UNLUCK WOULD MORTALLY WOUND ME...
...YOU ENDED UP SUMMONING A CAPTURE TOOL.
THE SAME UNLUCK THAT ONLY DEALT PHYSICAL DAMAGE BEFORE...
...TRANSFORMED INTO UNLUCK *PERSONALIZED* FOR THE TARGET.
NO DOUBT JOURNEYING WITH MY COUNTER-PART...
...YIELDED A BETTER UNDERSTANDING OF YOUR TARGET.

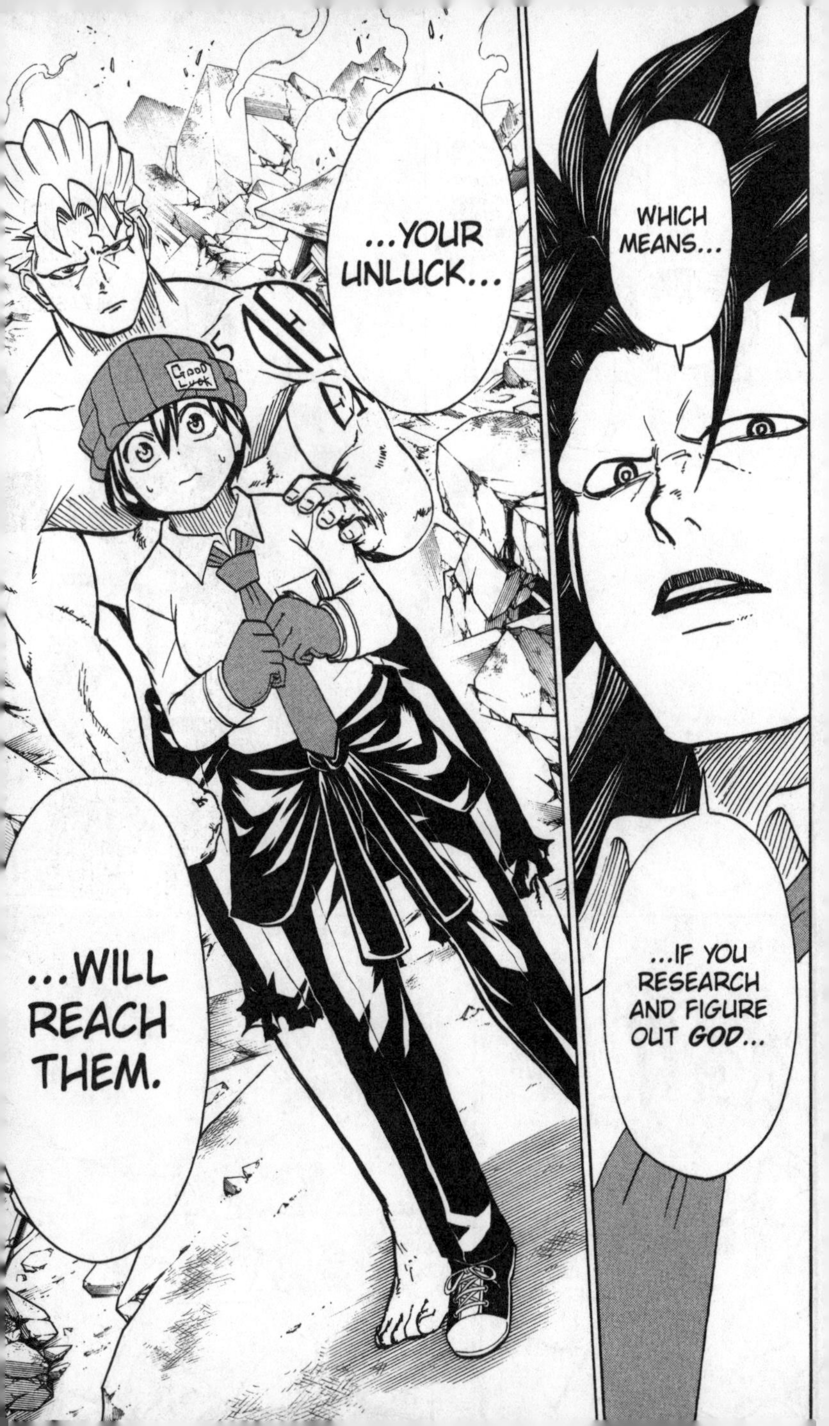
WHICH MEANS...
...IF YOU RESEARCH AND FIGURE OUT GOD...
...YOUR UNLUCK...
GOOD LUCK
...WILL REACH THEM.

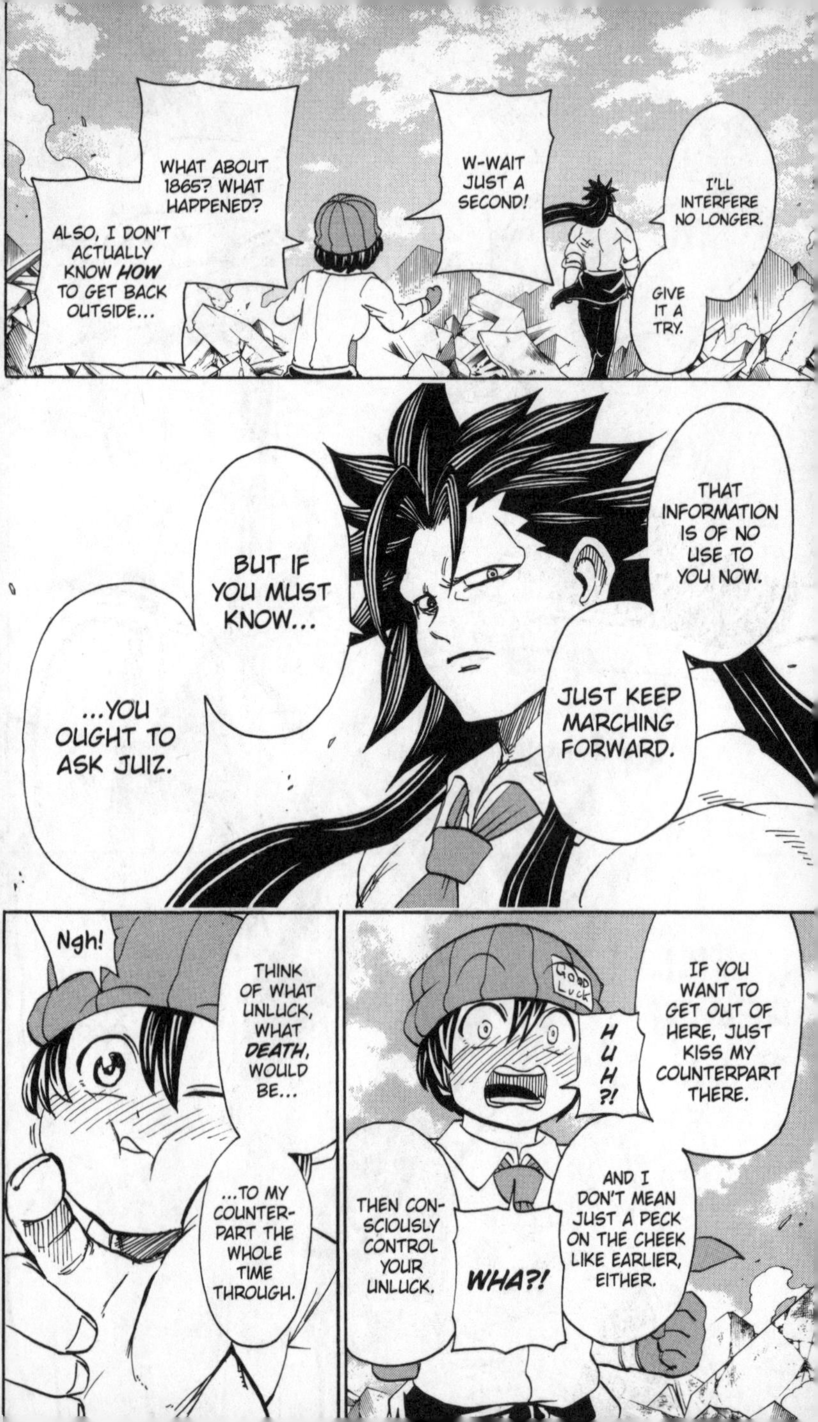
I'LL INTERFERE NO LONGER.
GIVE IT A TRY.
W-WAIT JUST A SECOND!
WHAT ABOUT 1865? WHAT HAPPENED?
ALSO, I DON'T ACTUALLY KNOW *HOW* TO GET BACK OUTSIDE...
THAT INFORMATION IS OF NO USE TO YOU NOW.
JUST KEEP MARCHING FORWARD.
BUT IF YOU MUST KNOW...
...YOU OUGHT TO ASK JUIZ.
GOOD LUCK
IF YOU WANT TO GET OUT OF HERE, JUST KISS MY COUNTERPART THERE.
HUH?!
AND I DON'T MEAN JUST A PECK ON THE CHEEK LIKE EARLIER, EITHER.
WHA?!
THEN CONSCIOUSLY CONTROL YOUR UNLUCK.
THINK OF WHAT UNLUCK, WHAT *DEATH*, WOULD BE...
Ngh!
...TO MY COUNTER-PART THE WHOLE TIME THROUGH.

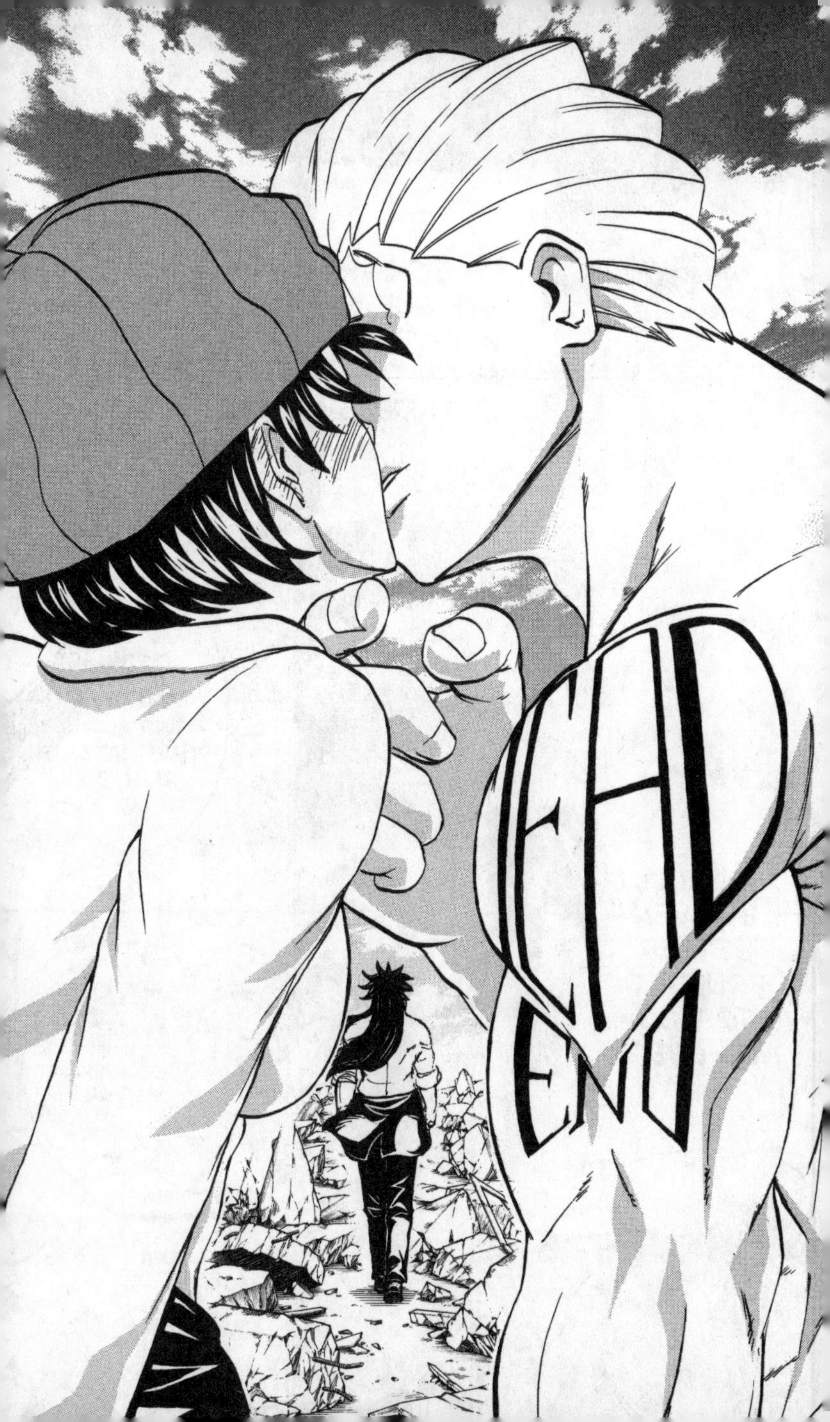
EAD
END

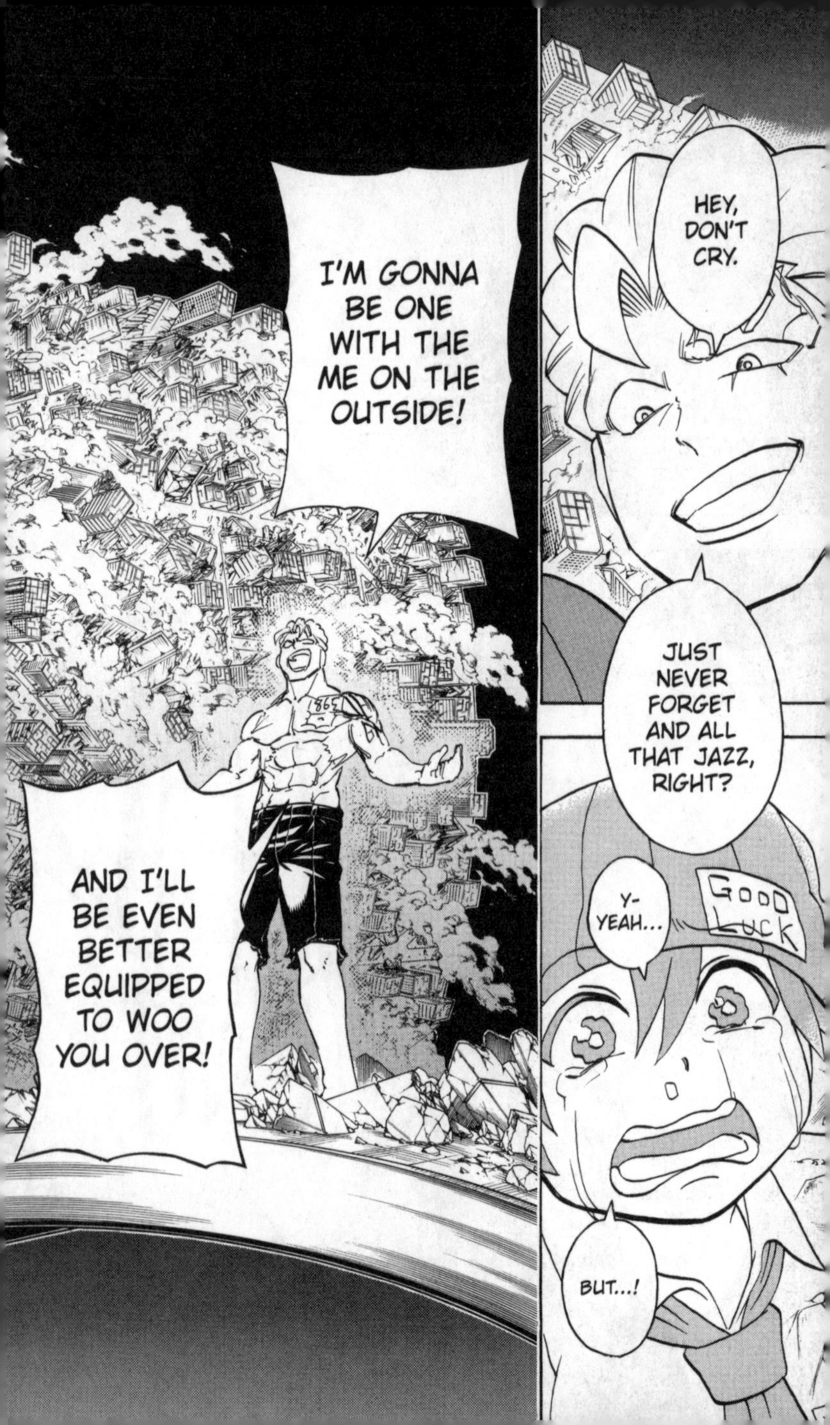
HEY, DON'T CRY.
JUST NEVER FORGET AND ALL THAT JAZZ, RIGHT?
GOOD LUCK
Y-YEAH...
BUT...!
I'M GONNA BE ONE WITH THE ME ON THE OUTSIDE!
865
AND I'LL BE EVEN BETTER EQUIPPED TO WOO YOU OVER!

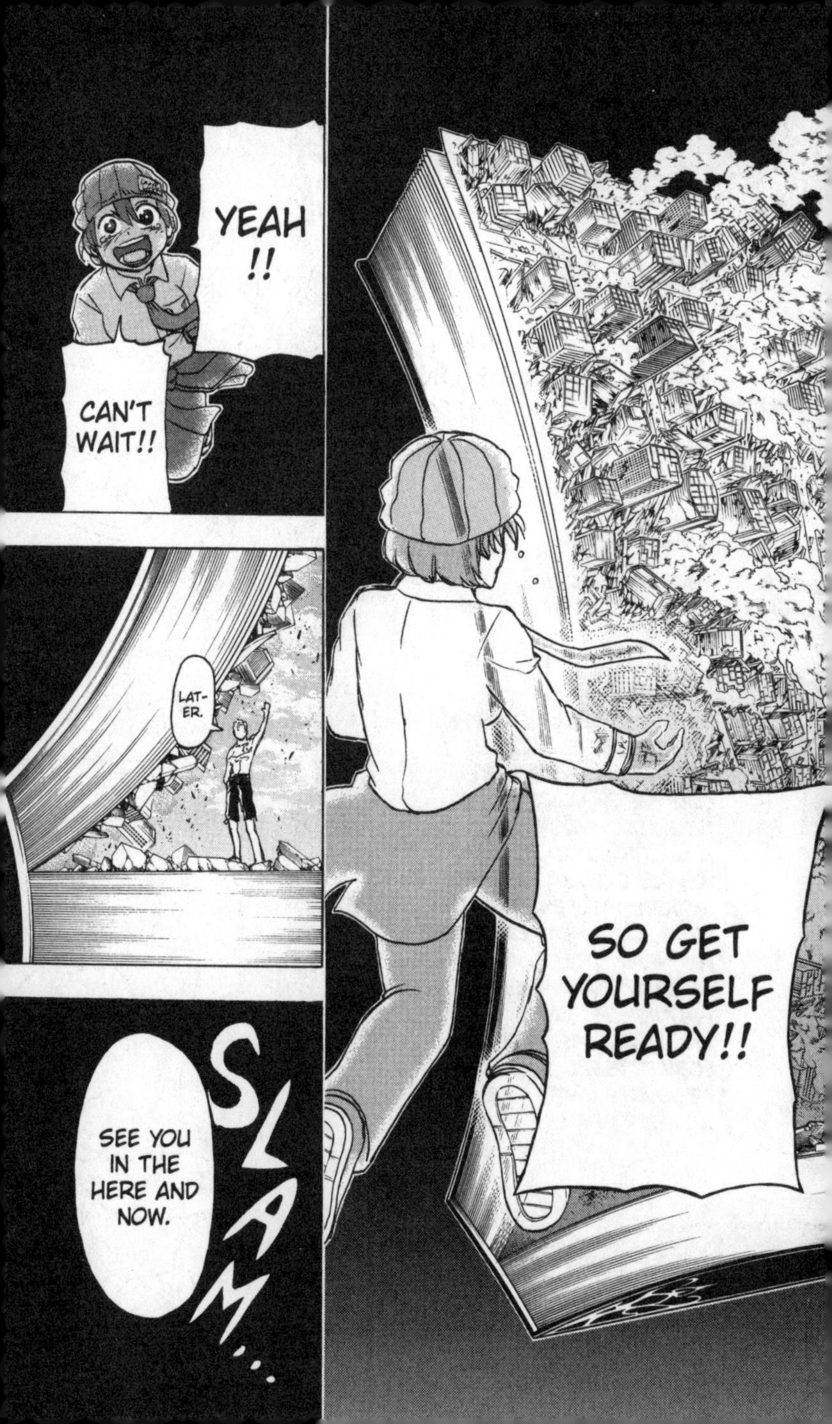
SO GET YOURSELF READY!!
YEAH!!
CAN'T WAIT!!
LATER.
SEE YOU IN THE HERE AND NOW.
SLAM...

VICTOR

AGE: HASN'T COUNTED

HEIGHT: WAS 189 CM, BUT BODY HAS GROWN, INFLATED WITH MUSCLE

WEIGHT: NO CLUE

HOBBIES: WORLD TRAVEL, TEA LEAF COLLECTING, RUIN EXPLORATION

SPECIAL SKILLS: TAIJUTSU, ABILITY CONTROL, ACCOMPANYING JUIZ SHOPPING

ABILITY: UNDEAD

BY CONSCIOUSLY CHANGING THE INTERPRETATION OF "DEATH" OVER THE COURSE OF MANY EONS, HE'S ALLOWED HIMSELF A MULTIFACETED USE OF HIS REGENERATION, WHICH INCLUDES REGENERATION FROM AREAS OTHER THAN HIS HEAD, CREATING CLONES (ALBEIT FOR A SHORT AMOUNT OF TIME), AND FIRING HIS BLOOD (COMPRESSED TO ITS ABSOLUTE LIMIT) LIKE A LASER BEAM.

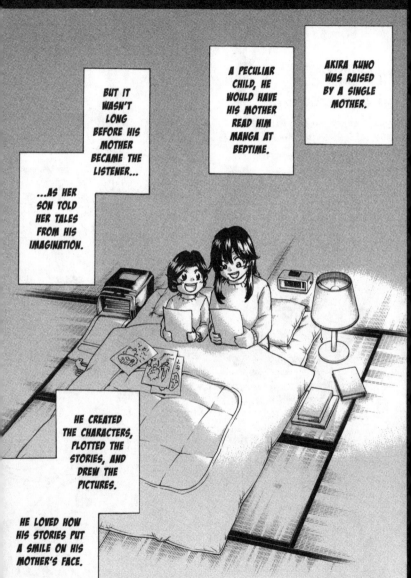

AKIRA KUNO WAS RAISED BY A SINGLE MOTHER.
A PECULIAR CHILD, HE WOULD HAVE HIS MOTHER READ HIM MANGA AT BEDTIME.
BUT IT WASN'T LONG BEFORE HIS MOTHER BECAME THE LISTENER...
...AS HER SON TOLD HER TALES FROM HIS IMAGINATION.
HE CREATED THE CHARACTERS, PLOTTED THE STORIES, AND DREW THE PICTURES.
HE LOVED HOW HIS STORIES PUT A SMILE ON HIS MOTHER'S FACE.

No. 047 Akira Kuno

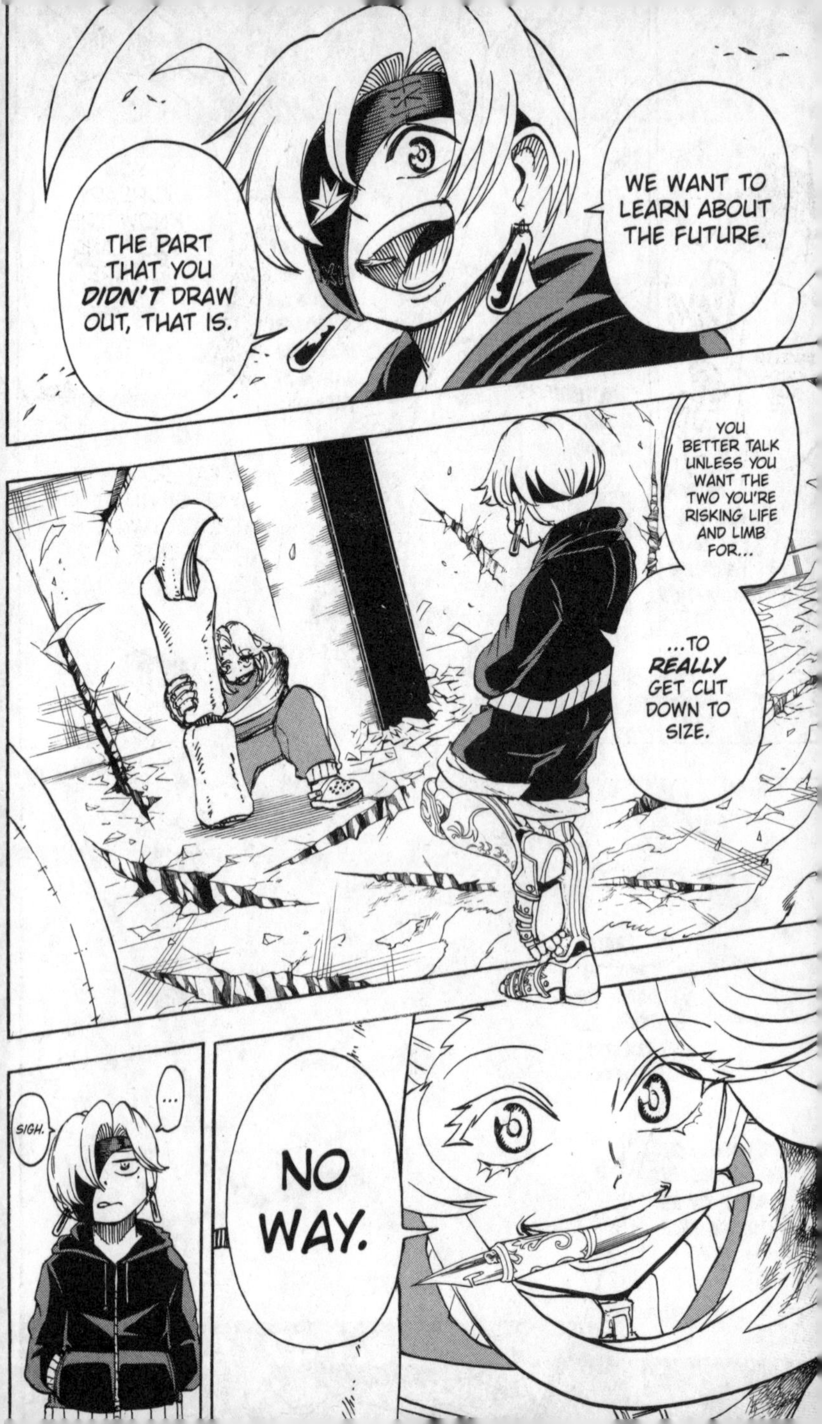
WE WANT TO LEARN ABOUT THE FUTURE.
THE PART THAT YOU *DIDN'T* DRAW OUT, THAT IS.
YOU BETTER TALK UNLESS YOU WANT THE TWO YOU'RE RISKING LIFE AND LIMB FOR...
...TO *REALLY* GET CUT DOWN TO SIZE.
NO WAY.
...
SIGH.

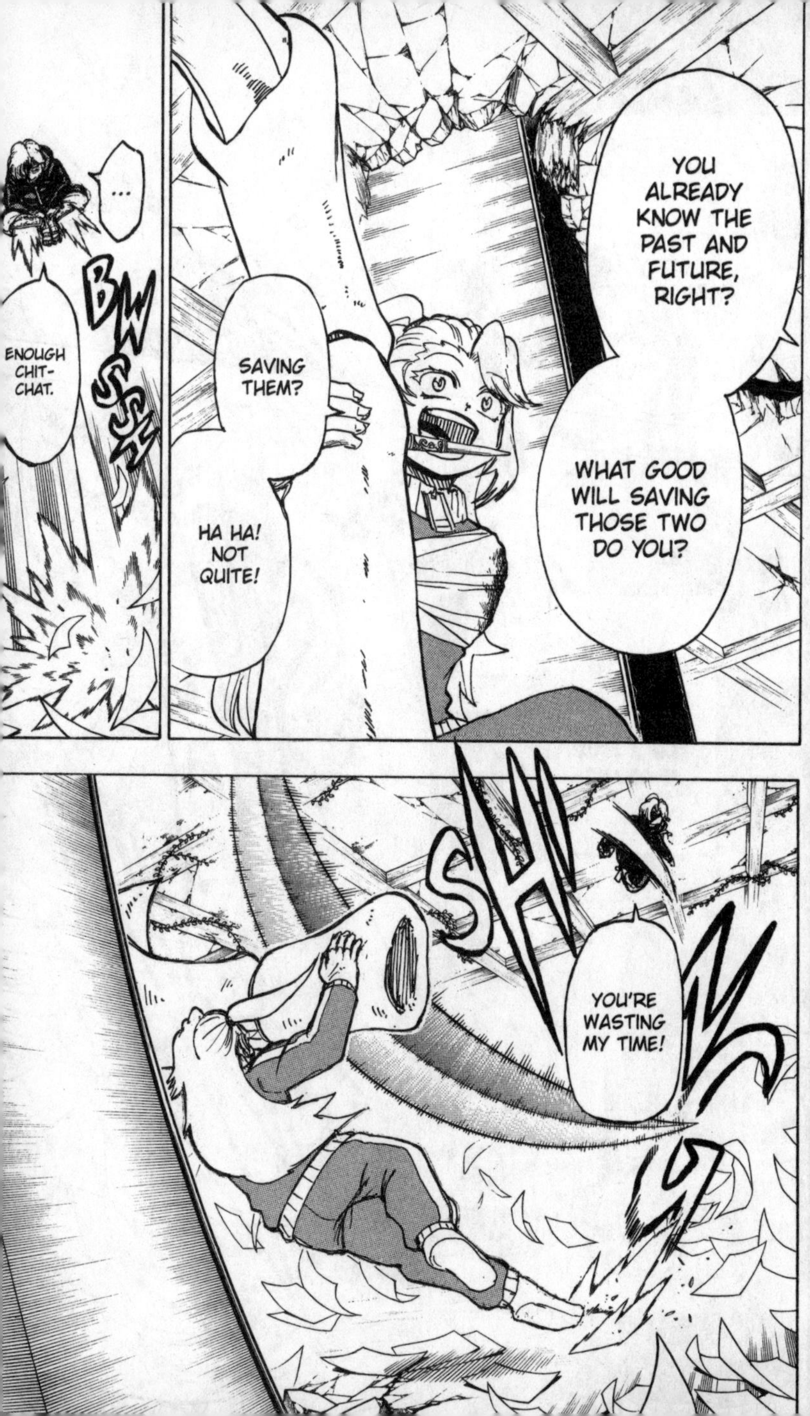
YOU ALREADY KNOW THE PAST AND FUTURE, RIGHT?
WHAT GOOD WILL SAVING THOSE TWO DO YOU?
SAVING THEM?
HA HA! NOT QUITE!
...
BWSSH
ENOUGH CHIT-CHAT.
SH
YOU'RE WASTING MY TIME!

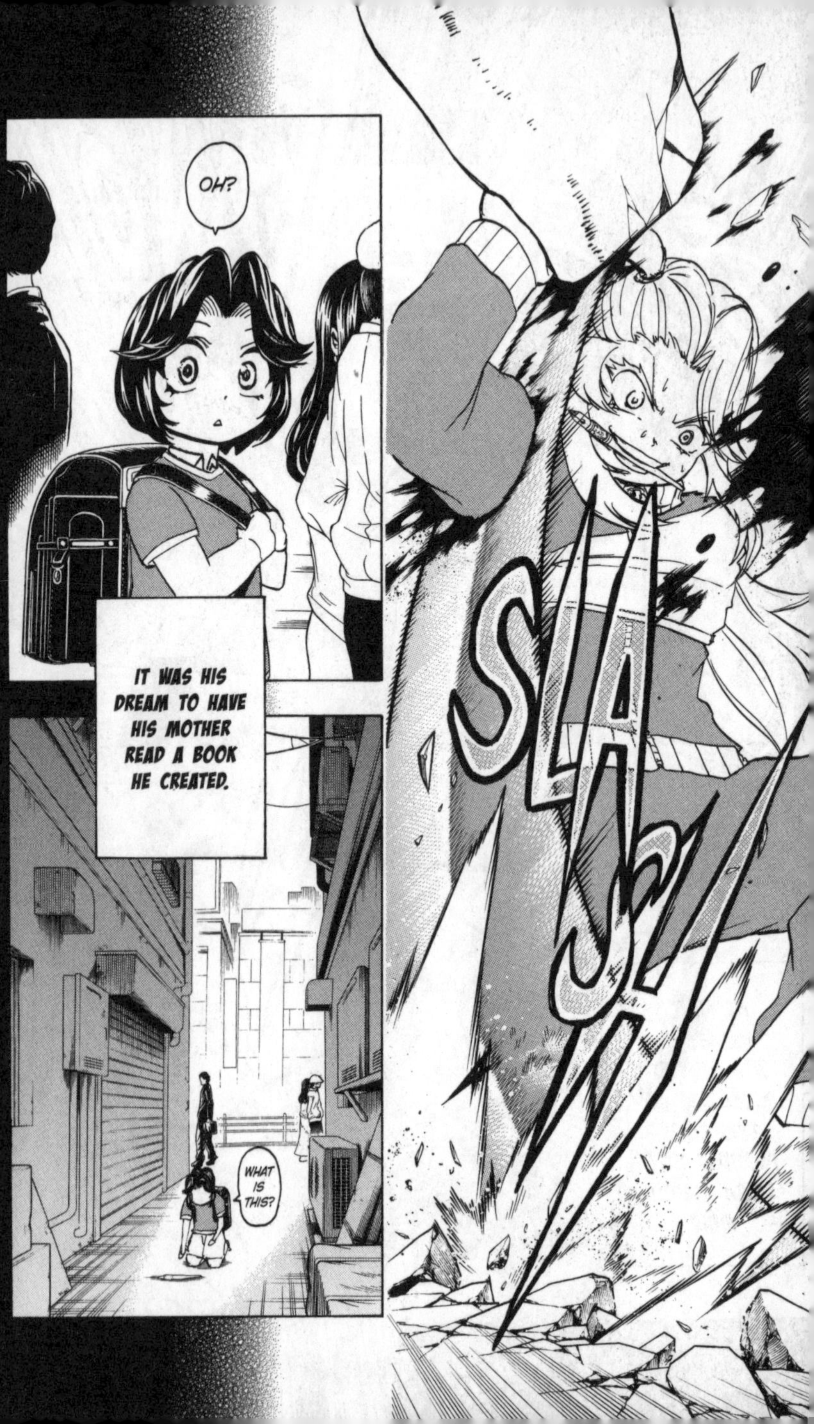
SLASH
OH?
IT WAS HIS DREAM TO HAVE HIS MOTHER READ A BOOK HE CREATED.
WHAT IS THIS?

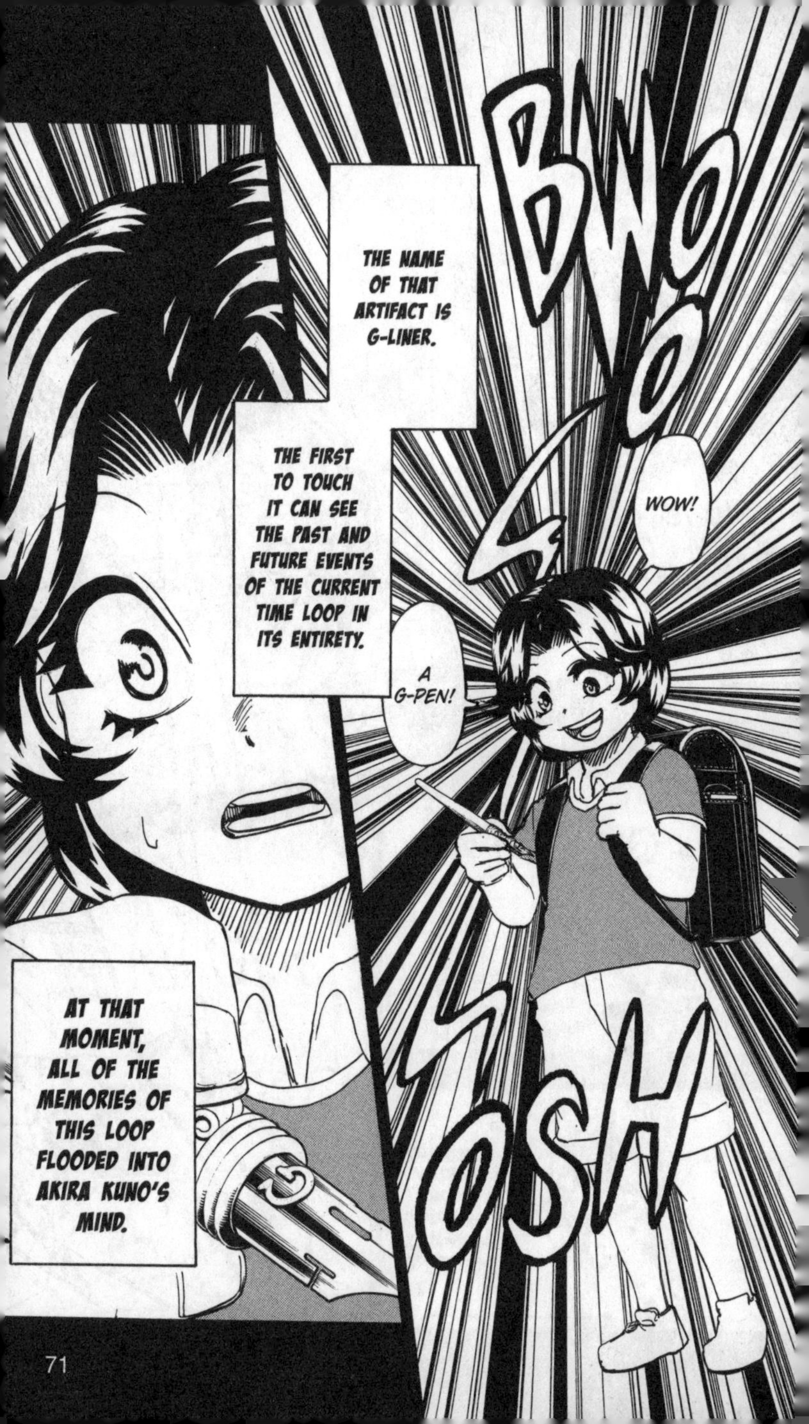
BWOOSH
WOW!
A G-PEN!
THE NAME OF THAT ARTIFACT IS G-LINER.
THE FIRST TO TOUCH IT CAN SEE THE PAST AND FUTURE EVENTS OF THE CURRENT TIME LOOP IN ITS ENTIRETY.
AT THAT MOMENT, ALL OF THE MEMORIES OF THIS LOOP FLOODED INTO AKIRA KUNO'S MIND.

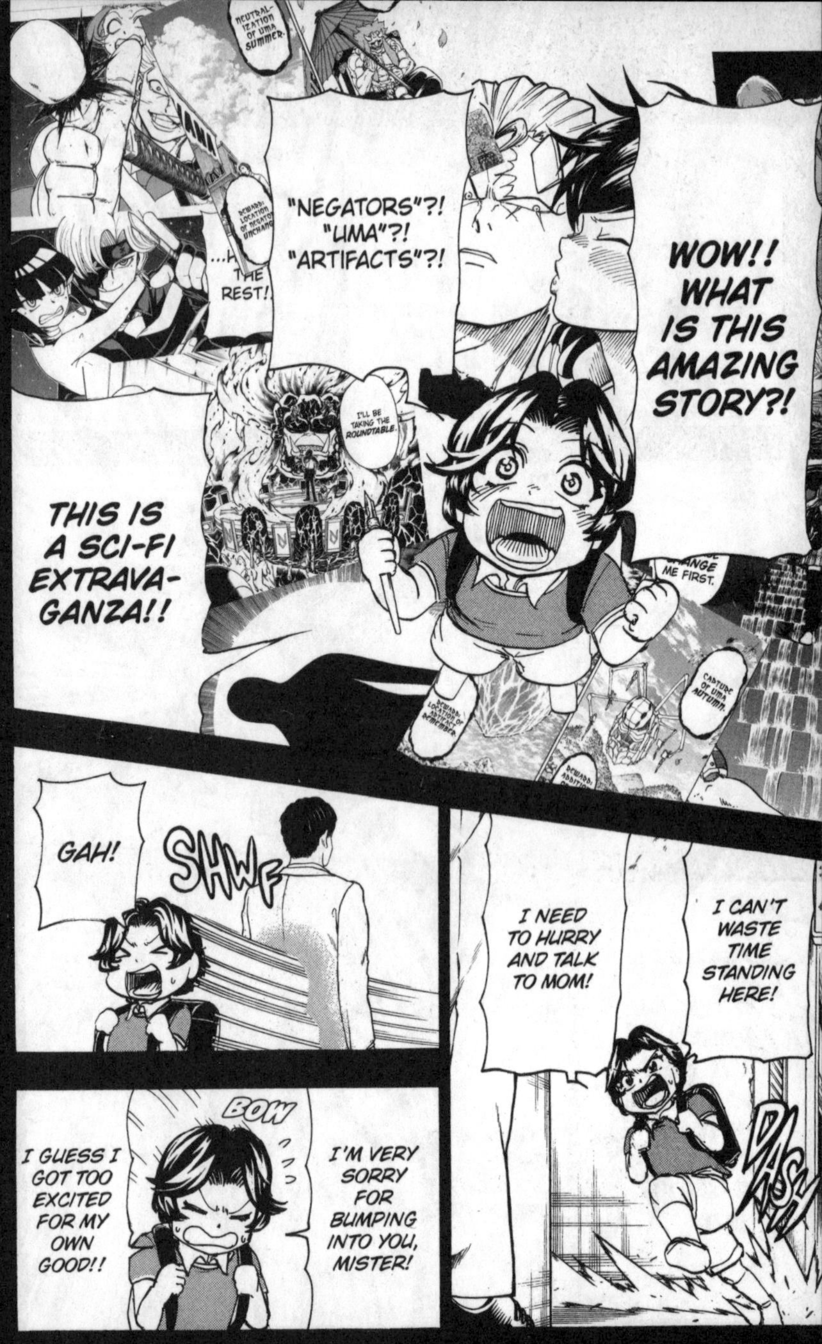
NEUTRALIZATION OF UMA SUMMER
WOW!! WHAT IS THIS AMAZING STORY?!
"NEGATORS"?! "UMA"?! "ARTIFACTS"?!
I'LL BE TAKING THE ROUNDTABLE.
THIS IS A SCI-FI EXTRAVAGANZA!!
CAPTURE OF UMA AUTUMN
REWARD: LOCATION OF ARTIFACT DECEMBER
I CAN'T WASTE TIME STANDING HERE!
I NEED TO HURRY AND TALK TO MOM!
DASH
GAH!
SHWF
BOW
I'M VERY SORRY FOR BUMPING INTO YOU, MISTER!
I GUESS I GOT TOO EXCITED FOR MY OWN GOOD!!

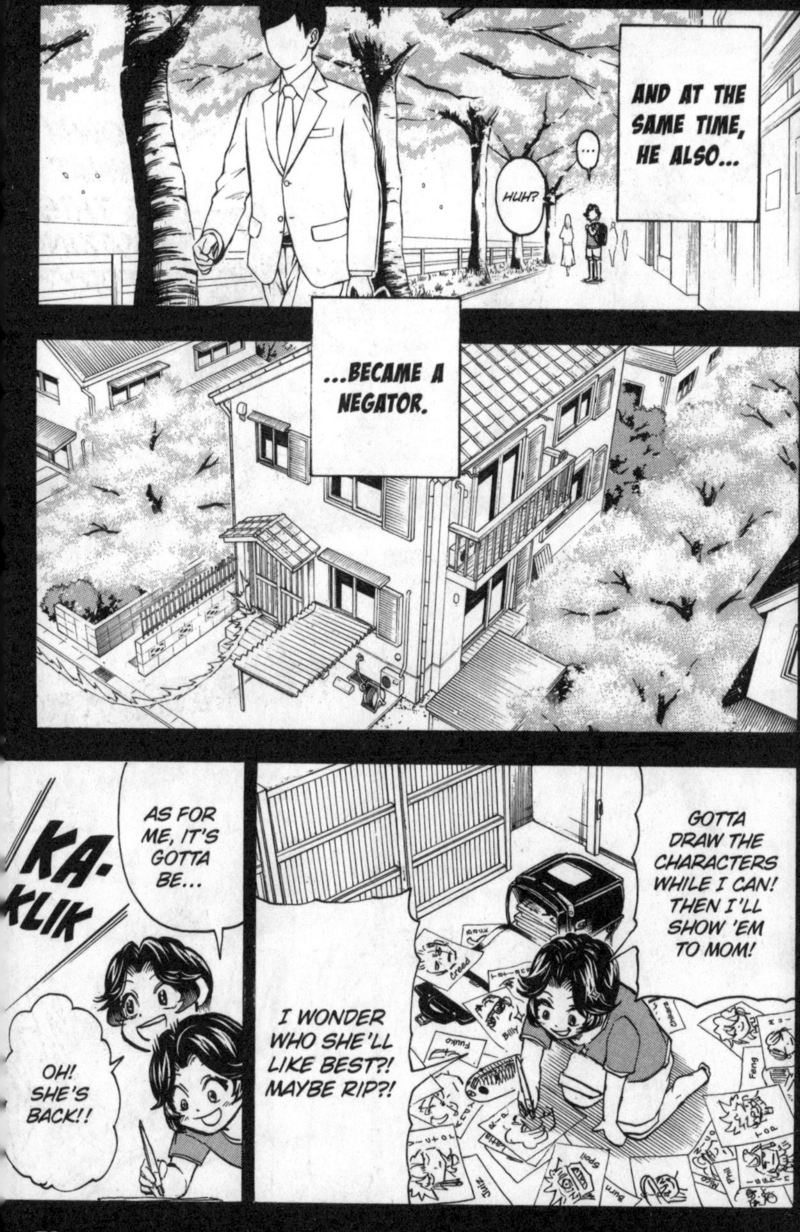
AND AT THE SAME TIME, HE ALSO...
...
HUH?
...BECAME A NEGATOR.
GOTTA DRAW THE CHARACTERS WHILE I CAN! THEN I'LL SHOW 'EM TO MOM!
I WONDER WHO SHE'LL LIKE BEST?! MAYBE RIP?!
KA-KLIK
AS FOR ME, IT'S GOTTA BE...
OH! SHE'S BACK!!

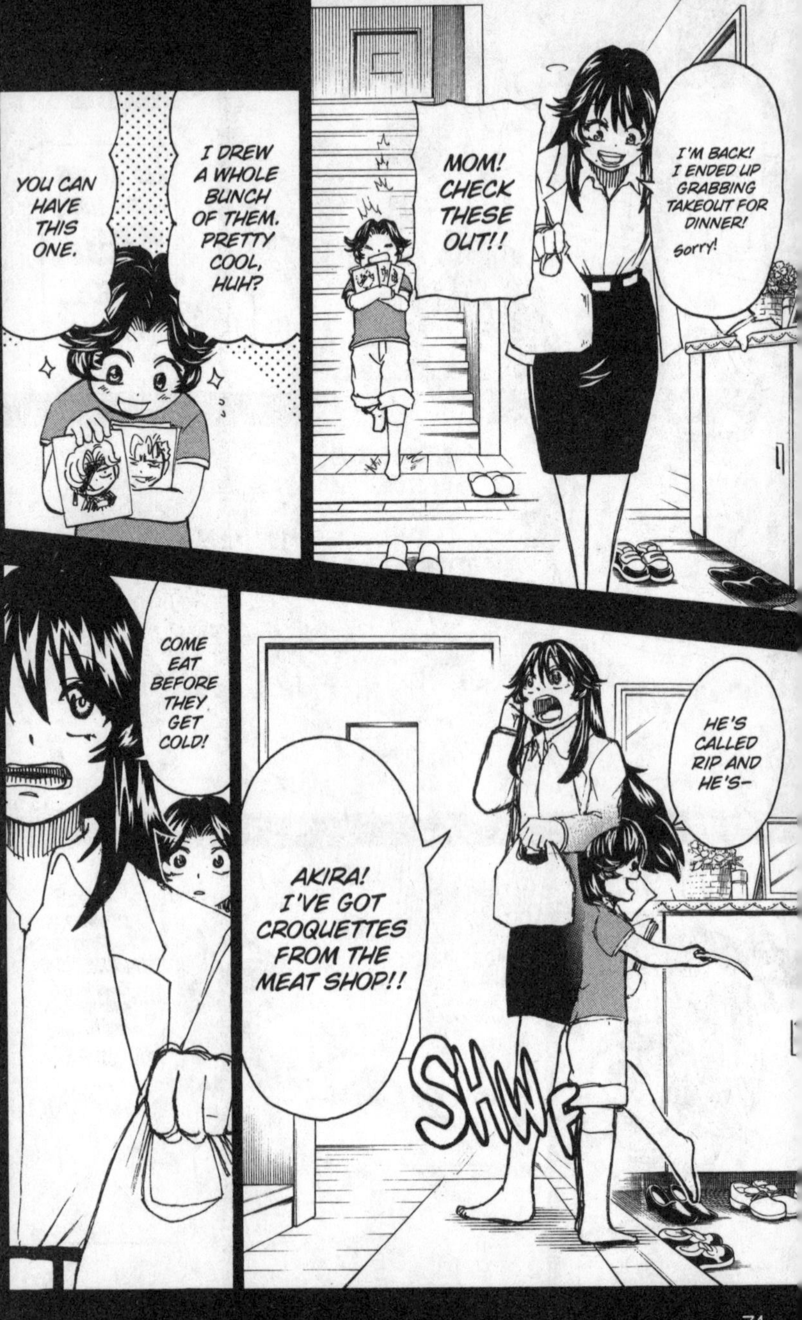
I'M BACK! I ENDED UP GRABBING TAKEOUT FOR DINNER! Sorry!
MOM! CHECK THESE OUT!!
I DREW A WHOLE BUNCH OF THEM. PRETTY COOL, HUH?
YOU CAN HAVE THIS ONE.
HE'S CALLED RIP AND HE'S-
SHWF
AKIRA! I'VE GOT CROQUETTES FROM THE MEAT SHOP!!
COME EAT BEFORE THEY GET COLD!

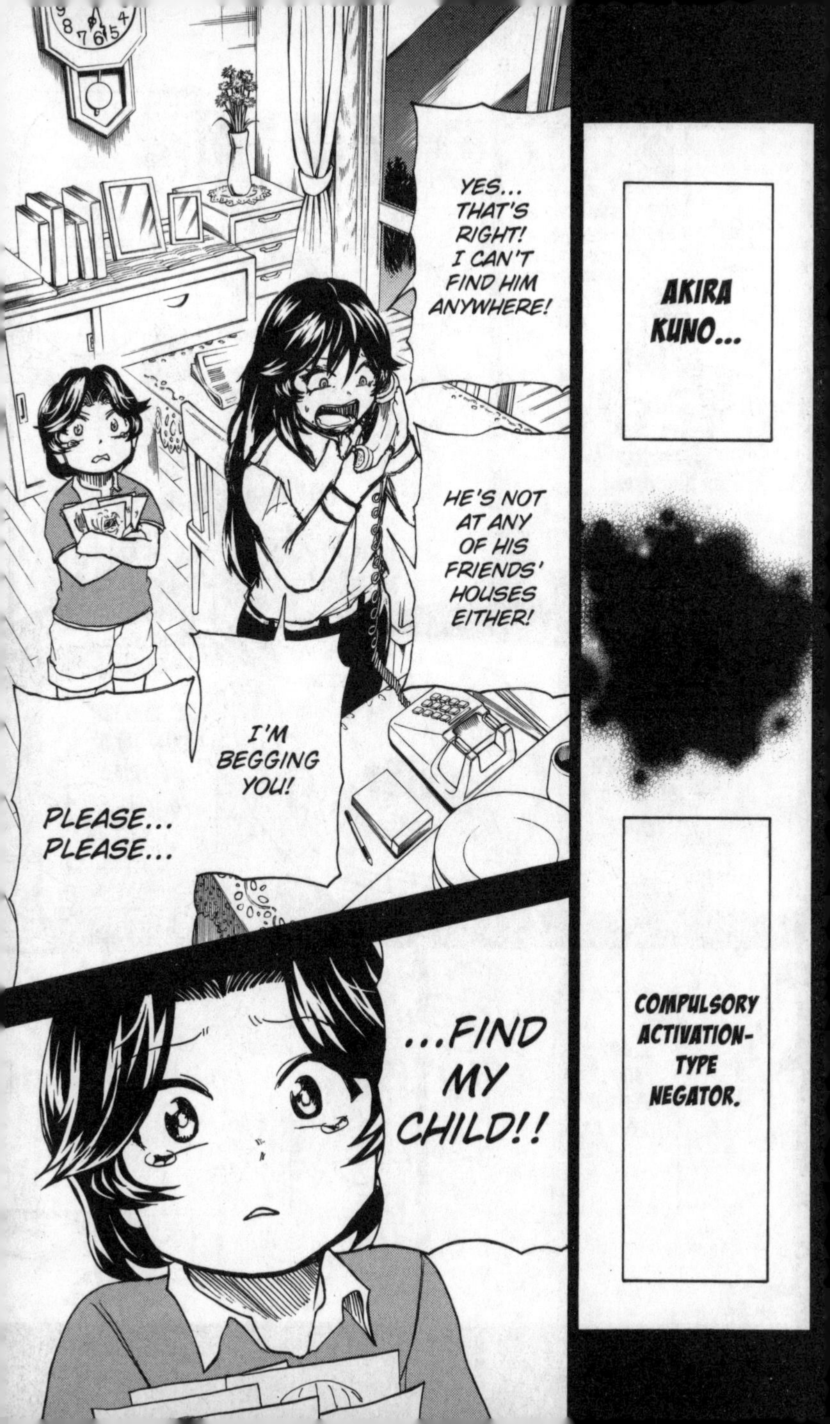
AKIRA KUNO...
COMPULSORY ACTIVATION-TYPE NEGATOR.
YES... THAT'S RIGHT! I CAN'T FIND HIM ANYWHERE!
HE'S NOT AT ANY OF HIS FRIENDS' HOUSES EITHER!
I'M BEGGING YOU!
PLEASE... PLEASE...
...FIND MY CHILD!!

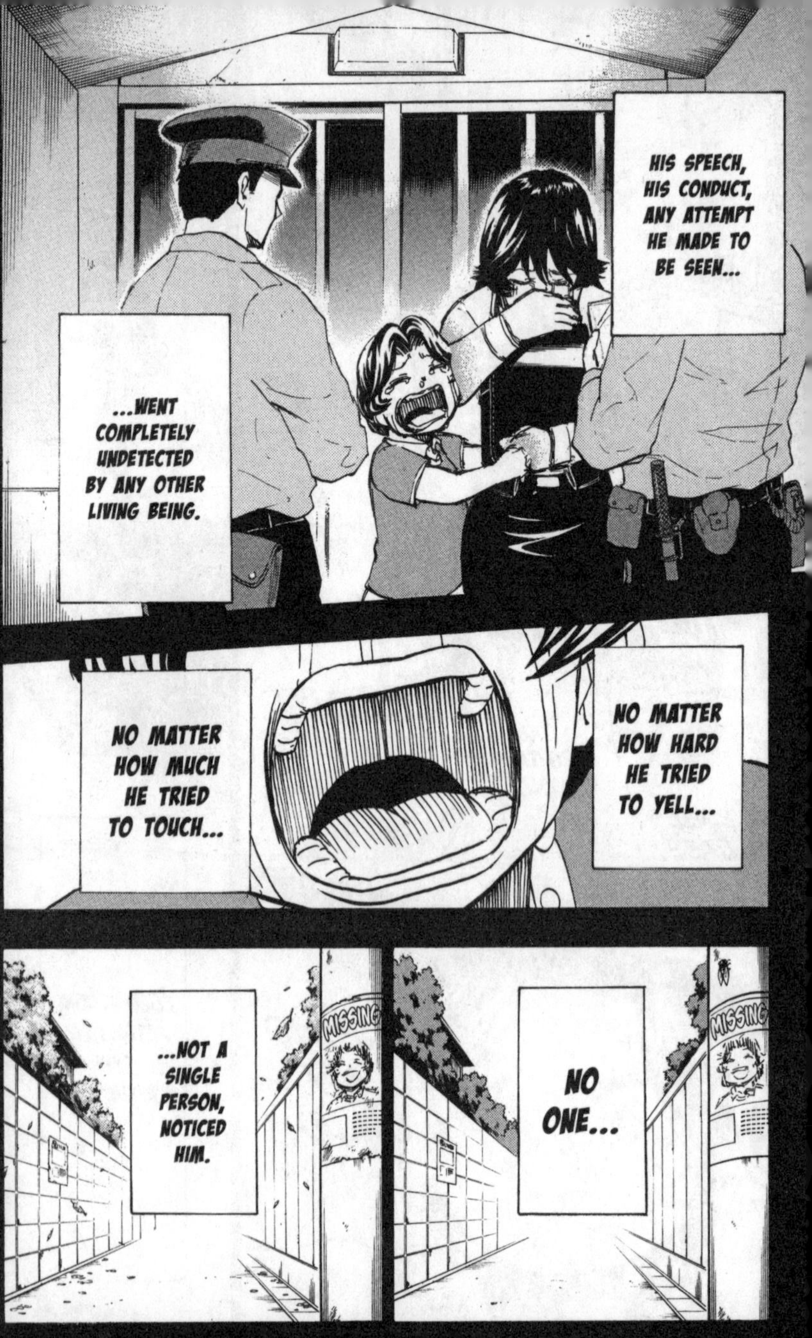
HIS SPEECH, HIS CONDUCT, ANY ATTEMPT HE MADE TO BE SEEN...
...WENT COMPLETELY UNDETECTED BY ANY OTHER LIVING BEING.
NO MATTER HOW HARD HE TRIED TO YELL...
NO MATTER HOW MUCH HE TRIED TO TOUCH...
MISSING
NO ONE...
MISSING
...NOT A SINGLE PERSON, NOTICED HIM.

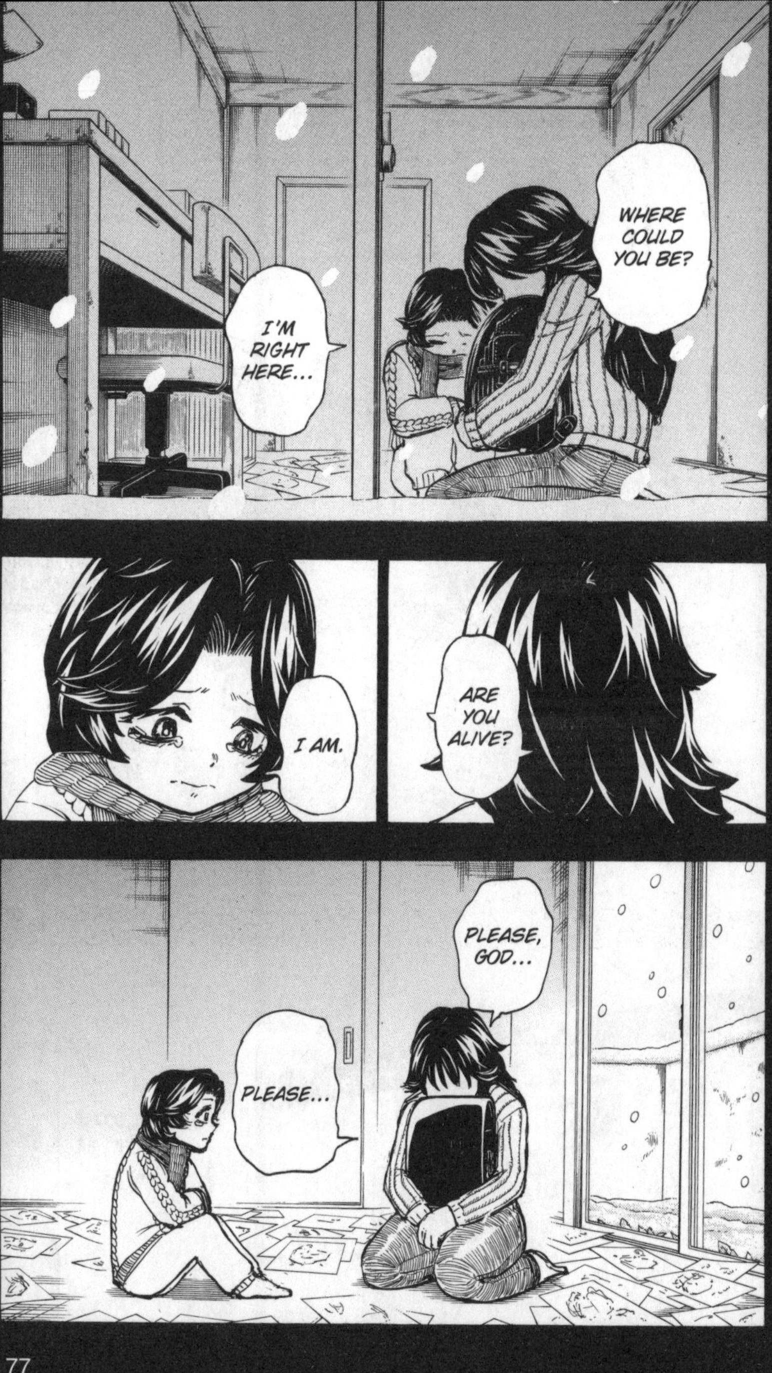
WHERE COULD YOU BE?
I'M RIGHT HERE...
ARE YOU ALIVE?
I AM.
PLEASE, GOD...
PLEASE...

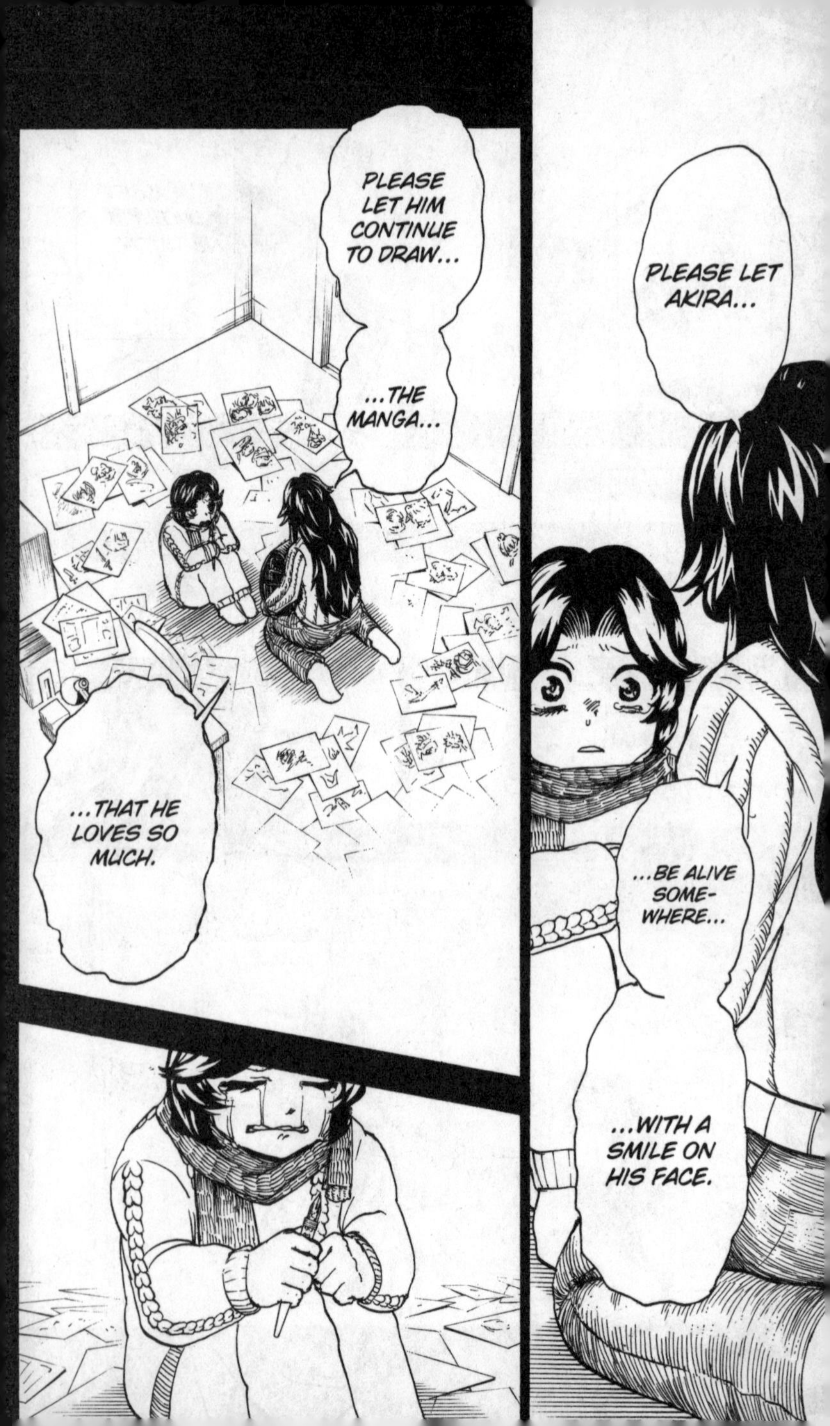
PLEASE LET AKIRA...
...BE ALIVE SOME-WHERE...
...WITH A SMILE ON HIS FACE.
PLEASE LET HIM CONTINUE TO DRAW...
...THE MANGA...
...THAT HE LOVES SO MUCH.

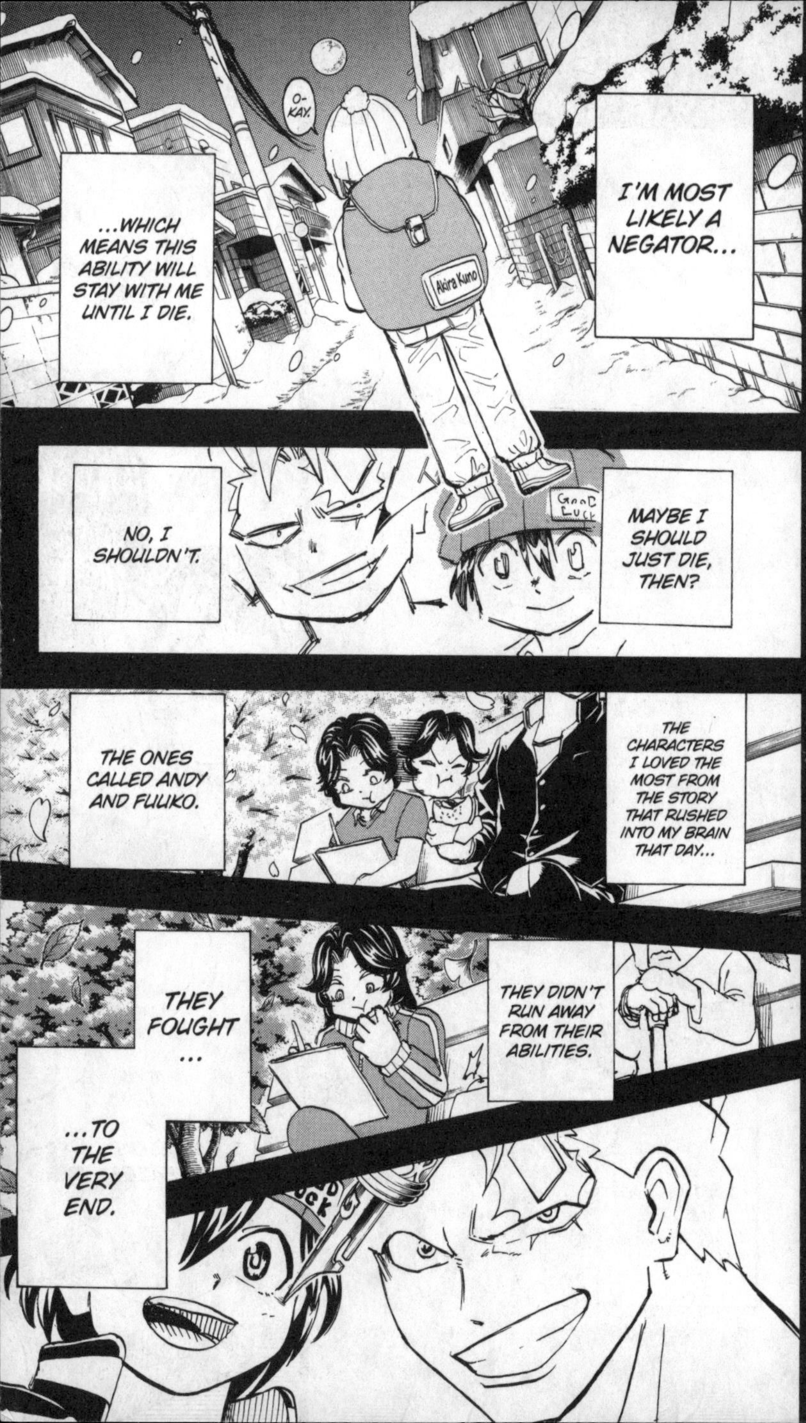
I'M MOST LIKELY A NEGATOR...
O-KAY.
Akira Kuno
...WHICH MEANS THIS ABILITY WILL STAY WITH ME UNTIL I DIE.
MAYBE I SHOULD JUST DIE, THEN?
NO, I SHOULDN'T.
THE CHARACTERS I LOVED THE MOST FROM THE STORY THAT RUSHED INTO MY BRAIN THAT DAY...
THE ONES CALLED ANDY AND FUUKO.
THEY DIDN'T RUN AWAY FROM THEIR ABILITIES.
THEY FOUGHT ...
...TO THE VERY END.

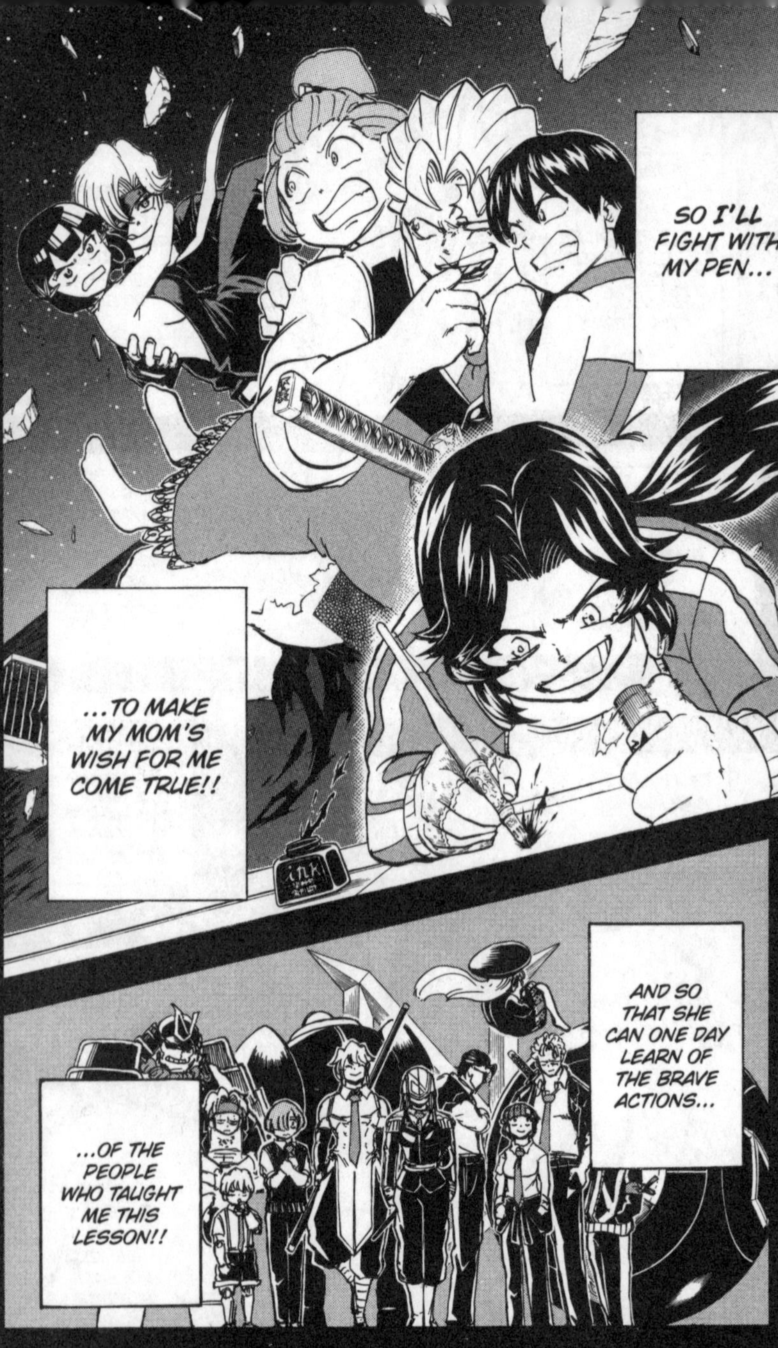
SO I'LL FIGHT WITH MY PEN...
...TO MAKE MY MOM'S WISH FOR ME COME TRUE!!
AND SO THAT SHE CAN ONE DAY LEARN OF THE BRAVE ACTIONS...
...OF THE PEOPLE WHO TAUGHT ME THIS LESSON!!

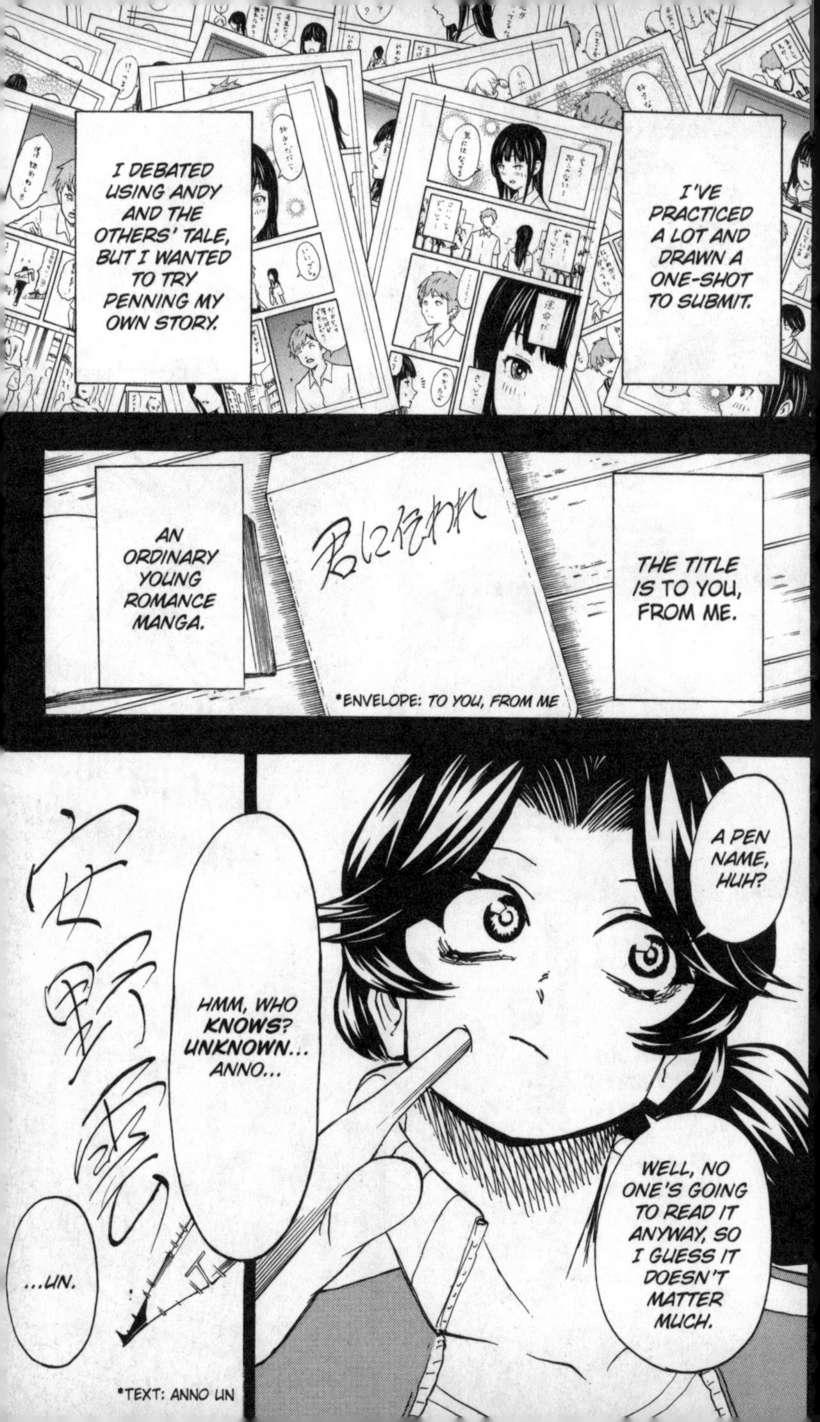
I'VE PRACTICED A LOT AND DRAWN A ONE-SHOT TO SUBMIT.
I DEBATED USING ANDY AND THE OTHERS' TALE, BUT I WANTED TO TRY PENNING MY OWN STORY.
THE TITLE IS TO YOU, FROM ME.
AN ORDINARY YOUNG ROMANCE MANGA.
*ENVELOPE: TO YOU, FROM ME
A PEN NAME, HUH?
WELL, NO ONE'S GOING TO READ IT ANYWAY, SO I GUESS IT DOESN'T MATTER MUCH.
HMM, WHO KNOWS? UNKNOWN... ANNO...
...UN.
*TEXT: ANNO UN

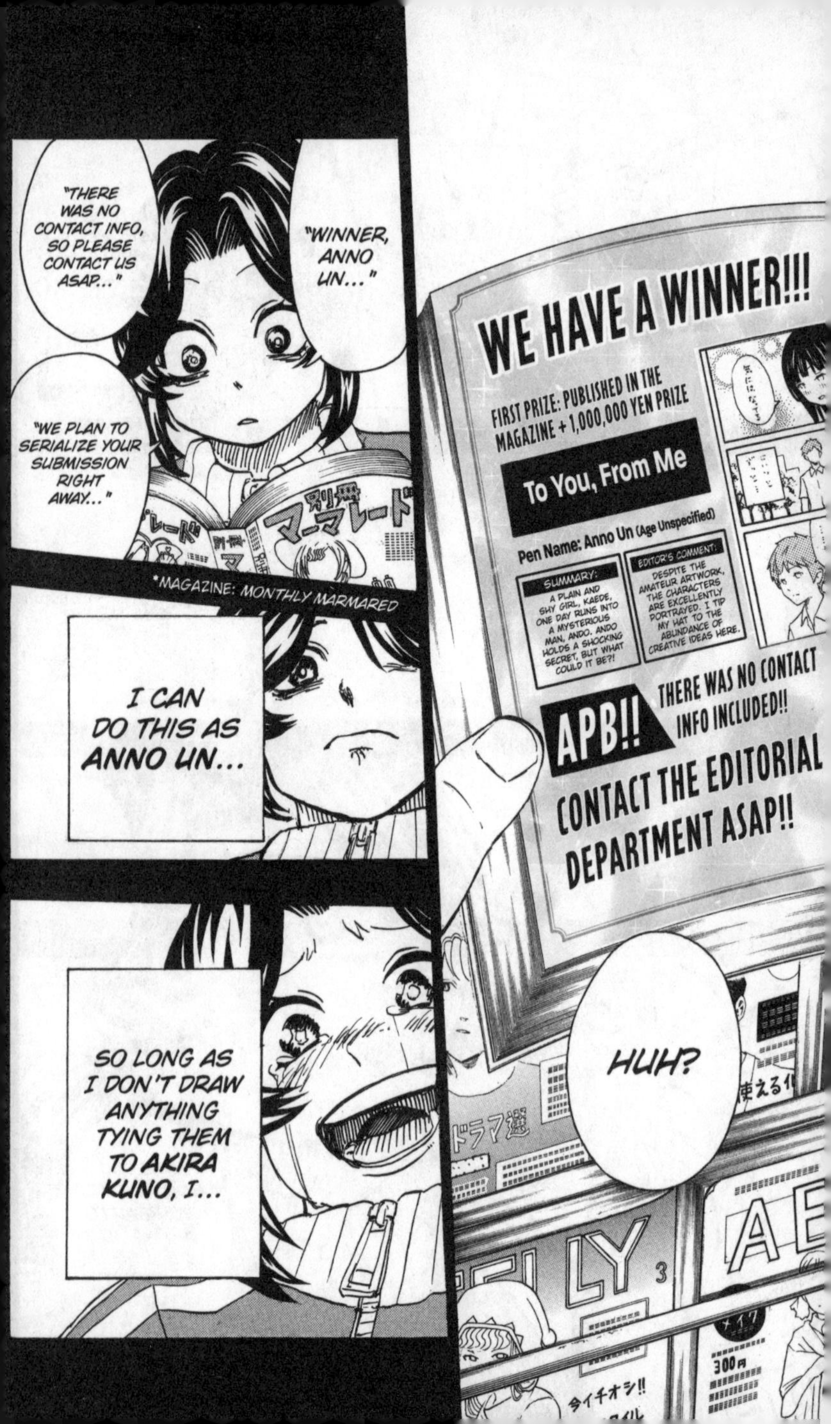
WE HAVE A WINNER!!!
FIRST PRIZE: PUBLISHED IN THE MAGAZINE + 1,000,000 YEN PRIZE
To You, From Me
Pen Name: Anno Un (Age Unspecified)
EDITOR'S COMMENT: DESPITE THE AMATEUR ARTWORK, THE CHARACTERS ARE EXCELLENTLY PORTRAYED. I TIP MY HAT TO THE ABUNDANCE OF CREATIVE IDEAS HERE.
SUMMARY: A PLAIN AND SHY GIRL, KAEDE, ONE DAY RUNS INTO A MYSTERIOUS MAN, ANDO. ANDO HOLDS A SHOCKING SECRET, BUT WHAT COULD IT BE?!
APB!! THERE WAS NO CONTACT INFO INCLUDED!!
CONTACT THE EDITORIAL DEPARTMENT ASAP!!
HUH?
"WINNER, ANNO UN..."
"THERE WAS NO CONTACT INFO, SO PLEASE CONTACT US ASAP..."
"WE PLAN TO SERIALIZE YOUR SUBMISSION RIGHT AWAY..."
別冊マーマレード
*MAGAZINE: MONTHLY MARMARED
I CAN DO THIS AS ANNO UN...
SO LONG AS I DON'T DRAW ANYTHING TYING THEM TO AKIRA KUNO, I...

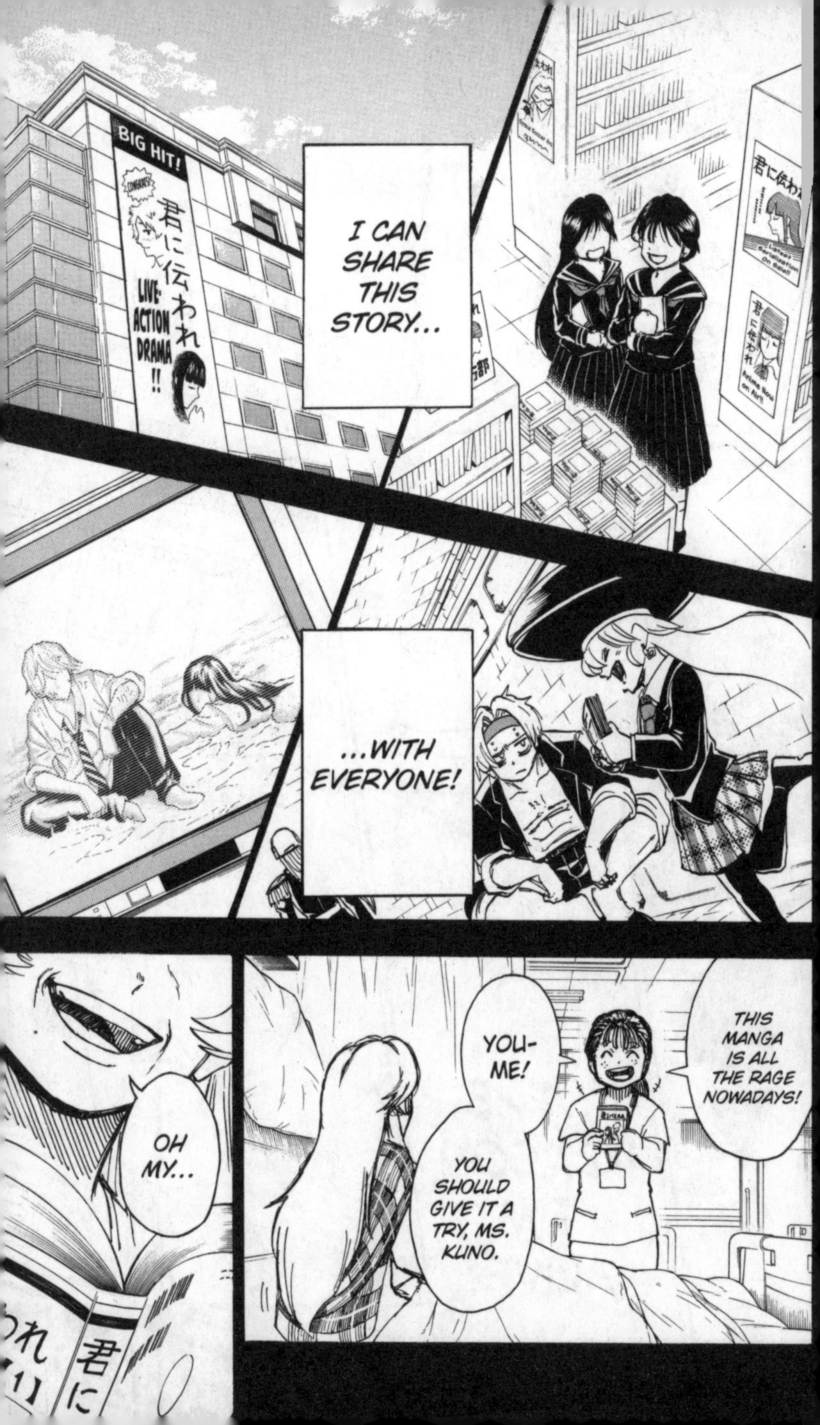
君に伝われ
Latest Serialization On Sale!
君に伝われ
Anime Now on Air!!
I CAN SHARE THIS STORY...
BIG HIT!
CONGRATS!
君に伝われ
LIVE-ACTION DRAMA!!
...WITH EVERYONE!
THIS MANGA IS ALL THE RAGE NOWADAYS!
YOU-ME!
YOU SHOULD GIVE IT A TRY, MS. KUNO.
OH MY...

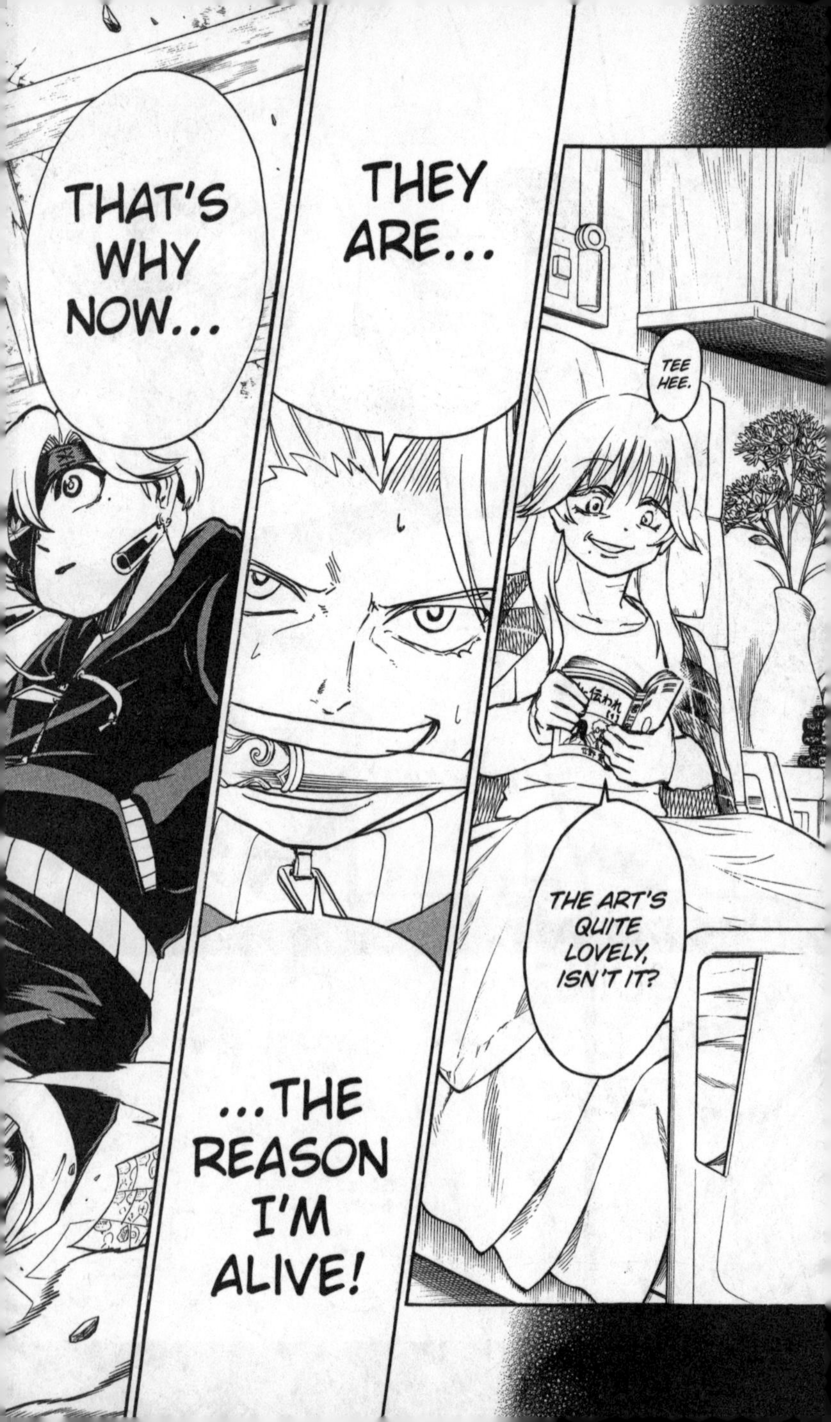
TEE HEE.
THE ART'S QUITE LOVELY, ISN'T IT?
THEY ARE...
...THE REASON I'M ALIVE!
THAT'S WHY NOW...

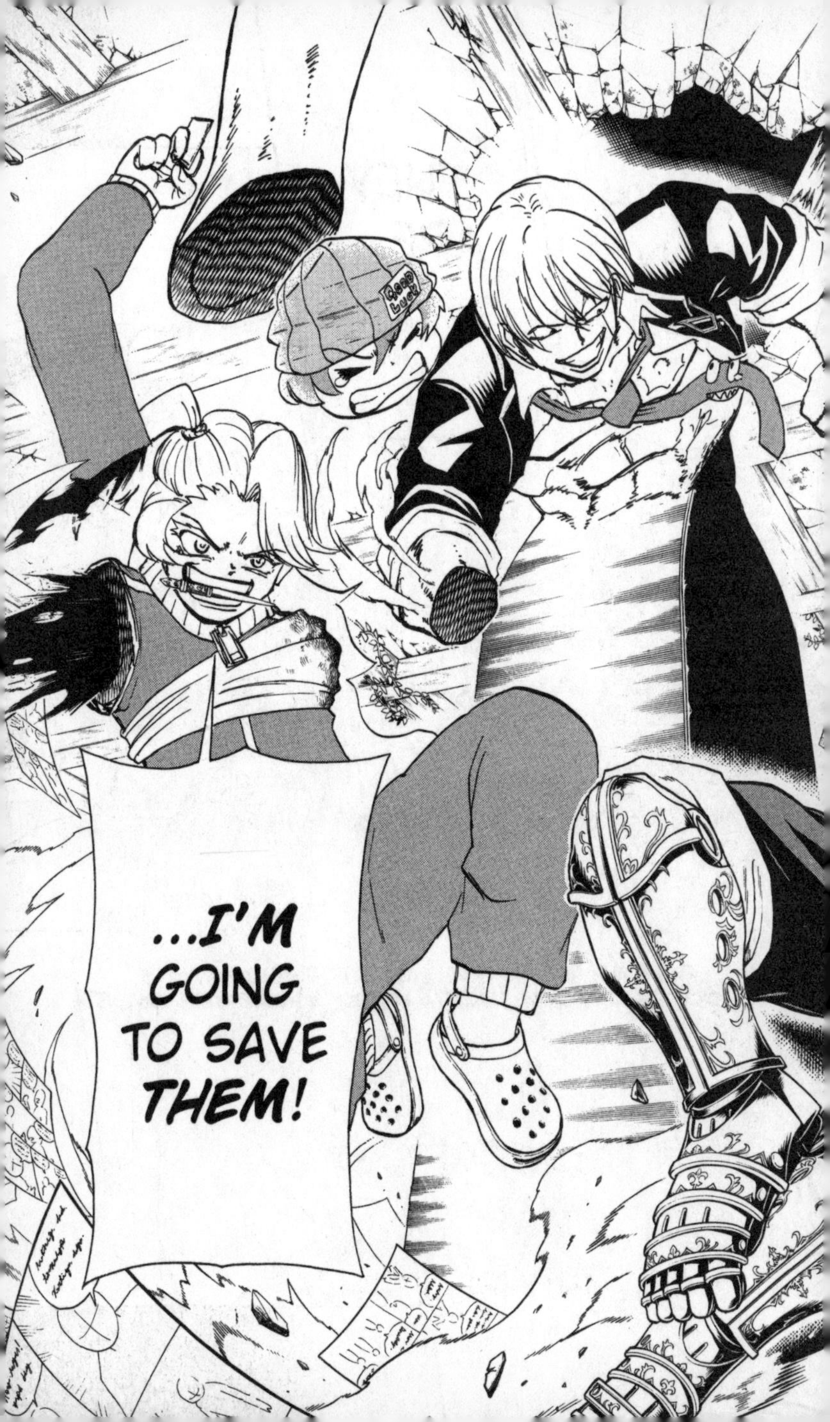
...I'M GOING TO SAVE THEM!

FROM THE VOLUME 6 RELEASE COMMEMORATION SITE
(SEARCH WITH KEYWORDS "UNDEAD UNLUCK VOLUME 6" IN JAPANESE!)

No. 048
A Story I Won't See Coming

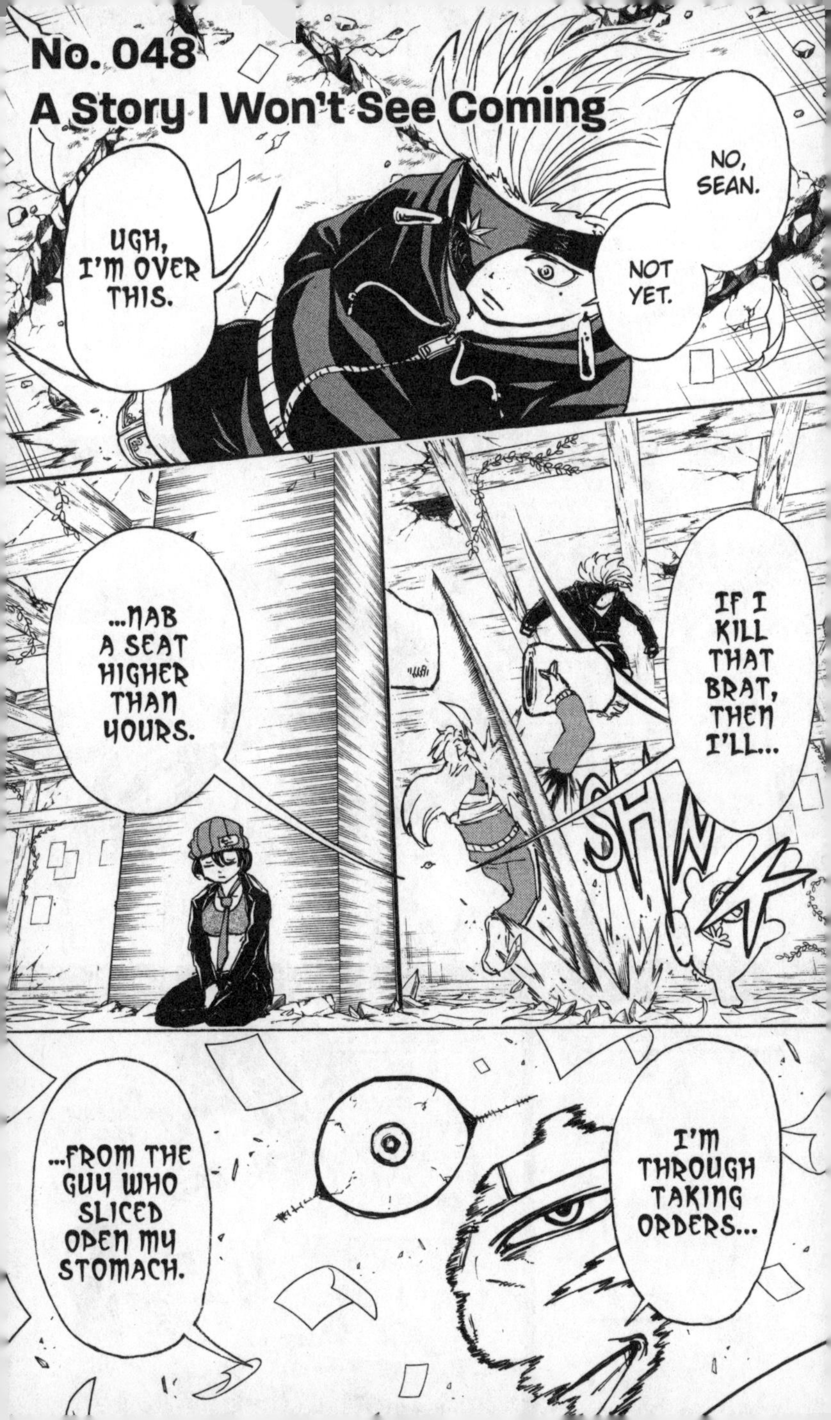
NO, SEAN.
NOT YET.
UGH, I'M OVER THIS.
IF I KILL THAT BRAT, THEN I'LL...
...NAB A SEAT HIGHER THAN YOURS.
SHNK
I'M THROUGH TAKING ORDERS...
...FROM THE GUY WHO SLICED OPEN MY STOMACH.

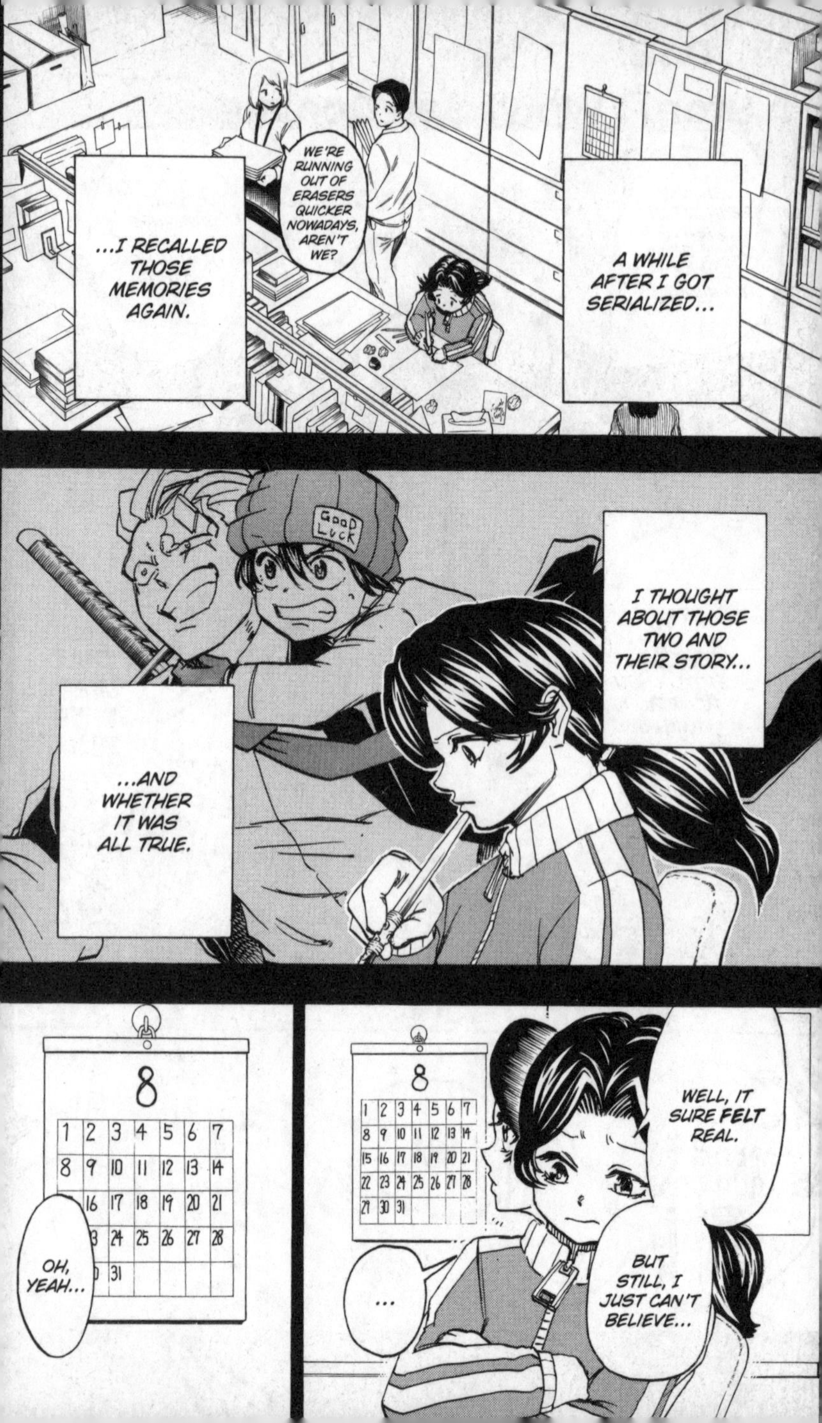
A WHILE AFTER I GOT SERIALIZED...
WE'RE RUNNING OUT OF ERASERS QUICKER NOWADAYS, AREN'T WE?
...I RECALLED THOSE MEMORIES AGAIN.
I THOUGHT ABOUT THOSE TWO AND THEIR STORY...
GOOD LUCK
...AND WHETHER IT WAS ALL TRUE.
WELL, IT SURE FELT REAL.
BUT STILL, I JUST CAN'T BELIEVE...
...
OH, YEAH...

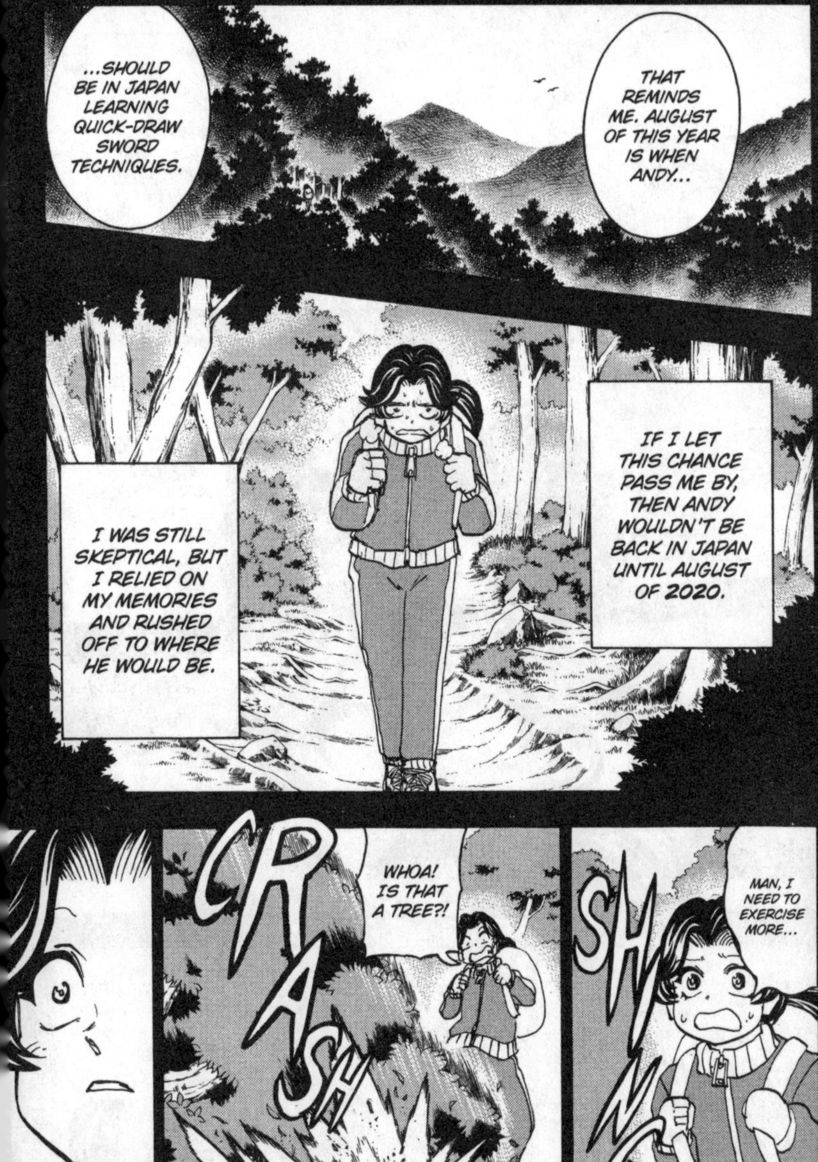
THAT REMINDS ME. AUGUST OF THIS YEAR IS WHEN ANDY...
...SHOULD BE IN JAPAN LEARNING QUICK-DRAW SWORD TECHNIQUES.
IF I LET THIS CHANCE PASS ME BY, THEN ANDY WOULDN'T BE BACK IN JAPAN UNTIL AUGUST OF 2020.
I WAS STILL SKEPTICAL, BUT I RELIED ON MY MEMORIES AND RUSHED OFF TO WHERE HE WOULD BE.
SHING
MAN, I NEED TO EXERCISE MORE...
CRASH
WHOA! IS THAT A TREE?!

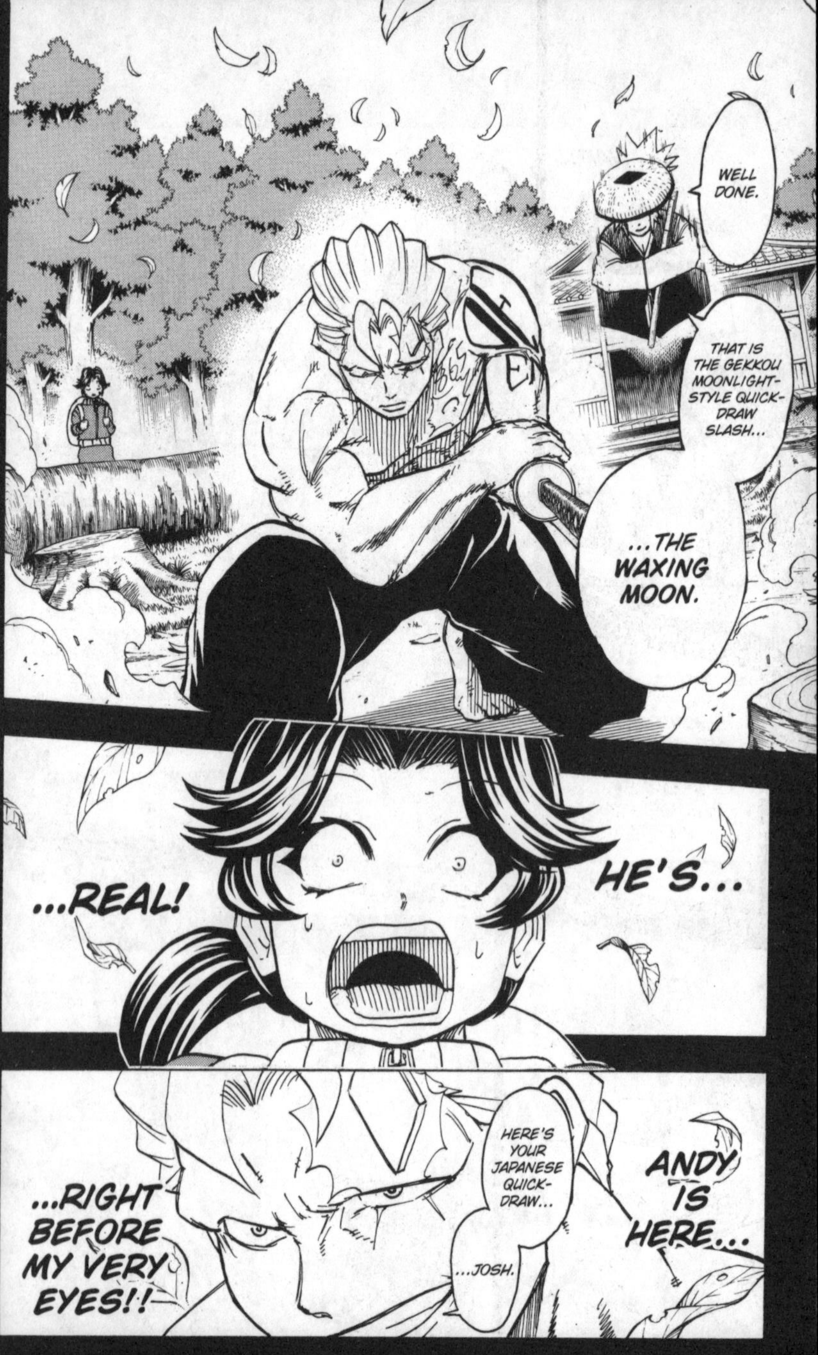
WELL DONE.
THAT IS THE GEKKOU MOONLIGHT-STYLE QUICK-DRAW SLASH...
...THE WAXING MOON.
HE'S...
...REAL!
ANDY IS HERE...
HERE'S YOUR JAPANESE QUICK-DRAW...
...JOSH.
...RIGHT BEFORE MY VERY EYES!!

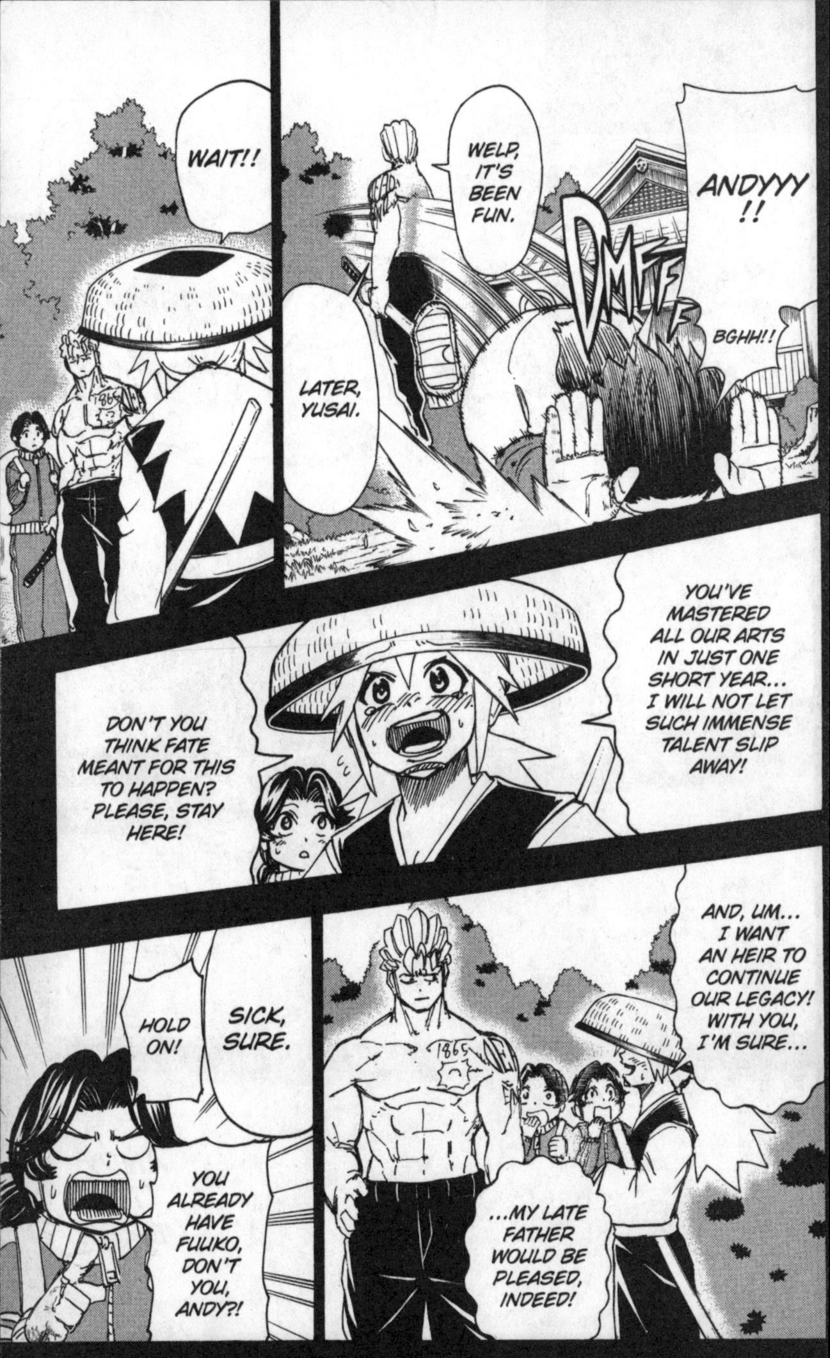
ANDYYY!!
DMFFF
BGHH!!
WELP, IT'S BEEN FUN.
LATER, YUSAI.
WAIT!!
YOU'VE MASTERED ALL OUR ARTS IN JUST ONE SHORT YEAR... I WILL NOT LET SUCH IMMENSE TALENT SLIP AWAY!
DON'T YOU THINK FATE MEANT FOR THIS TO HAPPEN? PLEASE, STAY HERE!
AND, UM... I WANT AN HEIR TO CONTINUE OUR LEGACY! WITH YOU, I'M SURE...
...MY LATE FATHER WOULD BE PLEASED, INDEED!
SICK, SURE.
HOLD ON!
YOU ALREADY HAVE FUUKO, DON'T YOU, ANDY?!

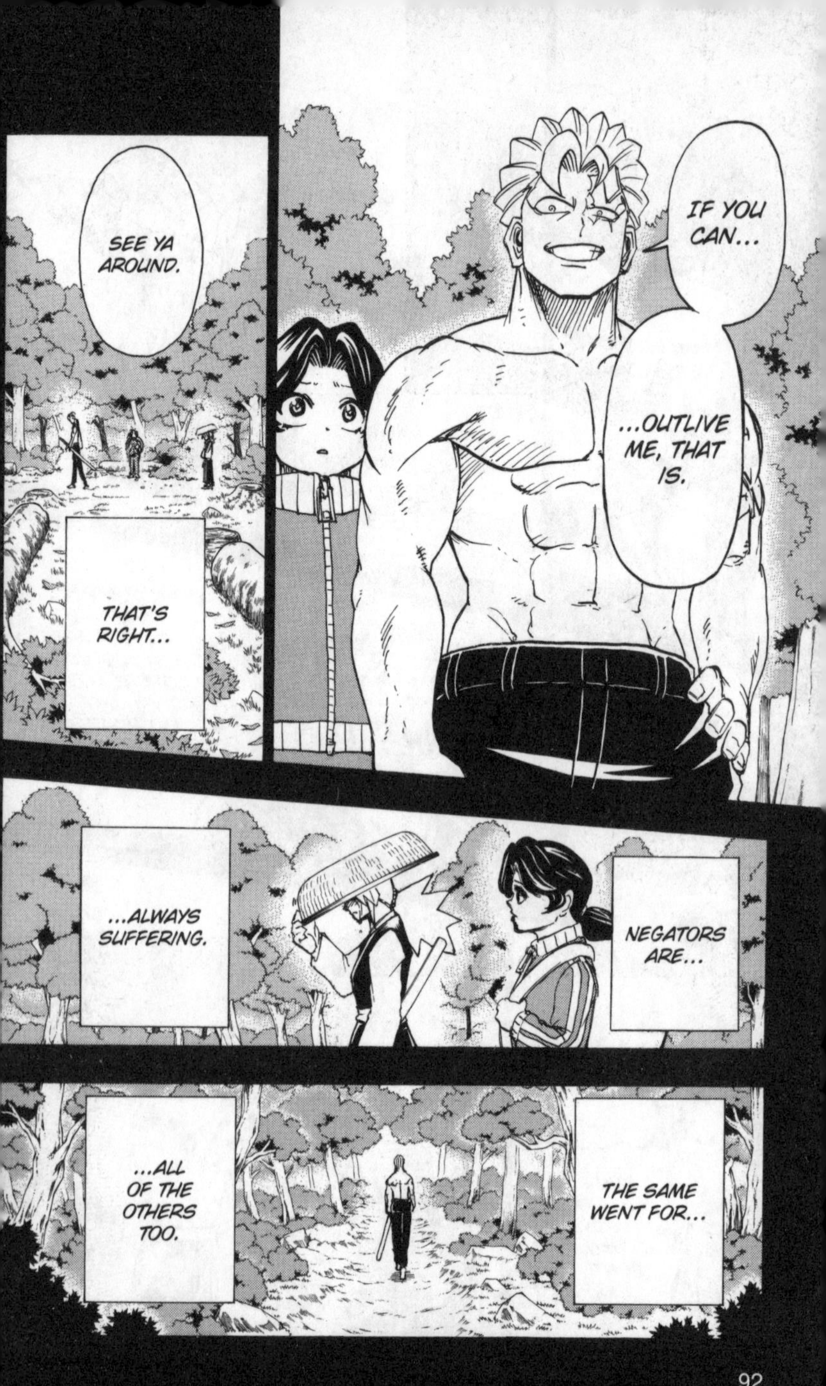
IF YOU CAN...
...OUTLIVE ME, THAT IS.
SEE YA AROUND.
THAT'S RIGHT...
NEGATORS ARE...
...ALWAYS SUFFERING.
THE SAME WENT FOR...
...ALL OF THE OTHERS TOO.

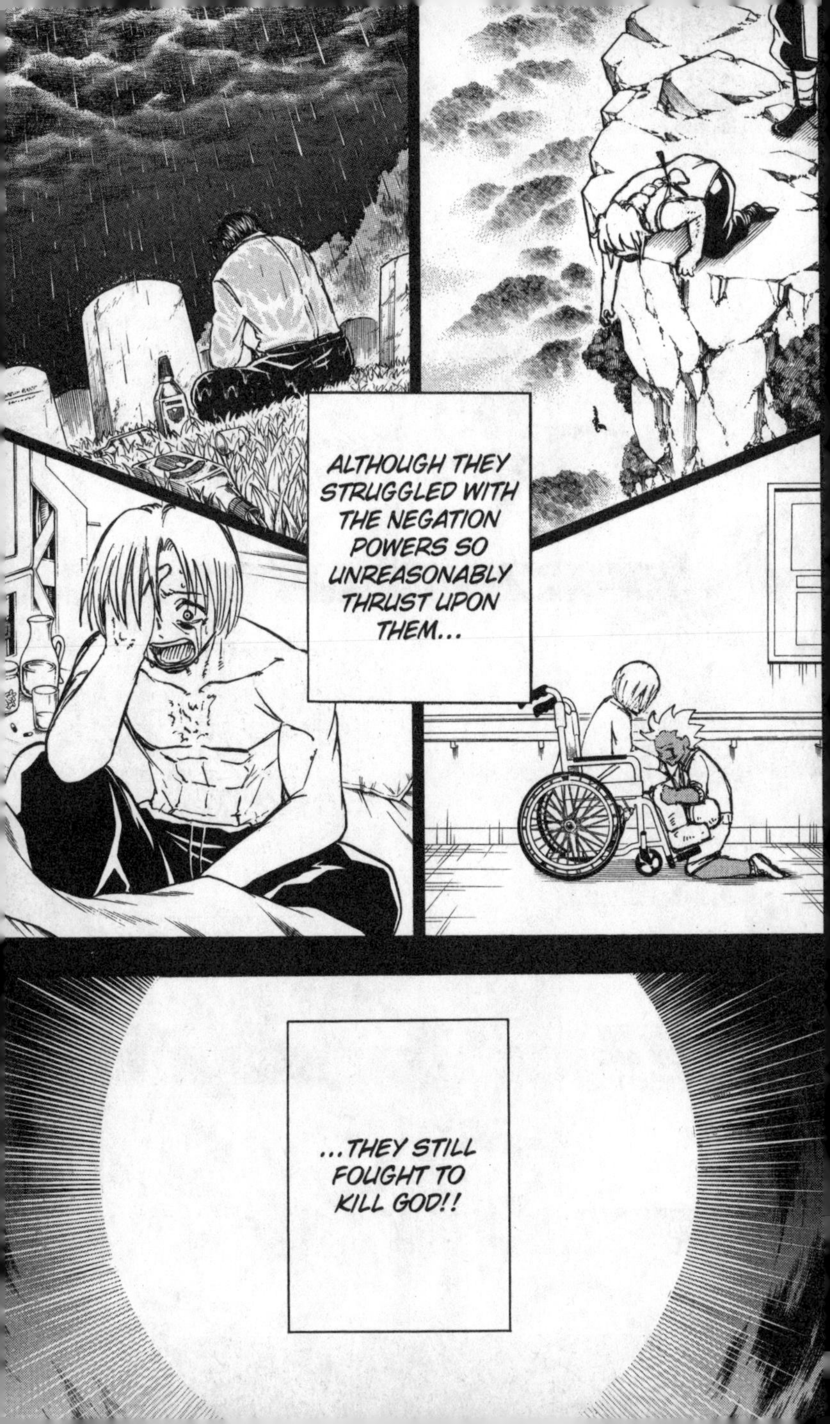
ALTHOUGH THEY STRUGGLED WITH THE NEGATION POWERS SO UNREASONABLY THRUST UPON THEM...
...THEY STILL FOUGHT TO KILL GOD!!

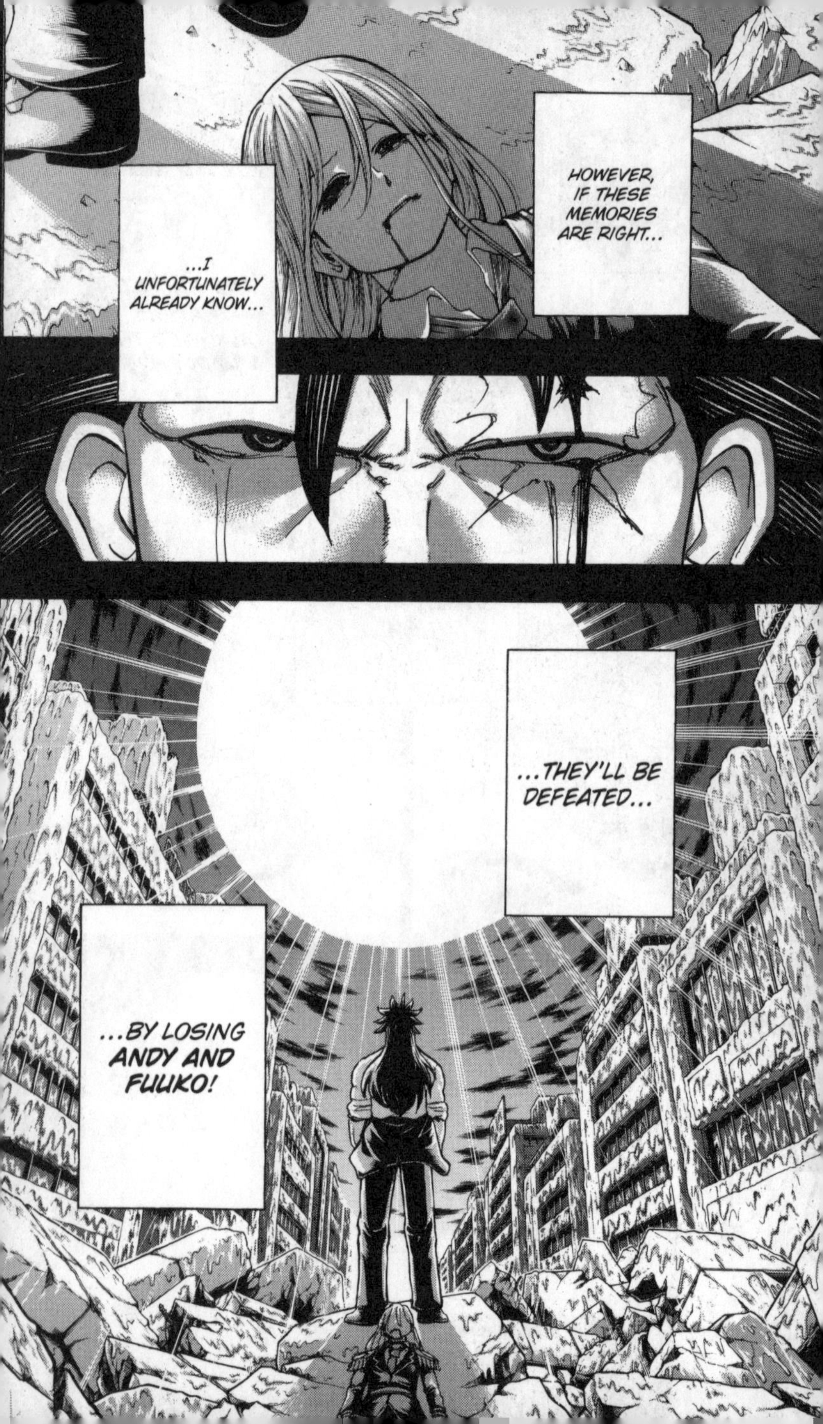
HOWEVER, IF THESE MEMORIES ARE RIGHT...
...I UNFORTUNATELY ALREADY KNOW...
...THEY'LL BE DEFEATED...
...BY LOSING ANDY AND FUUKO!

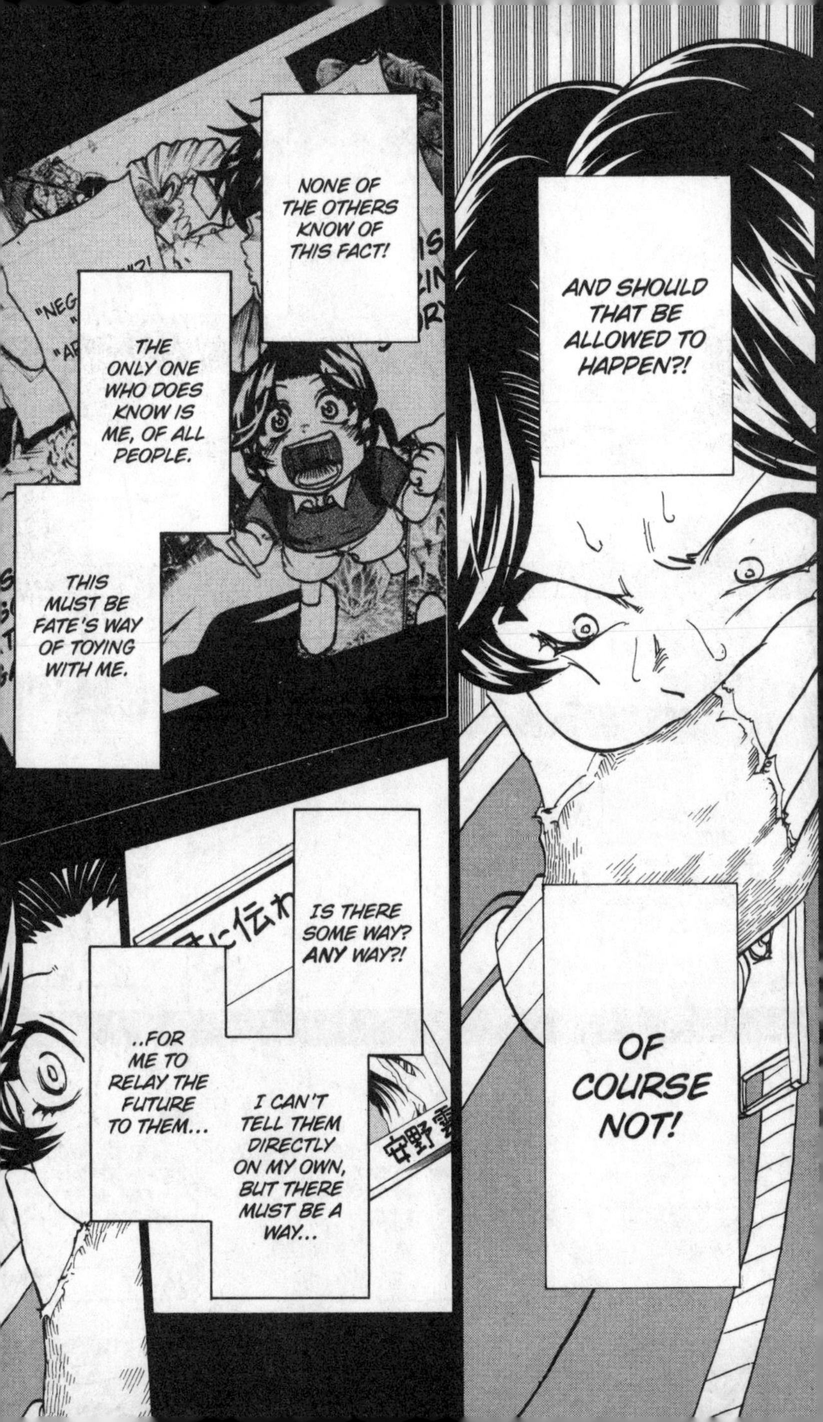

AND SHOULD THAT BE ALLOWED TO HAPPEN?!
OF COURSE NOT!
NONE OF THE OTHERS KNOW OF THIS FACT!
THE ONLY ONE WHO DOES KNOW IS ME, OF ALL PEOPLE.
THIS MUST BE FATE'S WAY OF TOYING WITH ME.
IS THERE SOME WAY? ANY WAY?!
...FOR ME TO RELAY THE FUTURE TO THEM...
I CAN'T TELL THEM DIRECTLY ON MY OWN, BUT THERE MUST BE A WAY...

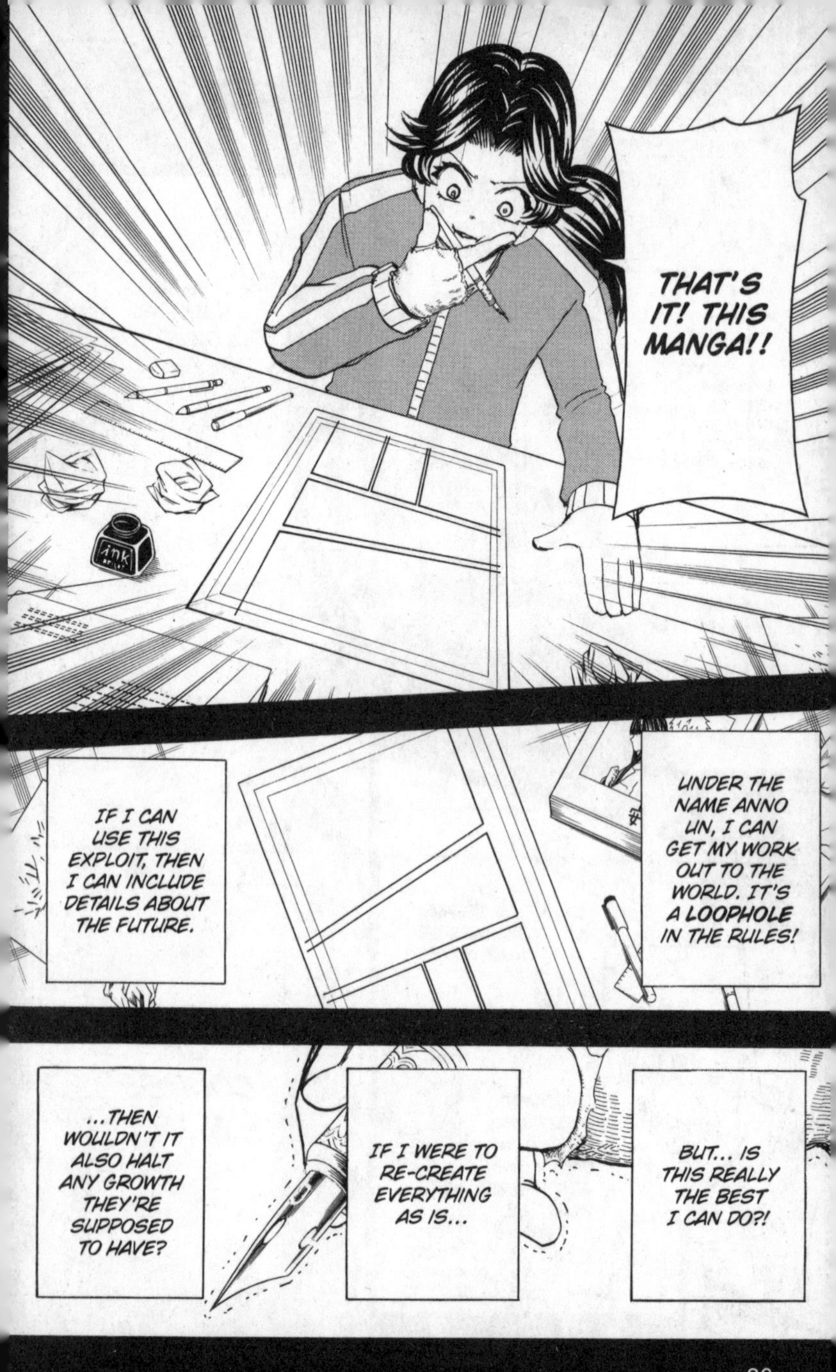
THAT'S IT! THIS MANGA!!
ink
UNDER THE NAME ANNO UN, I CAN GET MY WORK OUT TO THE WORLD. IT'S A LOOPHOLE IN THE RULES!
IF I CAN USE THIS EXPLOIT, THEN I CAN INCLUDE DETAILS ABOUT THE FUTURE.
BUT... IS THIS REALLY THE BEST I CAN DO?!
IF I WERE TO RE-CREATE EVERYTHING AS IS...
...THEN WOULDN'T IT ALSO HALT ANY GROWTH THEY'RE SUPPOSED TO HAVE?

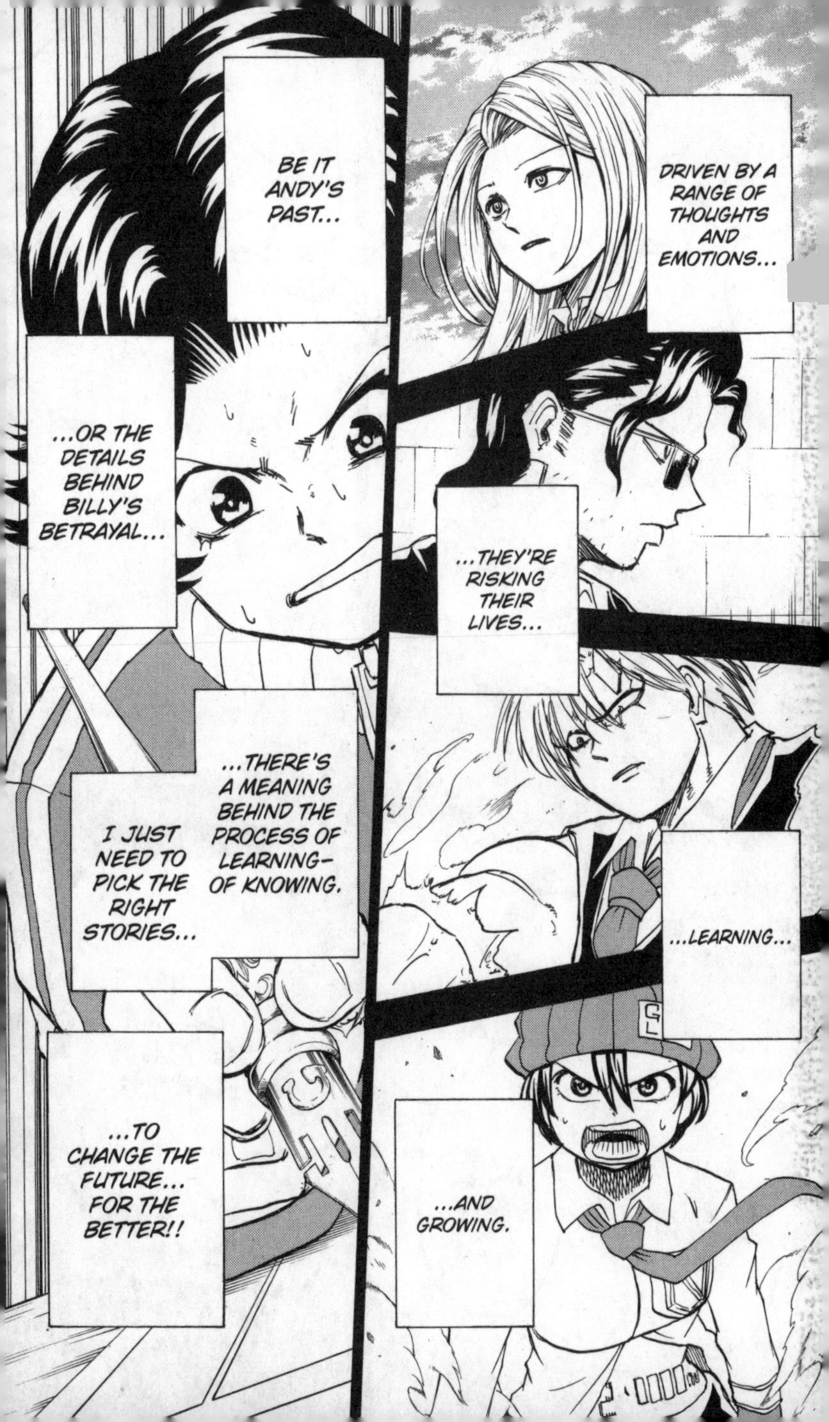
DRIVEN BY A RANGE OF THOUGHTS AND EMOTIONS...
...THEY'RE RISKING THEIR LIVES...
...LEARNING...
...AND GROWING.
BE IT ANDY'S PAST...
...OR THE DETAILS BEHIND BILLY'S BETRAYAL...
...THERE'S A MEANING BEHIND THE PROCESS OF LEARNING-OF KNOWING.
I JUST NEED TO PICK THE RIGHT STORIES...
...TO CHANGE THE FUTURE... FOR THE BETTER!!

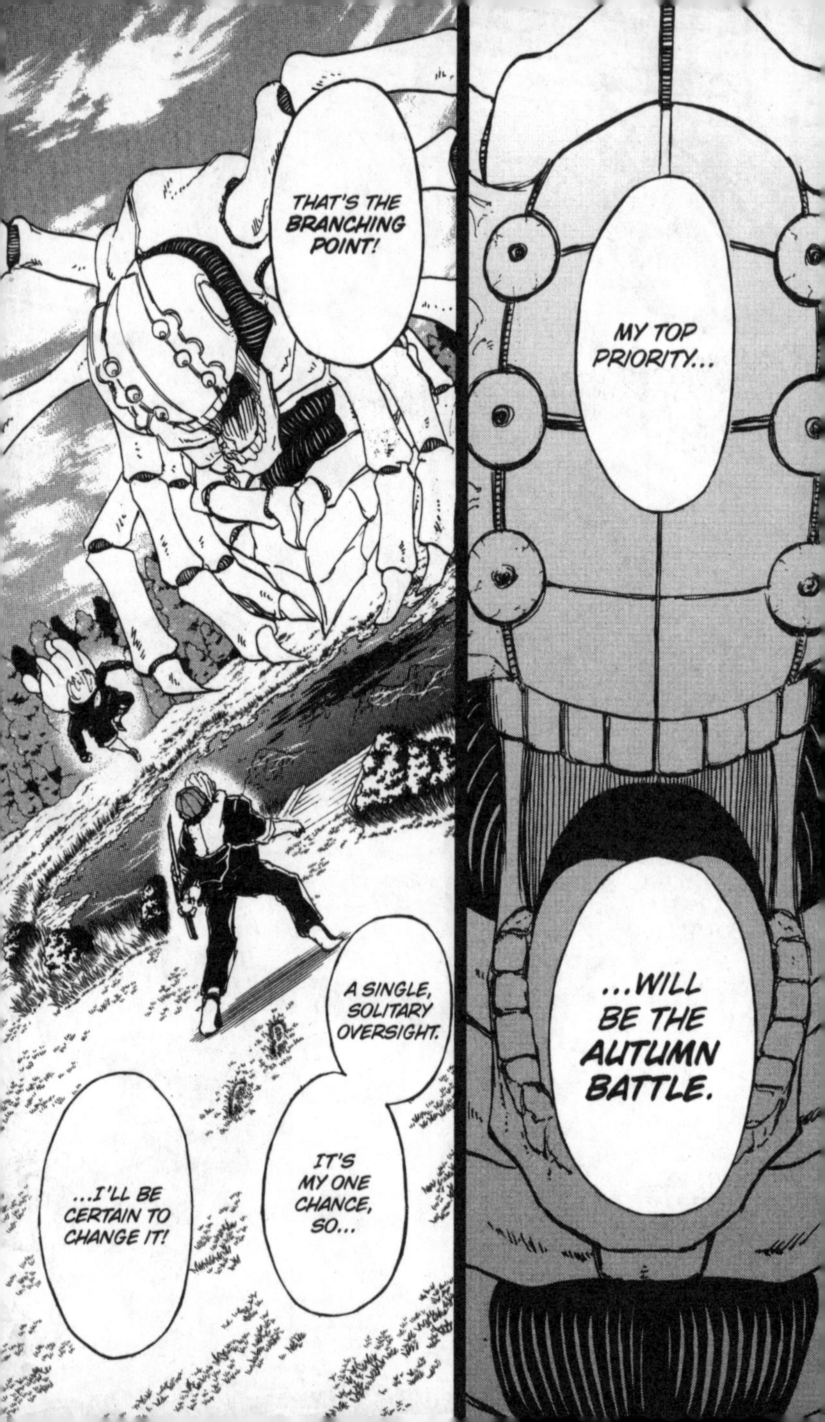
MY TOP PRIORITY...
...WILL BE THE AUTUMN BATTLE.
THAT'S THE BRANCHING POINT!
A SINGLE, SOLITARY OVERSIGHT.
IT'S MY ONE CHANCE, SO...
...I'LL BE CERTAIN TO CHANGE IT!

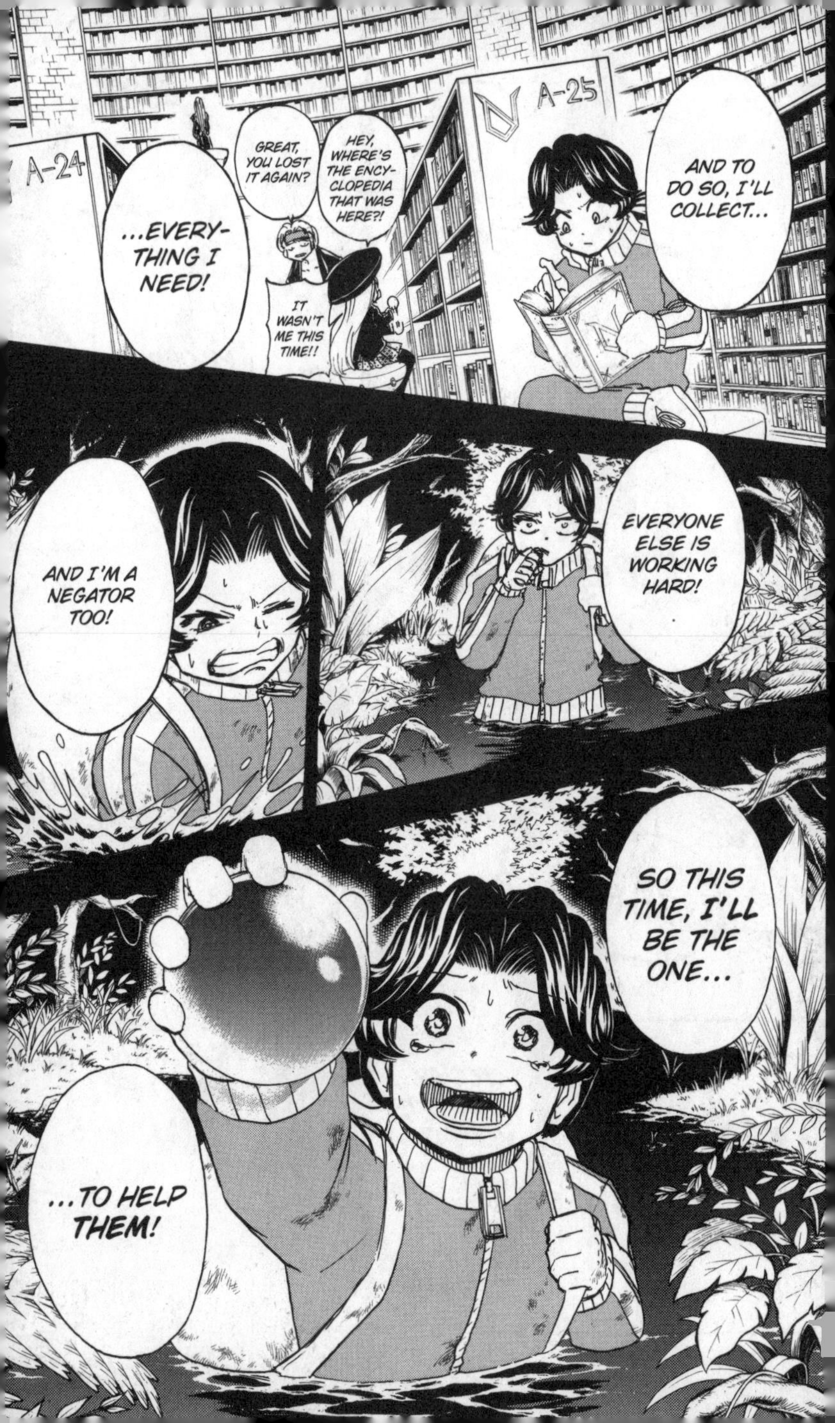

A-25
AND TO DO SO, I'LL COLLECT...
HEY, WHERE'S THE ENCYCLOPEDIA THAT WAS HERE?!
GREAT, YOU LOST IT AGAIN?
IT WASN'T ME THIS TIME!!
A-24
...EVERYTHING I NEED!
EVERYONE ELSE IS WORKING HARD!
AND I'M A NEGATOR TOO!
SO THIS TIME, I'LL BE THE ONE...
...TO HELP THEM!

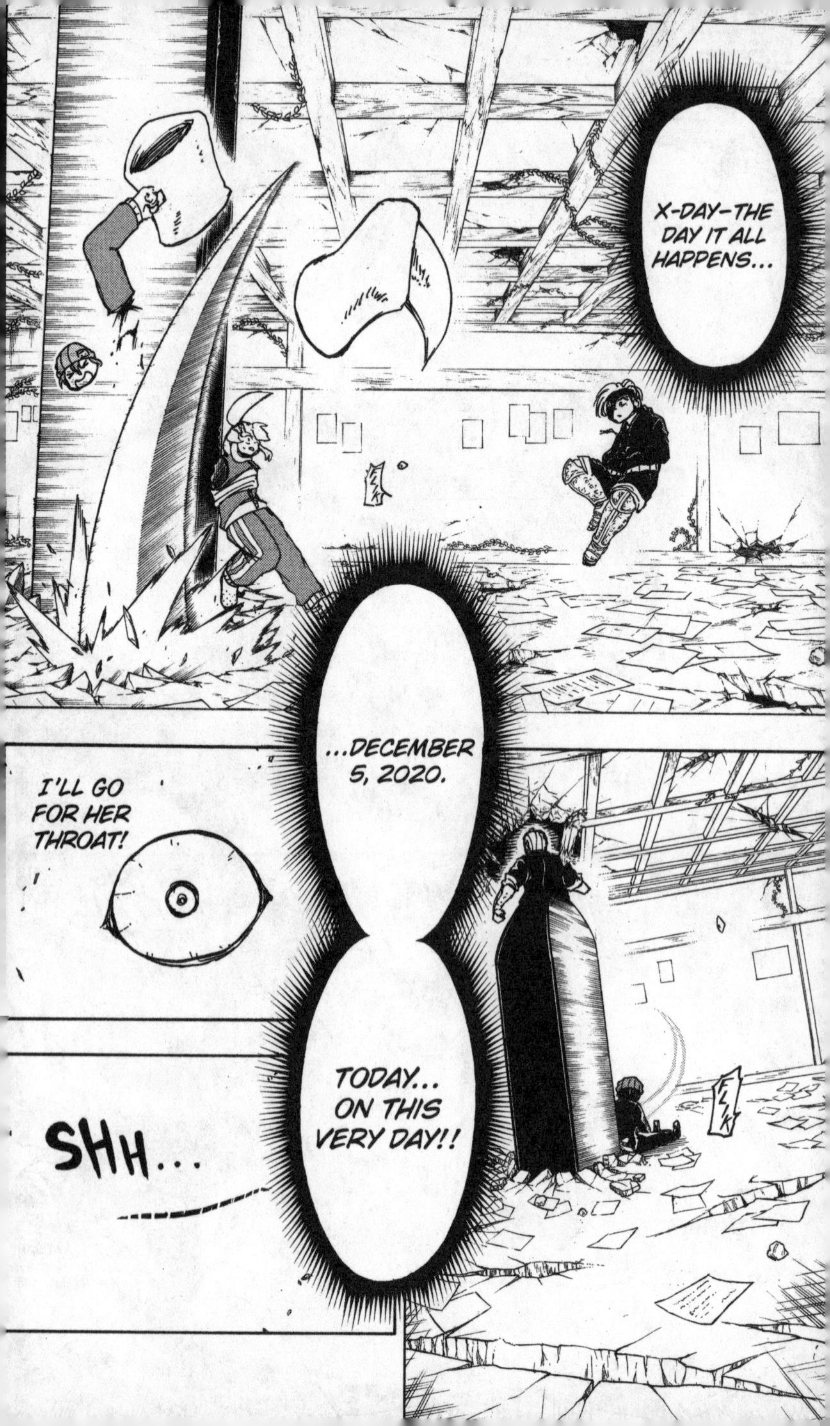
X-DAY—THE DAY IT ALL HAPPENS...
FLK
...DECEMBER 5, 2020.
TODAY... ON THIS VERY DAY!!
FLK
I'LL GO FOR HER THROAT!
SHH...

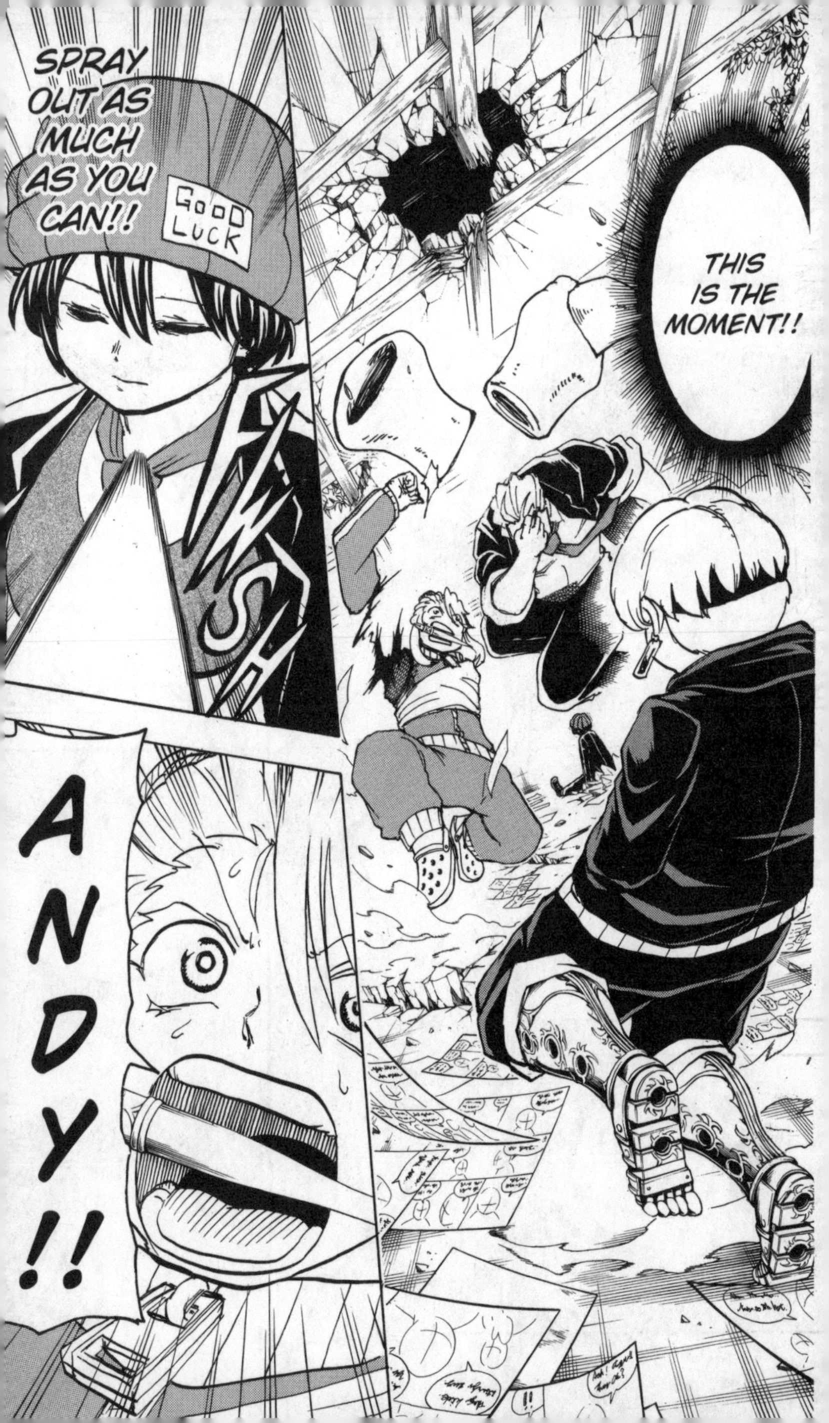

THIS IS THE MOMENT!!
SPRAY OUT AS MUCH AS YOU CAN!!
GOOD LUCK
ANDY!!

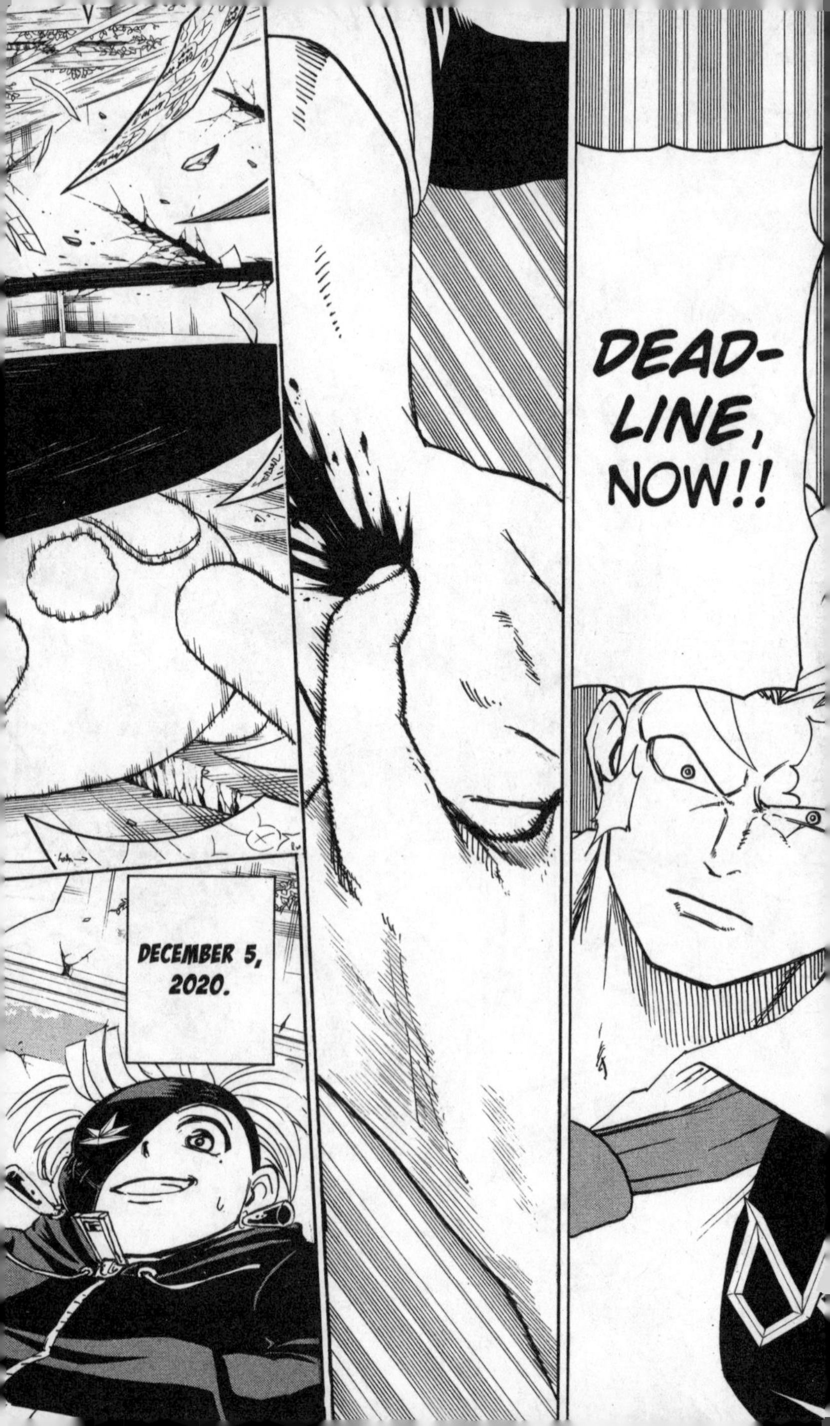
DEAD-
LINE,
NOW!!
DECEMBER 5,
2020.

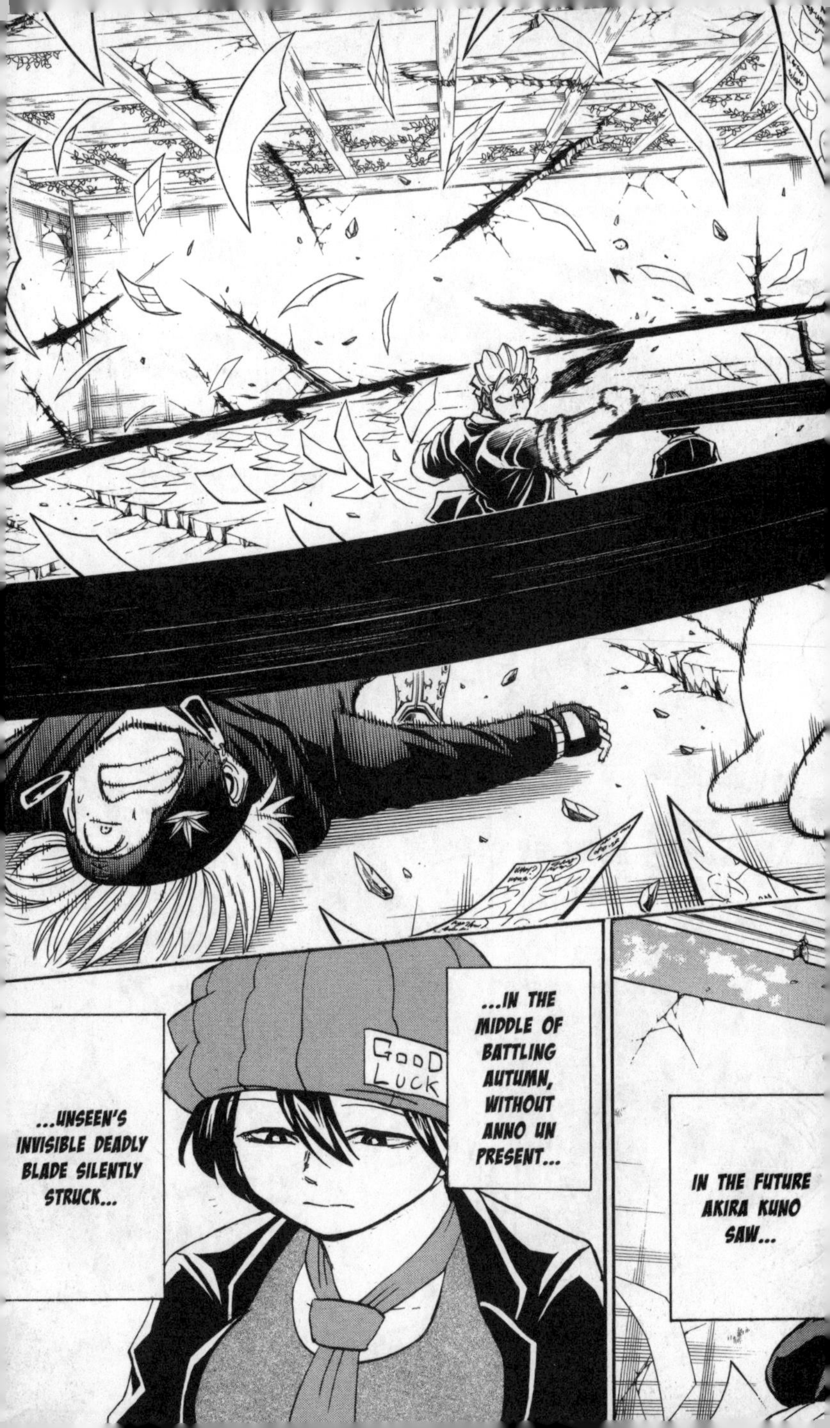
IN THE FUTURE AKIRA KUNO SAW...
...IN THE MIDDLE OF BATTLING AUTUMN, WITHOUT ANNO UN PRESENT...
...UNSEEN'S INVISIBLE DEADLY BLADE SILENTLY STRUCK...
GOOD LUCK

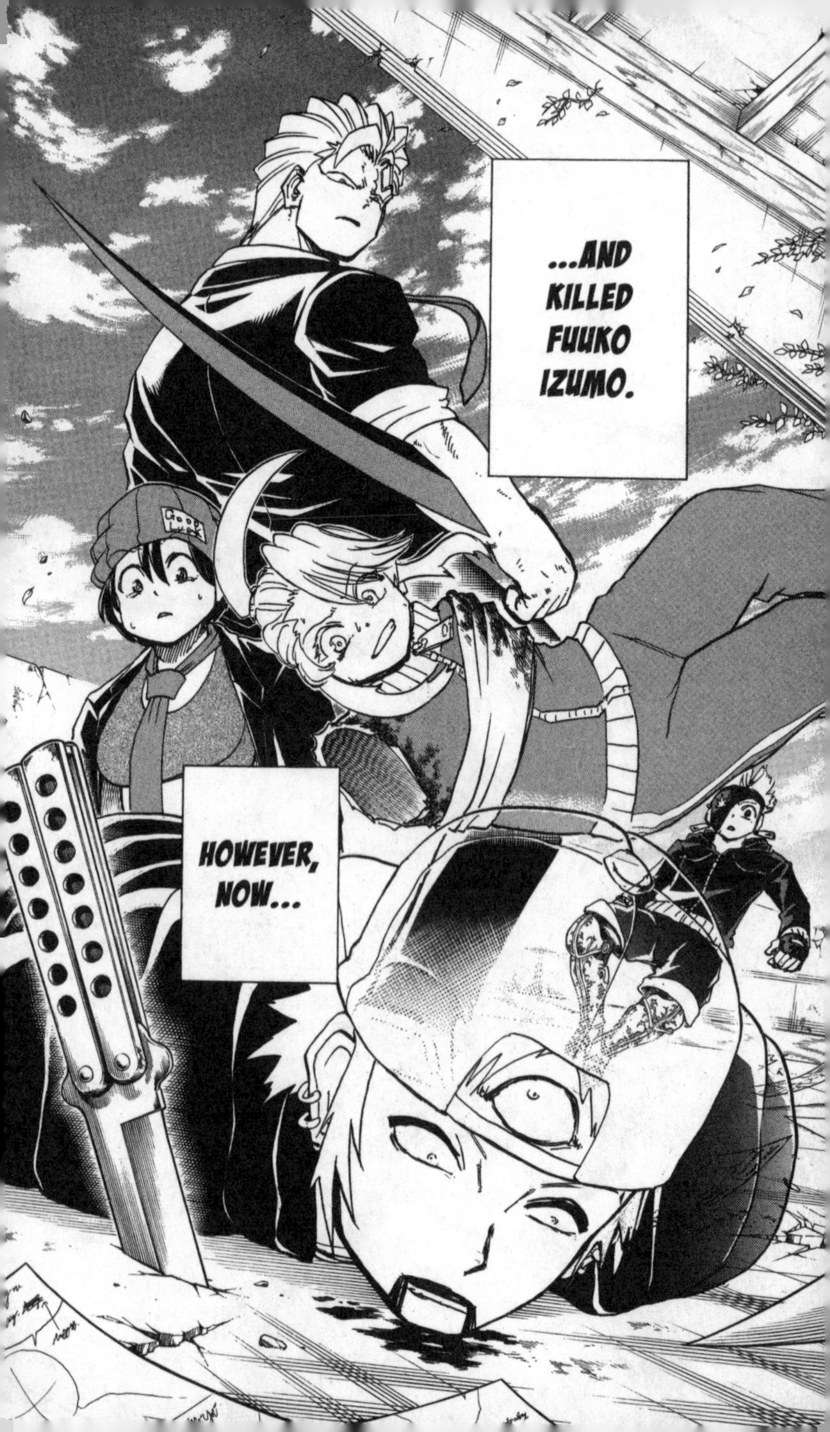
...AND KILLED FUUKO IZUMO.
HOWEVER, NOW...

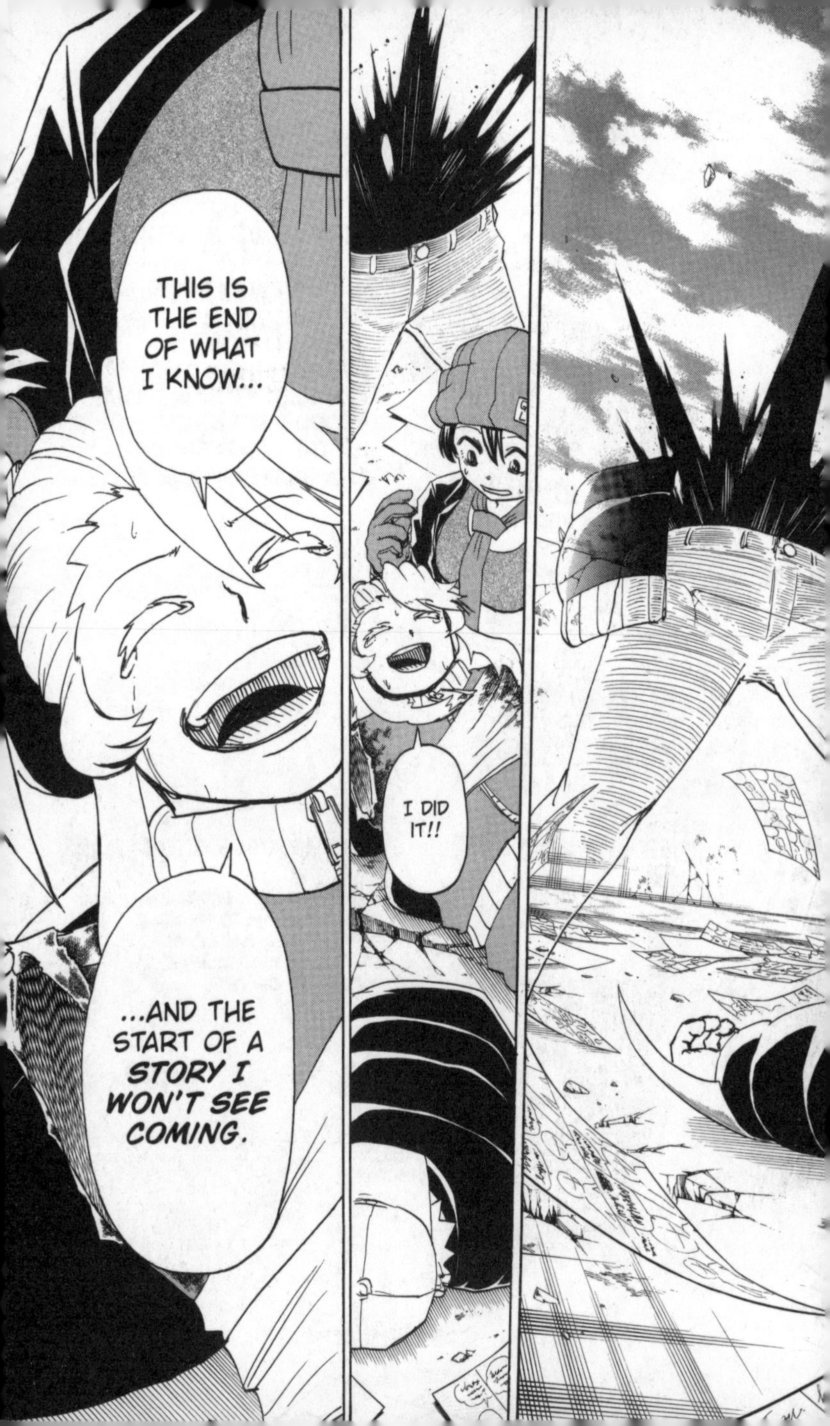
I DID IT!!
THIS IS THE END OF WHAT I KNOW...
...AND THE START OF A *STORY I WON'T SEE COMING*.

INTRODUCTION OF ANDY'S NEW MOVES ③

NEW MOVE 5: DEADBLADE

SPURTS AN OVERABUNDANCE OF BLOOD BY MAKING A WOUND HIMSELF TO PROMOTE BLEEDING AND REGENERATING THAT BLOOD WITH GREAT FORCE. HE THEN HARDENS IT IN THE SHAPE OF A BLADE.

BWSH

Oooh!

WELL, KINDA.

...

SO IT'S BASICALLY A REALLY HARD SCAB?

OH!

PoMF

NEW MOVE 6: DEADLINE

A WIDE-RANGE DEADBLADE. DOESN'T SEEM TO BE ABLE TO PERFORM THE MOVE ON THE SAME SCALE AS VICTOR AS OF YET.

WELL... KINDA.

...

SO IT'S BASICALLY A REALLY *BIG* SCAB?!

OH!

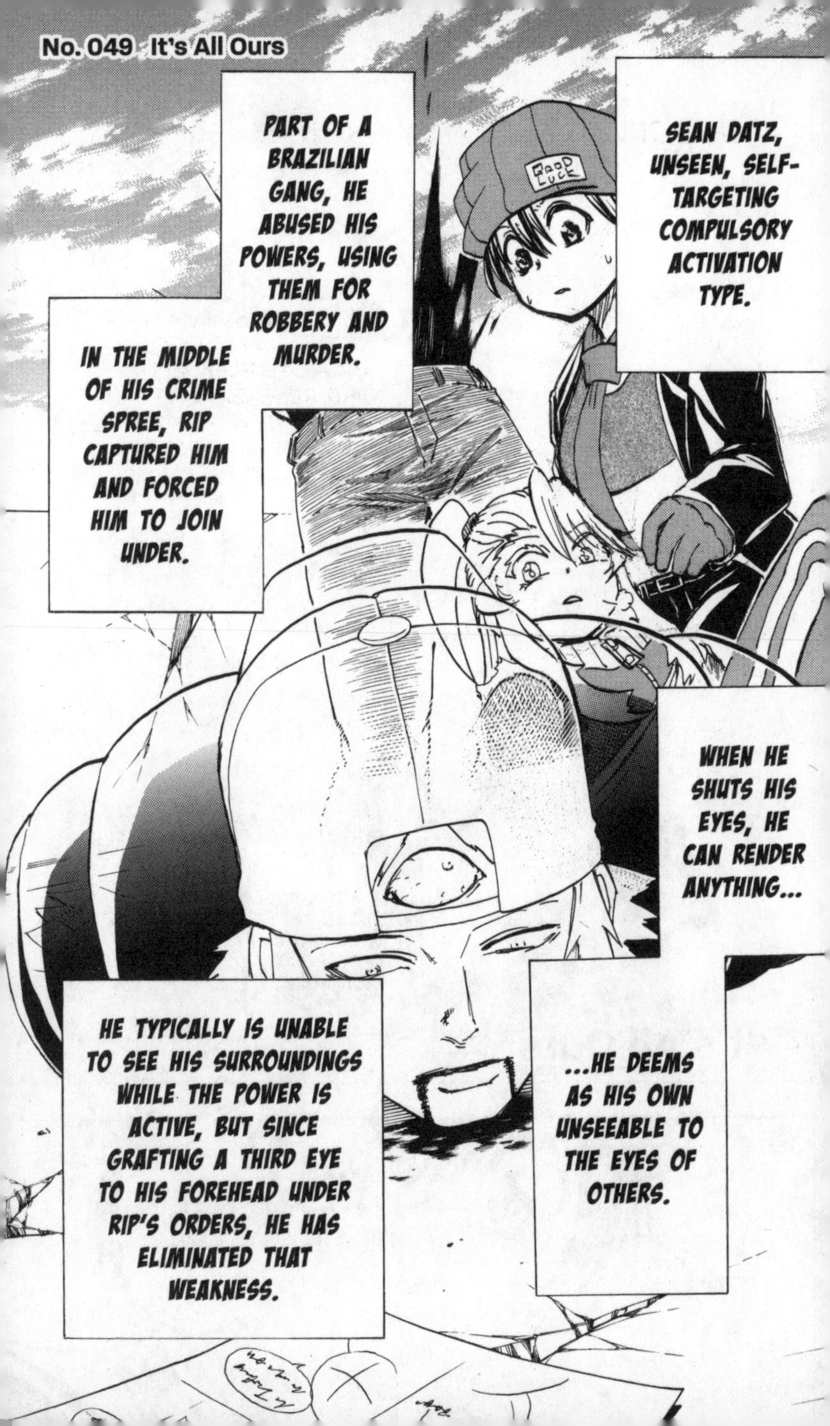
SEAN DATZ, UNSEEN, SELF-TARGETING COMPULSORY ACTIVATION TYPE.
GOOD LUCK
PART OF A BRAZILIAN GANG, HE ABUSED HIS POWERS, USING THEM FOR ROBBERY AND MURDER.
IN THE MIDDLE OF HIS CRIME SPREE, RIP CAPTURED HIM AND FORCED HIM TO JOIN UNDER.
WHEN HE SHUTS HIS EYES, HE CAN RENDER ANYTHING...
...HE DEEMS AS HIS OWN UNSEEABLE TO THE EYES OF OTHERS.
HE TYPICALLY IS UNABLE TO SEE HIS SURROUNDINGS WHILE THE POWER IS ACTIVE, BUT SINCE GRAFTING A THIRD EYE TO HIS FOREHEAD UNDER RIP'S ORDERS, HE HAS ELIMINATED THAT WEAKNESS.

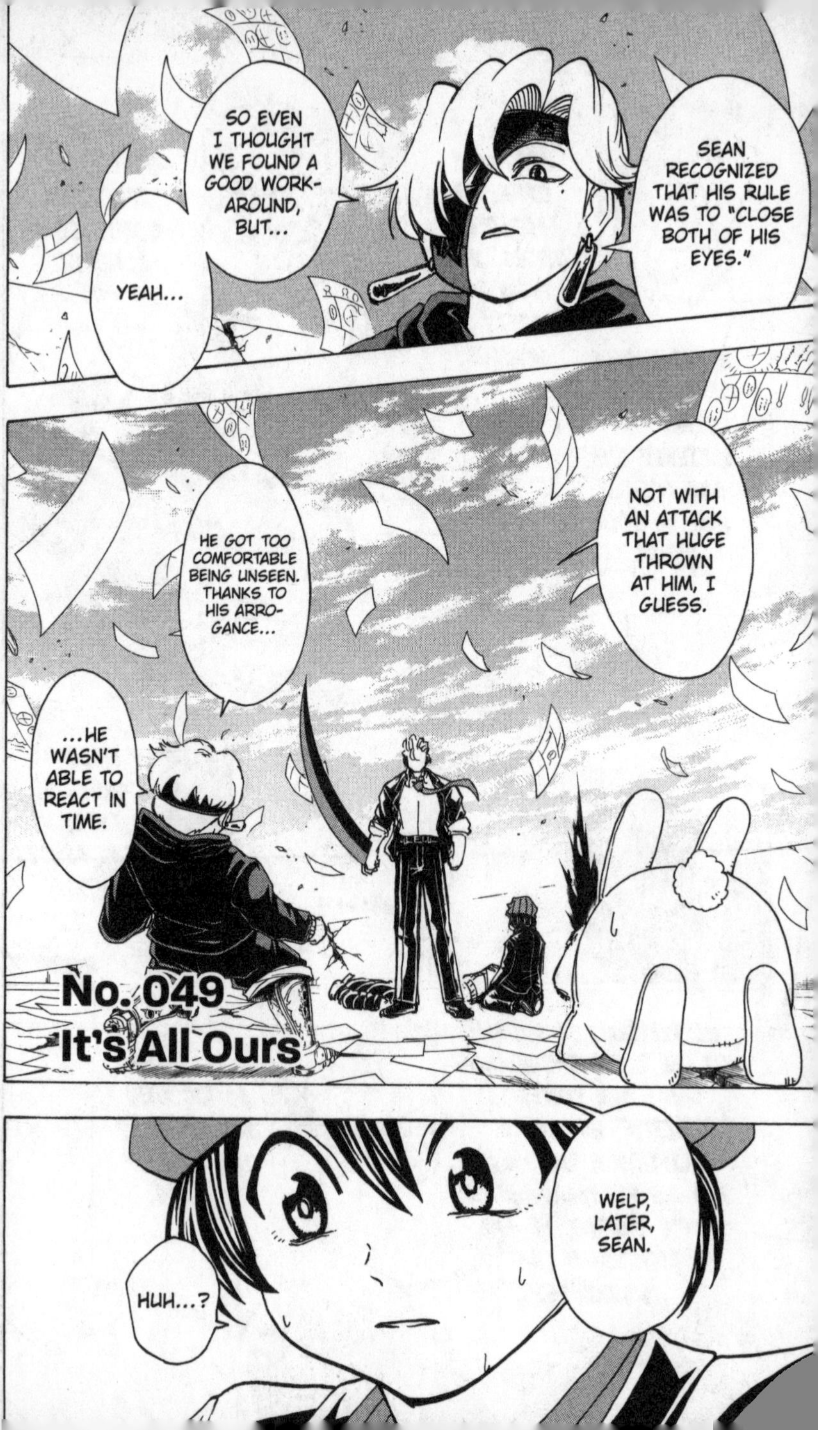
SEAN RECOGNIZED THAT HIS RULE WAS TO "CLOSE BOTH OF HIS EYES."
SO EVEN I THOUGHT WE FOUND A GOOD WORK-AROUND, BUT...
YEAH...
NOT WITH AN ATTACK THAT HUGE THROWN AT HIM, I GUESS.
HE GOT TOO COMFORTABLE BEING UNSEEN. THANKS TO HIS ARROGANCE...
...HE WASN'T ABLE TO REACT IN TIME.
No. 049
It's All Ours
WELP, LATER, SEAN.
HUH...?

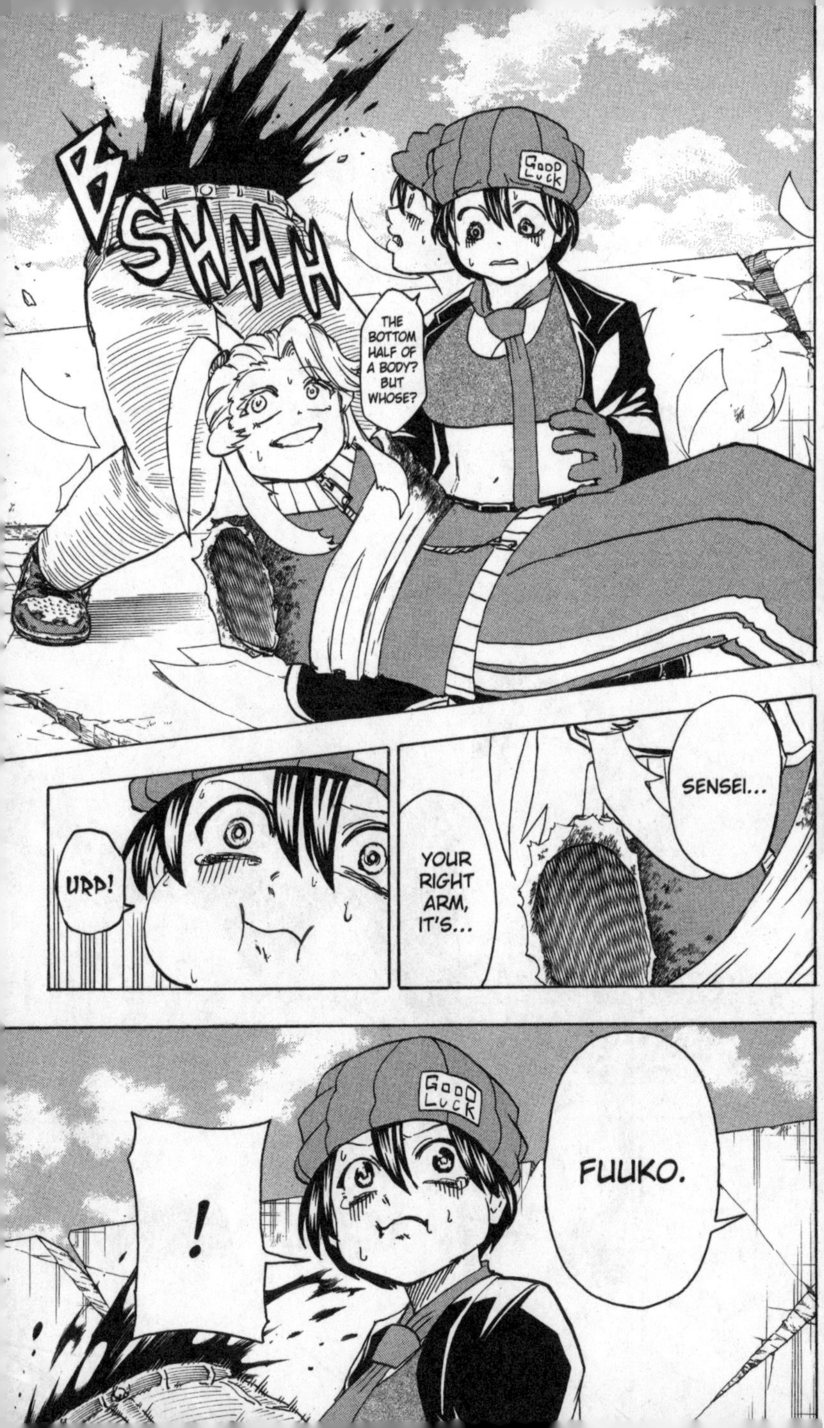
BSHHH
THE BOTTOM HALF OF A BODY? BUT WHOSE?
SENSEI...
YOUR RIGHT ARM, IT'S...
URP!
FUUKO.
!

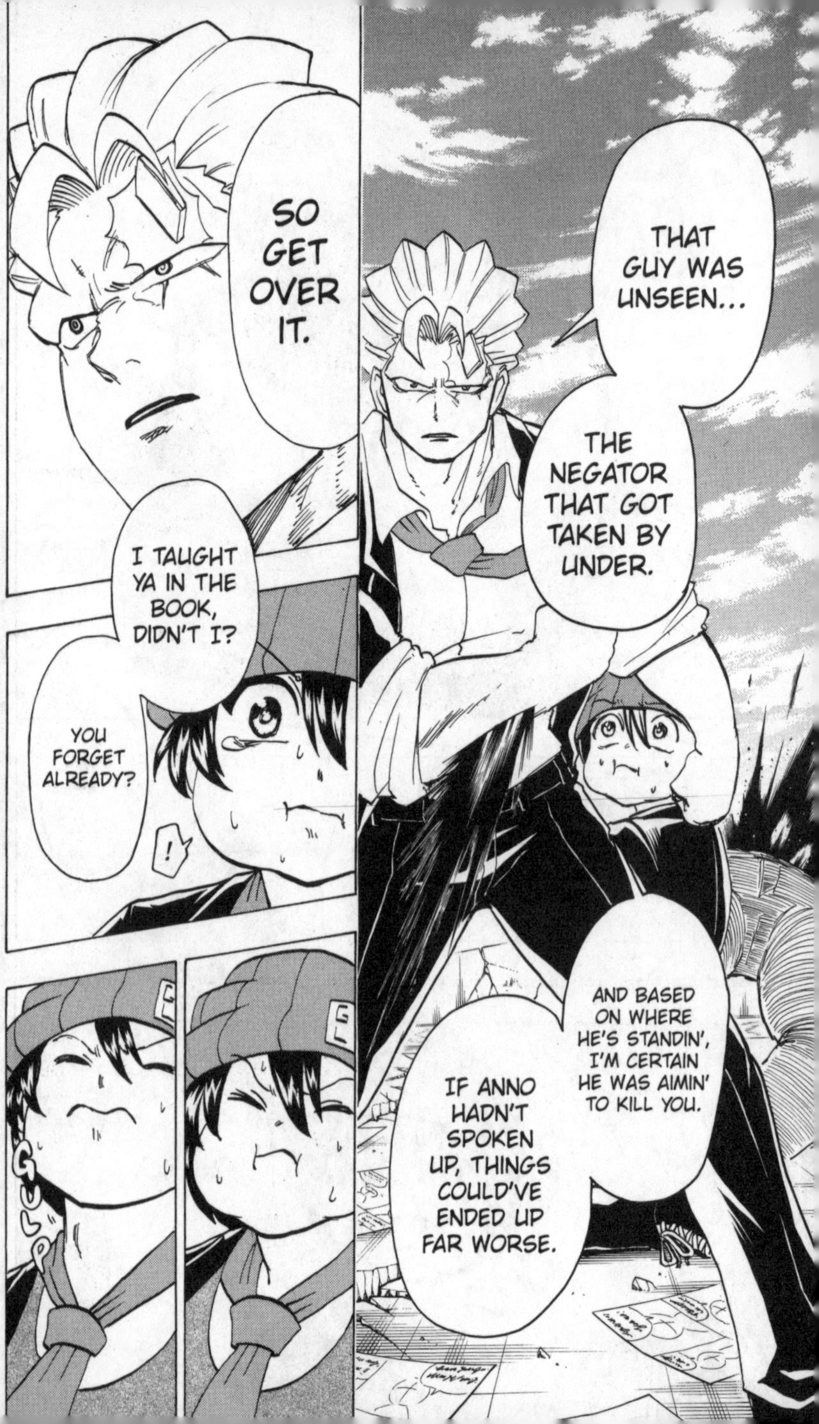

THAT GUY WAS UNSEEN...
THE NEGATOR THAT GOT TAKEN BY UNDER.
AND BASED ON WHERE HE'S STANDIN', I'M CERTAIN HE WAS AIMIN' TO KILL YOU.
IF ANNO HADN'T SPOKEN UP, THINGS COULD'VE ENDED UP FAR WORSE.
SO GET OVER IT.
I TAUGHT YA IN THE BOOK, DIDN'T I?
YOU FORGET ALREADY?
!
GULP

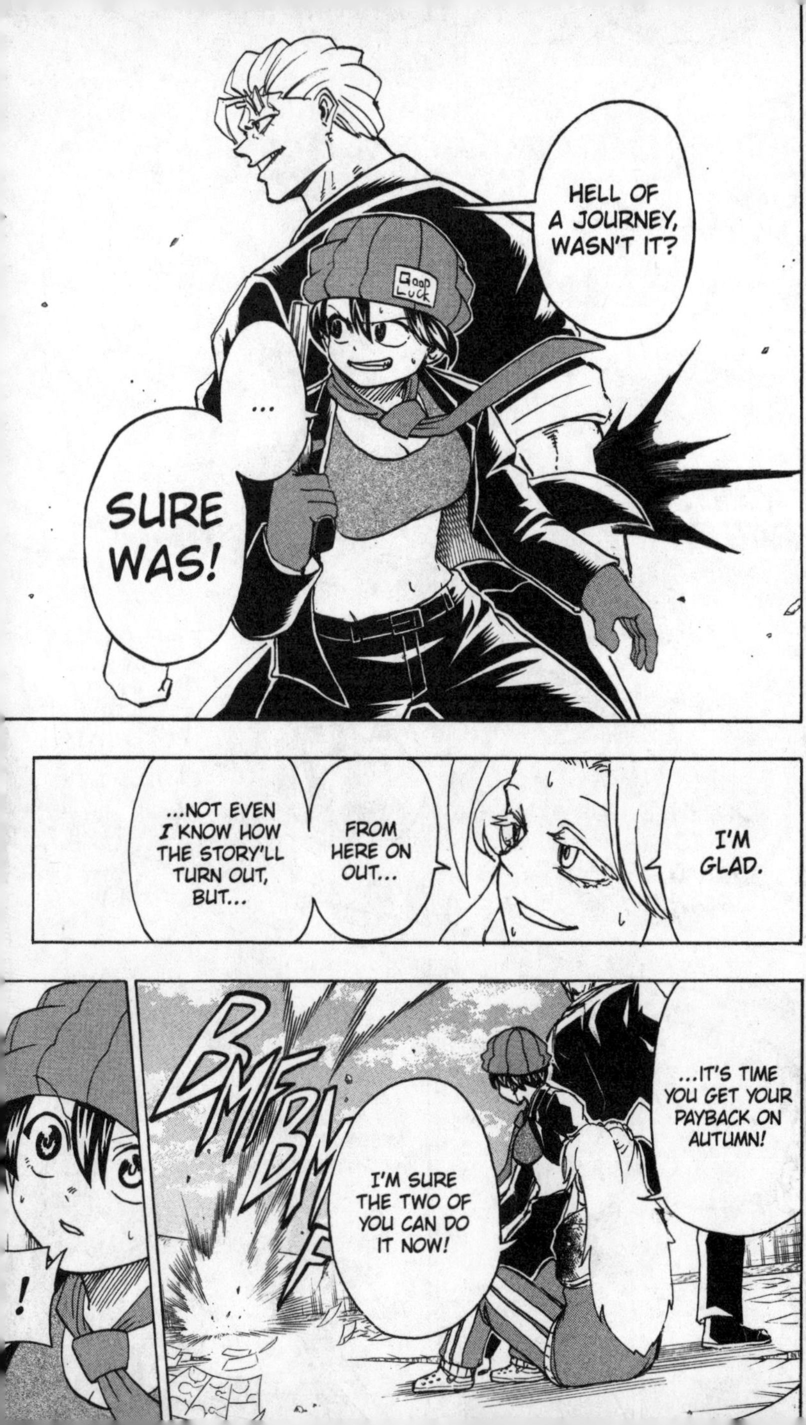
HELL OF A JOURNEY, WASN'T IT?
GOOD LUCK
...
SURE WAS!
I'M GLAD.
FROM HERE ON OUT...
...NOT EVEN I KNOW HOW THE STORY'LL TURN OUT, BUT...
...IT'S TIME YOU GET YOUR PAYBACK ON AUTUMN!
I'M SURE THE TWO OF YOU CAN DO IT NOW!
!

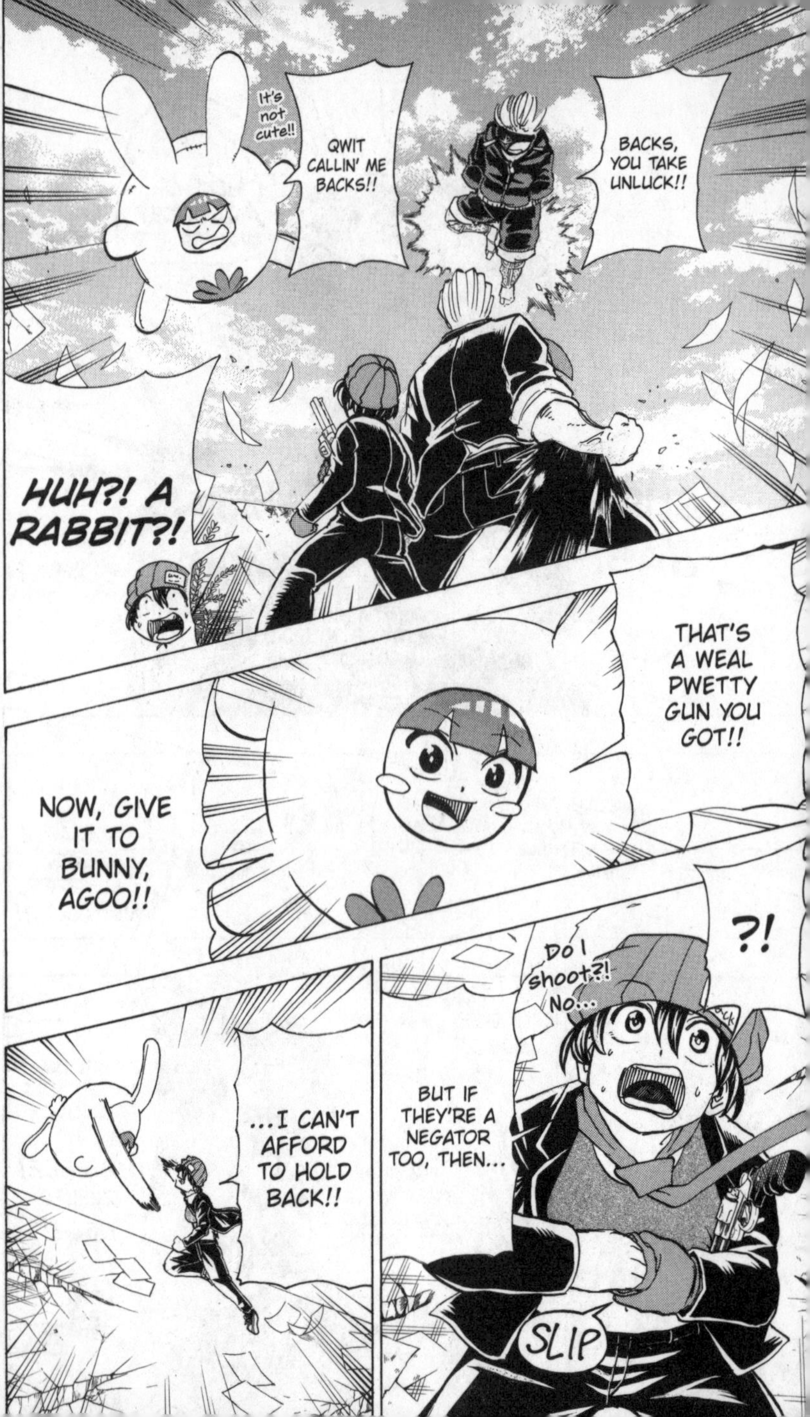
BACKS, YOU TAKE UNLUCK!!
QWIT CALLIN' ME BACKS!!
It's not cute!!
HUH?! A RABBIT?!
THAT'S A WEAL PWETTY GUN YOU GOT!!
NOW, GIVE IT TO BUNNY, AGOO!!
?!
Do I shoot?! No...
BUT IF THEY'RE A NEGATOR TOO, THEN...
SLIP
...I CAN'T AFFORD TO HOLD BACK!!

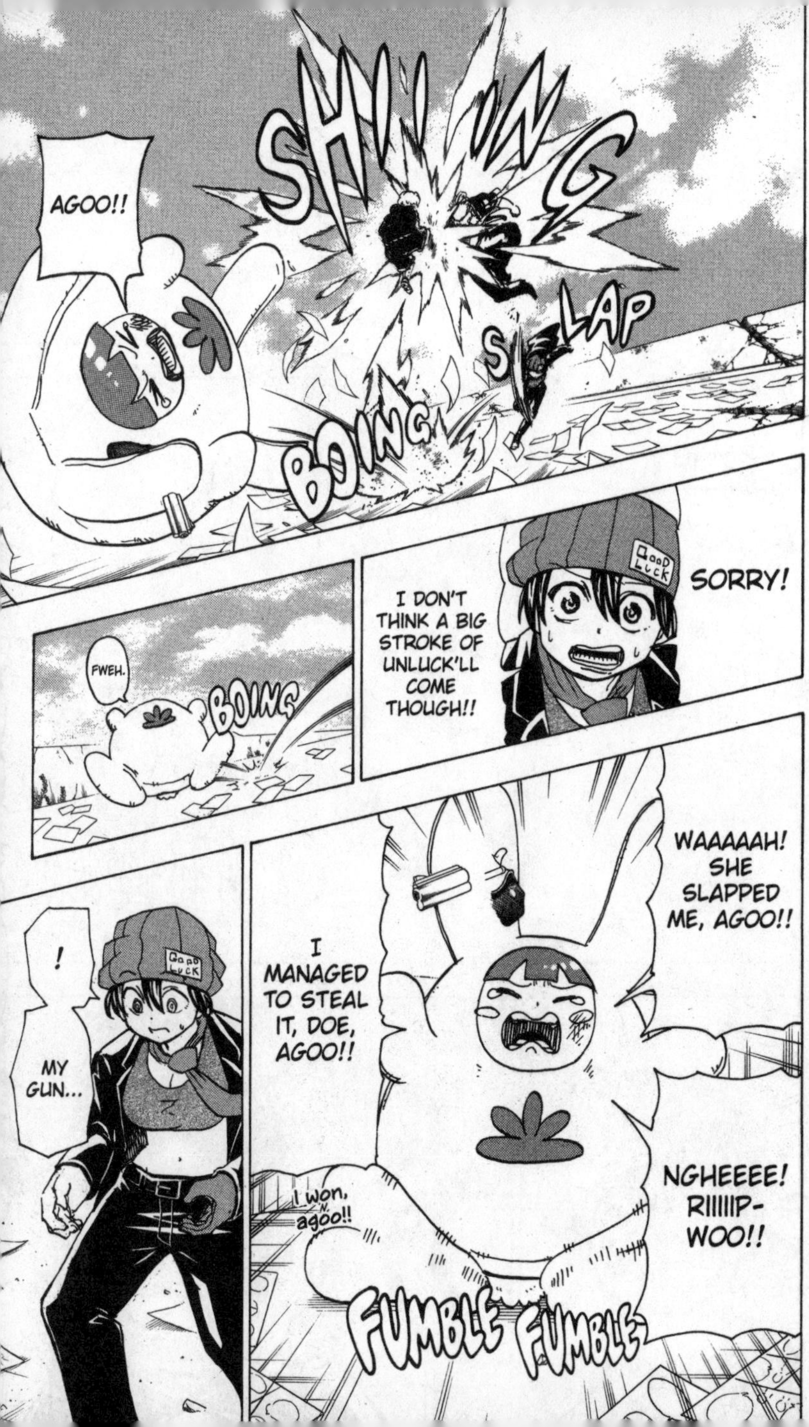
SHIIING
AGOO!!
SLAP
BOING
SORRY!
I DON'T THINK A BIG STROKE OF UNLUCK'LL COME THOUGH!!
GOOD LUCK
FWEH.
BOING
WAAAAAH! SHE SLAPPED ME, AGOO!!
I MANAGED TO STEAL IT, DOE, AGOO!!
NGHEEEE! RIIIIP-WOO!!
I won, agoo!!
FUMBLE FUMBLE
!
MY GUN...
GOOD LUCK

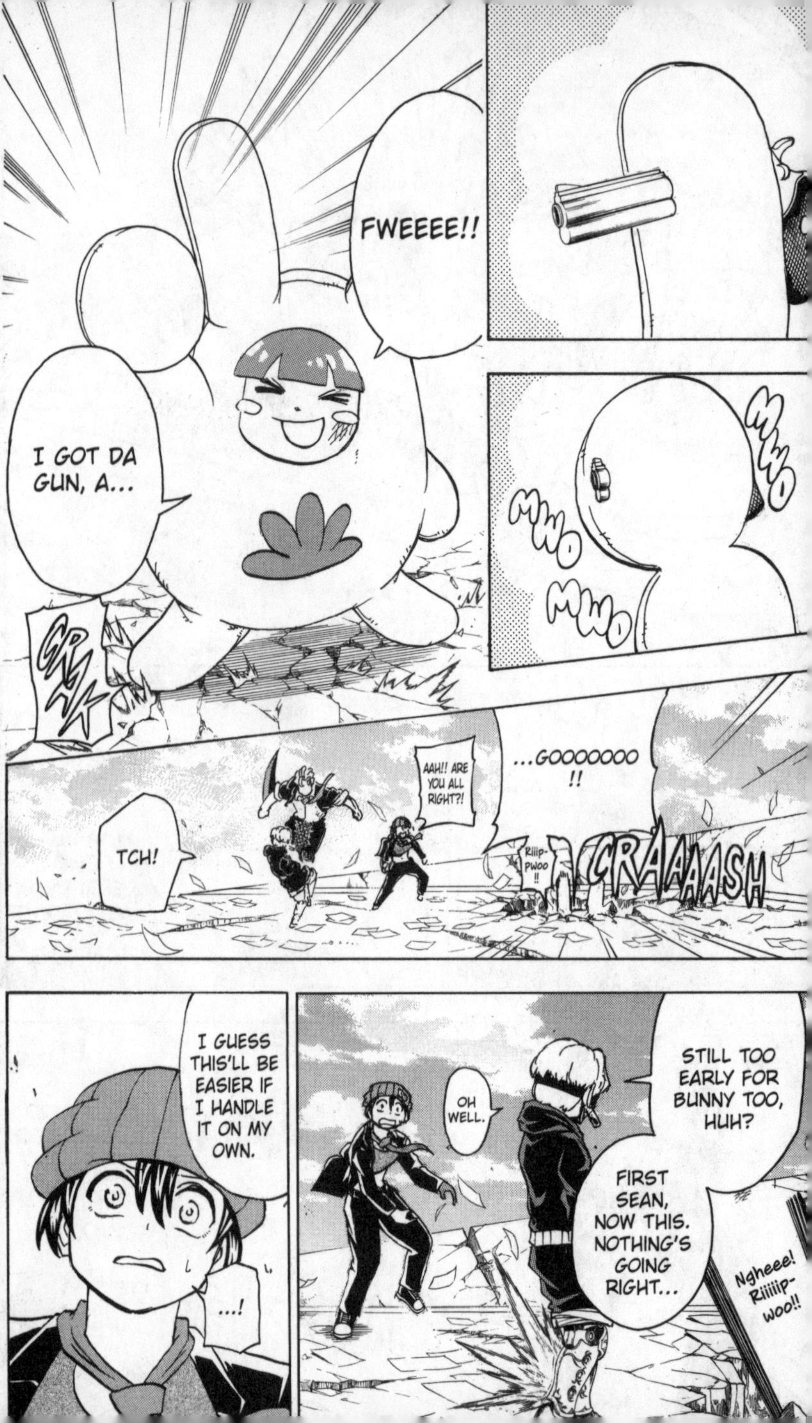
MWO MWO MWO MWO
FWEEEE!!
I GOT DA GUN, A...
CRAK
...GOOOOOOO!!
CRAAAASH
Riiip-pwoo!!
AAH!! ARE YOU ALL RIGHT?!
TCH!
STILL TOO EARLY FOR BUNNY TOO, HUH?
FIRST SEAN, NOW THIS. NOTHING'S GOING RIGHT...
Ngheee! Riiiiip-woo!!
OH WELL.
I GUESS THIS'LL BE EASIER IF I HANDLE IT ON MY OWN.
...!

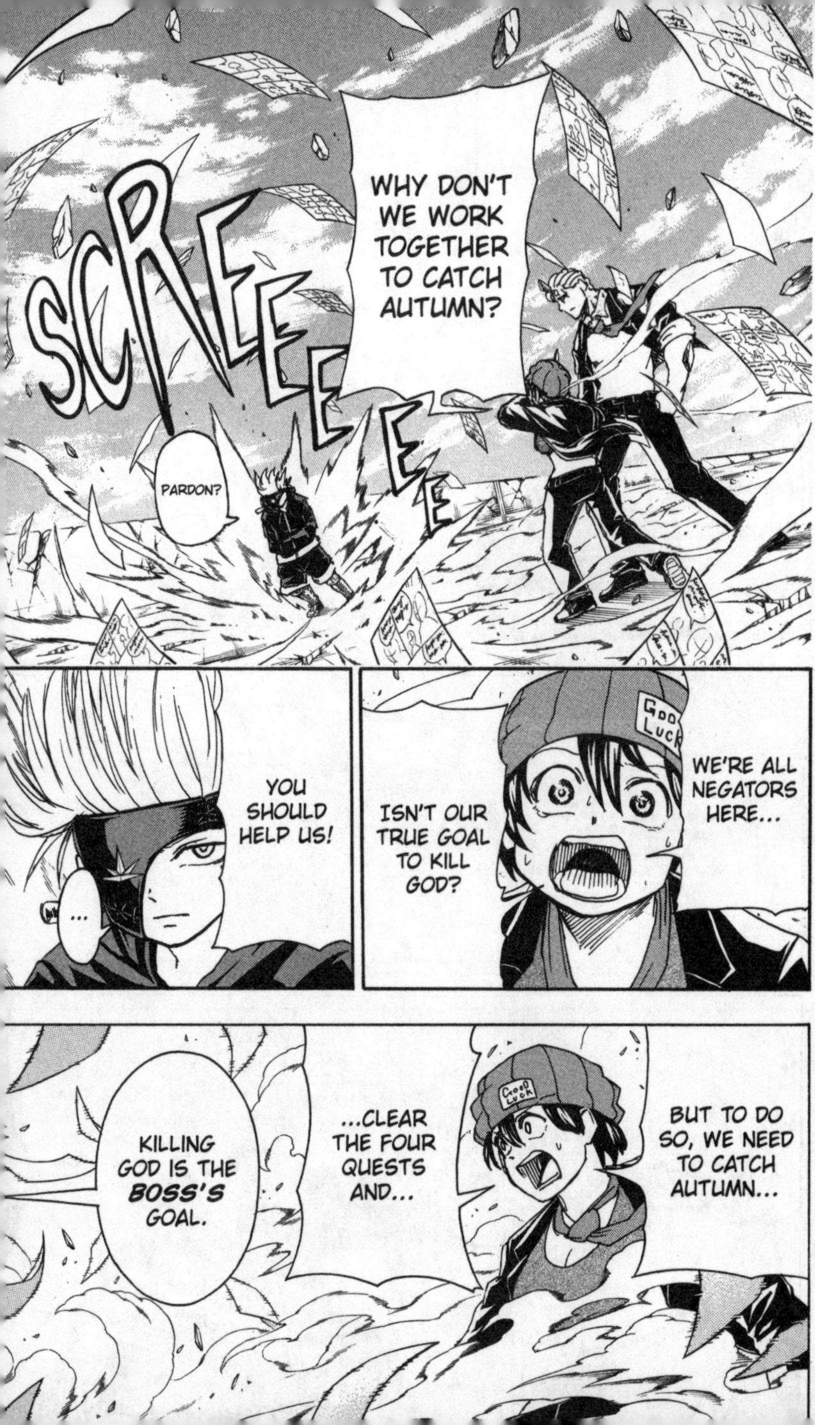
WHY DON'T WE WORK TOGETHER TO CATCH AUTUMN?
SCREEEEE
PARDON?
WE'RE ALL NEGATORS HERE...
ISN'T OUR TRUE GOAL TO KILL GOD?
YOU SHOULD HELP US!
...
BUT TO DO SO, WE NEED TO CATCH AUTUMN...
...CLEAR THE FOUR QUESTS AND...
KILLING GOD IS THE *BOSS'S* GOAL.

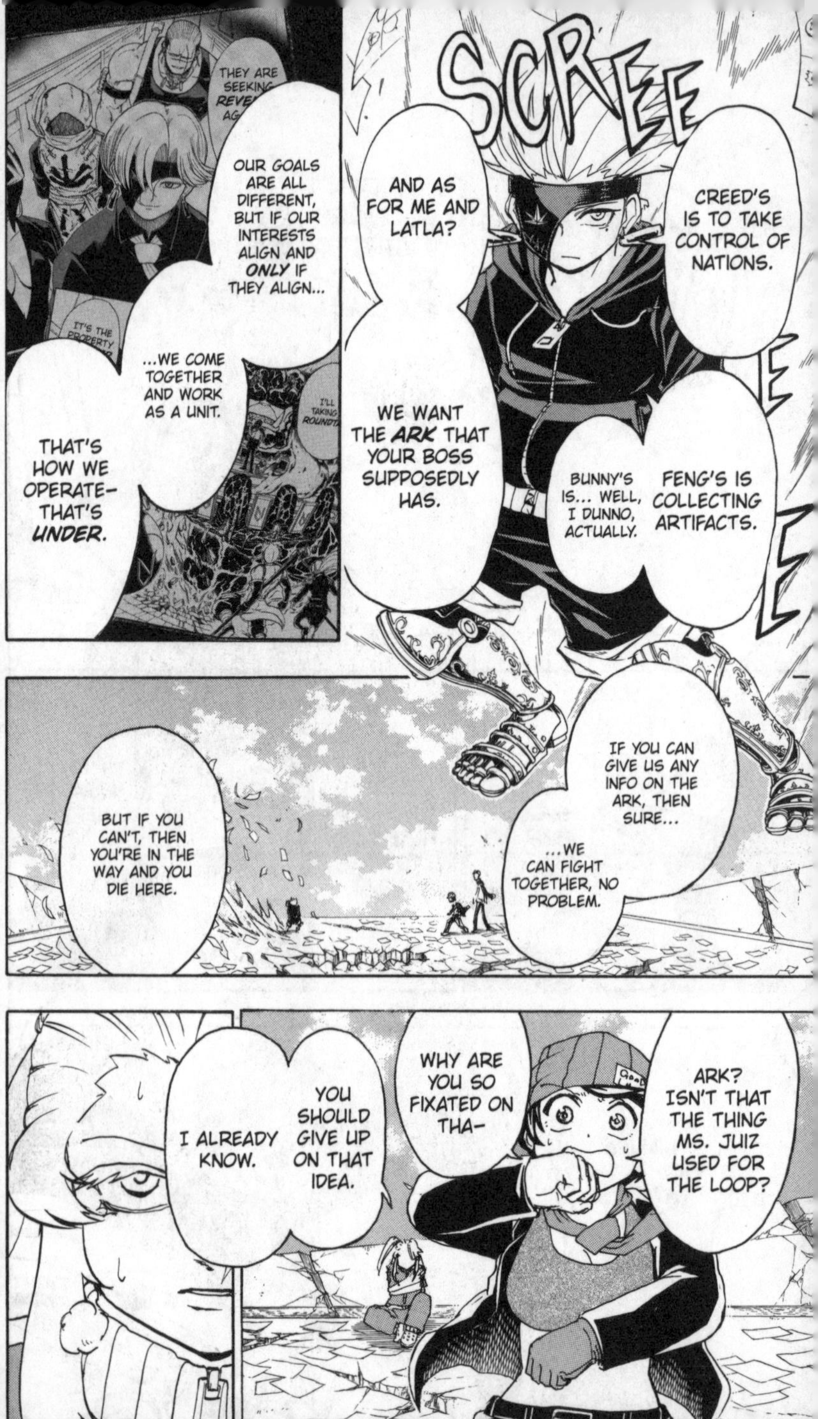

SCREE
CREED'S IS TO TAKE CONTROL OF NATIONS.
AND AS FOR ME AND LATLA?
FENG'S IS COLLECTING ARTIFACTS.
BUNNY'S IS... WELL, I DUNNO, ACTUALLY.
WE WANT THE ARK THAT YOUR BOSS SUPPOSEDLY HAS.
THEY ARE SEEKING
OUR GOALS ARE ALL DIFFERENT, BUT IF OUR INTERESTS ALIGN AND ONLY IF THEY ALIGN...
...WE COME TOGETHER AND WORK AS A UNIT.
IT'S THE PROPERTY
THAT'S HOW WE OPERATE-THAT'S UNDER.
IF YOU CAN GIVE US ANY INFO ON THE ARK, THEN SURE...
...WE CAN FIGHT TOGETHER, NO PROBLEM.
BUT IF YOU CAN'T, THEN YOU'RE IN THE WAY AND YOU DIE HERE.
ARK? ISN'T THAT THE THING MS. JUIZ USED FOR THE LOOP?
WHY ARE YOU SO FIXATED ON THA-
YOU SHOULD GIVE UP ON THAT IDEA.
I ALREADY KNOW.

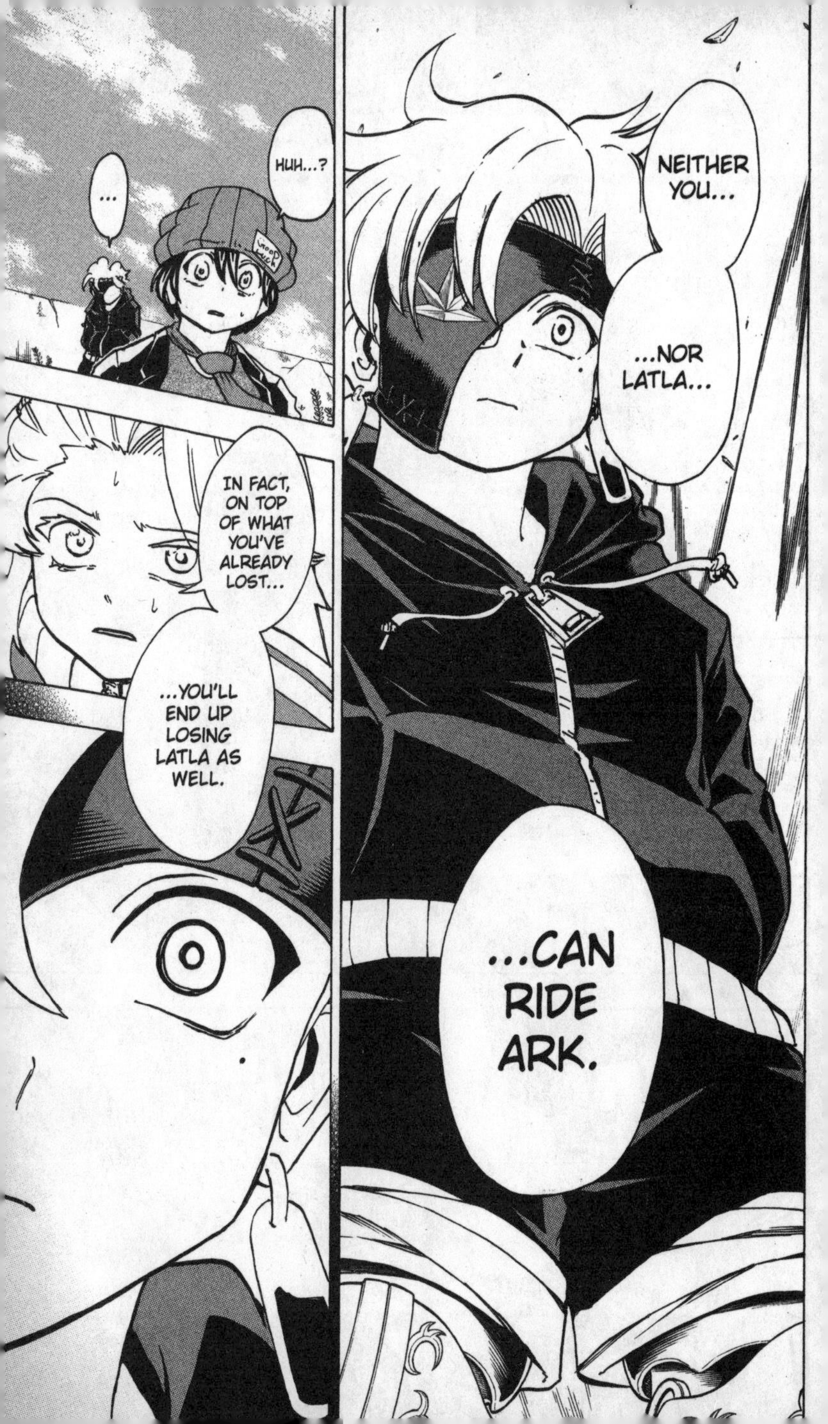
NEITHER YOU...
...NOR LATLA...
...CAN RIDE ARK.
HUH...?
...
IN FACT, ON TOP OF WHAT YOU'VE ALREADY LOST...
...YOU'LL END UP LOSING LATLA AS WELL.

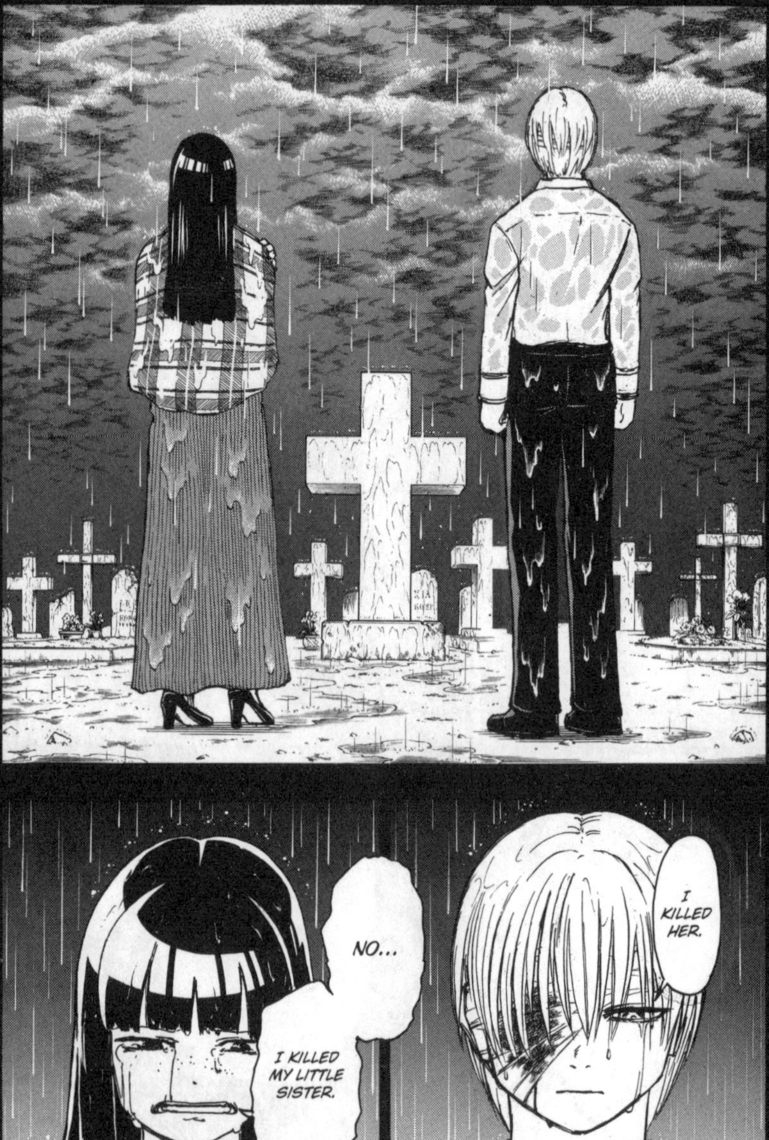
I KILLED HER.
NO...
I KILLED MY LITTLE SISTER.

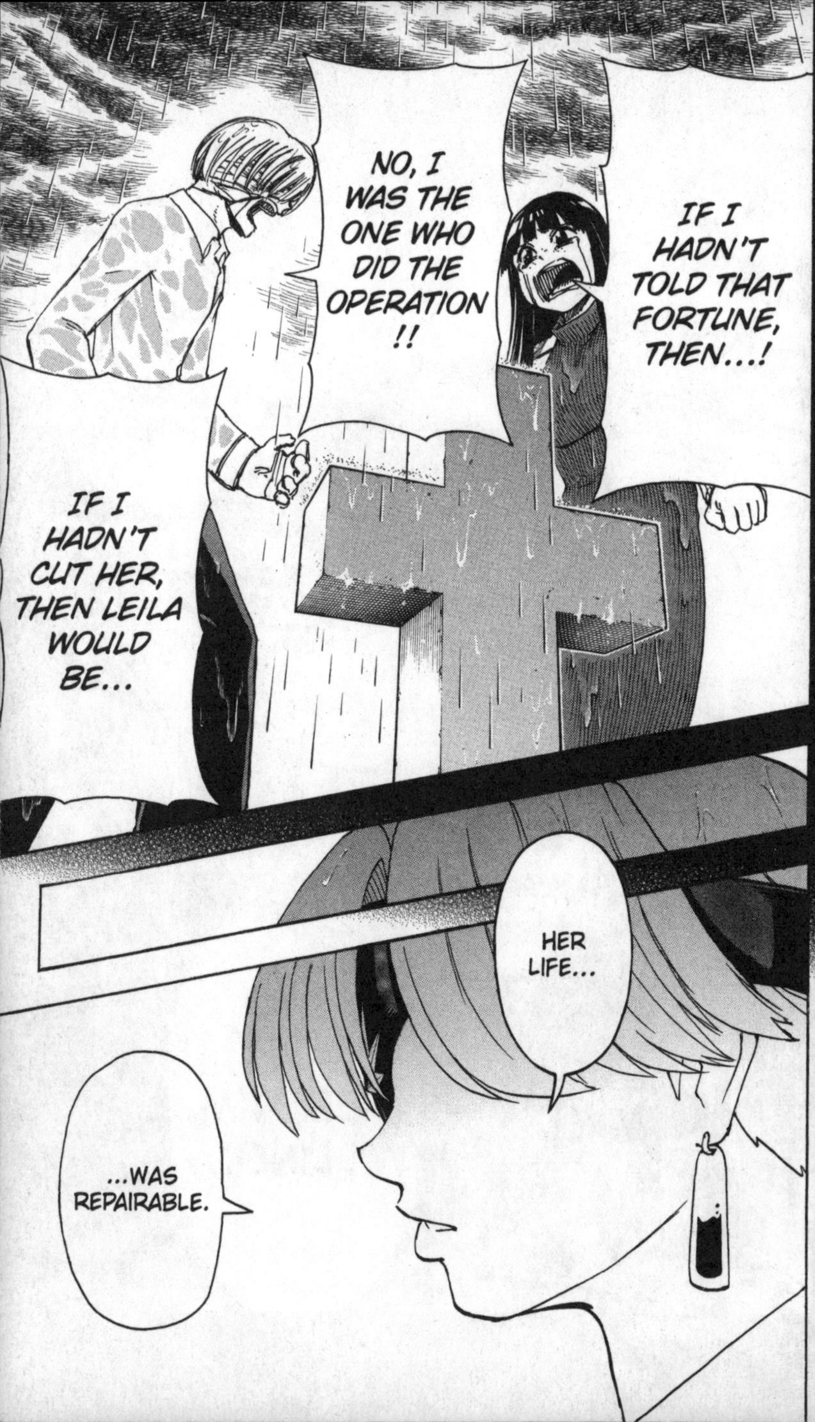
IF I HADN'T TOLD THAT FORTUNE, THEN...!
NO, I WAS THE ONE WHO DID THE OPERATION!!
IF I HADN'T CUT HER, THEN LEILA WOULD BE...
HER LIFE...
...WAS REPAIRABLE.

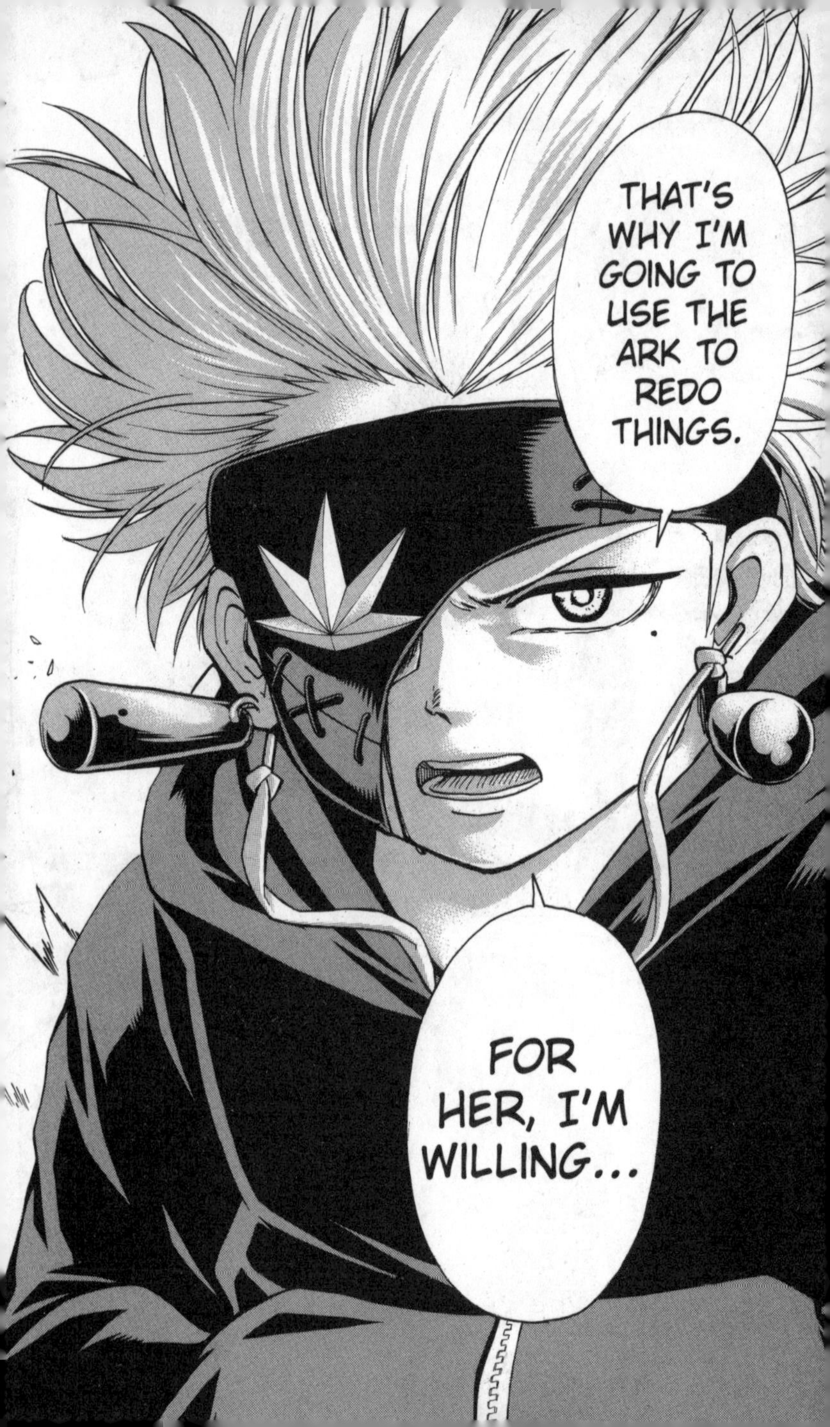
THAT'S WHY I'M GOING TO USE THE ARK TO REDO THINGS.
FOR HER, I'M WILLING...

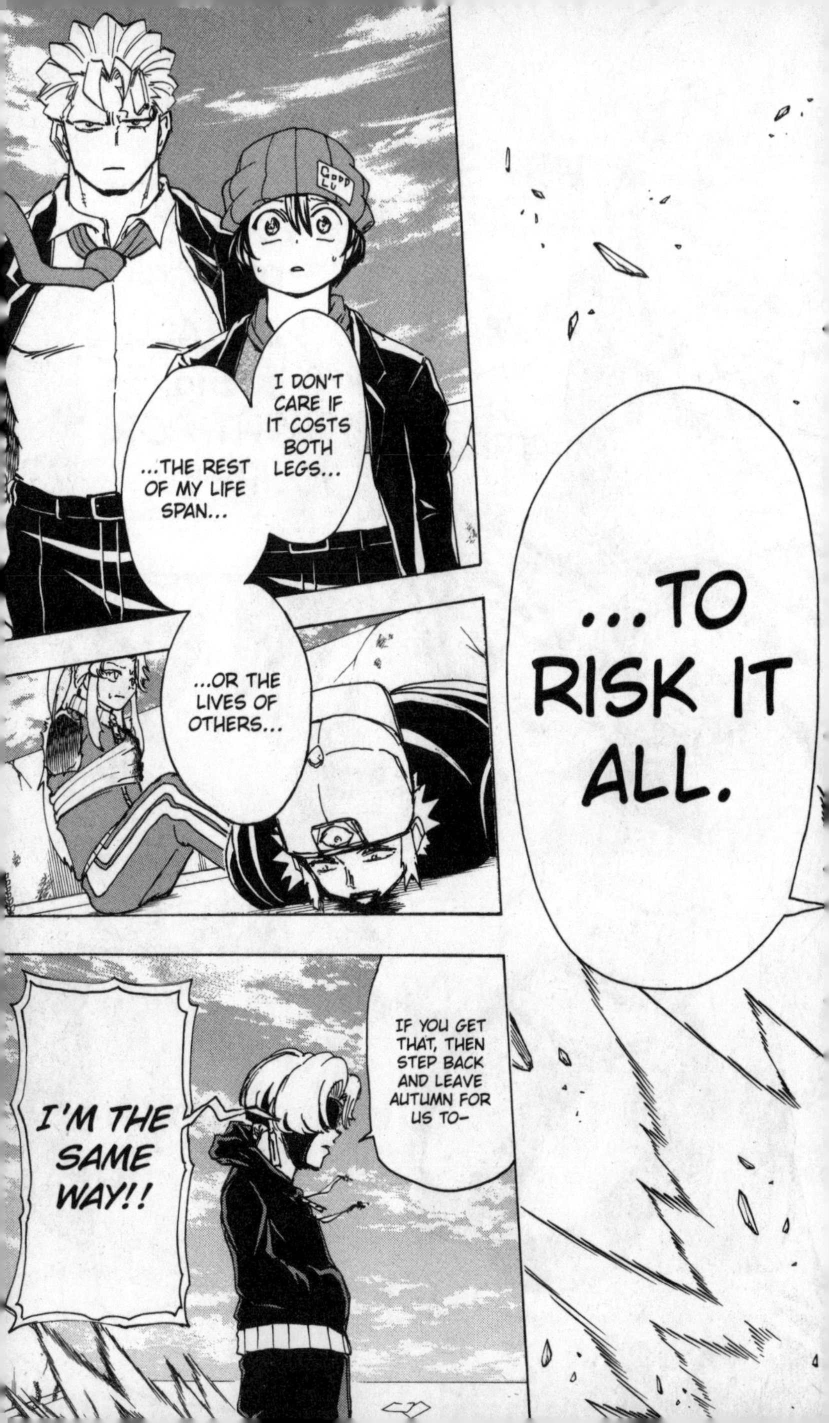
I DON'T CARE IF IT COSTS BOTH LEGS...
...THE REST OF MY LIFE SPAN...
...OR THE LIVES OF OTHERS...
...TO RISK IT ALL.
IF YOU GET THAT, THEN STEP BACK AND LEAVE AUTUMN FOR US TO-
I'M THE SAME WAY!!

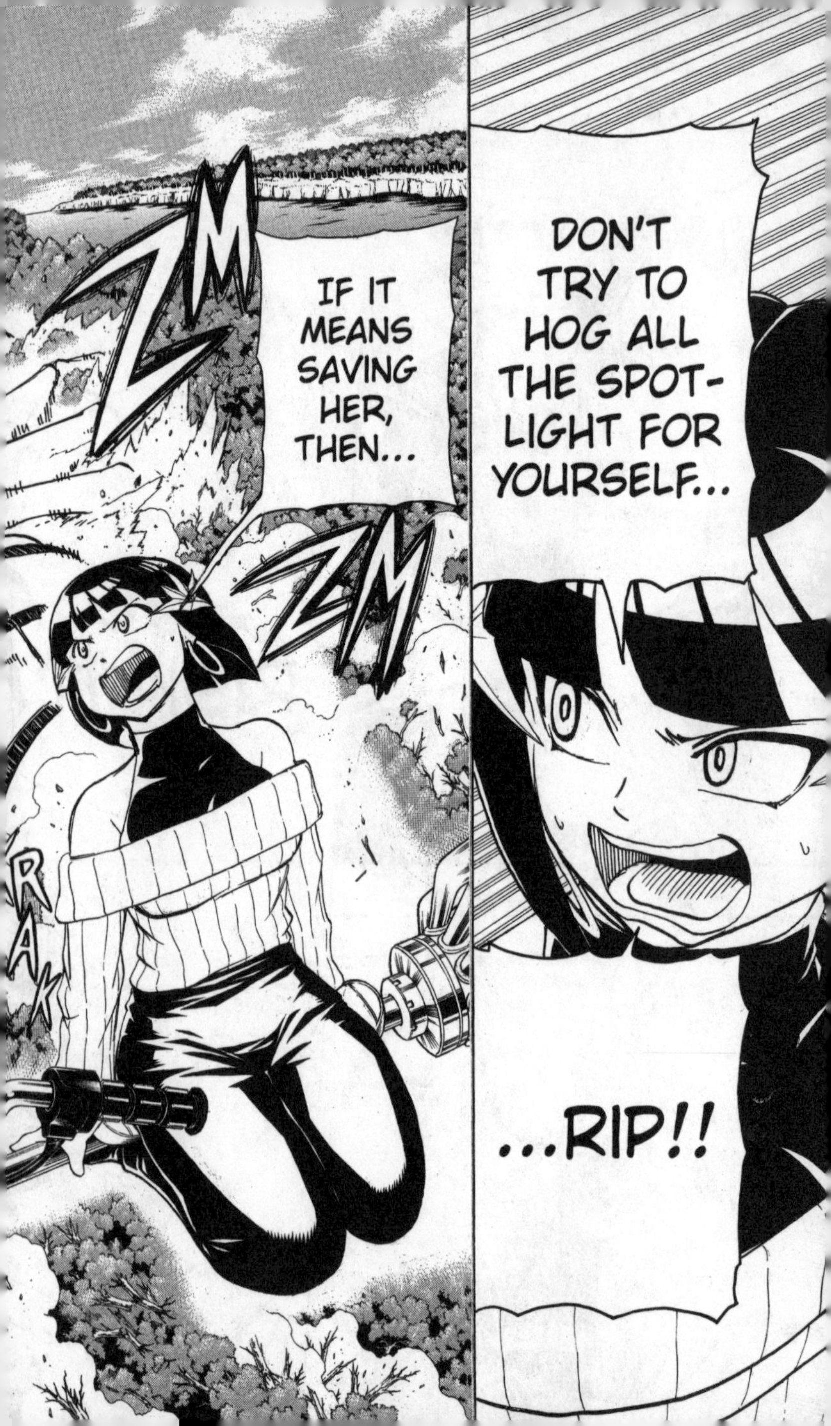
DON'T TRY TO HOG ALL THE SPOT-LIGHT FOR YOURSELF...
...RIP!!
ZM
IF IT MEANS SAVING HER, THEN...
ZM
RAK

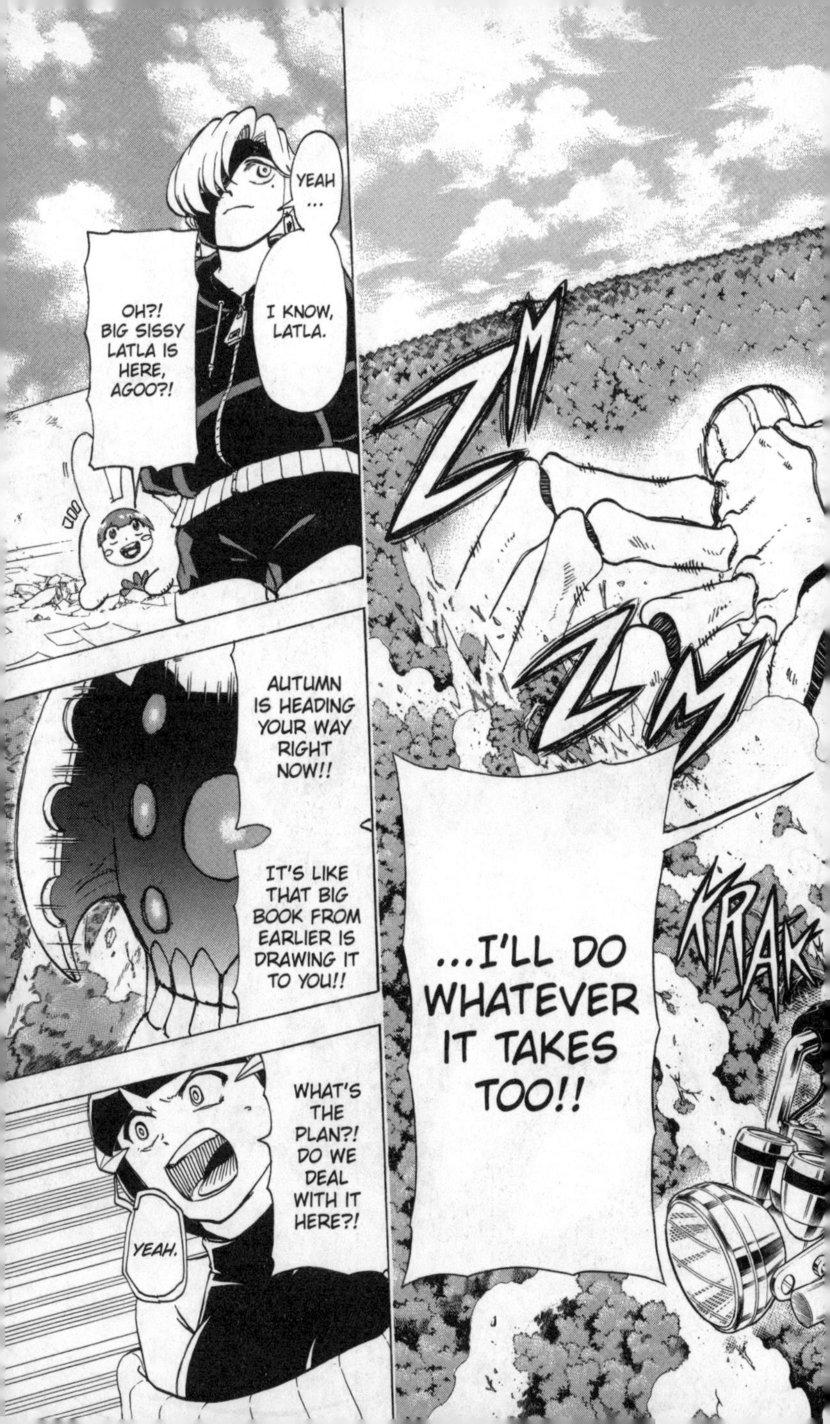

ZM
ZM
...I'LL DO WHATEVER IT TAKES TOO!!
KRAK
YEAH ...
I KNOW, LATLA.
OH?! BIG SISSY LATLA IS HERE, AGOO?!
AUTUMN IS HEADING YOUR WAY RIGHT NOW!!
IT'S LIKE THAT BIG BOOK FROM EARLIER IS DRAWING IT TO YOU!!
WHAT'S THE PLAN?! DO WE DEAL WITH IT HERE?!
YEAH.

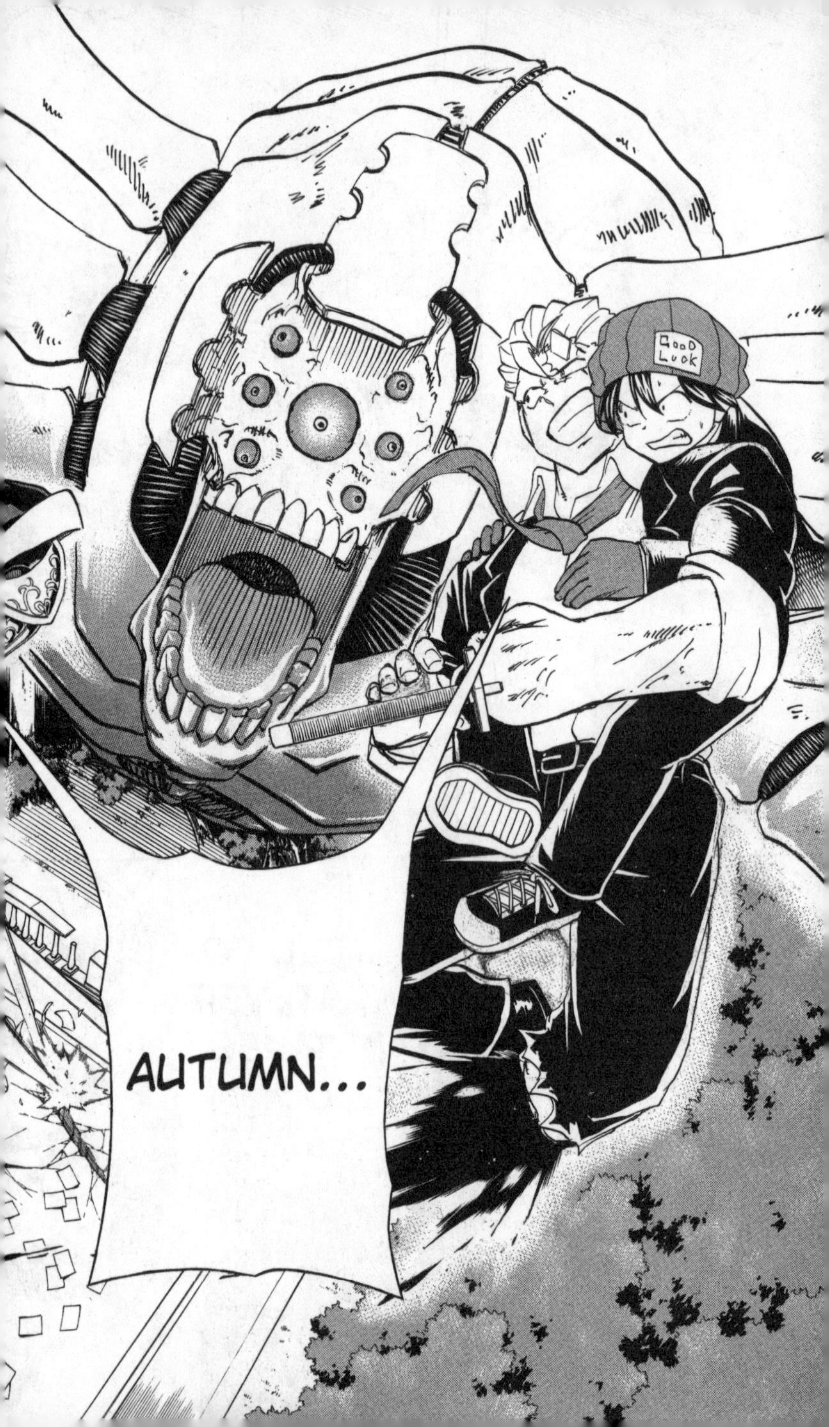
GOOD LUCK
AUTUMN...

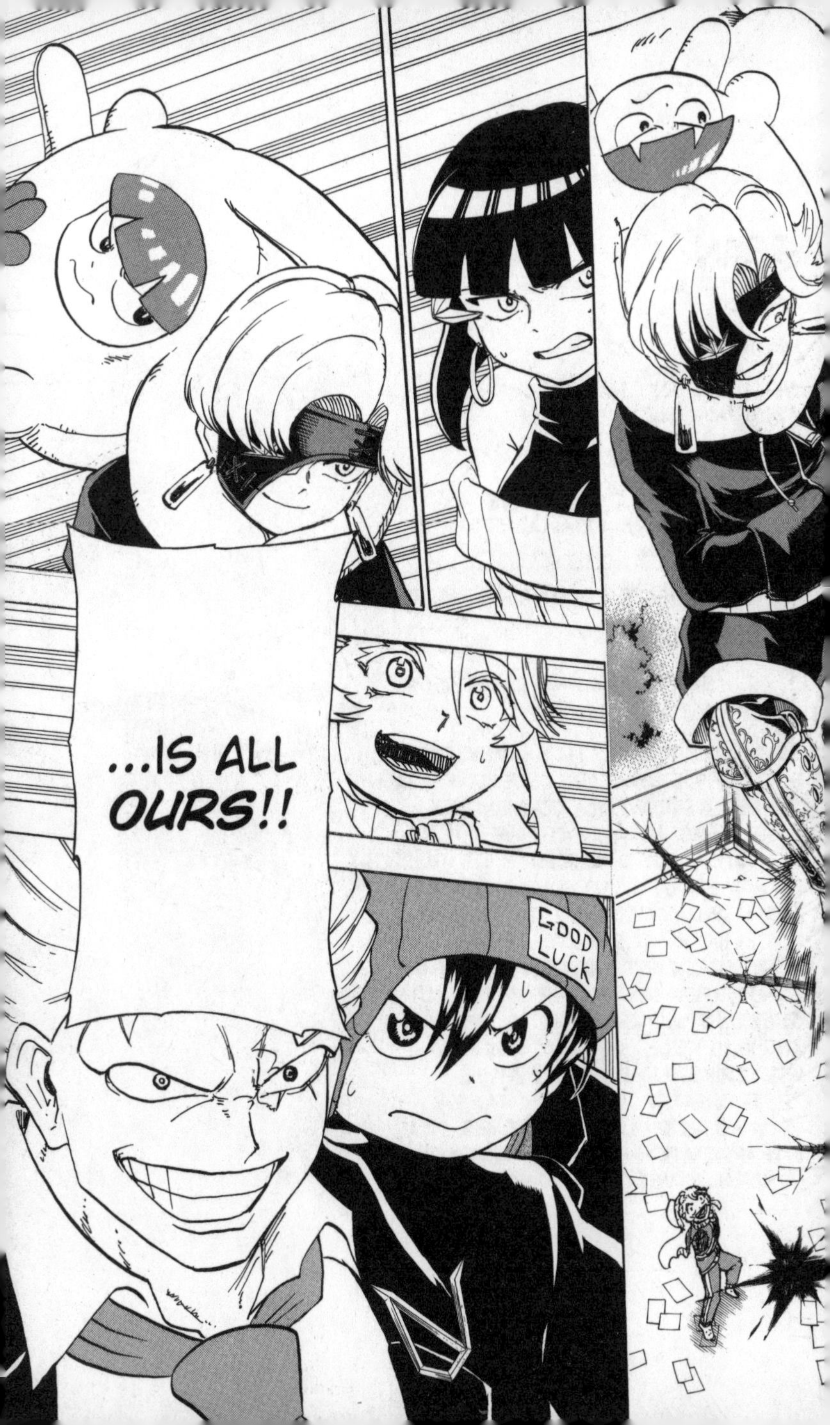
...IS ALL OURS!!
GOOD LUCK

SEAN

AGE: 18

HEIGHT: ABOUT 170 CM

WEIGHT: HASN'T HAD A CHANCE TO WEIGH HIMSELF

HOBBIES: HAT COLLECTING

SPECIAL SKILLS: TWIRLING HIS BUTTERFLY KNIFE, PICKPOCKETING, ASSASSINATION

FAVORITES: FRUITS IN GENERAL, MONEY

ABILITY: UNSEEN

> SELF-TARGETING COMPULSORY ACTIVATION TYPE

HE CAN COMPLETELY HIDE HIMSELF WHILE BOTH OF HIS EYES ARE CLOSED. HE HADN'T TURNED A PROFIT DUE TO BEING UNABLE TO SEE AROUND HIM WITH HIS ABILITY ACTIVATED, BUT UNDER RIP'S INSTRUCTIONS, HE HAD SURGERY TO HAVE A THIRD EYE ADDED AND CONQUERED THAT DRAWBACK. HOWEVER, EVER SINCE THEN, HE'S GROWN MORE ARROGANT AND DRIVEN BY THE HUNGER FOR GLORY. DURING THE AUTUMN QUEST, HE OVERSTEPPED TO THE FRONT AND WAS KILLED BY ANDY. ANYONE WHO TRIES TO FORCIBLY BYPASS THEIR NEGATOR ABILITIES' DRAWBACKS VIA A METHOD OUTSIDE OF THEIR OWN INTERPRETATION OF THEIR ABILITY GENERALLY MEETS A SAD END.

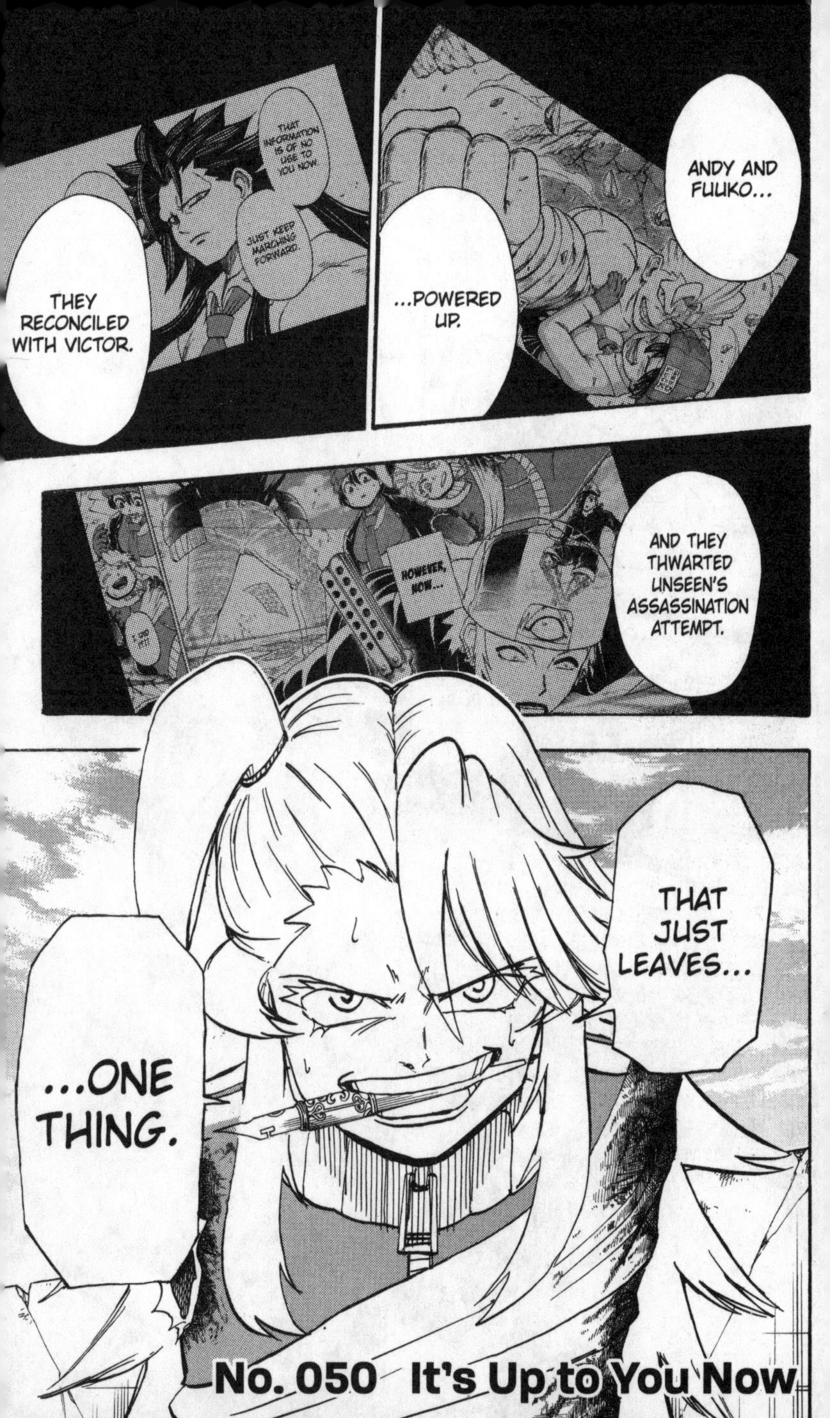
ANDY AND FUUKO...
...POWERED UP.
THAT INFORMATION IS OF NO USE TO YOU NOW
JUST KEEP MARCHING FORWARD.
THEY RECONCILED WITH VICTOR.
AND THEY THWARTED UNSEEN'S ASSASSINATION ATTEMPT.
HOWEVER, NOW...
I DID IT!
THAT JUST LEAVES...
...ONE THING.
No. 050 It's Up to You Now

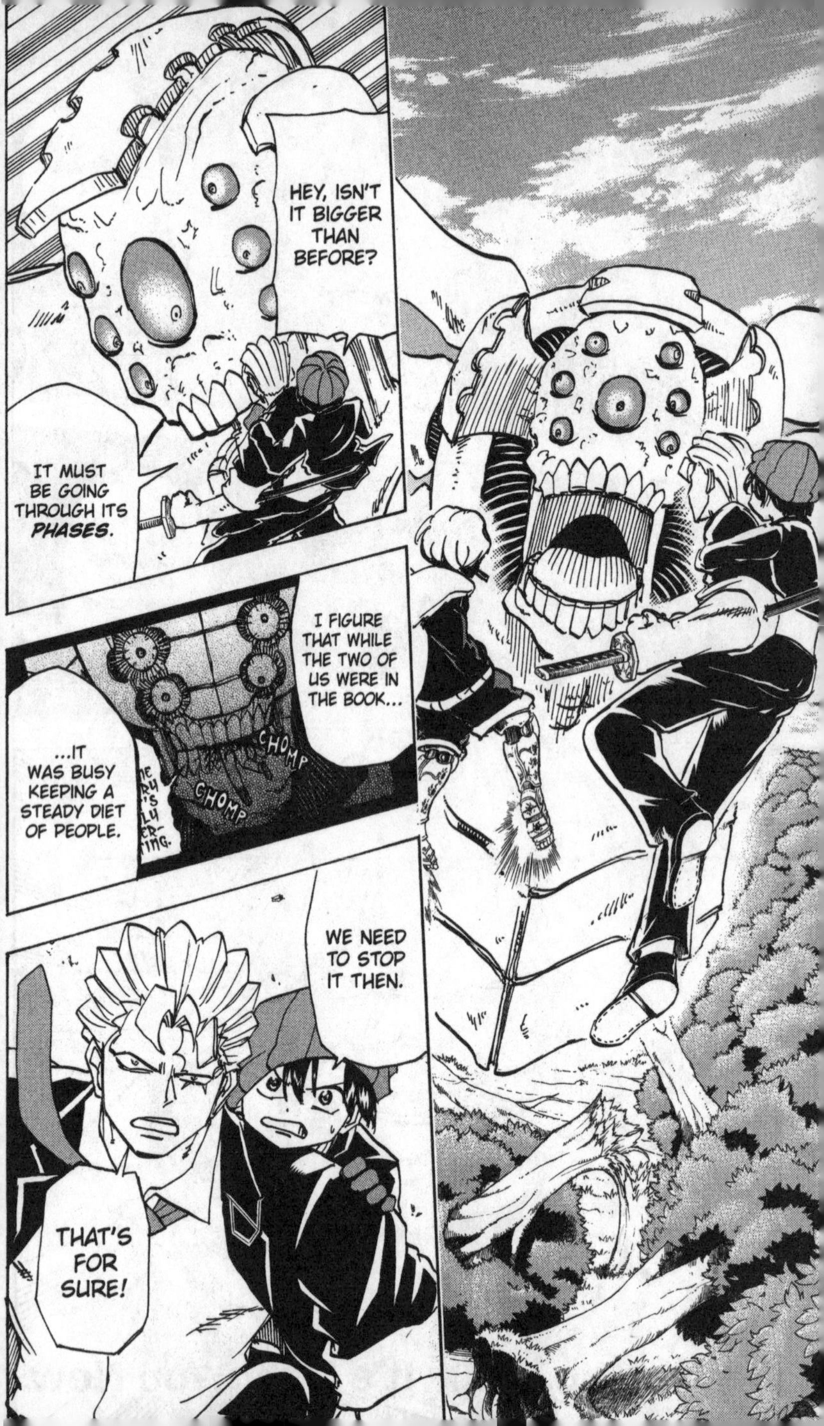
HEY, ISN'T IT BIGGER THAN BEFORE?
IT MUST BE GOING THROUGH ITS *PHASES*.
I FIGURE THAT WHILE THE TWO OF US WERE IN THE BOOK...
...IT WAS BUSY KEEPING A STEADY DIET OF PEOPLE.
CHOMP
CHOMP
WE NEED TO STOP IT THEN.
THAT'S FOR SURE!

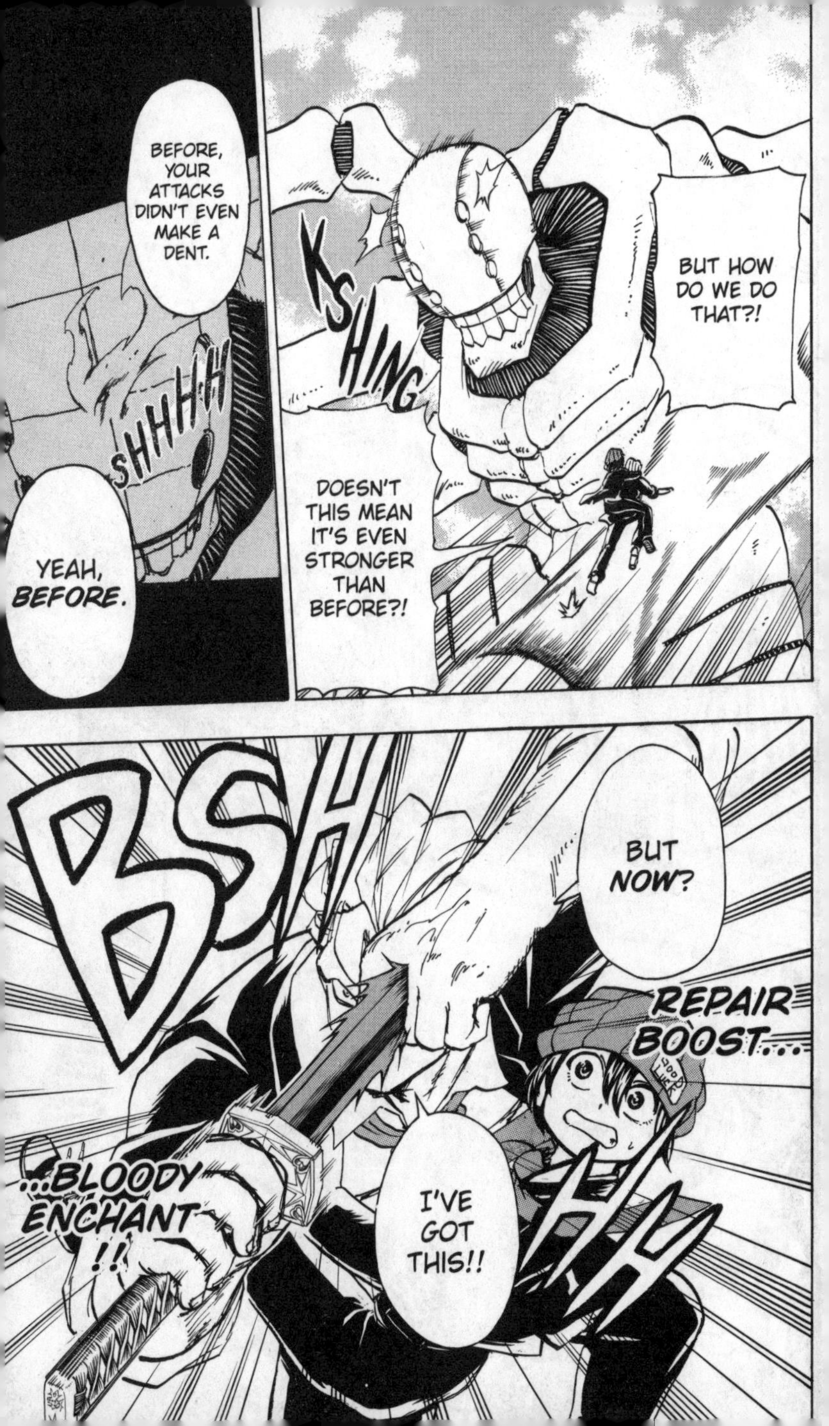
BUT HOW DO WE DO THAT?!
KSHING
DOESN'T THIS MEAN IT'S EVEN STRONGER THAN BEFORE?!
BEFORE, YOUR ATTACKS DIDN'T EVEN MAKE A DENT.
SHHHH
YEAH, BEFORE.
BUT NOW?
BSH
REPAIR BOOST...
I'VE GOT THIS!!
...BLOODY ENCHANT!!

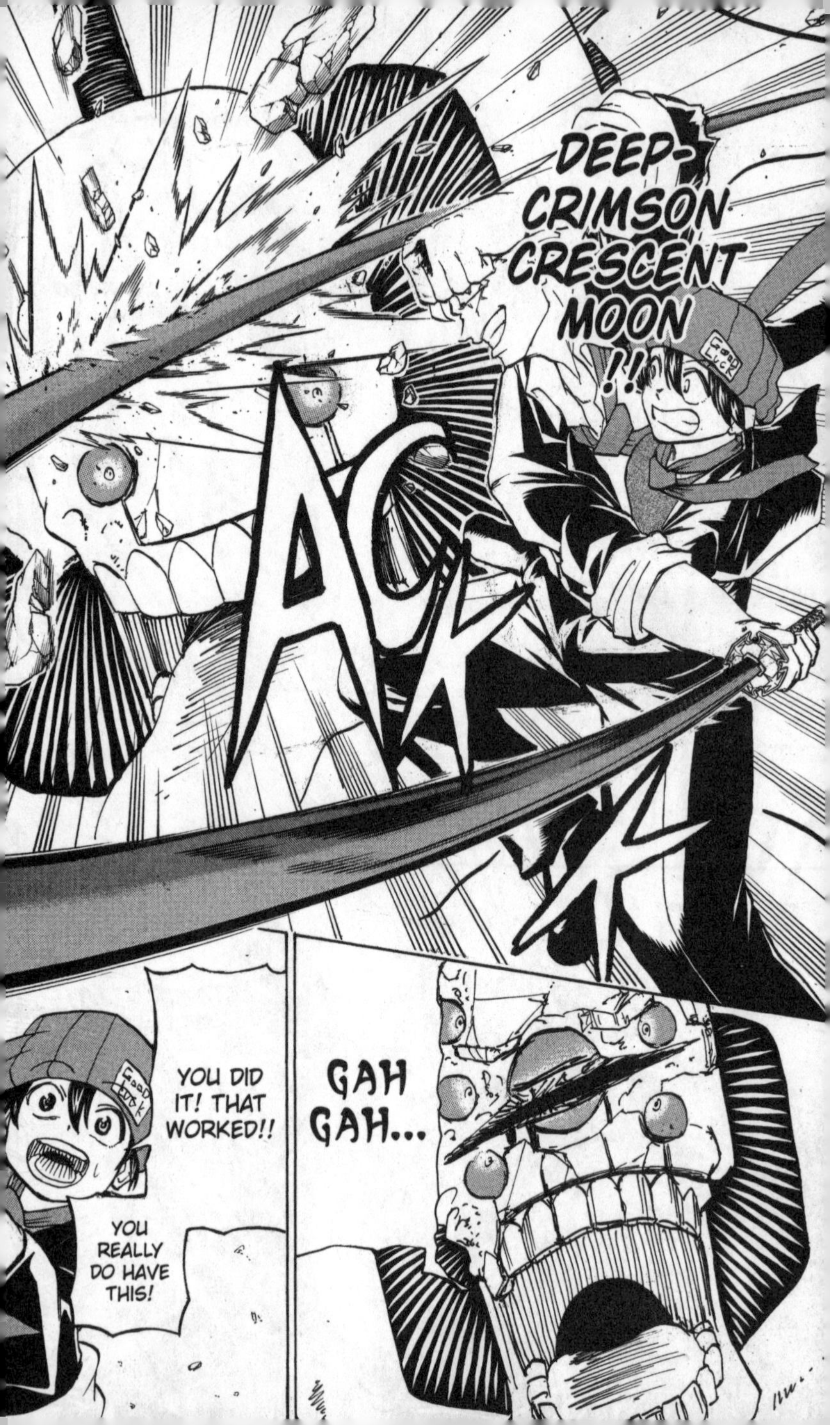
DEEP-CRIMSON CRESCENT MOON!!
GAH GAH...
YOU DID IT! THAT WORKED!!
YOU REALLY DO HAVE THIS!

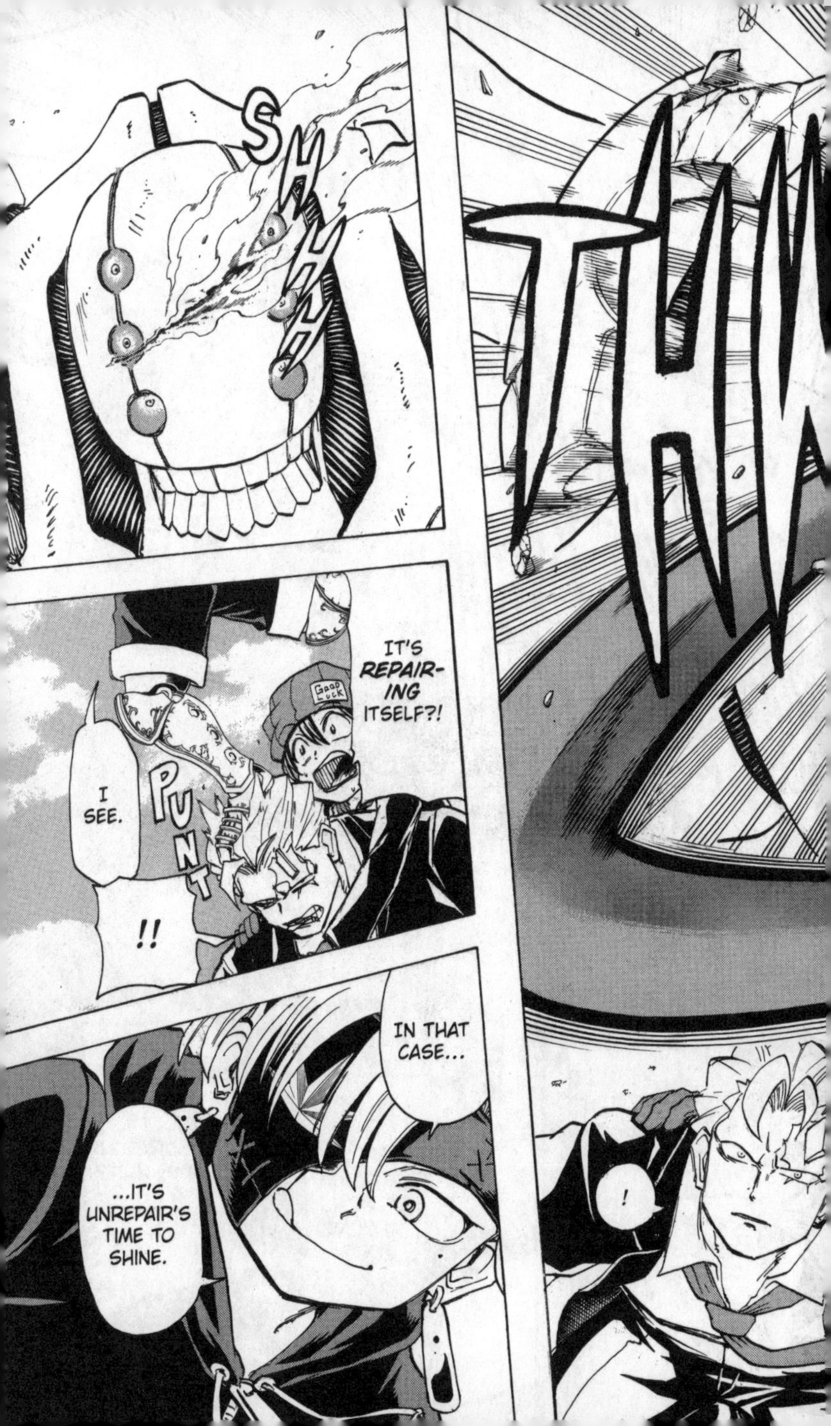

THM
SHHH
IT'S REPAIR-ING ITSELF?!
I SEE.
PUNT
!!
IN THAT CASE...
!
...IT'S UNREPAIR'S TIME TO SHINE.

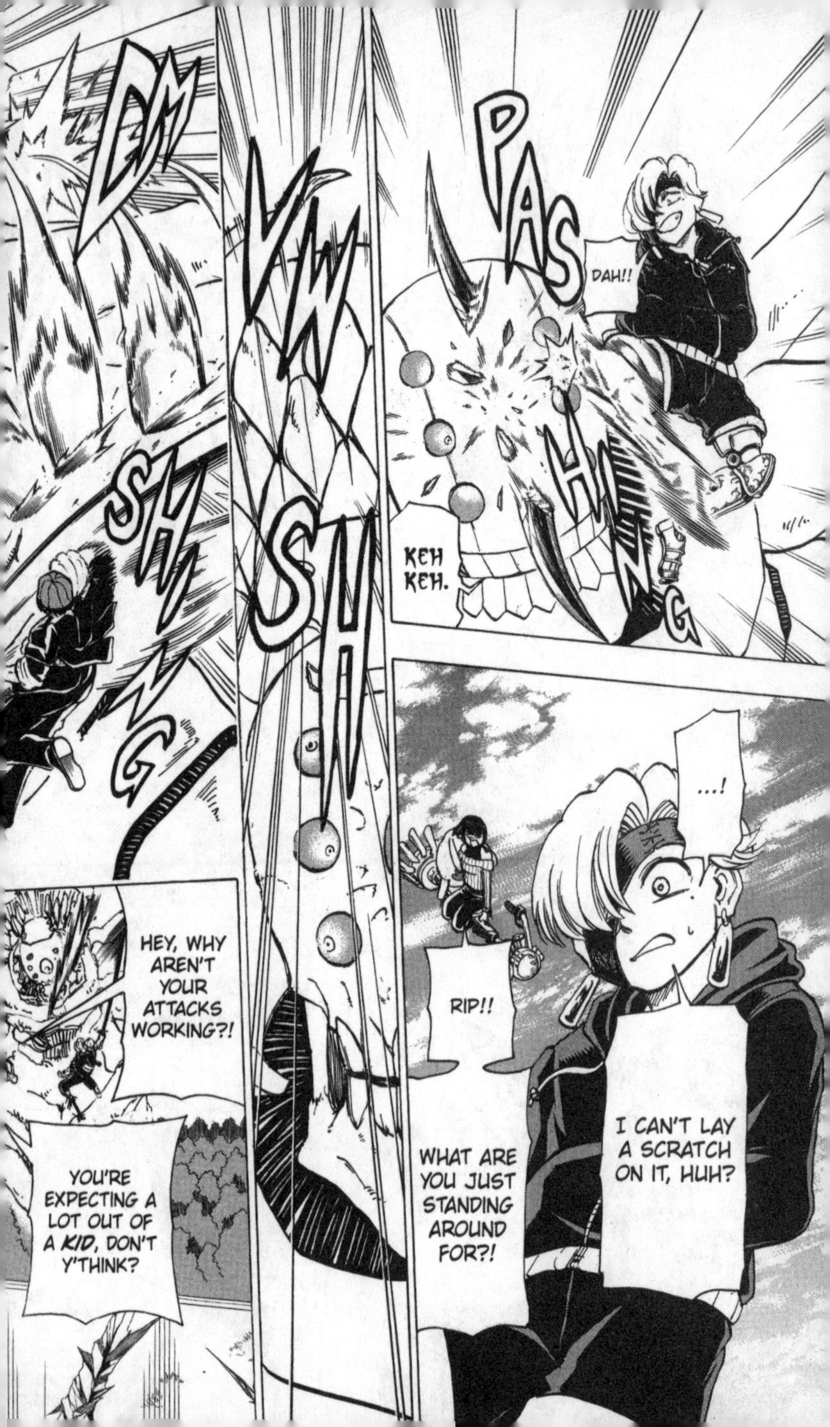
PAS
DAH!!
KEH KEH.
...!
RIP!!
I CAN'T LAY A SCRATCH ON IT, HUH?
WHAT ARE YOU JUST STANDING AROUND FOR?!
DM
HEY, WHY AREN'T YOUR ATTACKS WORKING?!
YOU'RE EXPECTING A LOT OUT OF A *KID*, DON'T Y'THINK?

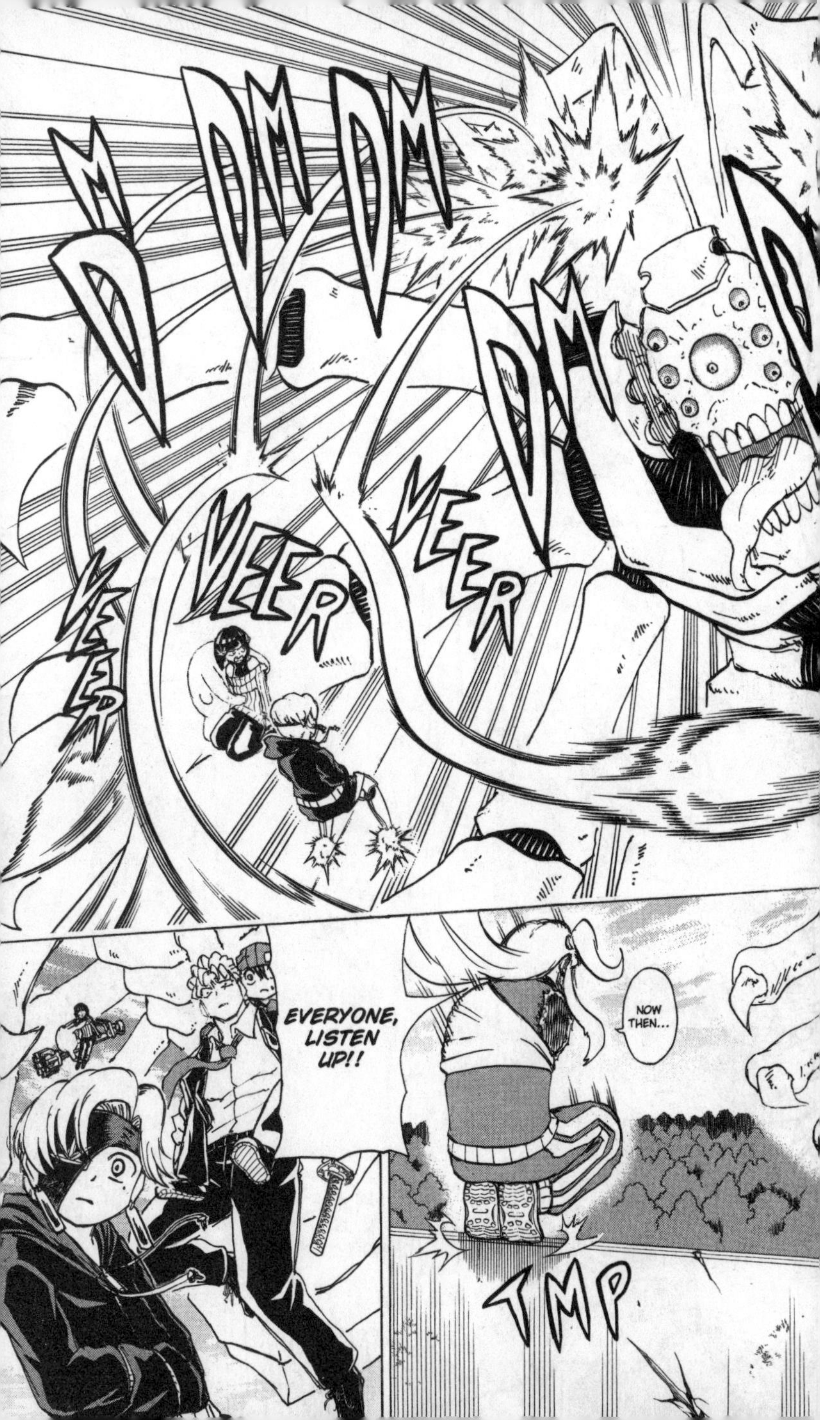

DM
DM DM DM
VEER
VEER
VEER
NOW THEN...
TMP
EVERYONE, LISTEN UP!!

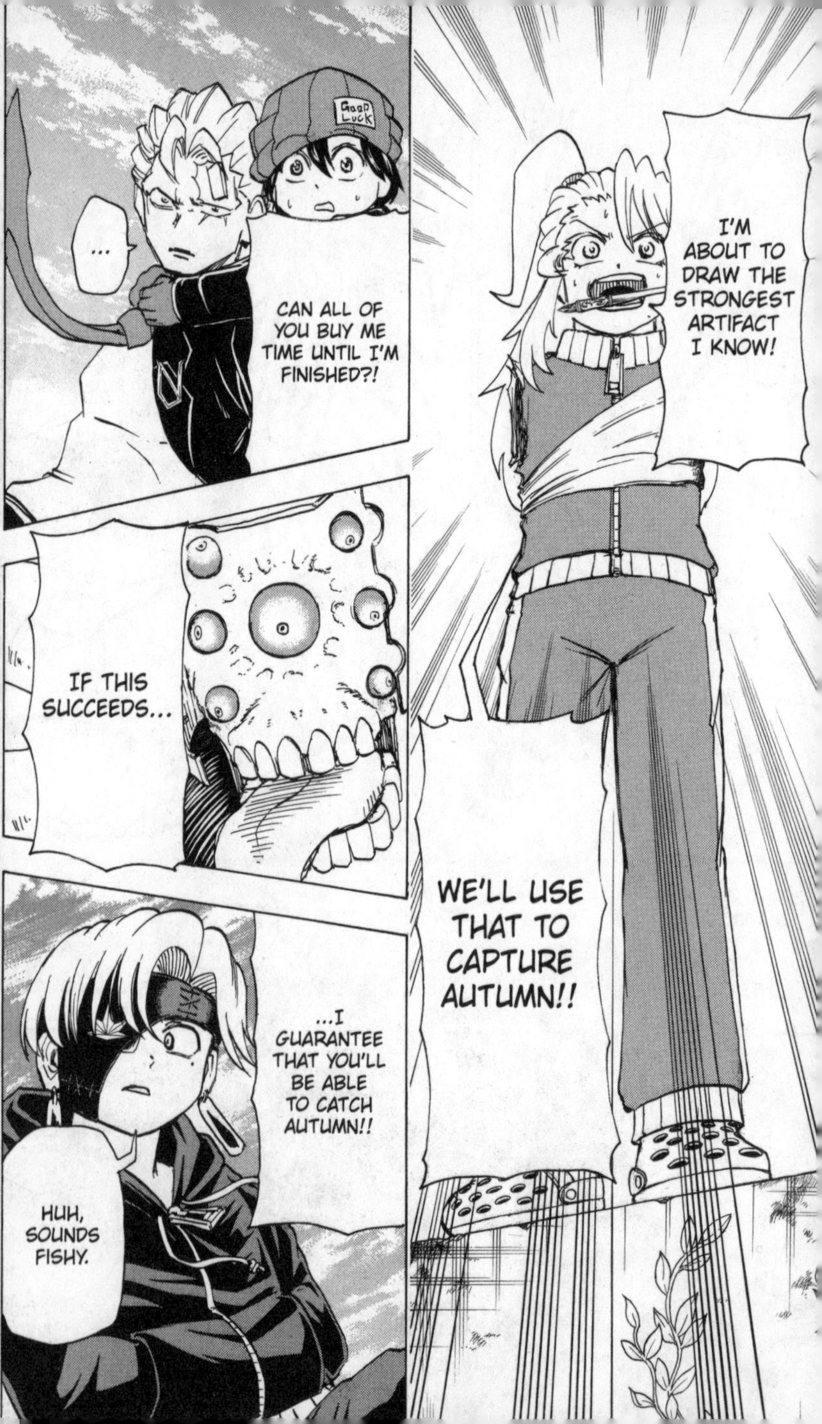
I'M ABOUT TO DRAW THE STRONGEST ARTIFACT I KNOW!
WE'LL USE THAT TO CAPTURE AUTUMN!!
...
CAN ALL OF YOU BUY ME TIME UNTIL I'M FINISHED?!
IF THIS SUCCEEDS...
...I GUARANTEE THAT YOU'LL BE ABLE TO CATCH AUTUMN!!
HUH, SOUNDS FISHY.

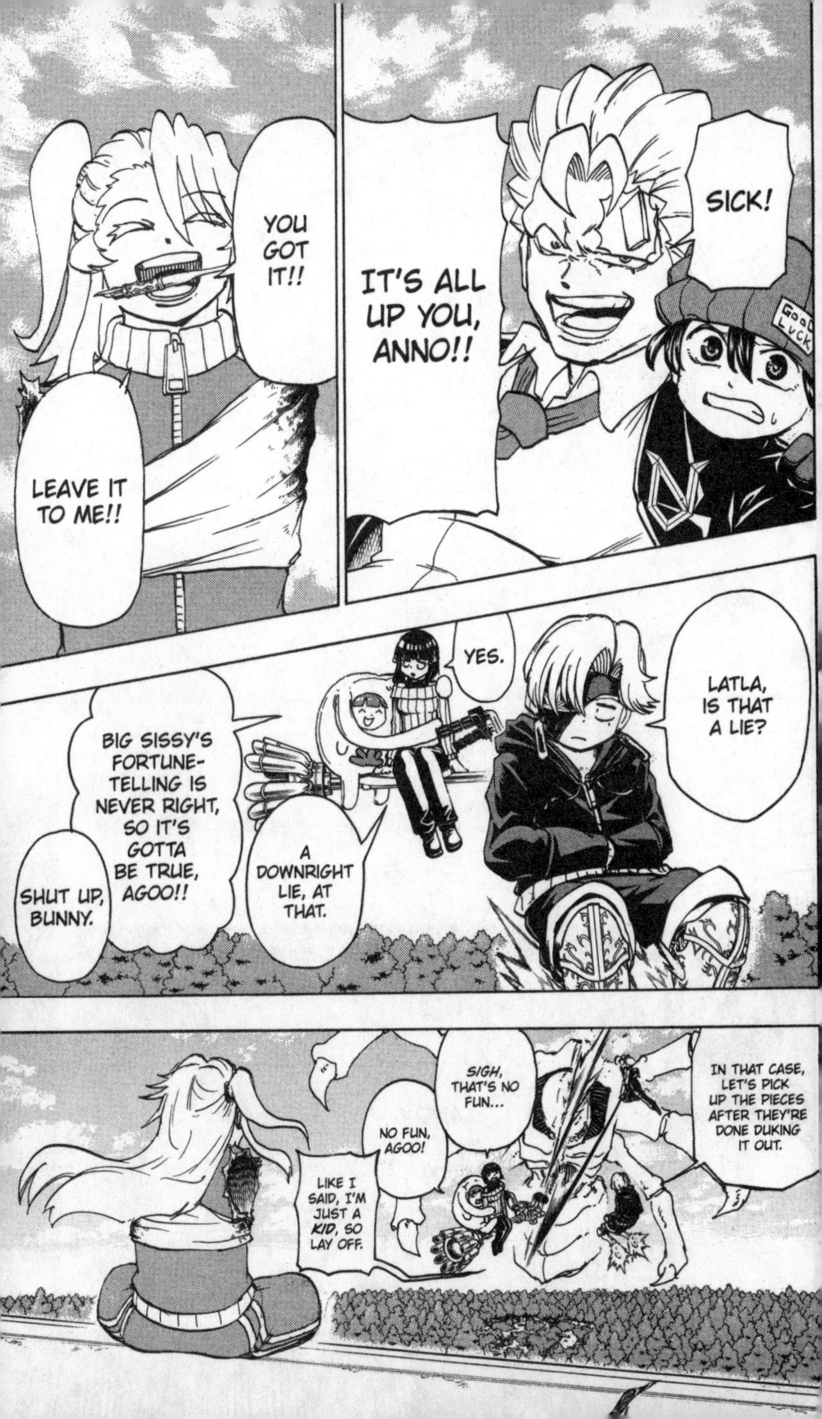
SICK!
GOOD LUCK
IT'S ALL UP YOU, ANNO!!
YOU GOT IT!!
LEAVE IT TO ME!!
LATLA, IS THAT A LIE?
YES.
A DOWNRIGHT LIE, AT THAT.
BIG SISSY'S FORTUNE-TELLING IS NEVER RIGHT, SO IT'S GOTTA BE TRUE, AGOO!!
SHUT UP, BUNNY.
IN THAT CASE, LET'S PICK UP THE PIECES AFTER THEY'RE DONE DUKING IT OUT.
SIGH, THAT'S NO FUN...
NO FUN, AGOO!
LIKE I SAID, I'M JUST A *KID*, SO LAY OFF.

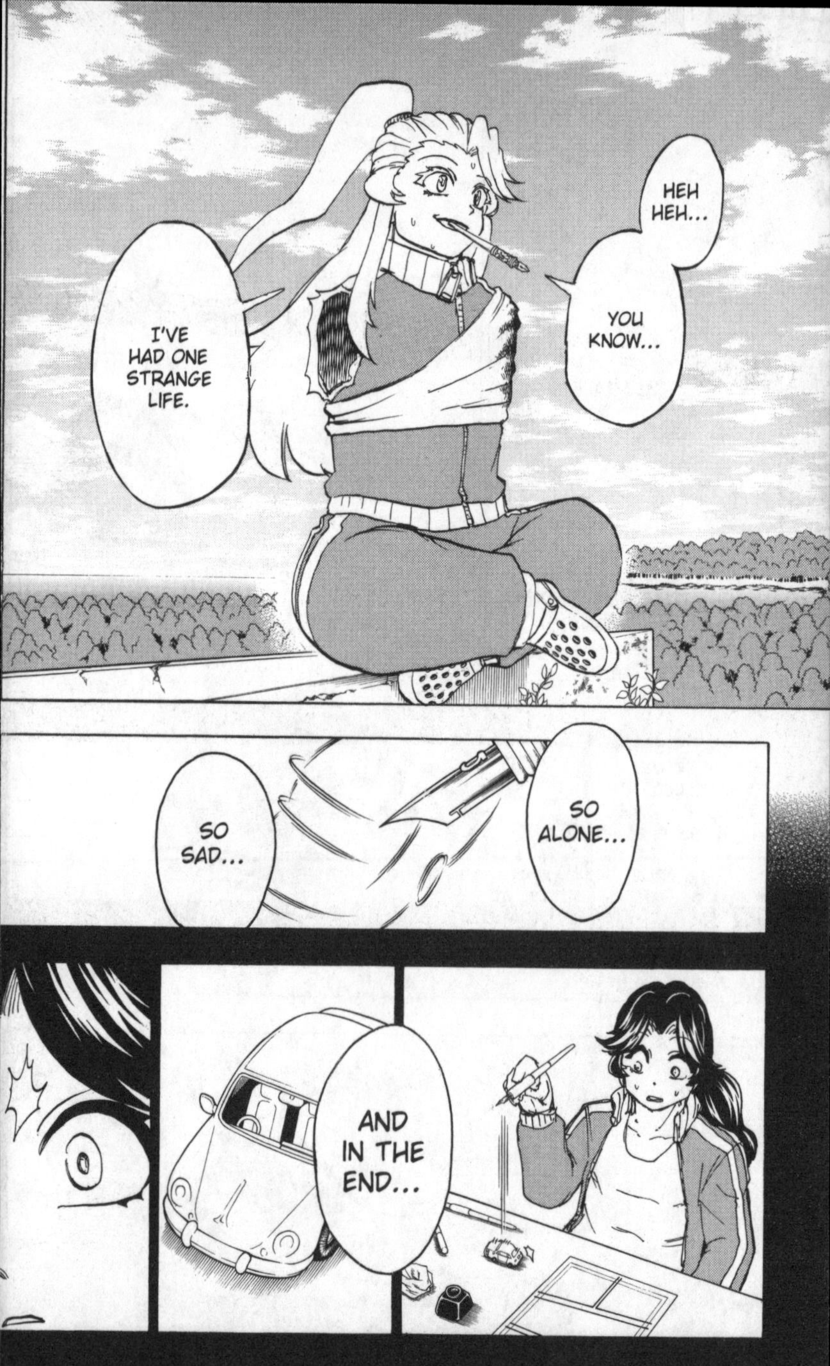
HEH HEH...
YOU KNOW...
I'VE HAD ONE STRANGE LIFE.
SO ALONE...
SO SAD...
AND IN THE END...

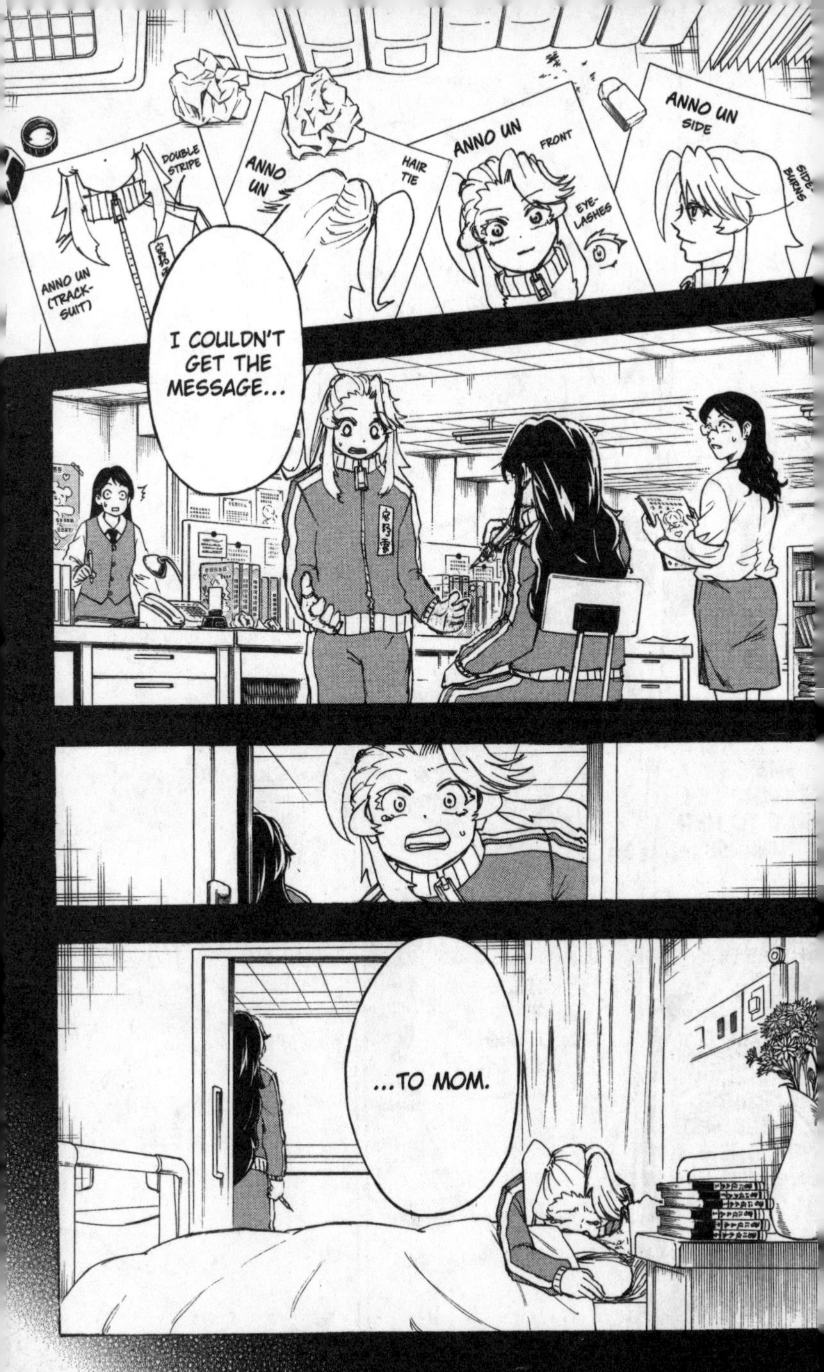
ANNO UN
SIDE
SIDEBURNS
ANNO UN
FRONT
EYE-LASHES
ANNO UN
HAIR TIE
DOUBLE STRIPE
ANNO UN (TRACK-SUIT)
I COULDN'T GET THE MESSAGE...
...TO MOM.

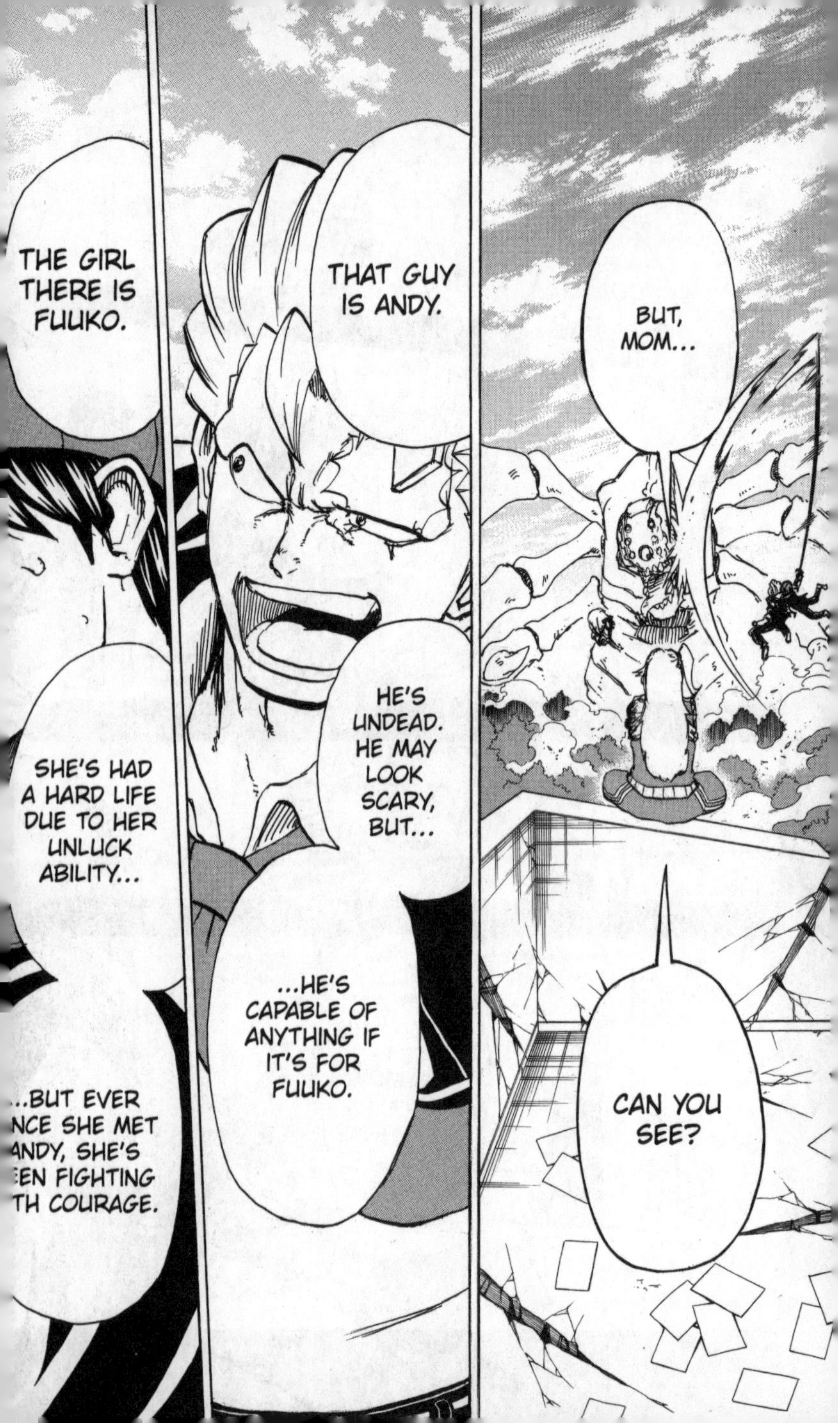
BUT, MOM...
CAN YOU SEE?
THAT GUY IS ANDY.
HE'S UNDEAD. HE MAY LOOK SCARY, BUT...
...HE'S CAPABLE OF ANYTHING IF IT'S FOR FUUKO.
THE GIRL THERE IS FUUKO.
SHE'S HAD A HARD LIFE DUE TO HER UNLUCK ABILITY...
...BUT EVER NCE SHE MET ANDY, SHE'S EEN FIGHTING TH COURAGE.

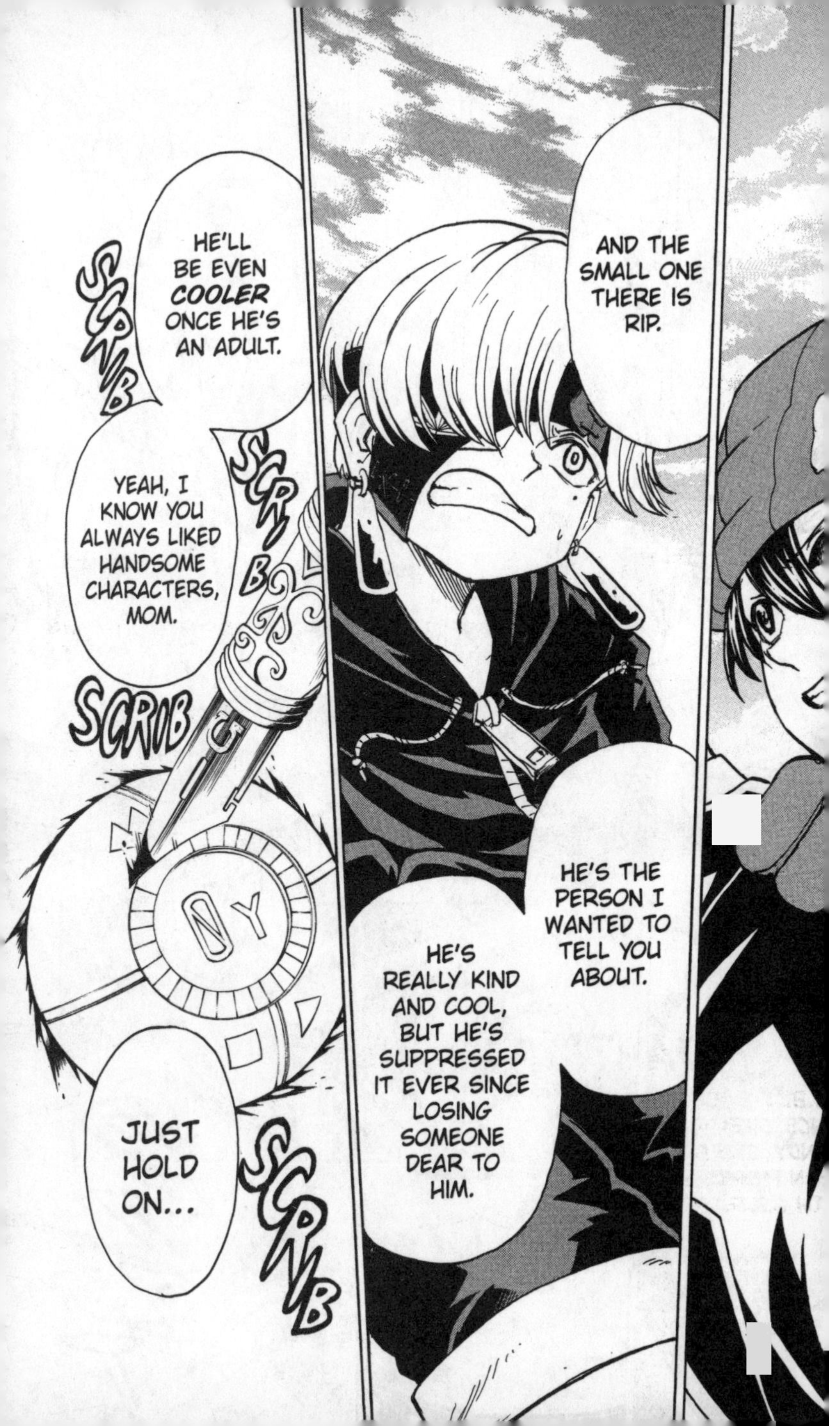
AND THE SMALL ONE THERE IS RIP.
HE'S THE PERSON I WANTED TO TELL YOU ABOUT.
HE'S REALLY KIND AND COOL, BUT HE'S SUPPRESSED IT EVER SINCE LOSING SOMEONE DEAR TO HIM.
HE'LL BE EVEN *COOLER* ONCE HE'S AN ADULT.
SCRIB
SCRIB
YEAH, I KNOW YOU ALWAYS LIKED HANDSOME CHARACTERS, MOM.
SCRIB
JUST HOLD ON...
SCRIB

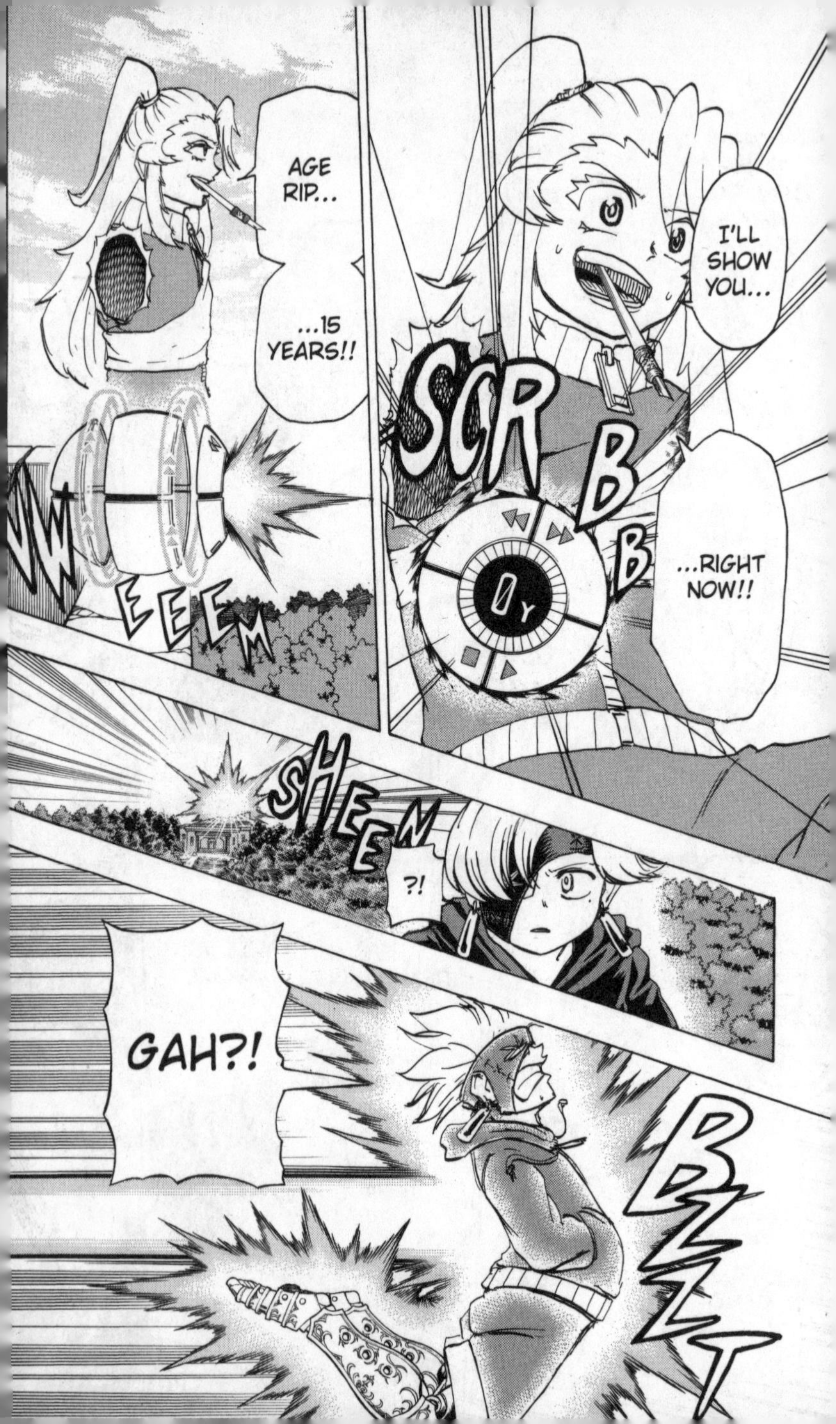
I'LL SHOW YOU...
SCR
BB
...RIGHT NOW!!
AGE RIP...
...15 YEARS!!
WEEEM
SHEEN
?!
GAH?!
BZZZT

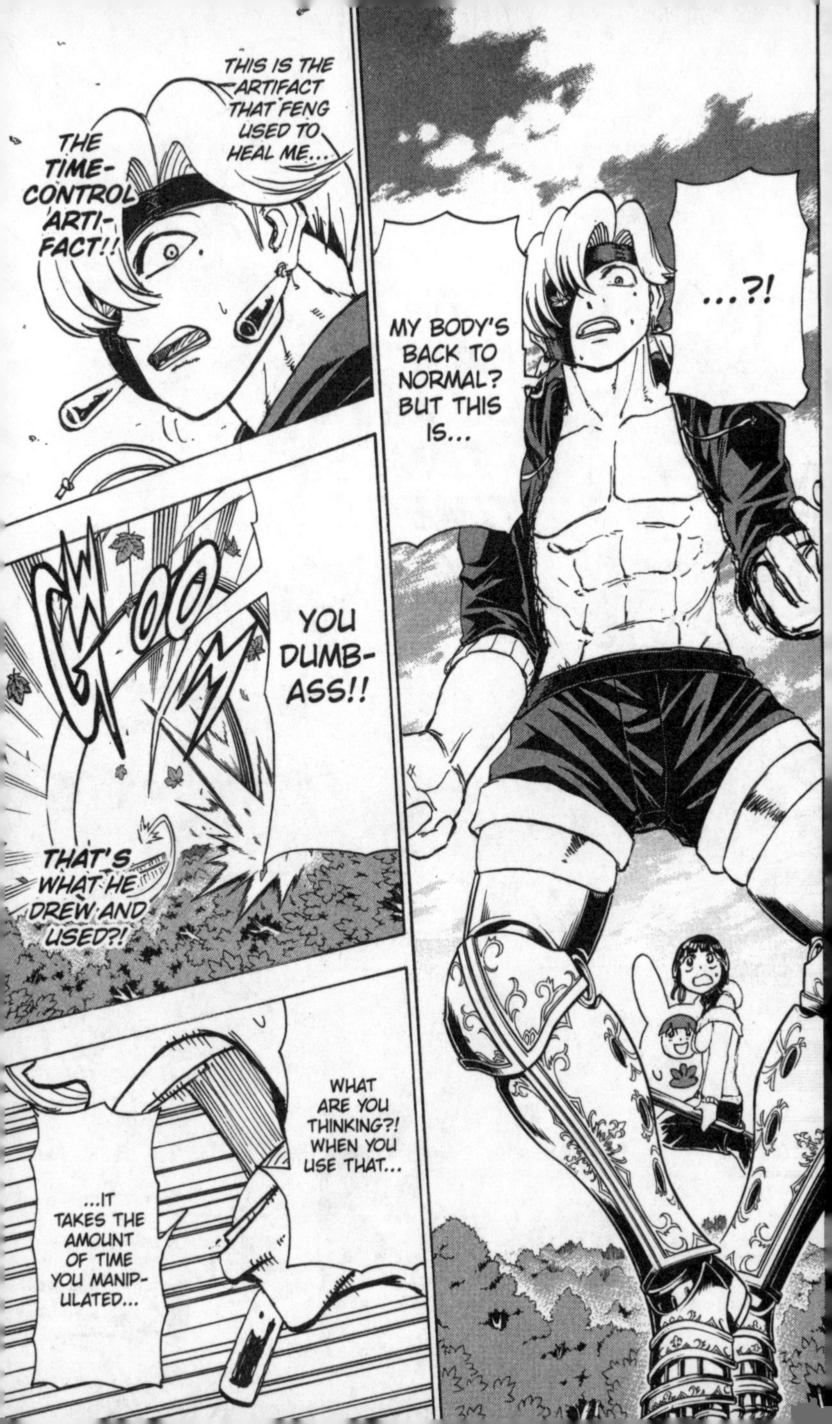
...?!
MY BODY'S BACK TO NORMAL? BUT THIS IS...
THIS IS THE ARTIFACT THAT FENG USED TO HEAL ME...
THE TIME-CONTROL ARTIFACT!!
YOU DUMB-ASS!!
THAT'S WHAT HE DREW AND USED?!
WHAT ARE YOU THINKING?! WHEN YOU USE THAT...
...IT TAKES THE AMOUNT OF TIME YOU MANIPULATED...

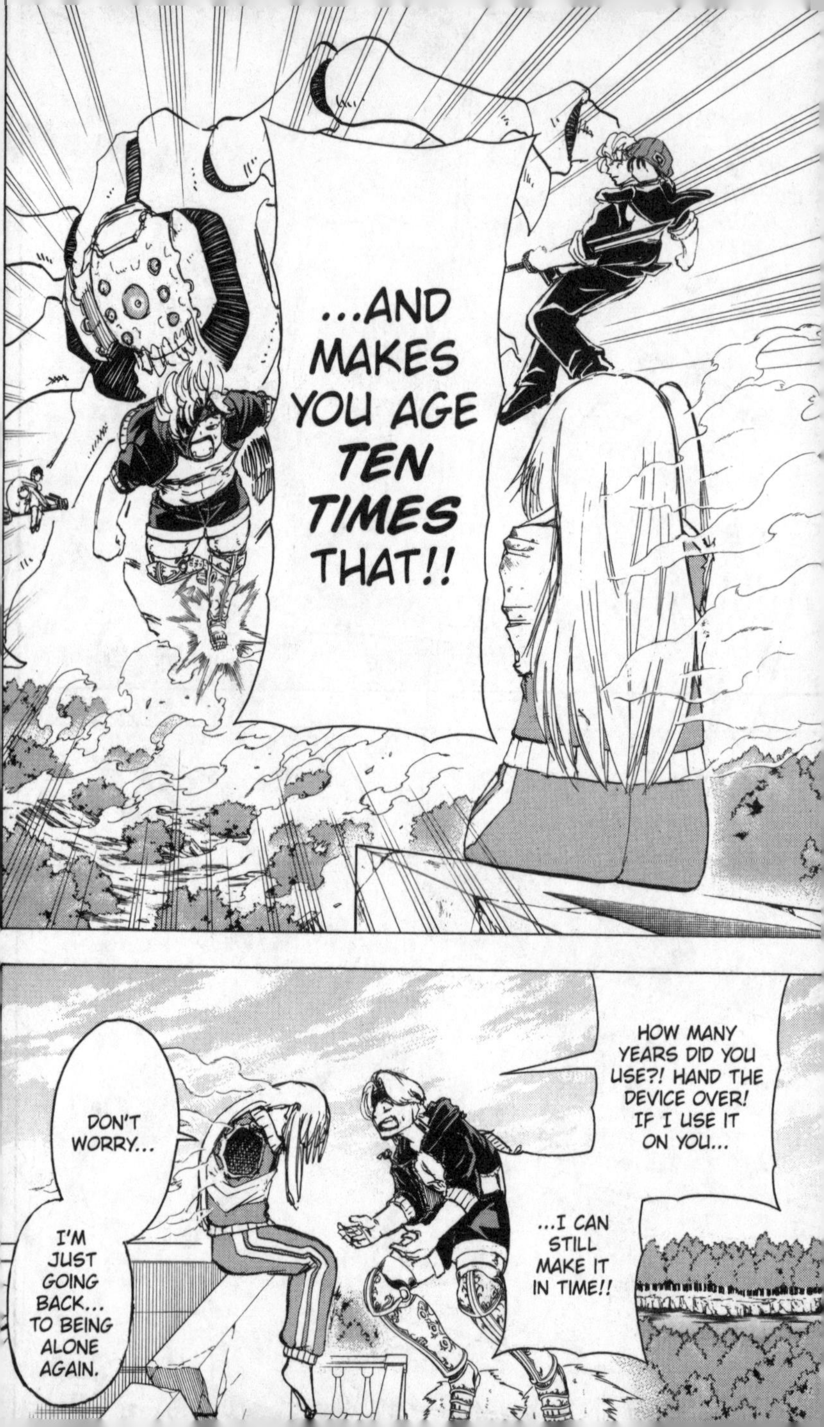
...AND MAKES YOU AGE TEN TIMES THAT!!
HOW MANY YEARS DID YOU USE?! HAND THE DEVICE OVER! IF I USE IT ON YOU...
...I CAN STILL MAKE IT IN TIME!!
DON'T WORRY...
I'M JUST GOING BACK... TO BEING ALONE AGAIN.

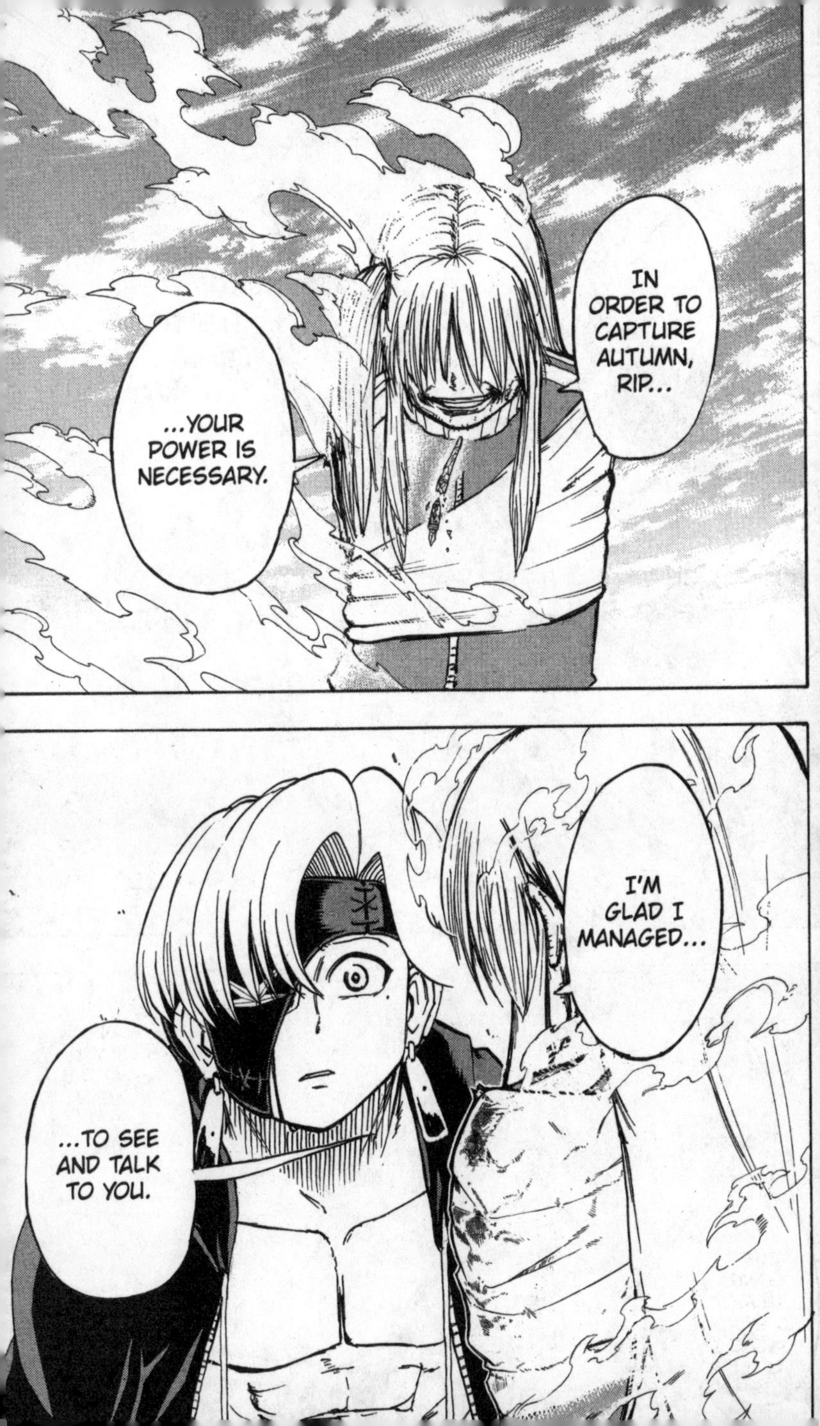
IN ORDER TO CAPTURE AUTUMN, RIP...
...YOUR POWER IS NECESSARY.
I'M GLAD I MANAGED...
...TO SEE AND TALK TO YOU.

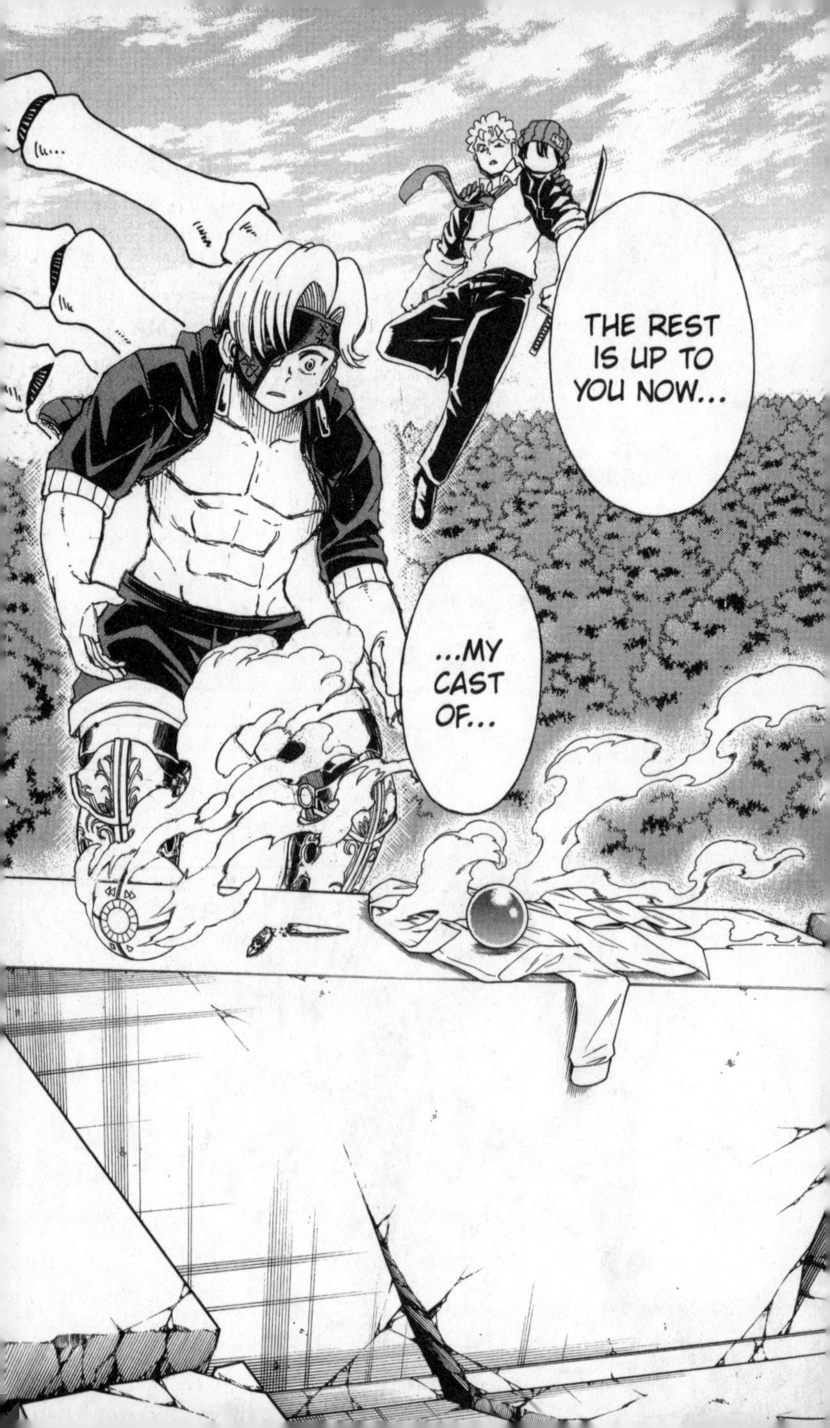
THE REST IS UP TO YOU NOW...
...MY CAST OF...

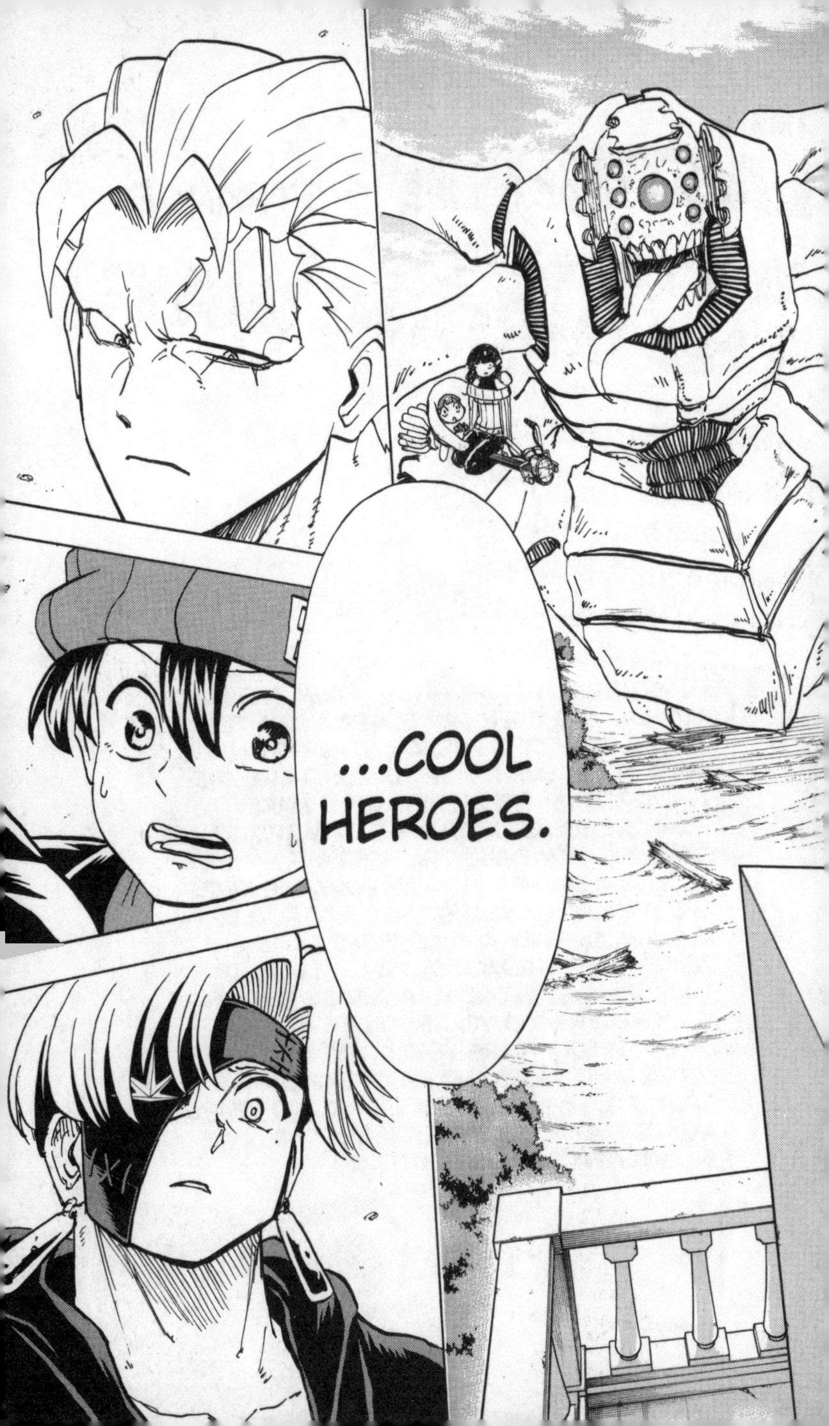
...COOL HEROES.

ARTIFACT, LIFE IS STRANGE

AN ARTIFACT THAT RIP STOLE FROM THE BLACK
AUCTION. THE USER CAN CONTROL THE TIME
OF THE BODY OF A PERSON OTHER THAN THE
USER IN INCREMENTS OF YEARS. THERE ARE
TWO OPTIONS: EITHER REWIND TO MAKE
SOMEONE YOUNGER OR FAST FORWARD TO AGE
SOMEONE. HOWEVER, THE USER'S BODY WILL
RECEIVE A CHANGE IN THEIR BODY TEN TIMES
THE AMOUNT OF YEARS THEY CONTROLLED IN
RETURN. IF THEY AGE SOMEONE BY TEN
YEARS, THEY GROW 100 YEARS OLDER. IF
THEY MAKE SOMEONE YOUNGER BY TEN YEARS,
THEY REVERT 100 YEARS. THOSE INCAPABLE
OF LIVING 100 YEARS WHO GROW 100 YEARS
OLDER WILL DECAY AND DISAPPEAR ON THE
SPOT. THOSE WHO HAVEN'T LIVED 100 YEARS
AND REVERT 100 YEARS YOUNGER WILL
SILENTLY FADE FROM EXISTENCE.

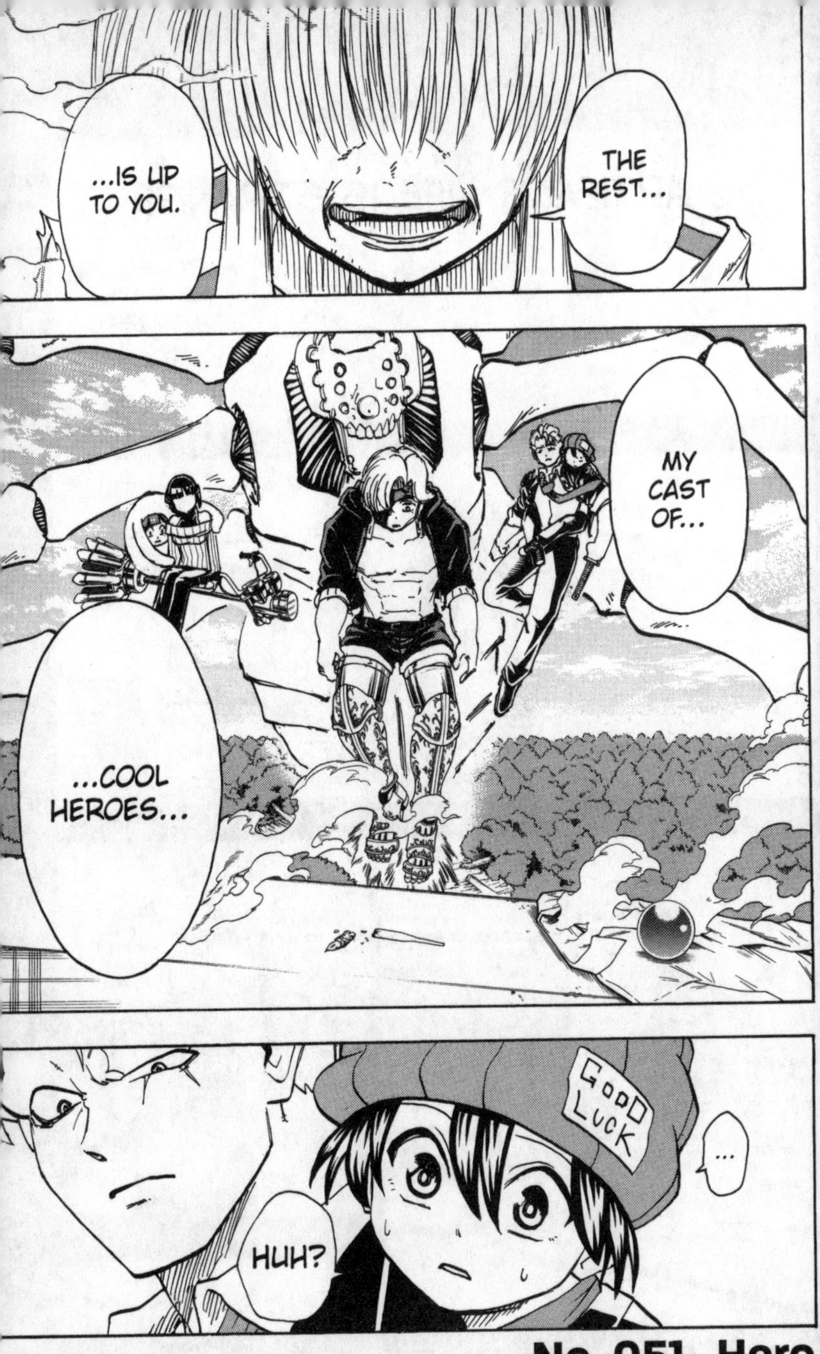
THE REST...
...IS UP TO YOU.
MY CAST OF...
...COOL HEROES...
...
HUH?
GOOD LUCK

No. 051 Hero

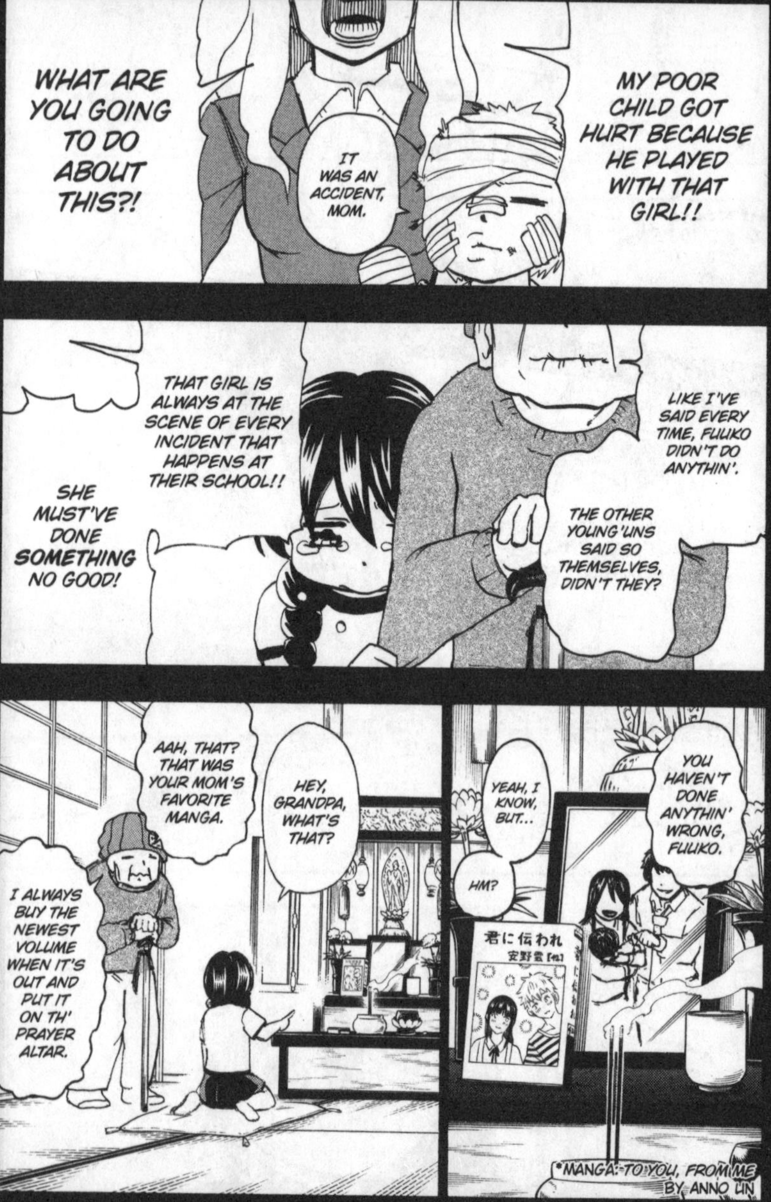
MY POOR CHILD GOT HURT BECAUSE HE PLAYED WITH THAT GIRL!!
IT WAS AN ACCIDENT, MOM.
WHAT ARE YOU GOING TO DO ABOUT THIS?!
LIKE I'VE SAID EVERY TIME, FUUKO DIDN'T DO ANYTHIN'.
THE OTHER YOUNG'UNS SAID SO THEMSELVES, DIDN'T THEY?
THAT GIRL IS ALWAYS AT THE SCENE OF EVERY INCIDENT THAT HAPPENS AT THEIR SCHOOL!!
SHE MUST'VE DONE **SOMETHING** NO GOOD!
YOU HAVEN'T DONE ANYTHIN' WRONG, FUUKO.
YEAH, I KNOW, BUT...
HM?
君に伝われ
安野雲
*MANGA: TO YOU, FROM ME BY ANNO UN
HEY, GRANDPA, WHAT'S THAT?
AAH, THAT? THAT WAS YOUR MOM'S FAVORITE MANGA.
I ALWAYS BUY THE NEWEST VOLUME WHEN IT'S OUT AND PUT IT ON TH' PRAYER ALTAR.

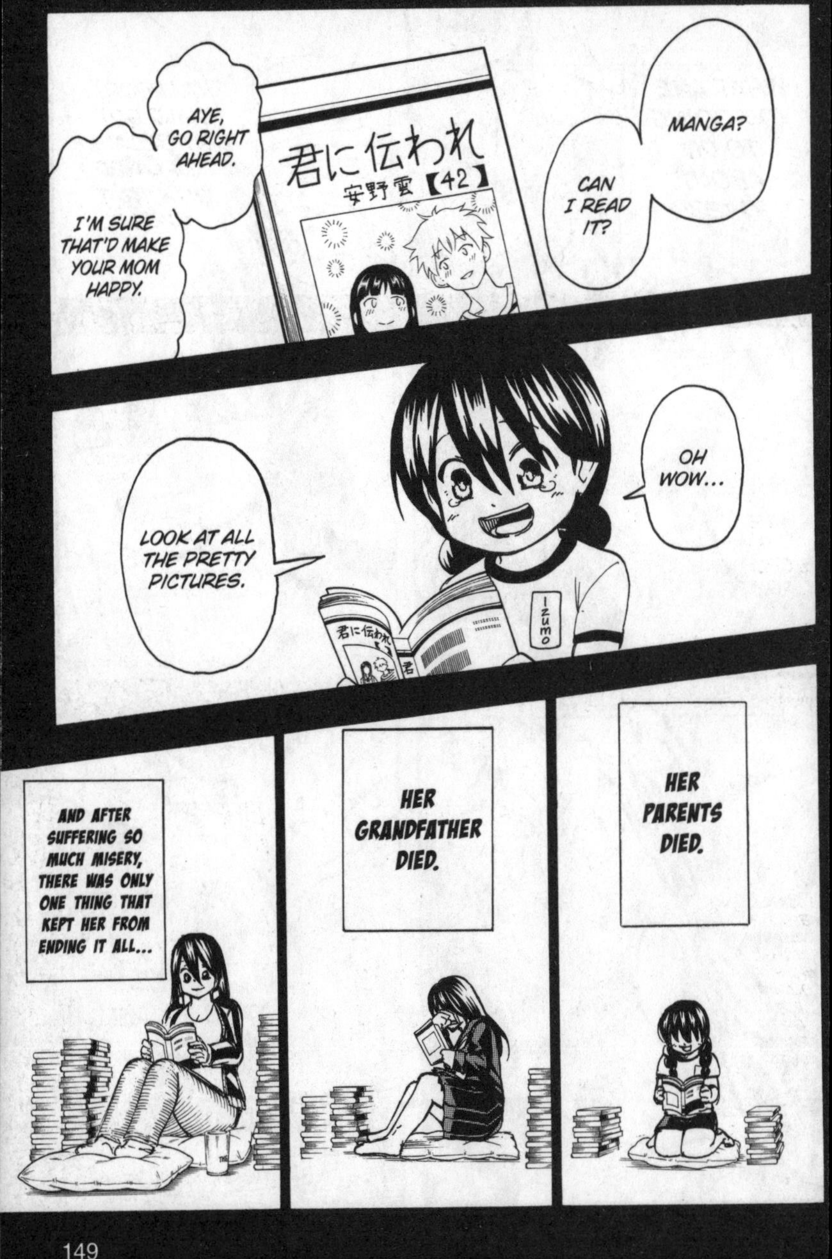
君に伝われ
安野雲【42】
MANGA?
CAN I READ IT?
AYE, GO RIGHT AHEAD.
I'M SURE THAT'D MAKE YOUR MOM HAPPY.
OH WOW...
LOOK AT ALL THE PRETTY PICTURES.
IZUMO
君に伝われ
HER PARENTS DIED.
HER GRANDFATHER DIED.
AND AFTER SUFFERING SO MUCH MISERY, THERE WAS ONLY ONE THING THAT KEPT HER FROM ENDING IT ALL...

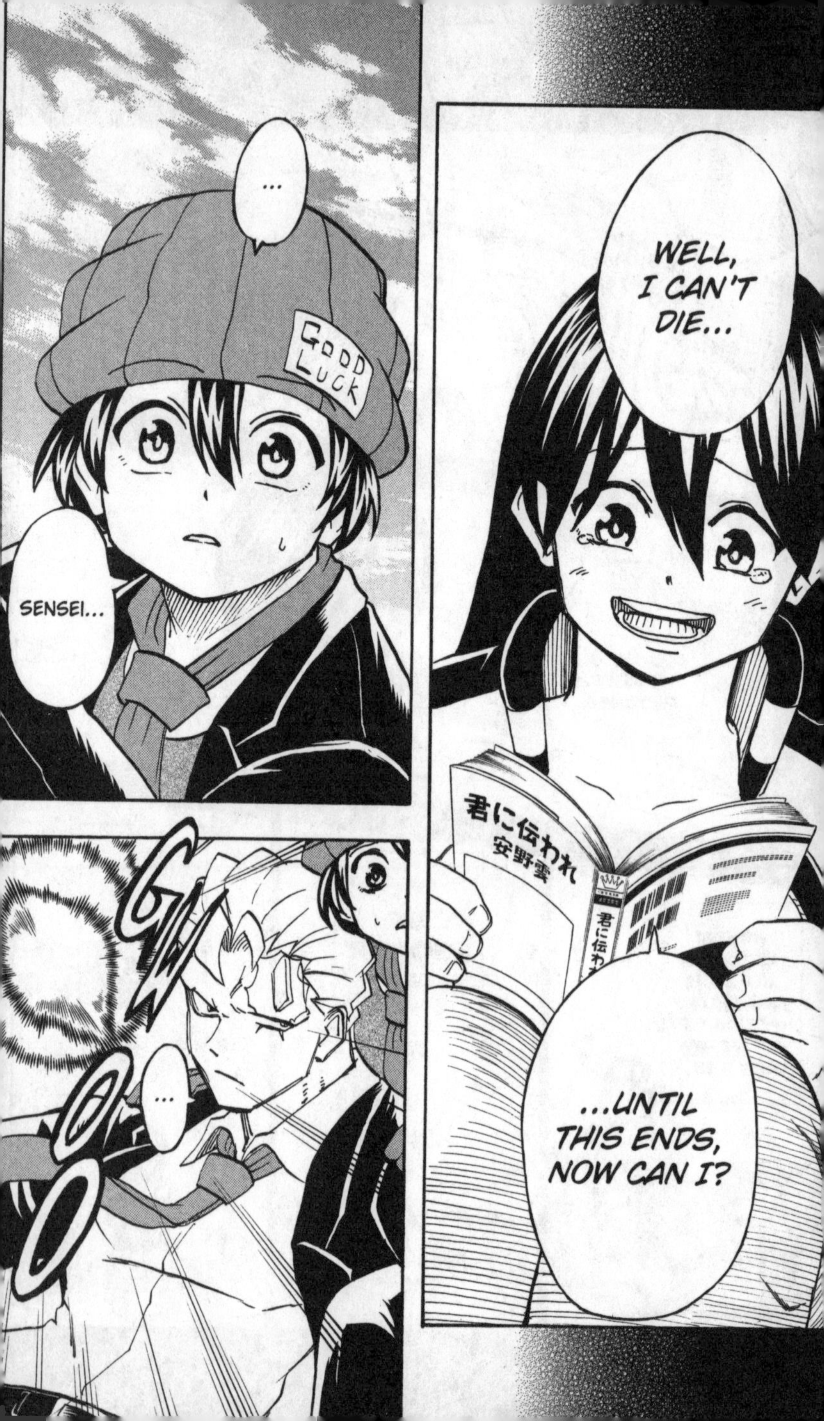
WELL, I CAN'T DIE...
君に伝われ
安野雲
...UNTIL THIS ENDS, NOW CAN I?
...
SENSEI...
...

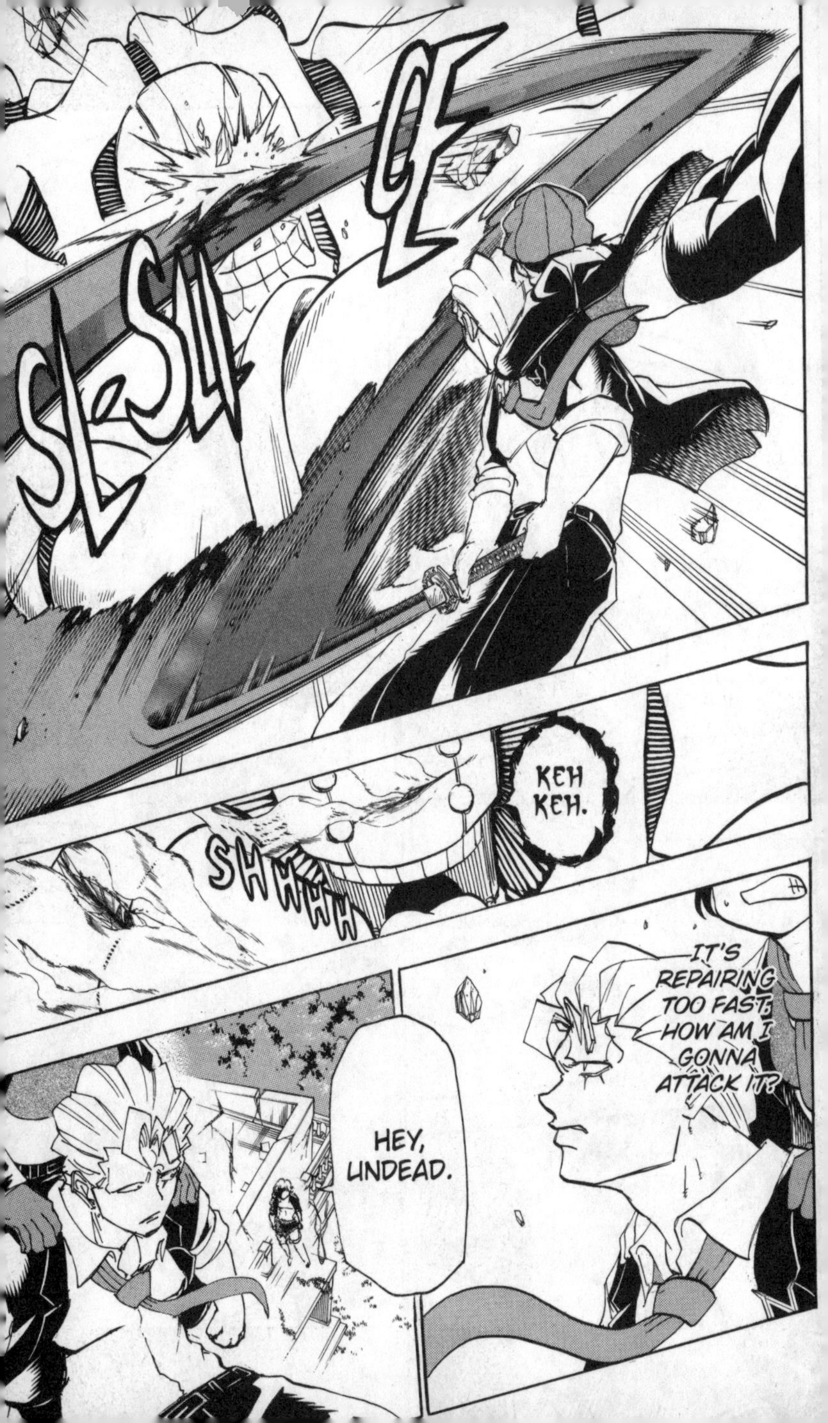

GF
SLASH
KEH KEH.
SHHHHH
IT'S REPAIRING TOO FAST. HOW AM I GONNA ATTACK IT?
HEY, UNDEAD.

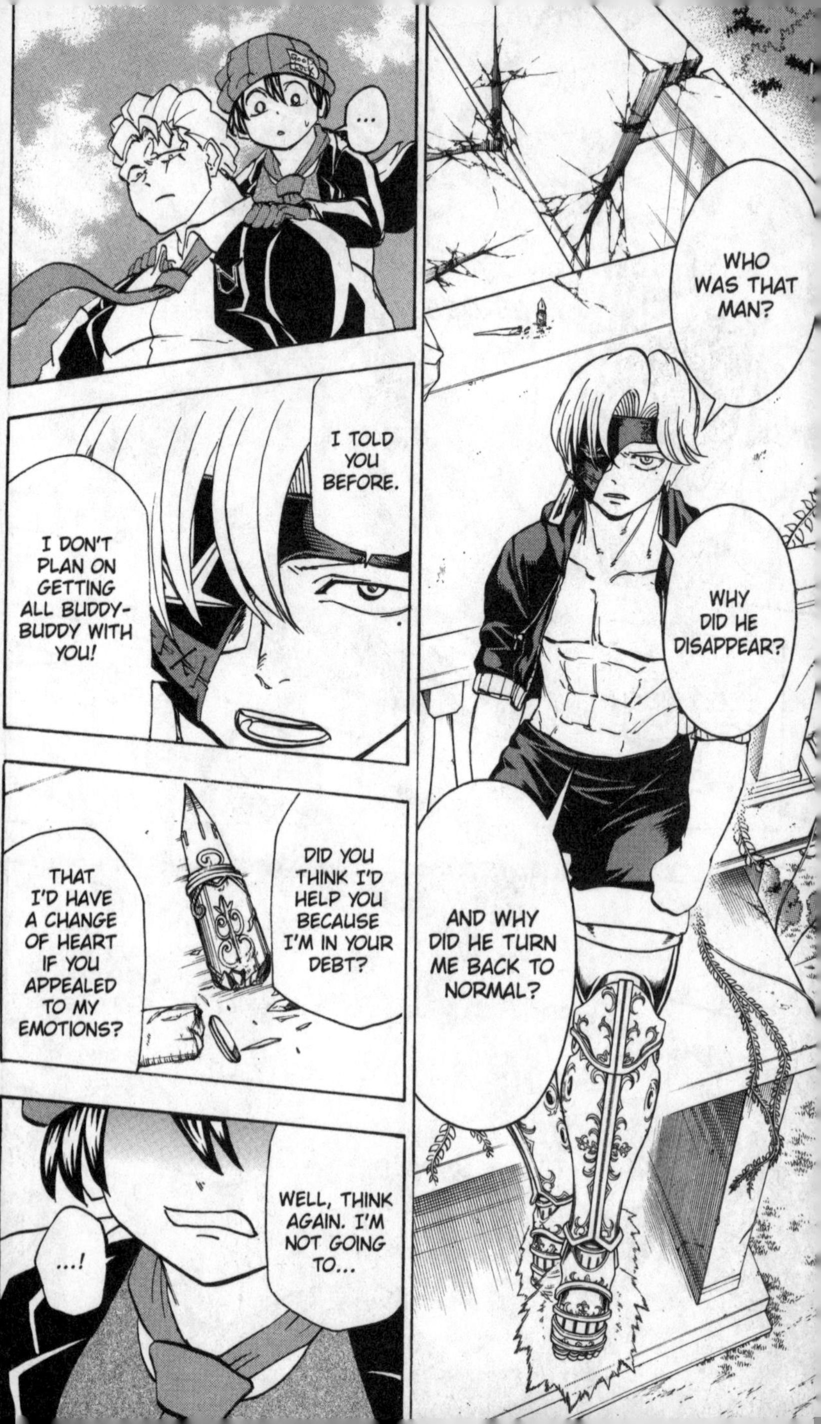
WHO WAS THAT MAN?
WHY DID HE DISAPPEAR?
AND WHY DID HE TURN ME BACK TO NORMAL?
...
I TOLD YOU BEFORE.
I DON'T PLAN ON GETTING ALL BUDDY-BUDDY WITH YOU!
DID YOU THINK I'D HELP YOU BECAUSE I'M IN YOUR DEBT?
THAT I'D HAVE A CHANGE OF HEART IF YOU APPEALED TO MY EMOTIONS?
WELL, THINK AGAIN. I'M NOT GOING TO...
...!

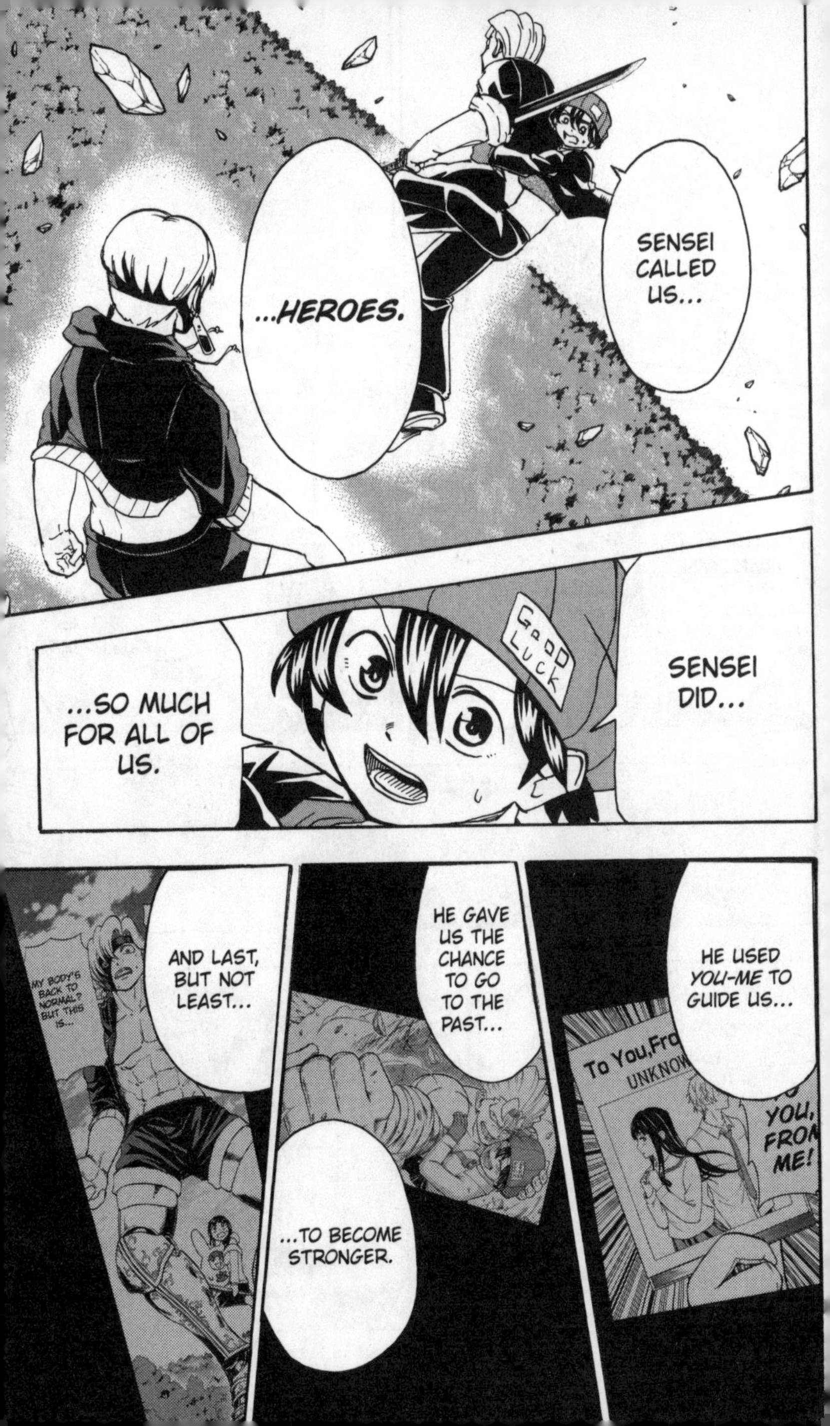
SENSEI CALLED US...
...HEROES.
SENSEI DID...
GOOD LUCK
...SO MUCH FOR ALL OF US.
HE USED *YOU-ME* TO GUIDE US...
HE GAVE US THE CHANCE TO GO TO THE PAST...
...TO BECOME STRONGER.
AND LAST, BUT NOT LEAST...
MY BODY'S BACK TO NORMAL? BUT THIS IS...

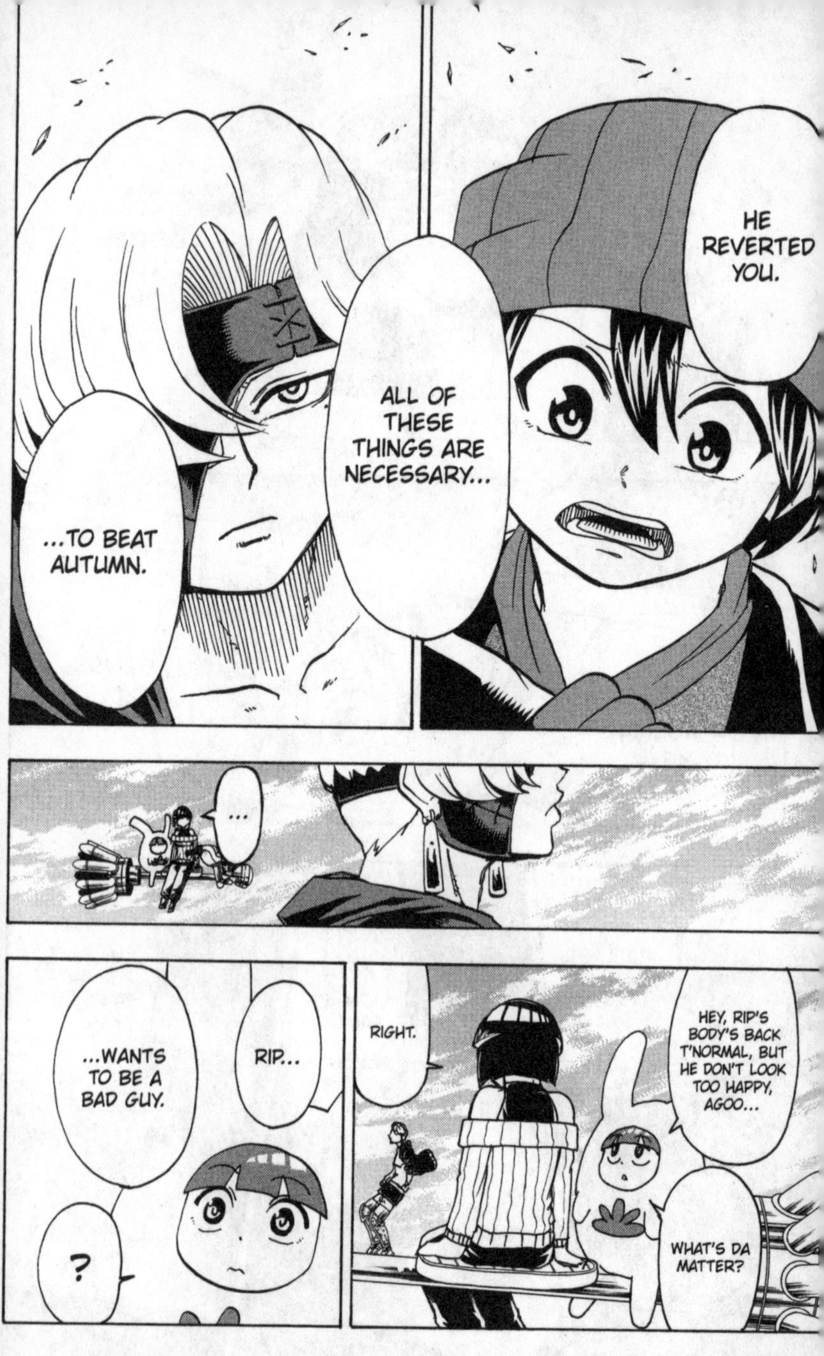
HE REVERTED YOU.
ALL OF THESE THINGS ARE NECESSARY...
...TO BEAT AUTUMN.
...
HEY, RIP'S BODY'S BACK T'NORMAL, BUT HE DON'T LOOK TOO HAPPY, AGOO...
WHAT'S DA MATTER?
RIGHT.
RIP...
...WANTS TO BE A BAD GUY.
?

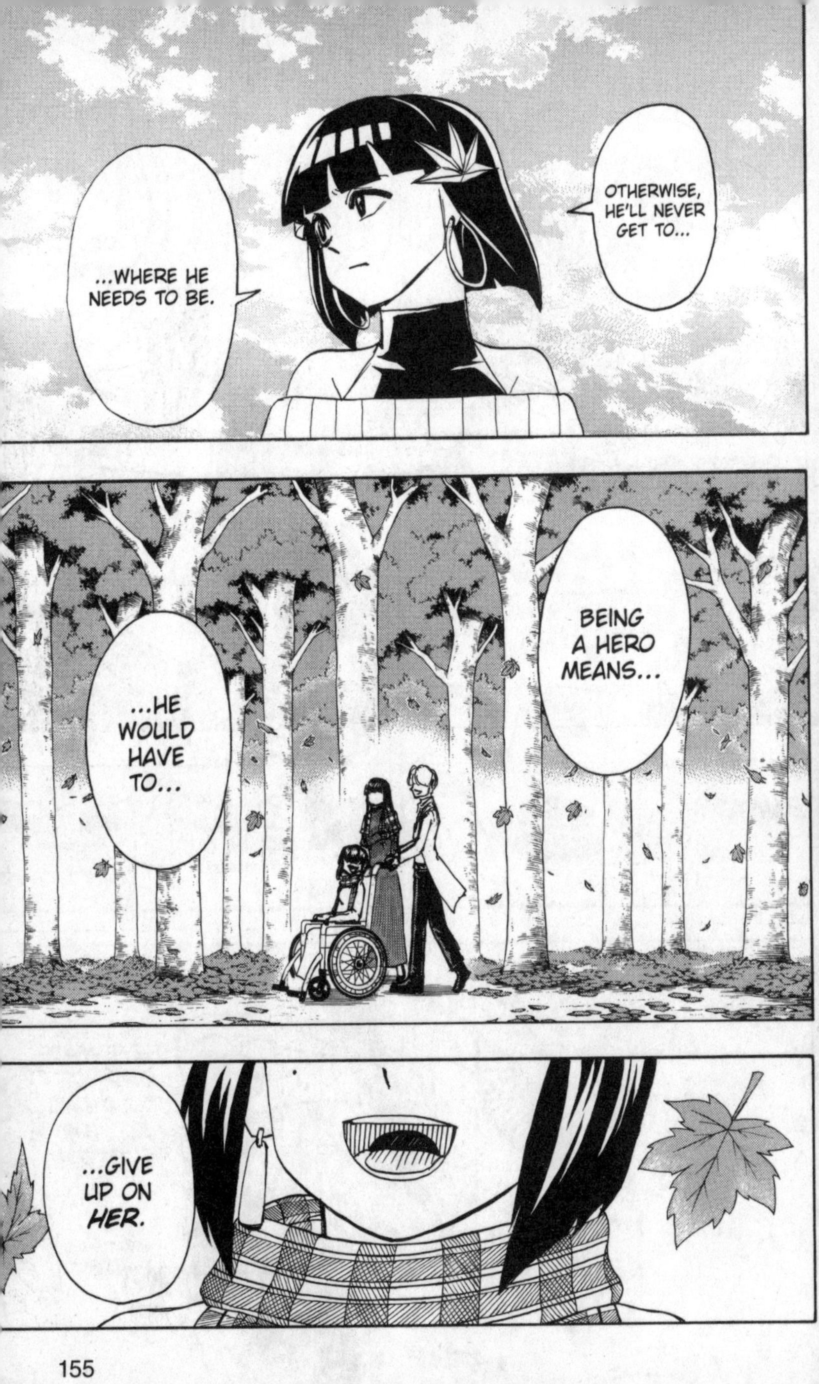
OTHERWISE, HE'LL NEVER GET TO...
...WHERE HE NEEDS TO BE.
BEING A HERO MEANS...
...HE WOULD HAVE TO...
...GIVE UP ON *HER*.

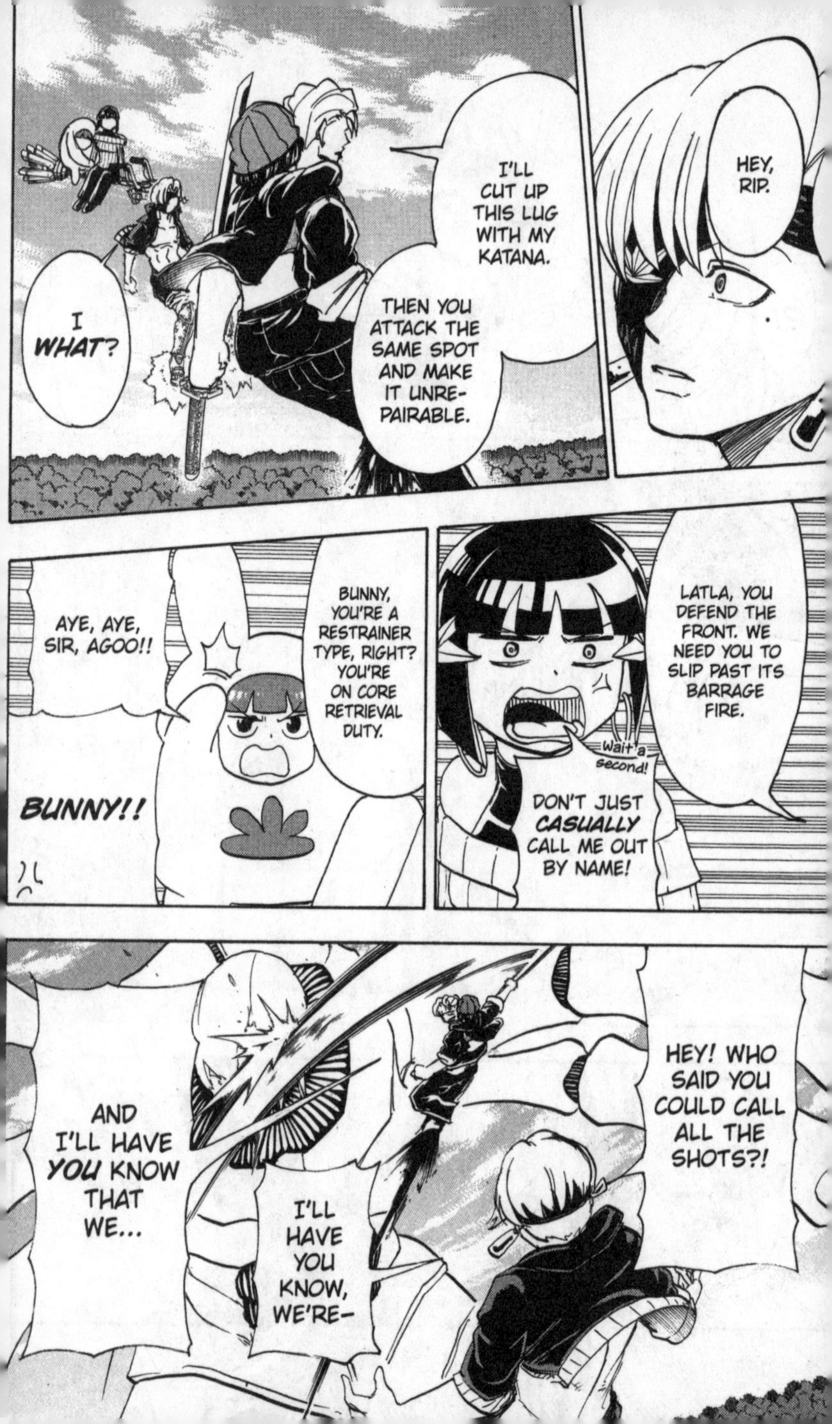
HEY, RIP.
I'LL CUT UP THIS LUG WITH MY KATANA.
THEN YOU ATTACK THE SAME SPOT AND MAKE IT UNRE-PAIRABLE.
I *WHAT*?
LATLA, YOU DEFEND THE FRONT. WE NEED YOU TO SLIP PAST ITS BARRAGE FIRE.
Wait a second!
DON'T JUST *CASUALLY* CALL ME OUT BY NAME!
BUNNY, YOU'RE A RESTRAINER TYPE, RIGHT? YOU'RE ON CORE RETRIEVAL DUTY.
AYE, AYE, SIR, AGOO!!
BUNNY!!
HEY! WHO SAID YOU COULD CALL ALL THE SHOTS?!
I'LL HAVE YOU KNOW, WE'RE-
AND I'LL HAVE *YOU* KNOW THAT WE...

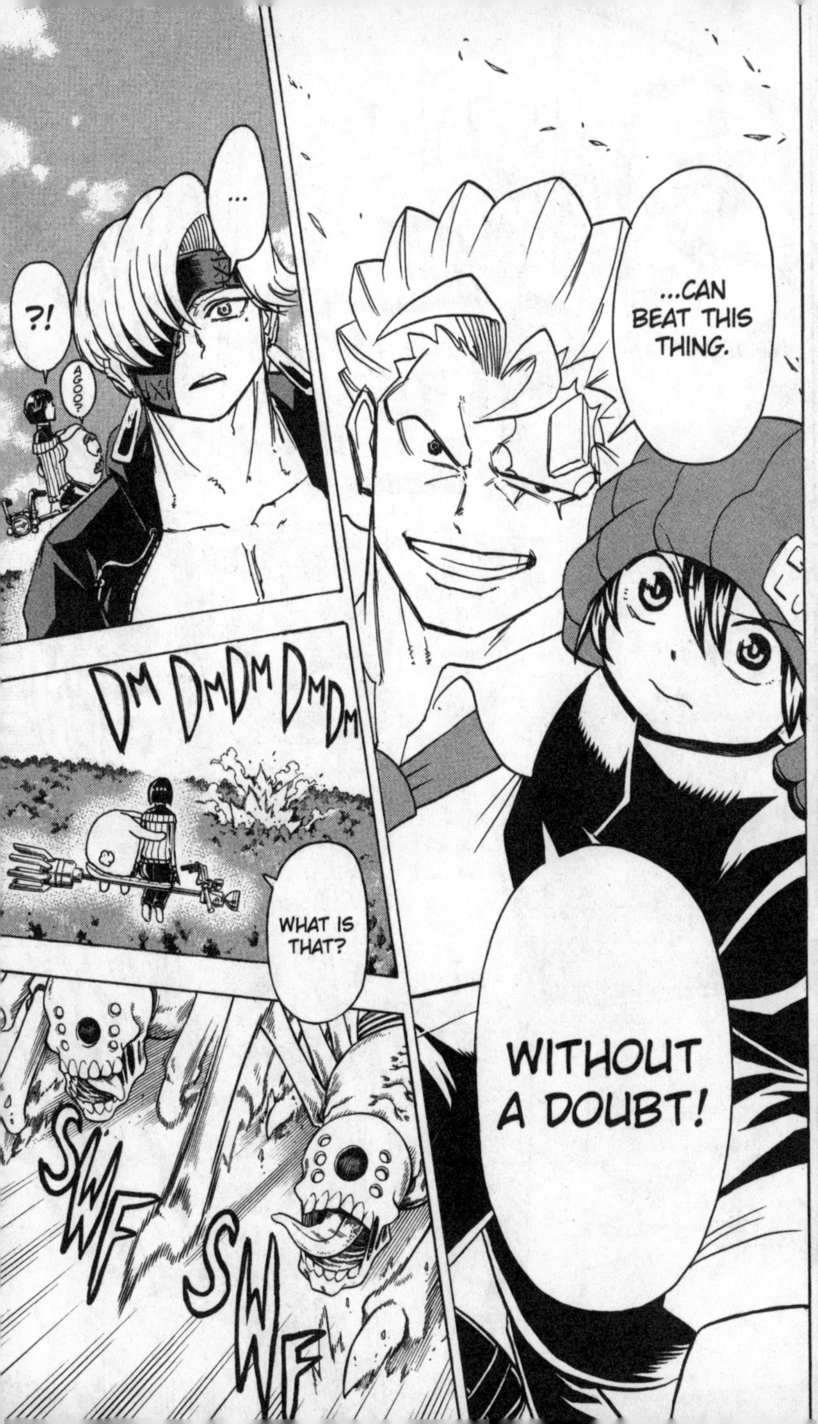
...CAN BEAT THIS THING.
WITHOUT A DOUBT!
...
?!
AGOO?
DM DM DM DM DM
WHAT IS THAT?
SWF SWF

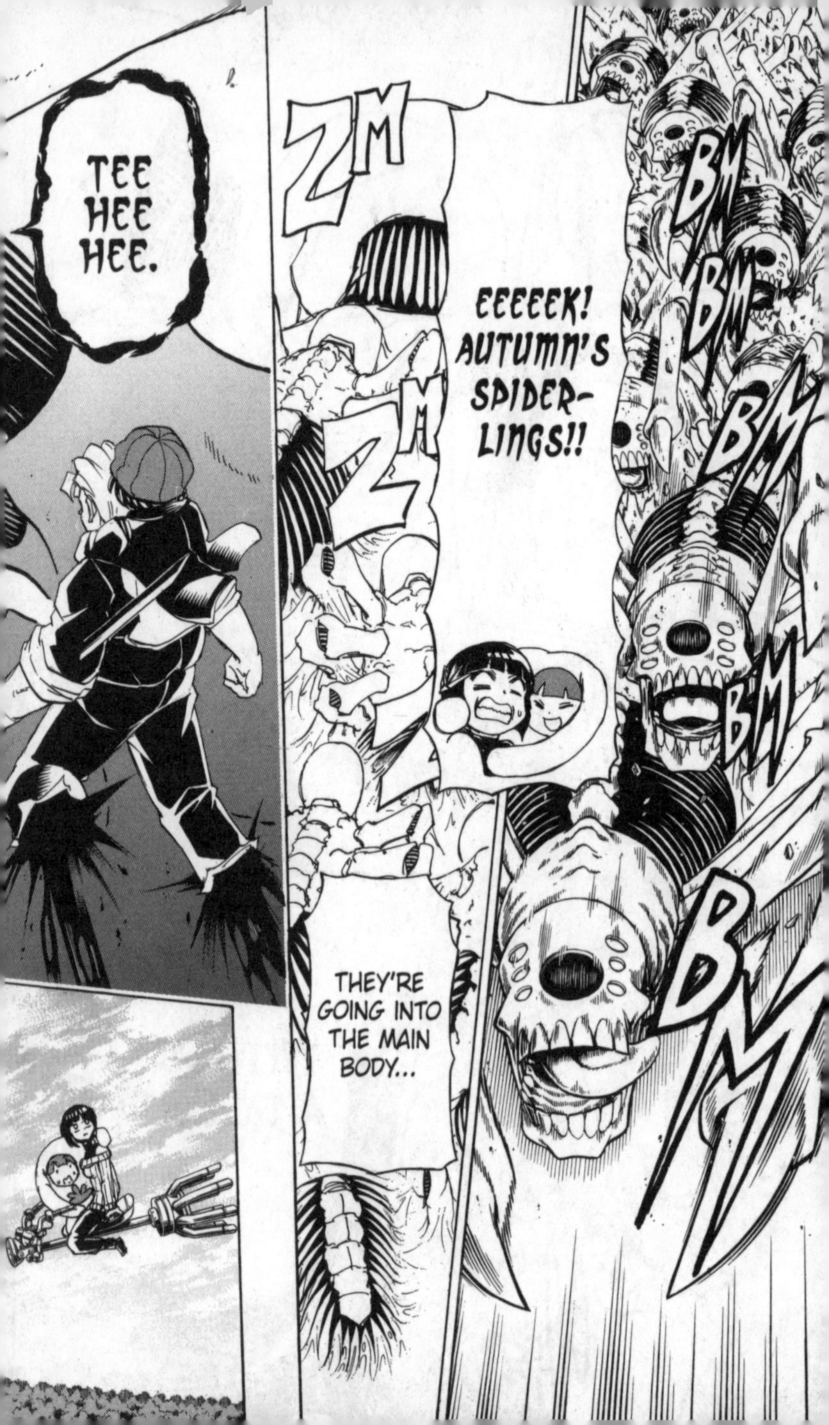
BM
BM
BM
BM
BM
EEEEEK! AUTUMN'S SPIDER-LINGS!!
ZM
ZM
THEY'RE GOING INTO THE MAIN BODY...
TEE HEE HEE.

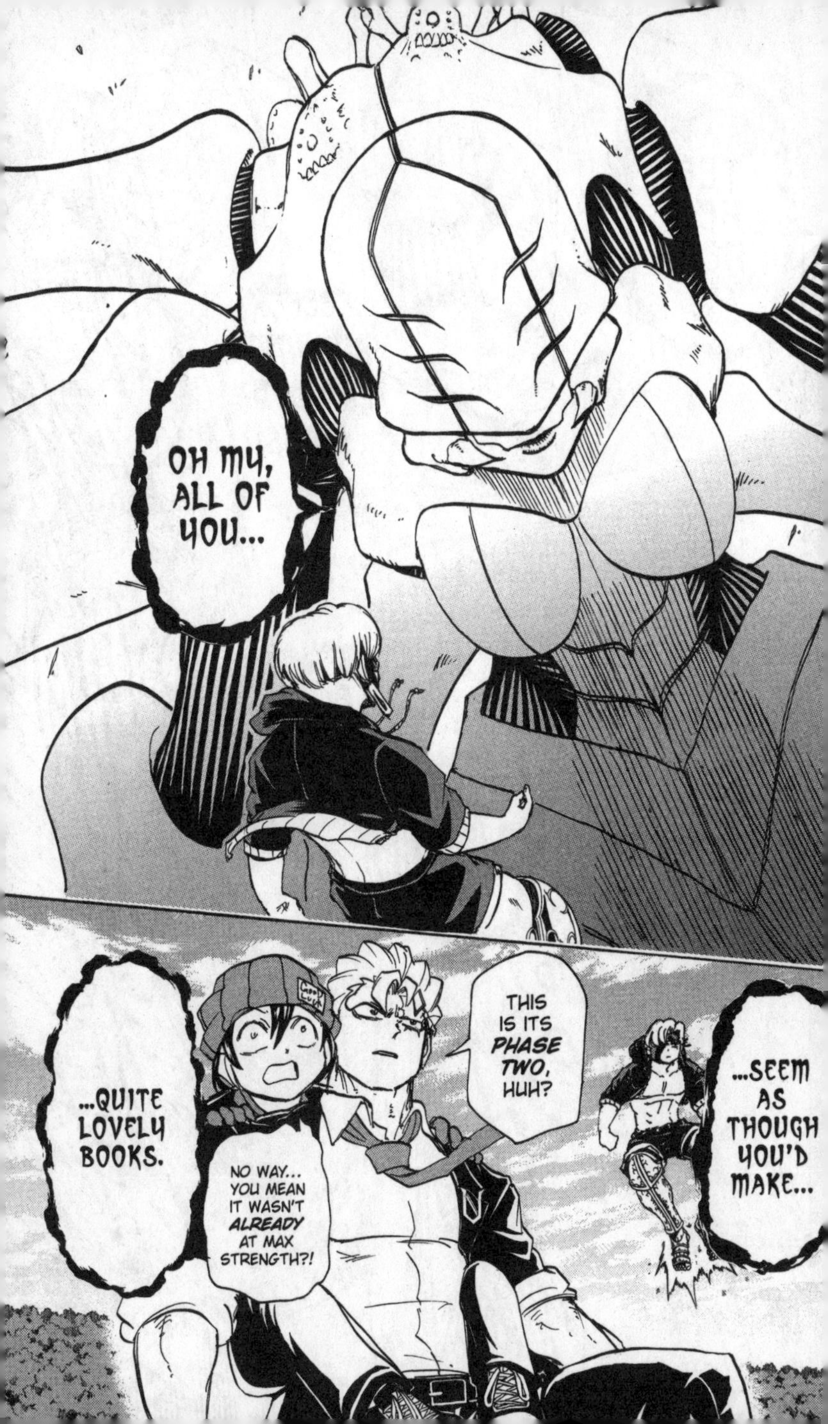
OH MY, ALL OF YOU...
...SEEM AS THOUGH YOU'D MAKE...
THIS IS ITS *PHASE TWO*, HUH?
NO WAY... YOU MEAN IT WASN'T *ALREADY* AT MAX STRENGTH?!
...QUITE LOVELY BOOKS.

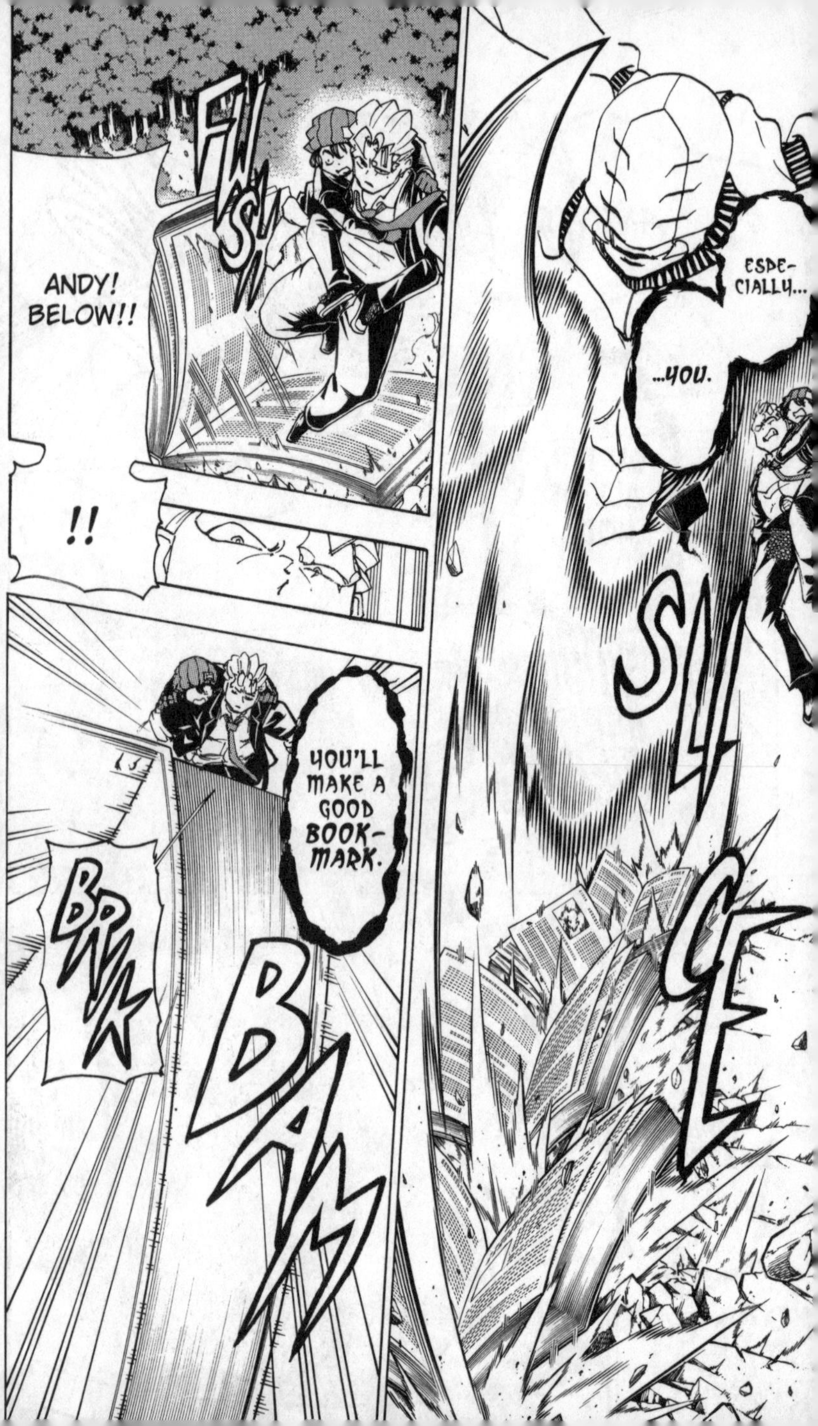
ESPE-
CIALLY...
...YOU.
SLI
CE
FWASH
ANDY! BELOW!!
!!
YOU'LL MAKE A GOOD BOOK-MARK.
BRINK
BAM

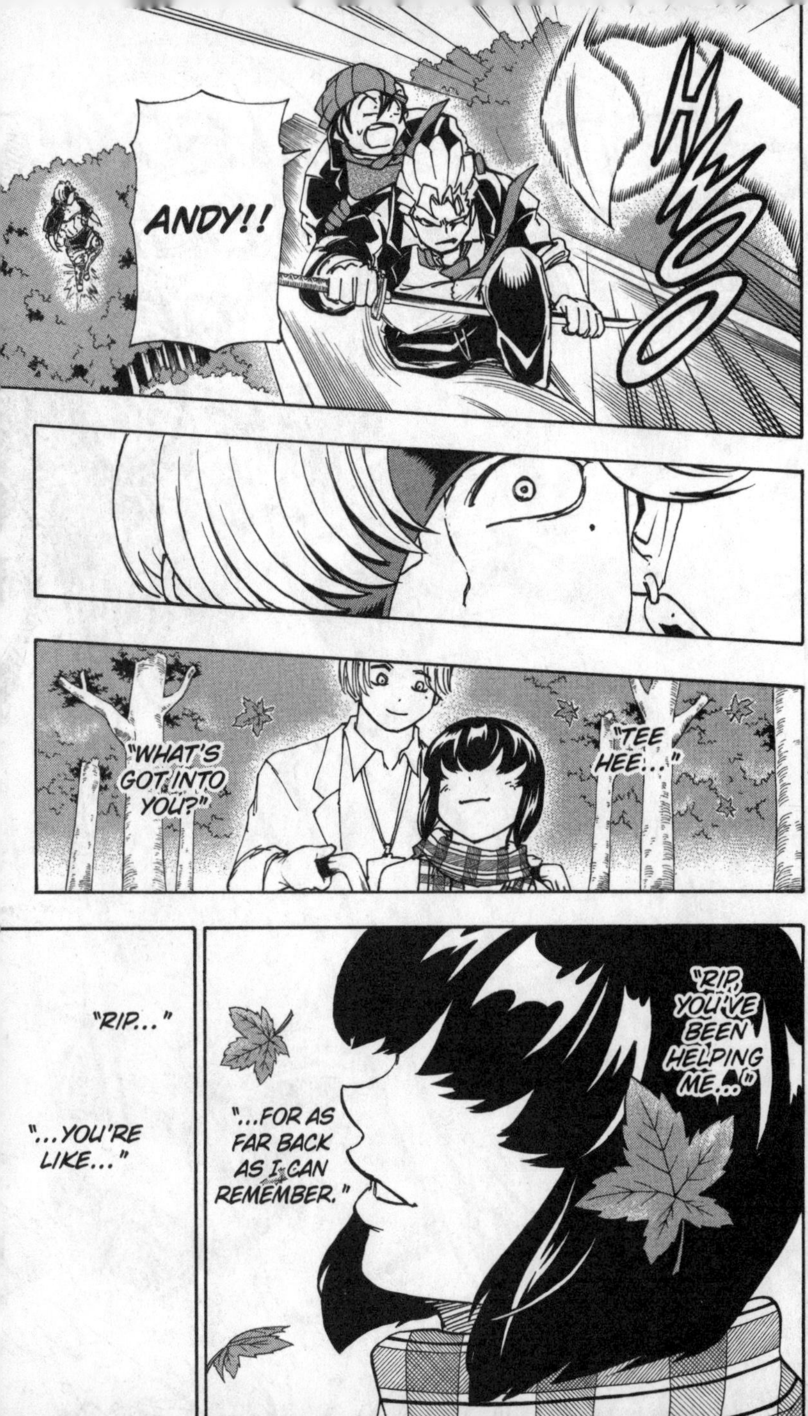
HWOO
ANDY!!
"TEE HEE..."
"WHAT'S GOT INTO YOU?"
"RIP, YOU'VE BEEN HELPING ME..."
"...FOR AS FAR BACK AS I CAN REMEMBER."
"RIP..."
"...YOU'RE LIKE..."

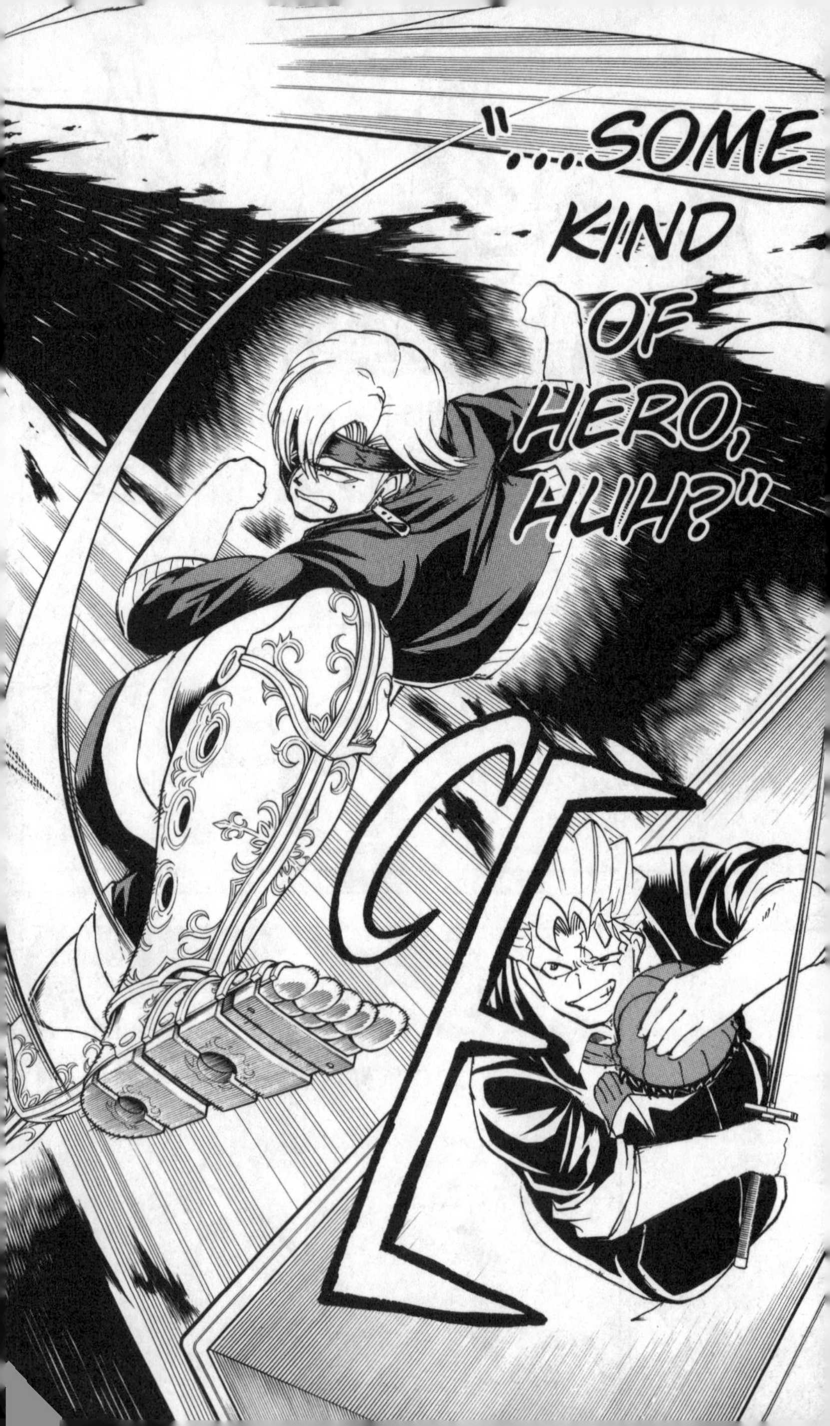
"...SOME KIND OF HERO, HUH?"

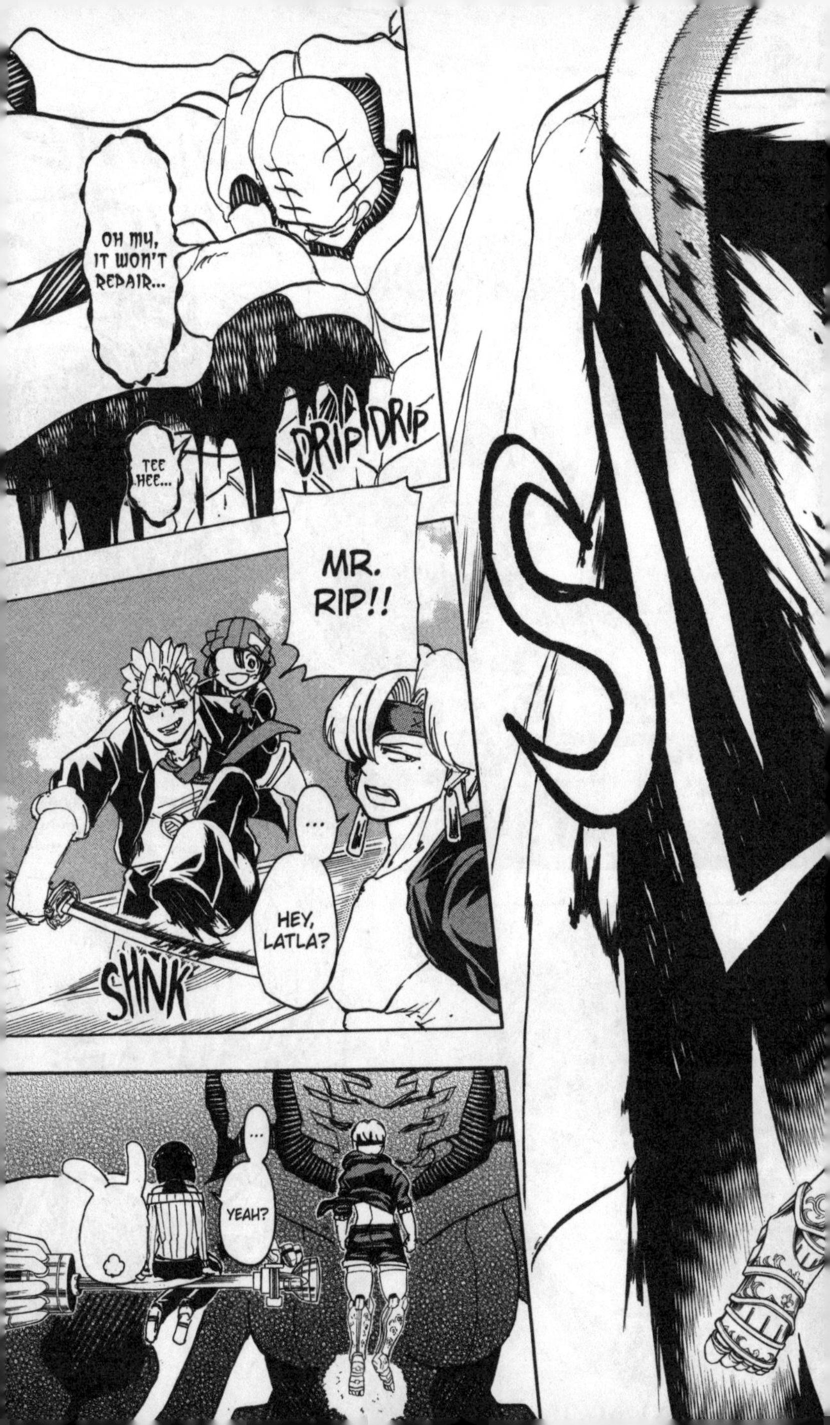
OH MY, IT WON'T REPAIR...
DRIP DRIP
TEE HEE...
MR. RIP!!
...
HEY, LATLA?
SHNK
...
YEAH?

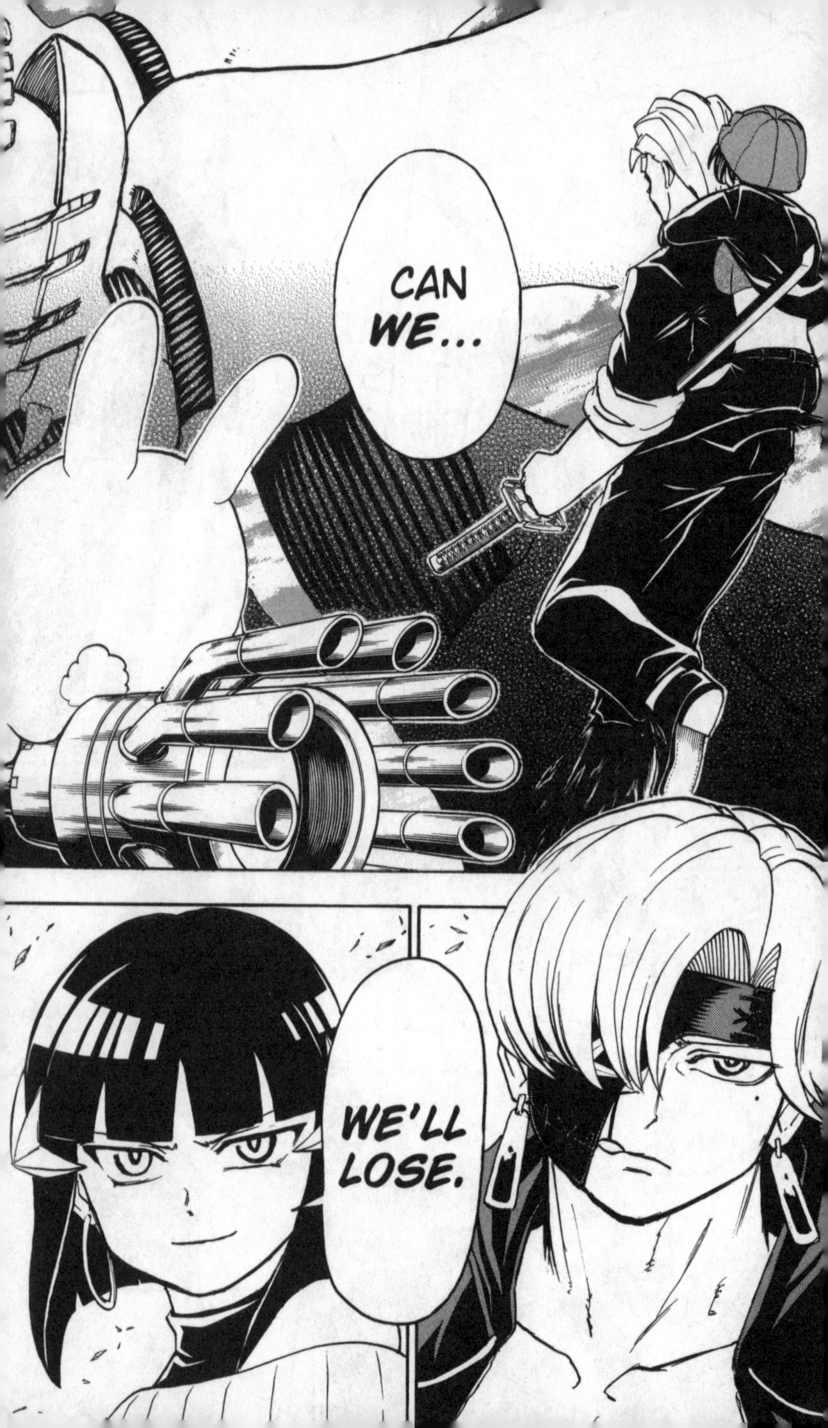
CAN WE...
WE'LL LOSE.

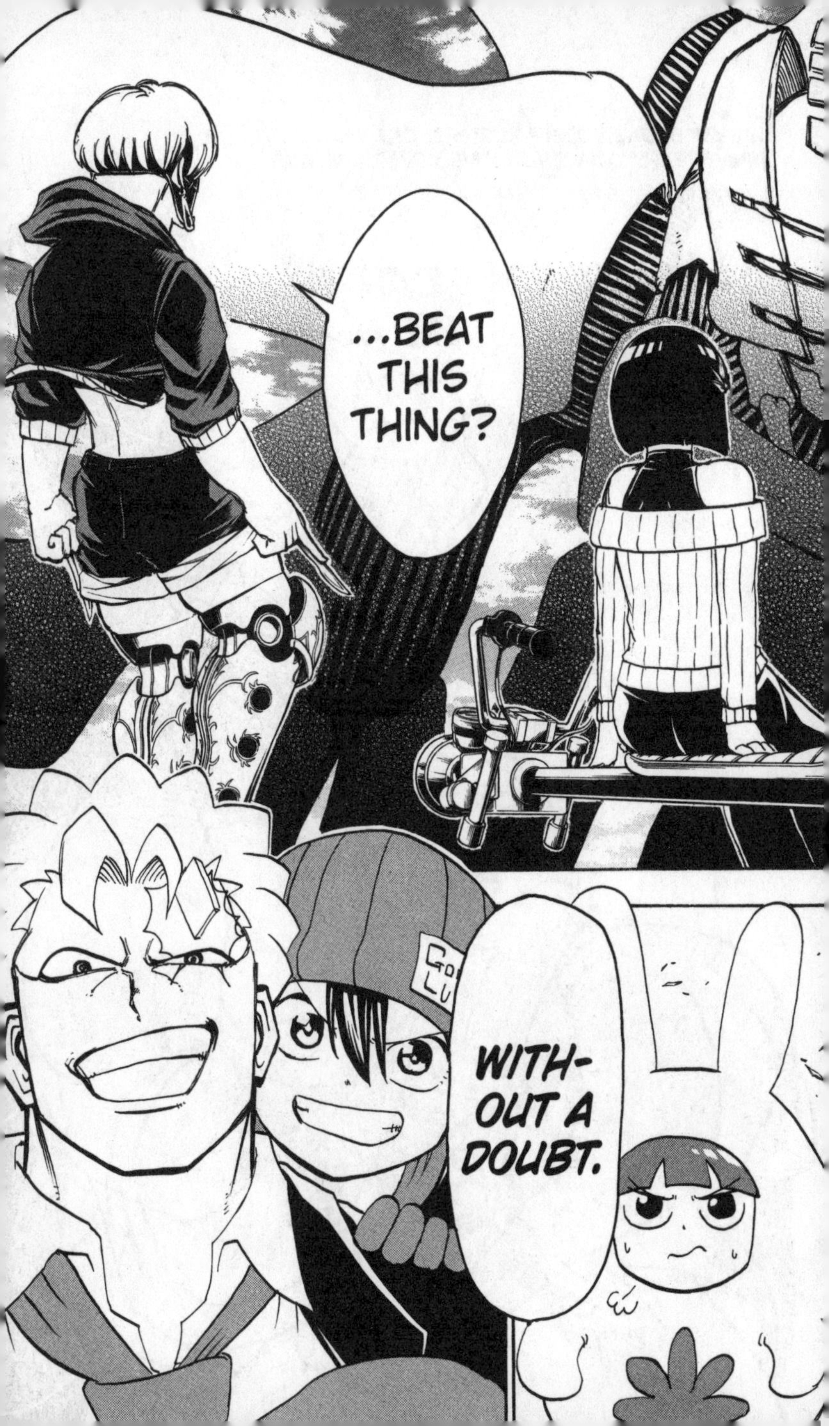
...BEAT THIS THING?
WITH- OUT A DOUBT.

WEEKLY SHONEN JUMP 2021 #12, ONE YEAR ANNIVERSARY COMMEMORATIVE COVER LINE ART

*HAT: ONE YEAR ANNIVERSARY

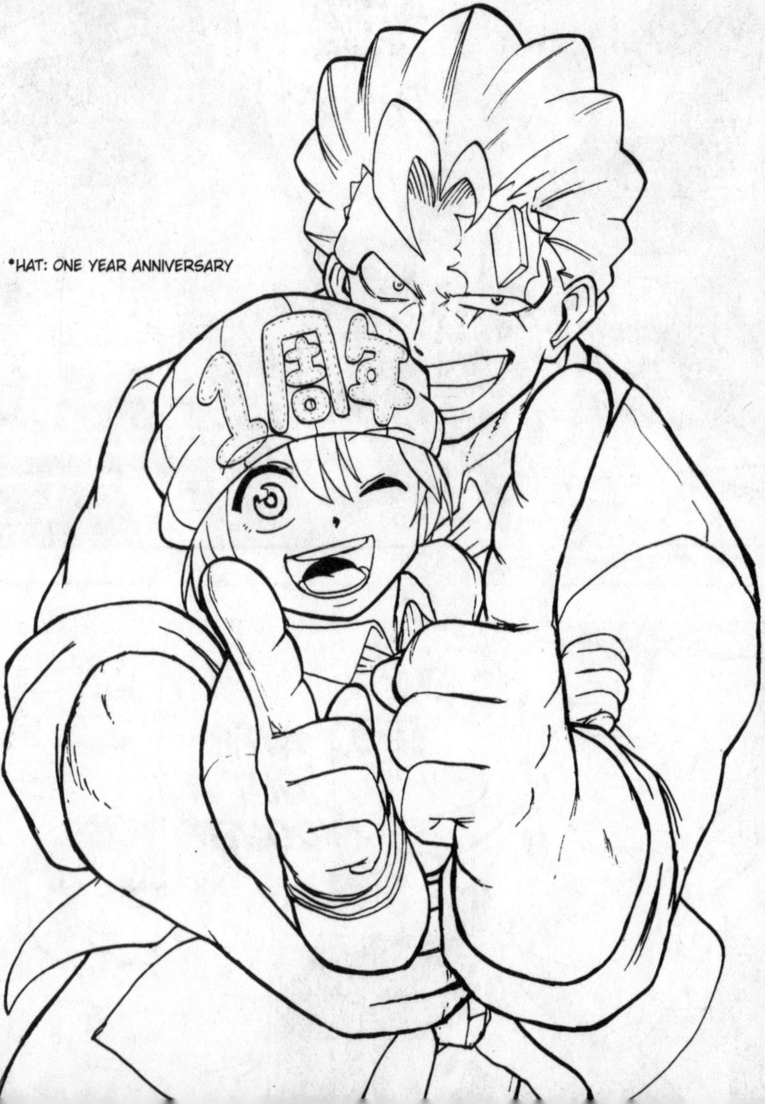
1周年

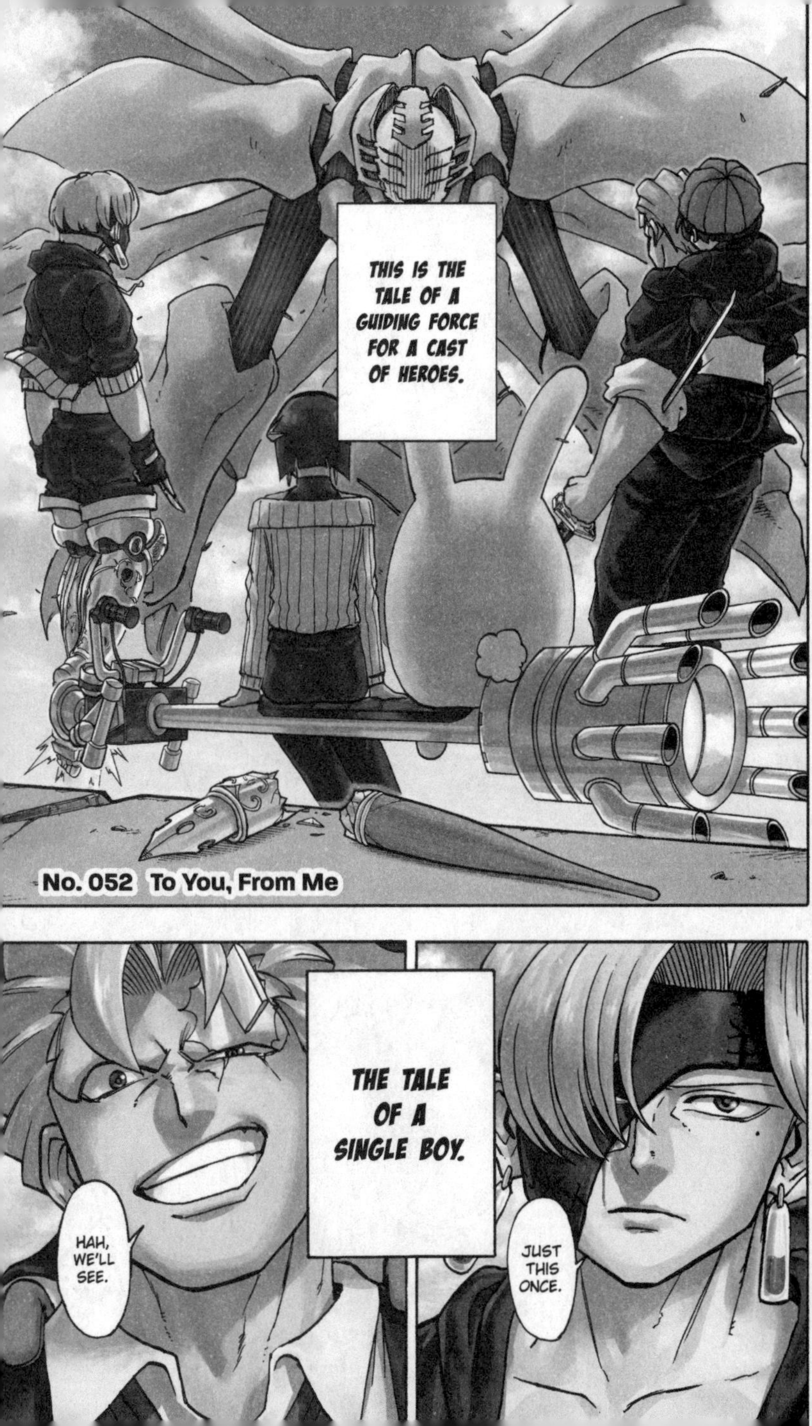
THIS IS THE TALE OF A GUIDING FORCE FOR A CAST OF HEROES.
No. 052 To You, From Me
THE TALE OF A SINGLE BOY.
JUST THIS ONCE.
HAH, WE'LL SEE.

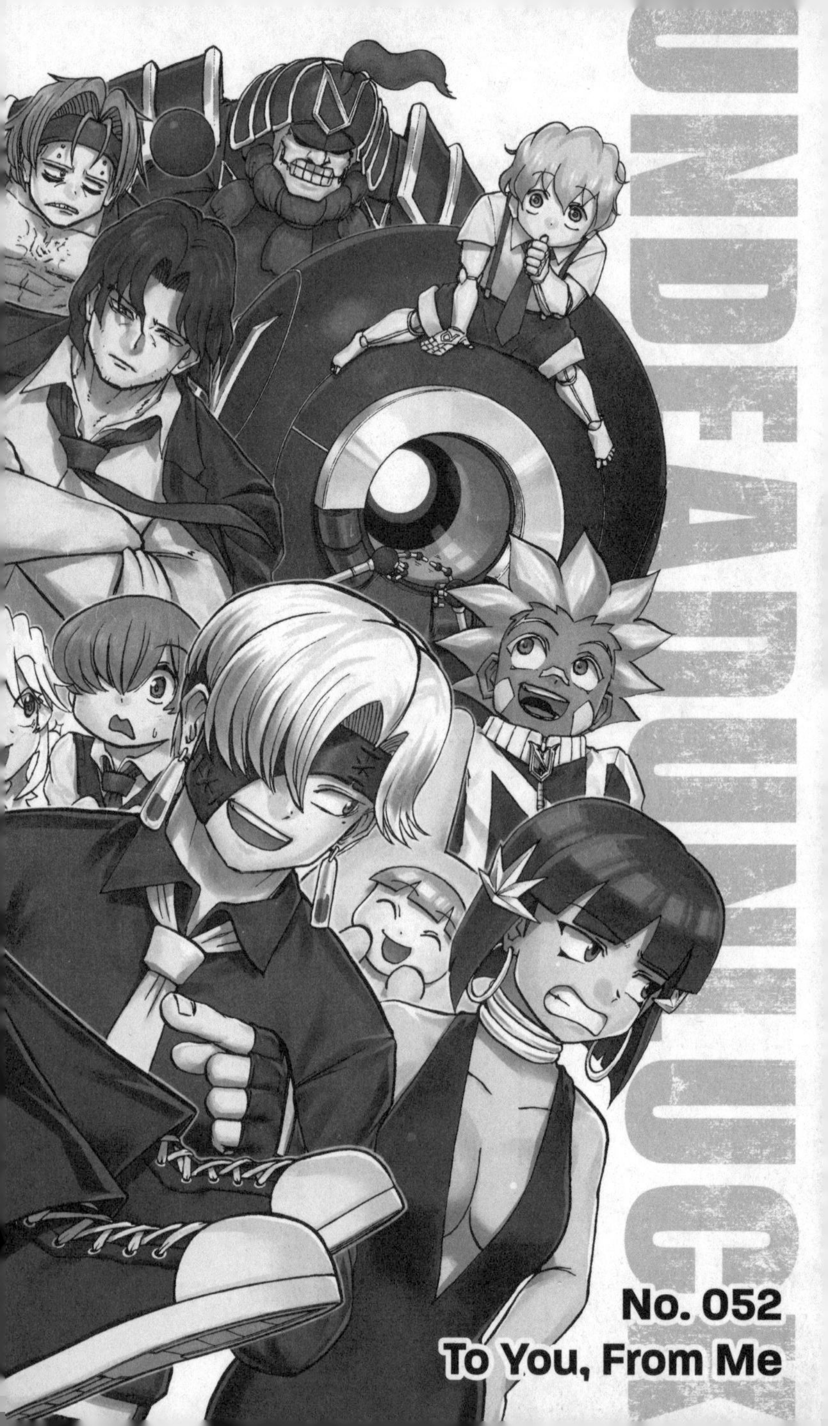
UNDEAD UNLUCK
No. 052
To You, From Me

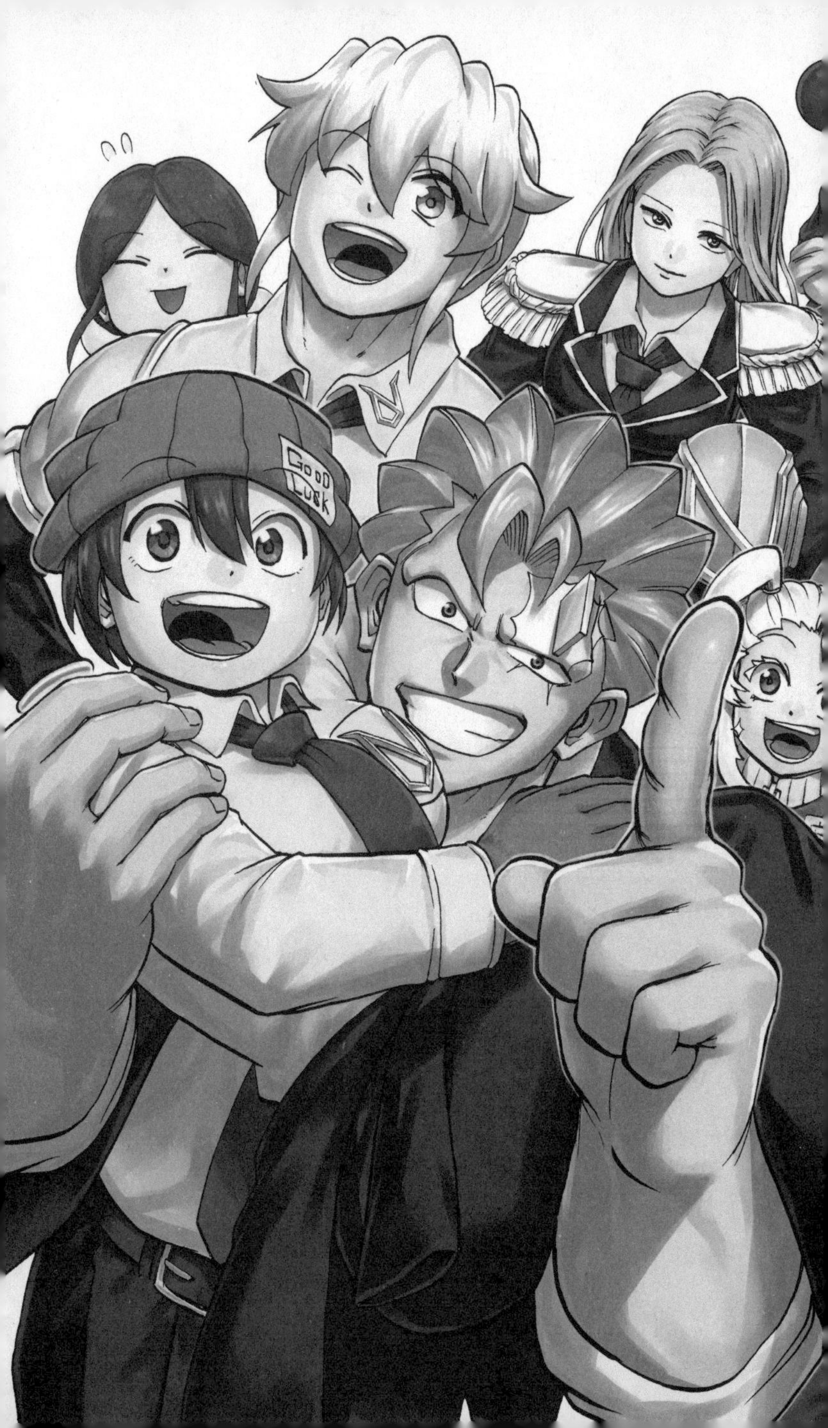
GOOD LUCK

**UNDEAD
UNLUCK**

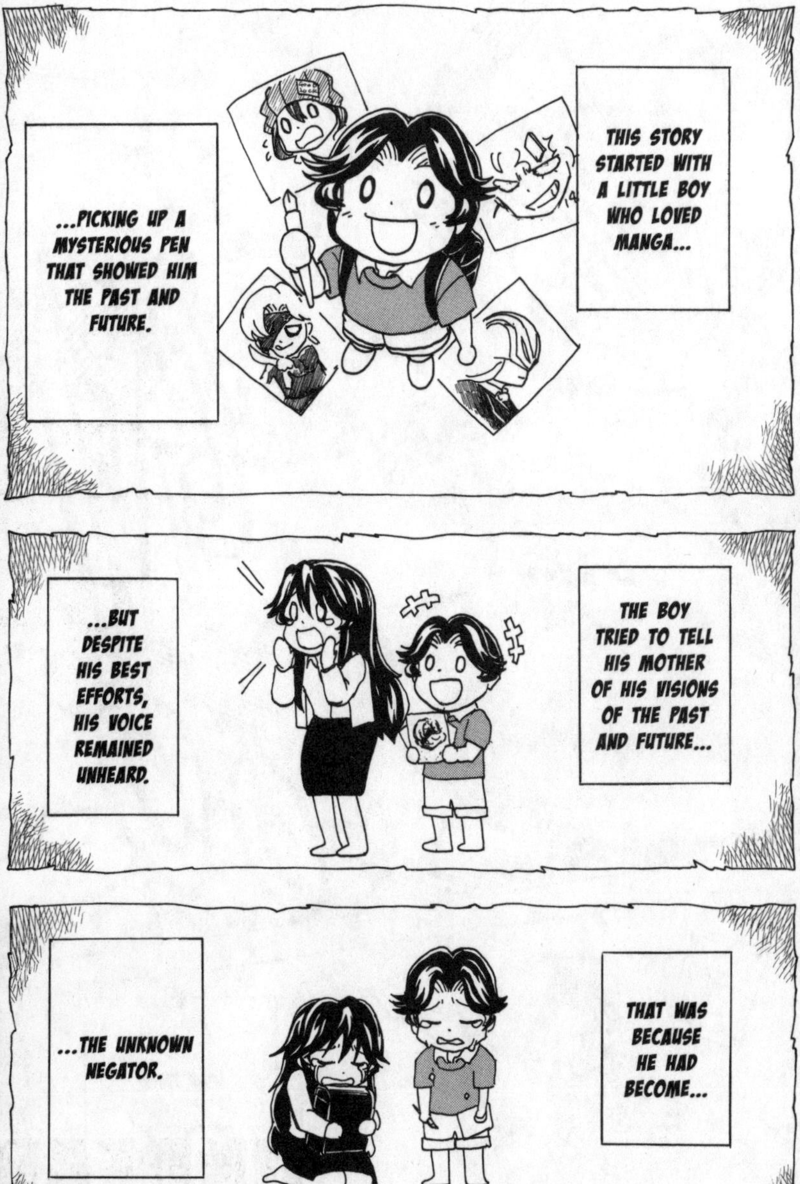
THIS STORY STARTED WITH A LITTLE BOY WHO LOVED MANGA...
...PICKING UP A MYSTERIOUS PEN THAT SHOWED HIM THE PAST AND FUTURE.
THE BOY TRIED TO TELL HIS MOTHER OF HIS VISIONS OF THE PAST AND FUTURE...
...BUT DESPITE HIS BEST EFFORTS, HIS VOICE REMAINED UNHEARD.
THAT WAS BECAUSE HE HAD BECOME...
...THE UNKNOWN NEGATOR.

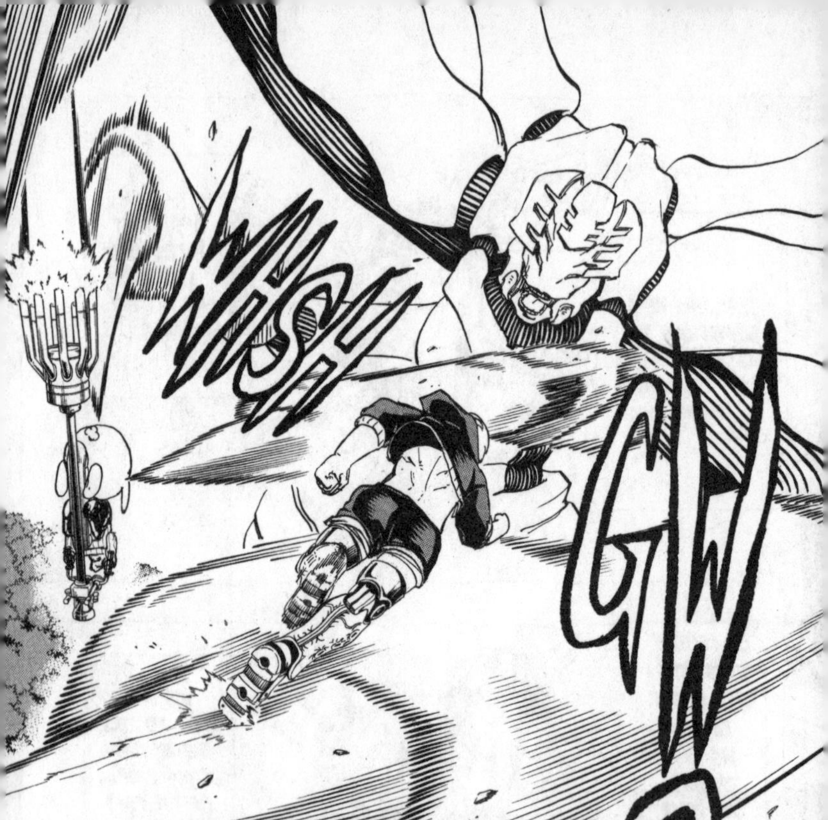
GWOO
WHSH
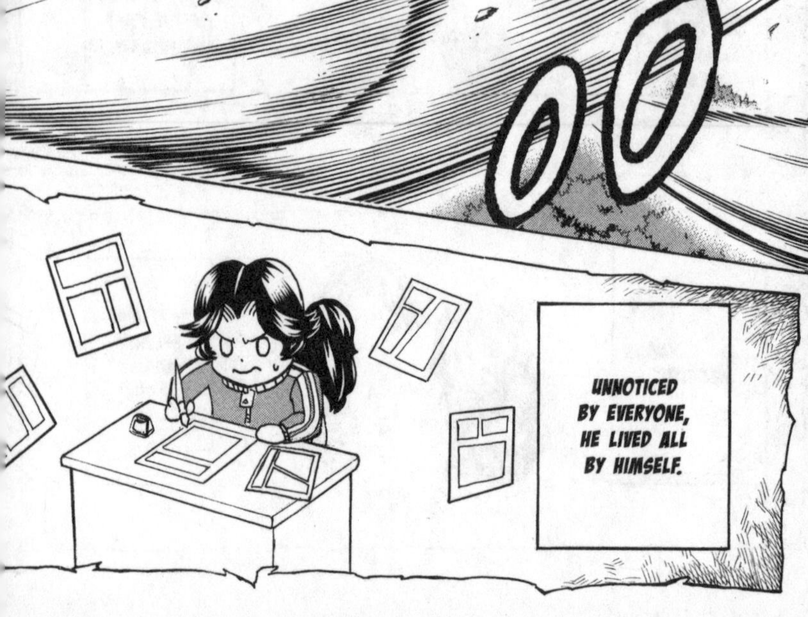
UNNOTICED BY EVERYONE, HE LIVED ALL BY HIMSELF.

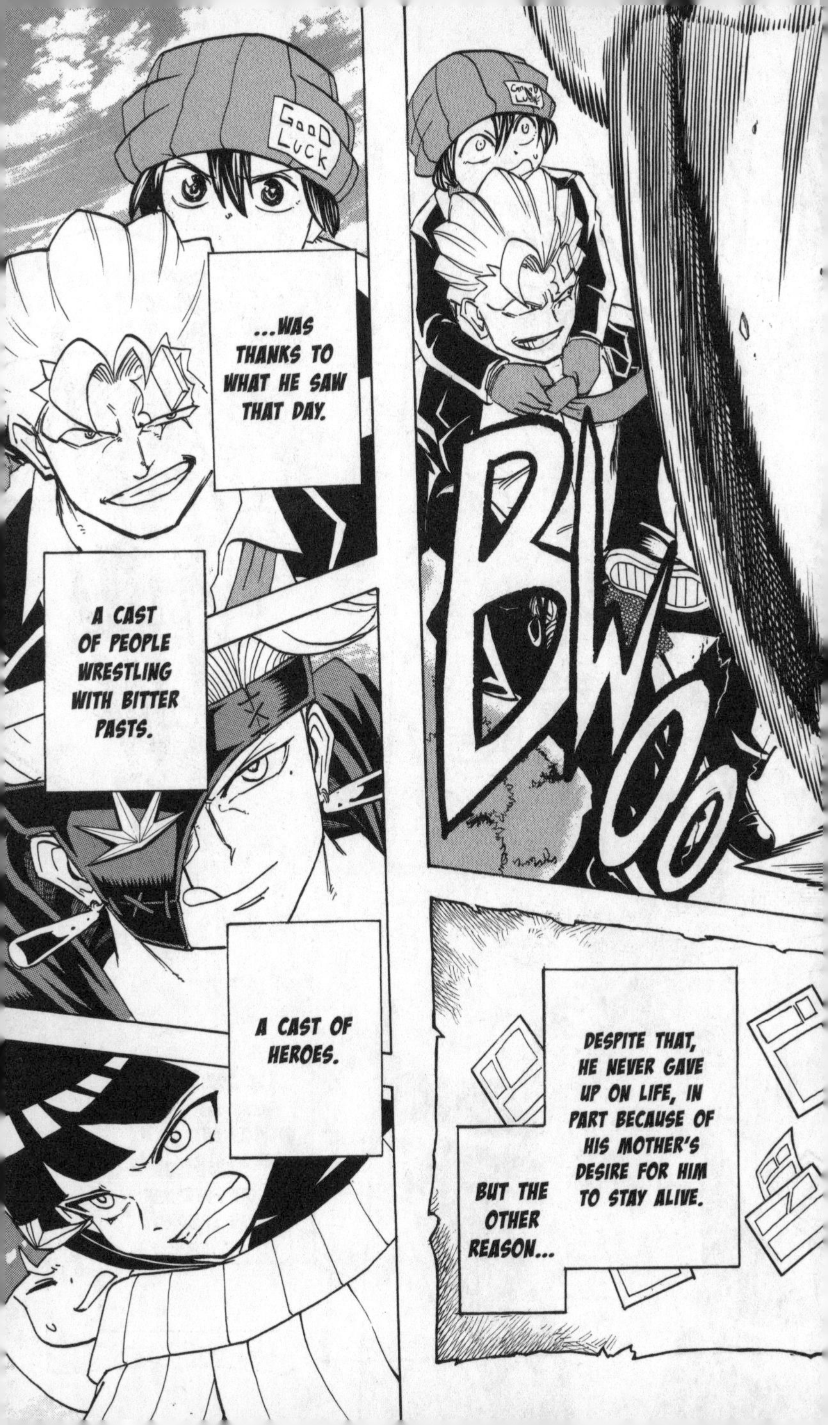
GOOD LUCK
BWOO
DESPITE THAT, HE NEVER GAVE UP ON LIFE, IN PART BECAUSE OF HIS MOTHER'S DESIRE FOR HIM TO STAY ALIVE.
BUT THE OTHER REASON...
GOOD LUCK
...WAS THANKS TO WHAT HE SAW THAT DAY.
A CAST OF PEOPLE WRESTLING WITH BITTER PASTS.
A CAST OF HEROES.

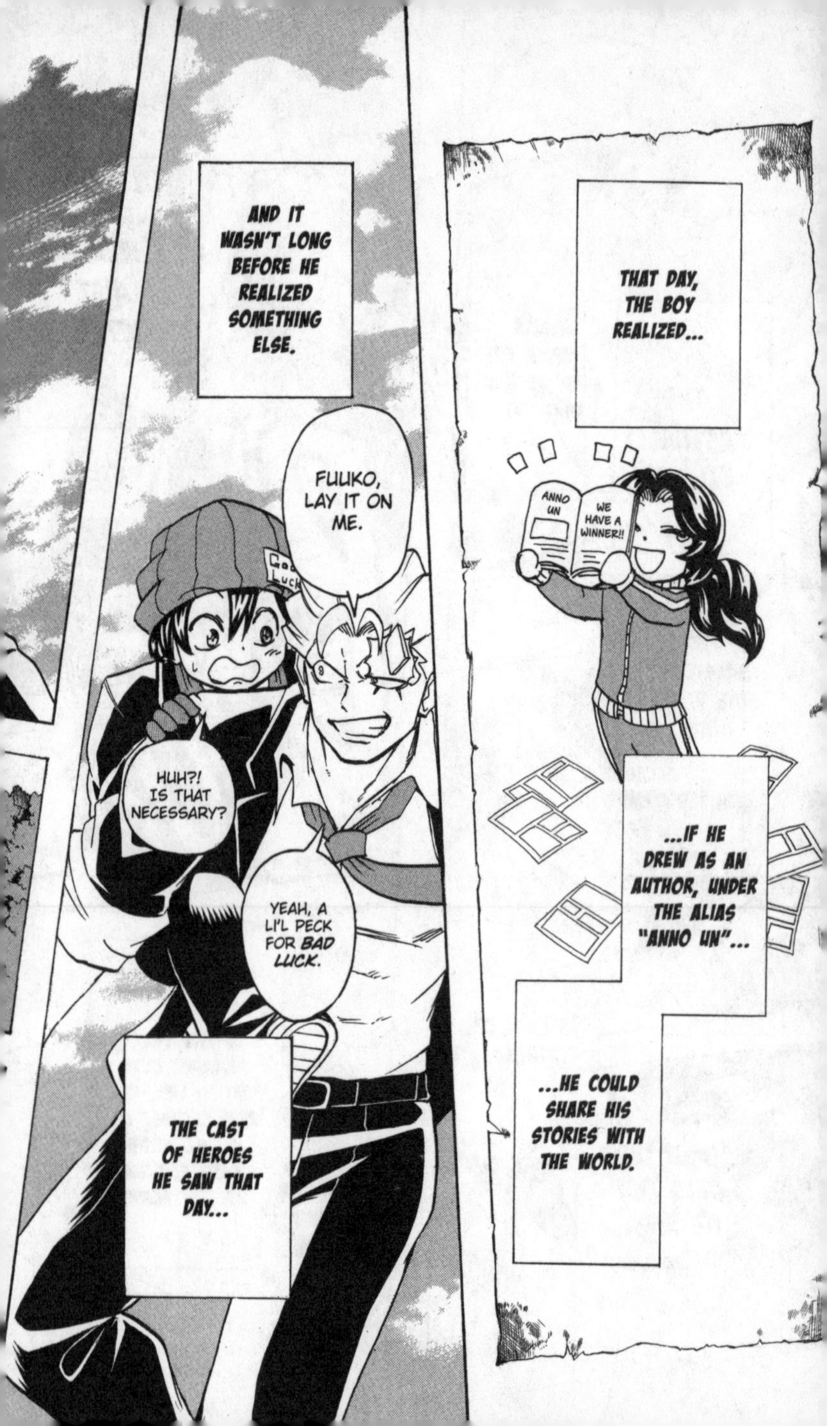
THAT DAY, THE BOY REALIZED...
ANNO UN
WE HAVE A WINNER!!
...IF HE DREW AS AN AUTHOR, UNDER THE ALIAS "ANNO UN"...
...HE COULD SHARE HIS STORIES WITH THE WORLD.
AND IT WASN'T LONG BEFORE HE REALIZED SOMETHING ELSE.
FUUKO, LAY IT ON ME.
HUH?! IS THAT NECESSARY?
YEAH, A LI'L PECK FOR *BAD LUCK*.
THE CAST OF HEROES HE SAW THAT DAY...

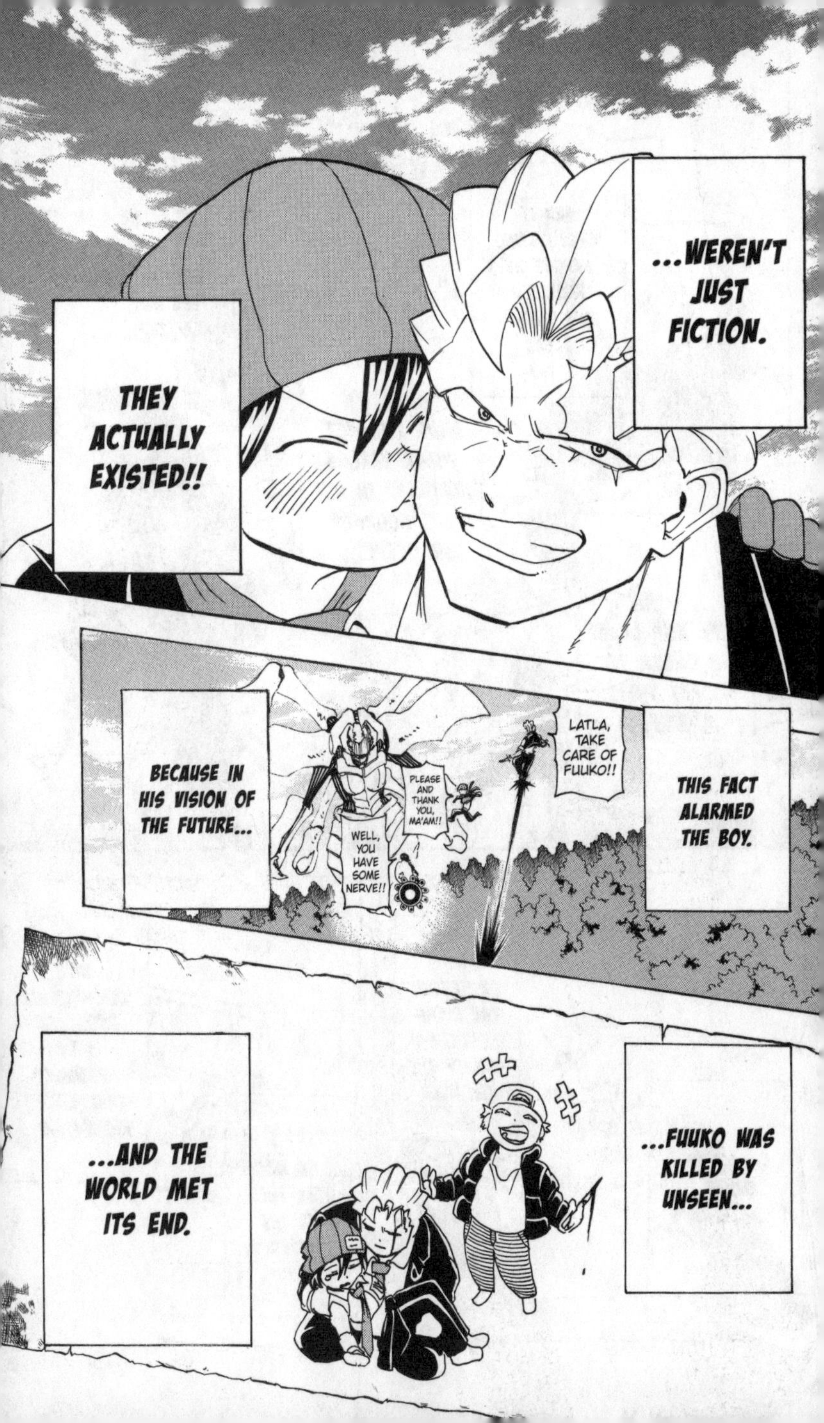
...WEREN'T JUST FICTION.
THEY ACTUALLY EXISTED!!
THIS FACT ALARMED THE BOY.
LATLA, TAKE CARE OF FUUKO!!
PLEASE AND THANK YOU, MA'AM!!
WELL, YOU HAVE SOME NERVE!!
BECAUSE IN HIS VISION OF THE FUTURE...
...FUUKO WAS KILLED BY UNSEEN...
...AND THE WORLD MET ITS END.

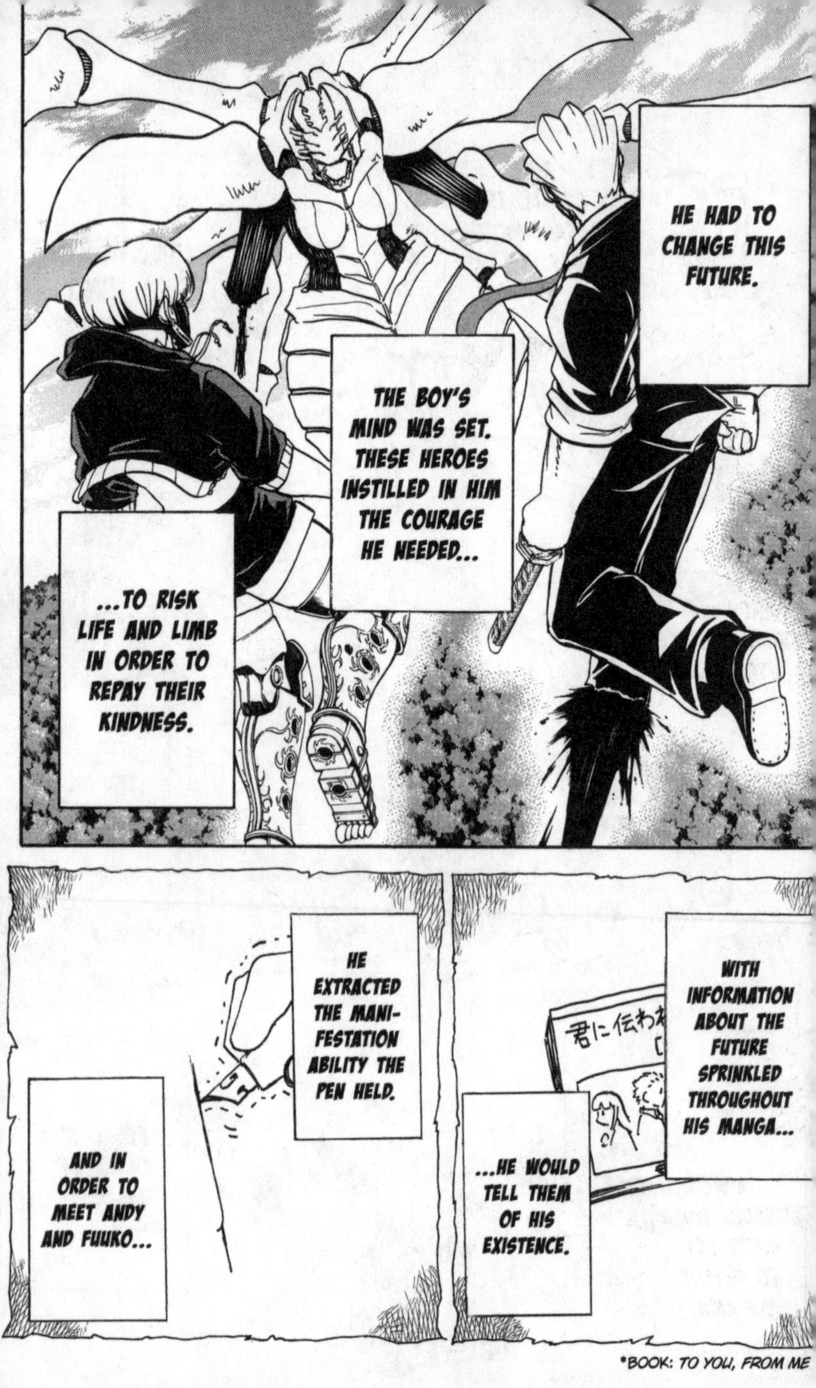
HE HAD TO CHANGE THIS FUTURE.
THE BOY'S MIND WAS SET. THESE HEROES INSTILLED IN HIM THE COURAGE HE NEEDED...
...TO RISK LIFE AND LIMB IN ORDER TO REPAY THEIR KINDNESS.
WITH INFORMATION ABOUT THE FUTURE SPRINKLED THROUGHOUT HIS MANGA...
...HE WOULD TELL THEM OF HIS EXISTENCE.
HE EXTRACTED THE MANI-FESTATION ABILITY THE PEN HELD.
AND IN ORDER TO MEET ANDY AND FUUKO...

*BOOK: *TO YOU, FROM ME*

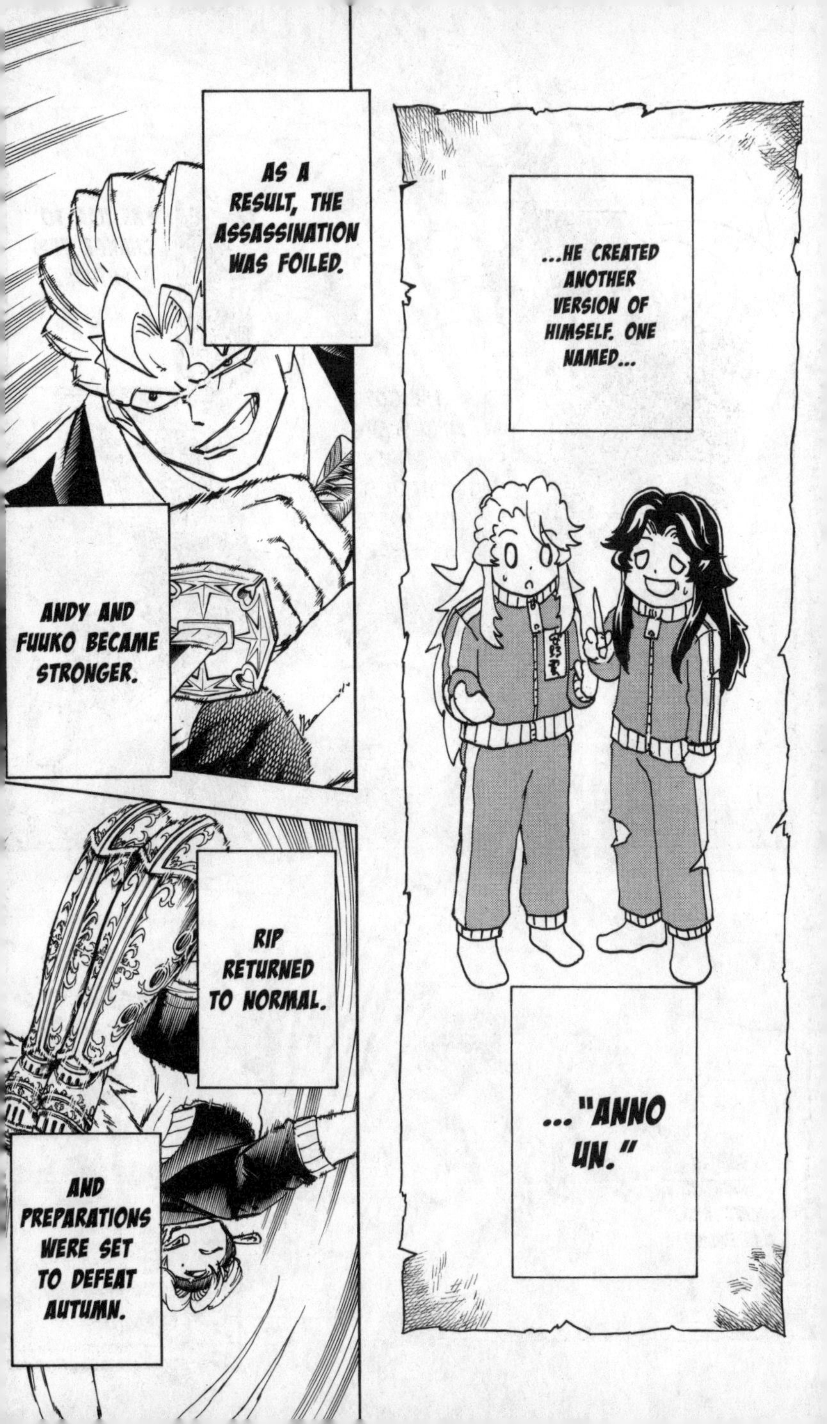
...HE CREATED ANOTHER VERSION OF HIMSELF. ONE NAMED...
..."ANNO UN."
AS A RESULT, THE ASSASSINATION WAS FOILED.
ANDY AND FUUKO BECAME STRONGER.
RIP RETURNED TO NORMAL.
AND PREPARATIONS WERE SET TO DEFEAT AUTUMN.

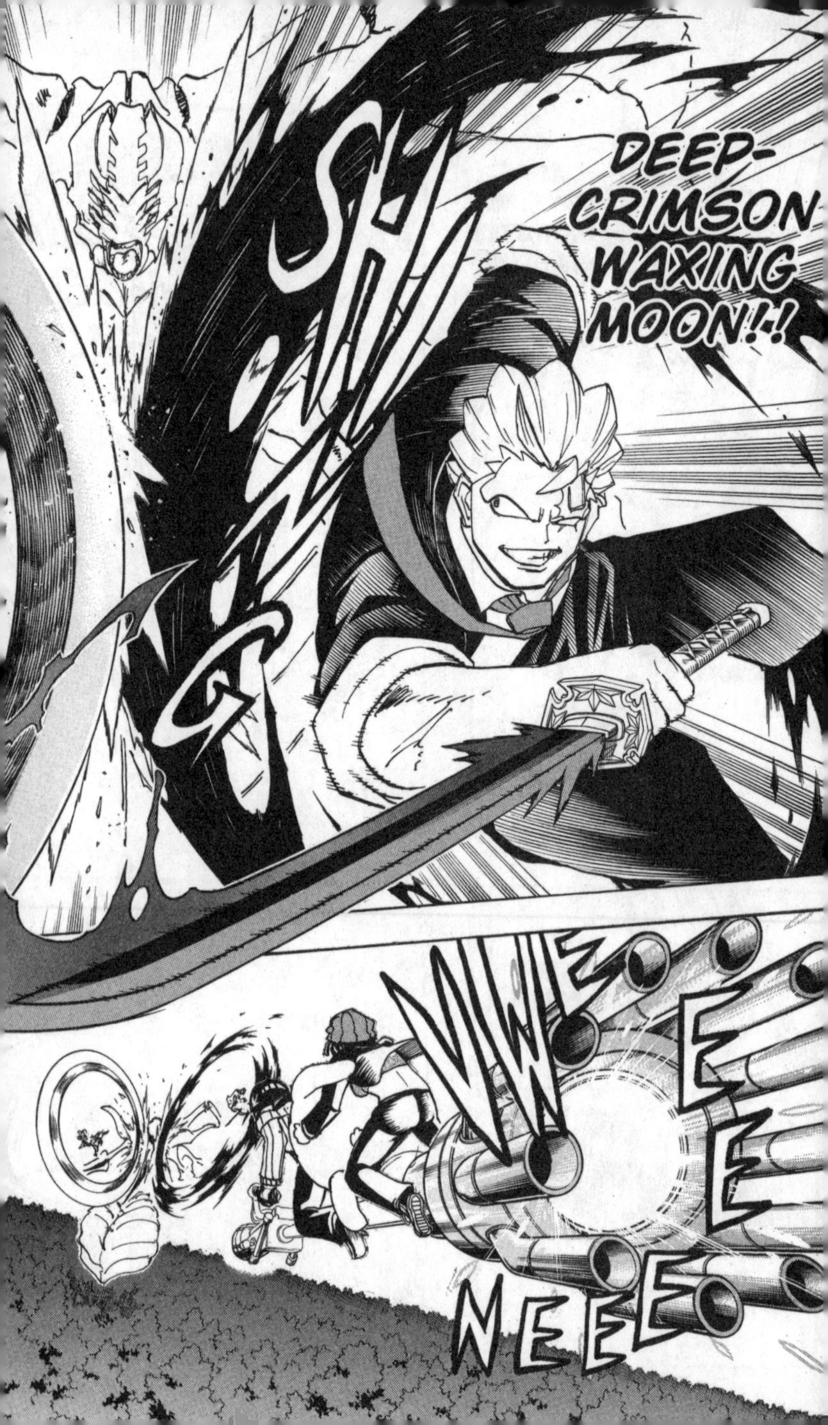
DEEP-CRIMSON WAXING MOON!!
SHING
VWEEEEEEE
NEEEE

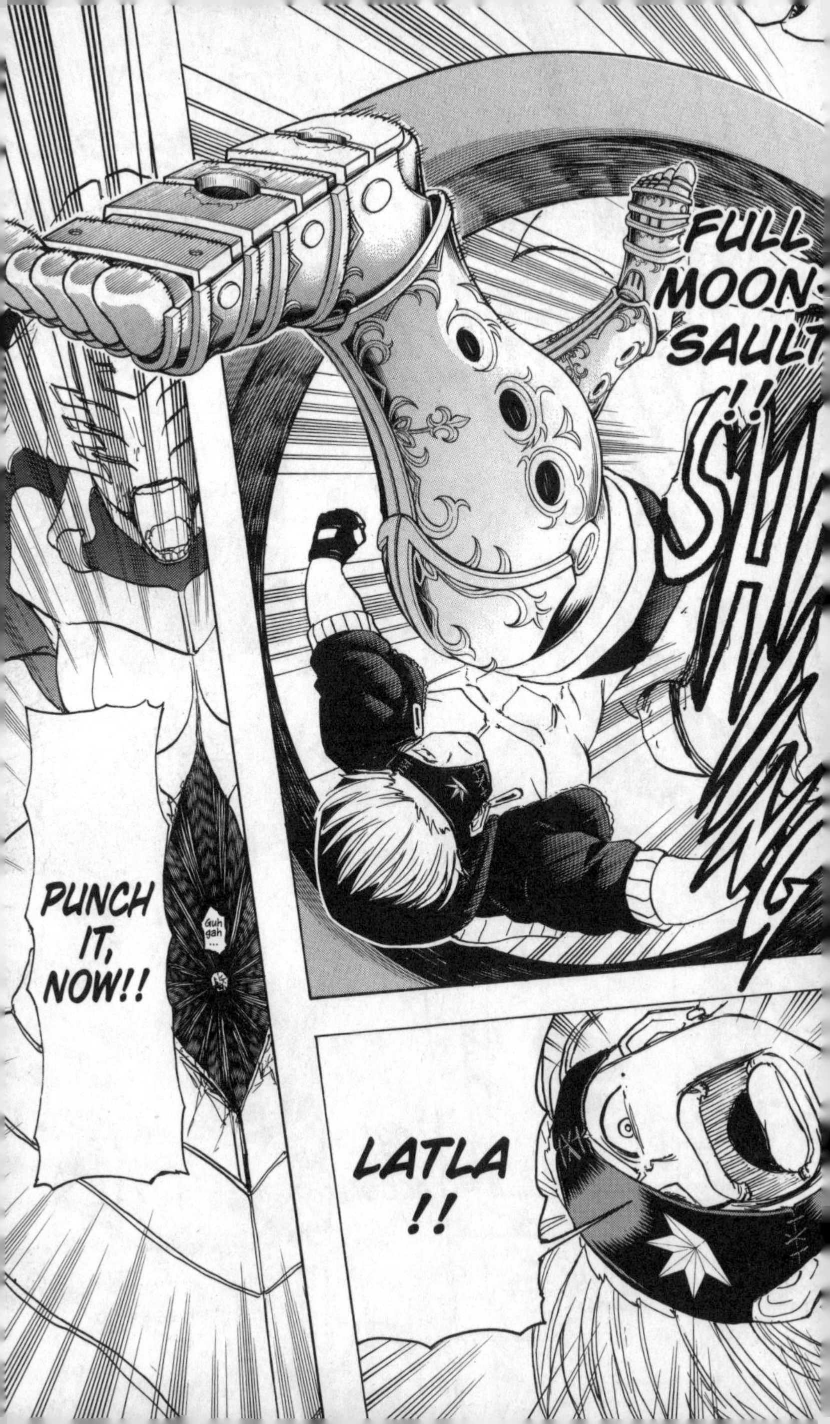
FULL MOONSAULT!!
LATLA!!
PUNCH IT, NOW!!
Guh gah...

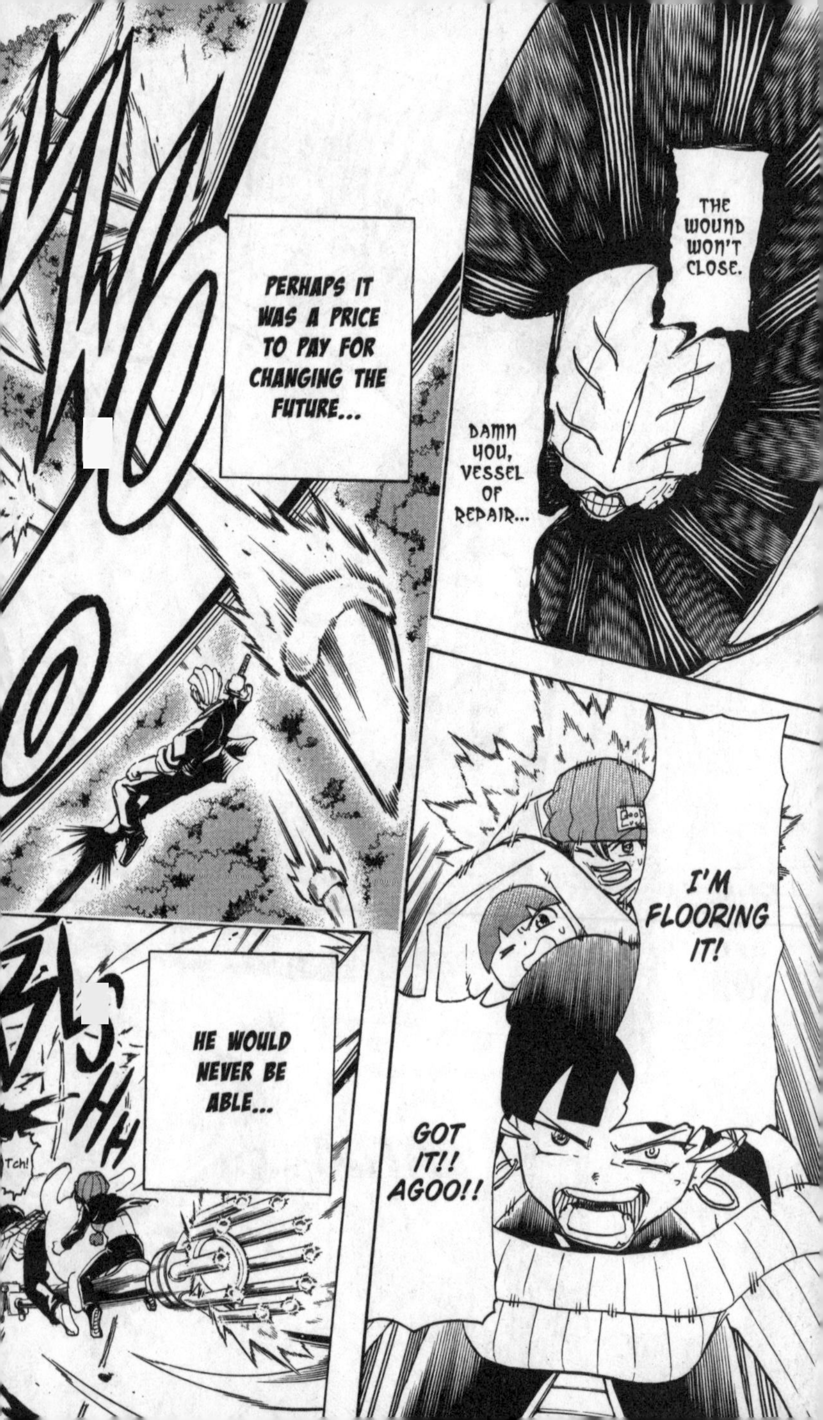
THE WOUND WON'T CLOSE.
DAMN YOU, VESSEL OF REPAIR...
PERHAPS IT WAS A PRICE TO PAY FOR CHANGING THE FUTURE...
I'M FLOORING IT!
GOT IT!! AGOO!!
HE WOULD NEVER BE ABLE...
Tch!

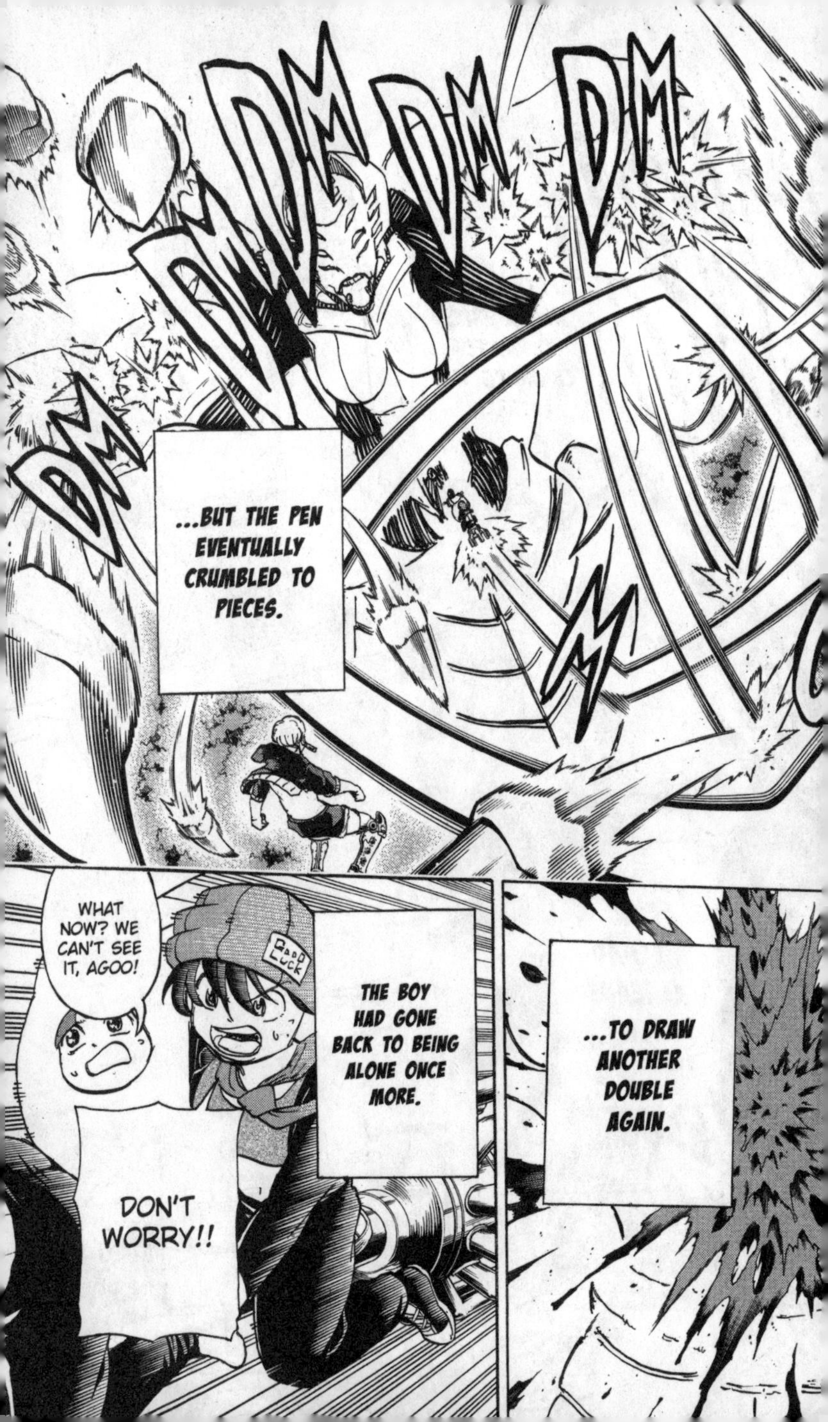
DM DM DM DM DM
...BUT THE PEN EVENTUALLY CRUMBLED TO PIECES.
...TO DRAW ANOTHER DOUBLE AGAIN.
THE BOY HAD GONE BACK TO BEING ALONE ONCE MORE.
WHAT NOW? WE CAN'T SEE IT, AGOO!
DON'T WORRY!!

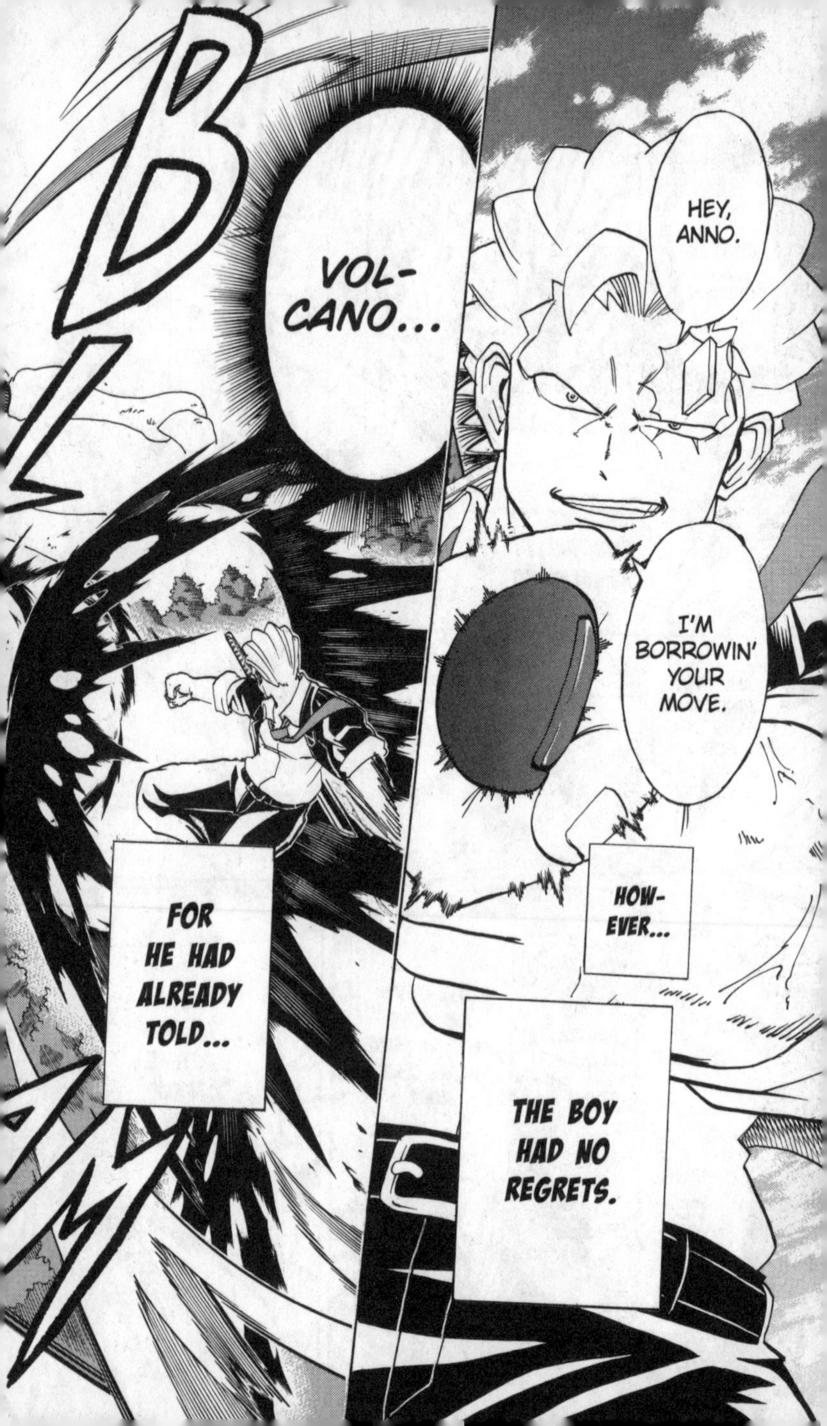
HEY, ANNO.
I'M BORROWIN' YOUR MOVE.
HOW-EVER...
THE BOY HAD NO REGRETS.
BLAM
VOL-CANO...
FOR HE HAD ALREADY TOLD...

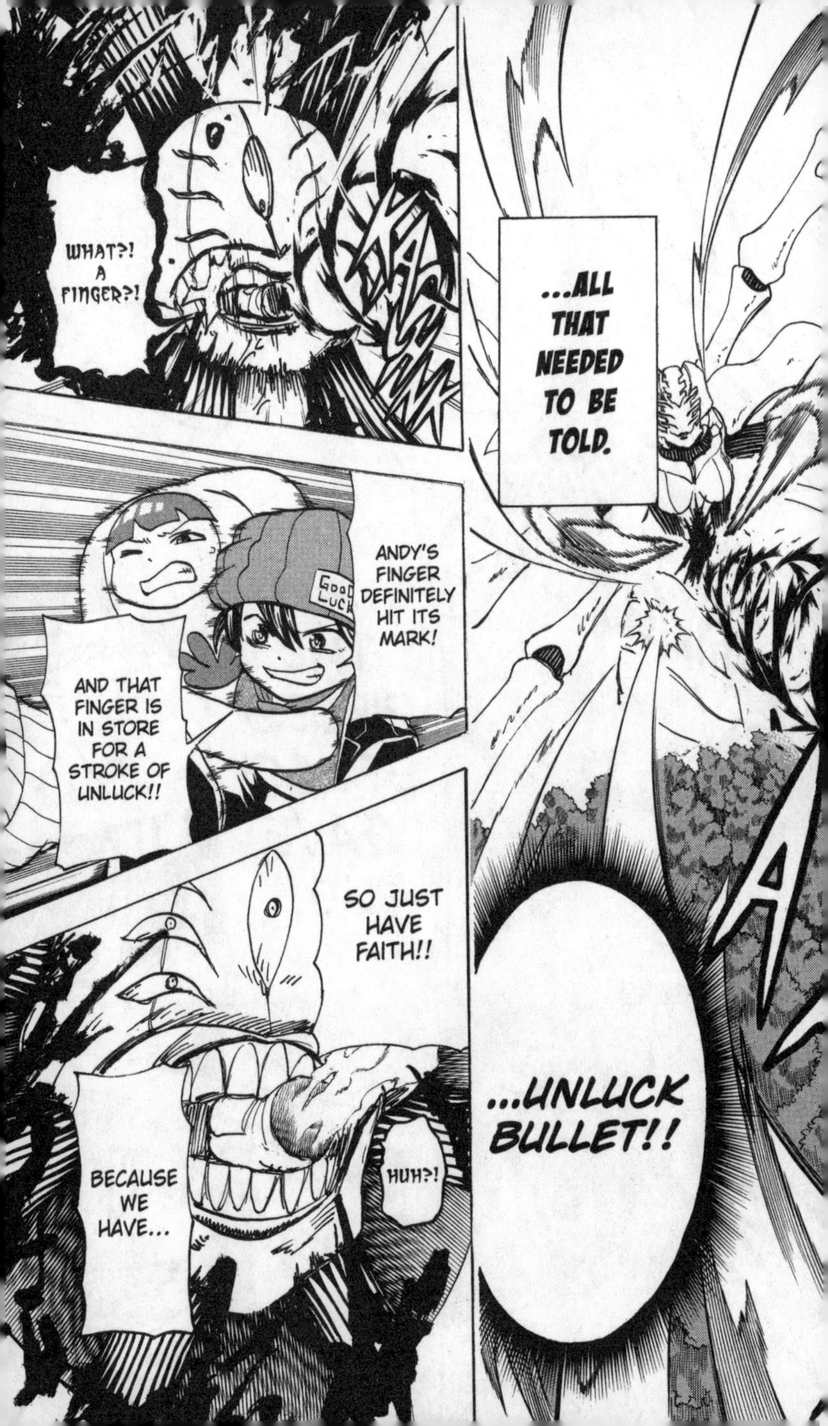
...ALL THAT NEEDED TO BE TOLD.
...UNLUCK BULLET!!
WHAT?! A FINGER?!
ANDY'S FINGER DEFINITELY HIT ITS MARK!
AND THAT FINGER IS IN STORE FOR A STROKE OF UNLUCK!!
SO JUST HAVE FAITH!!
HUH?!
BECAUSE WE HAVE...

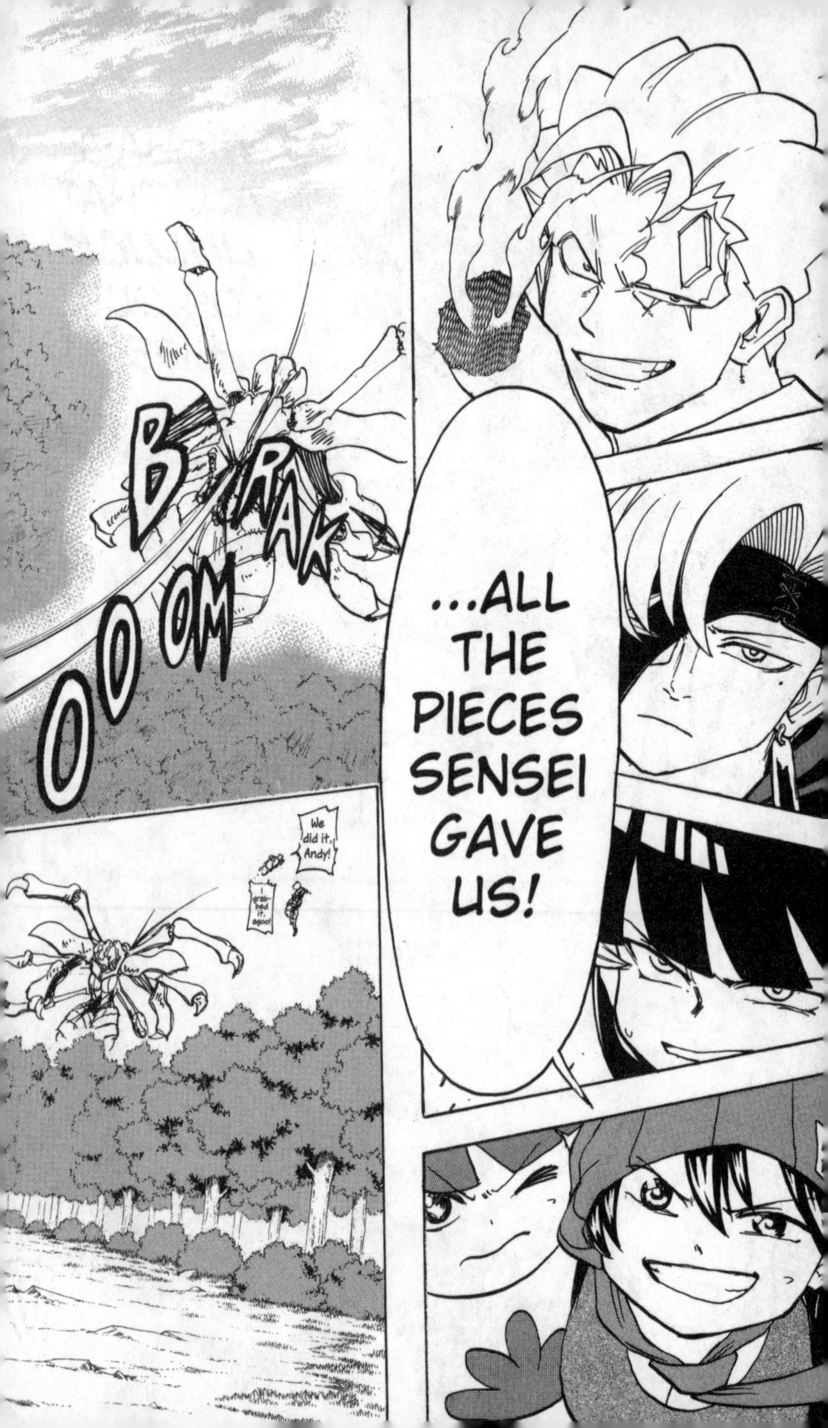
...ALL THE PIECES SENSEI GAVE US!
BRAK
BOOOM
We did it, Andy!
I grab-bed it, agoo!

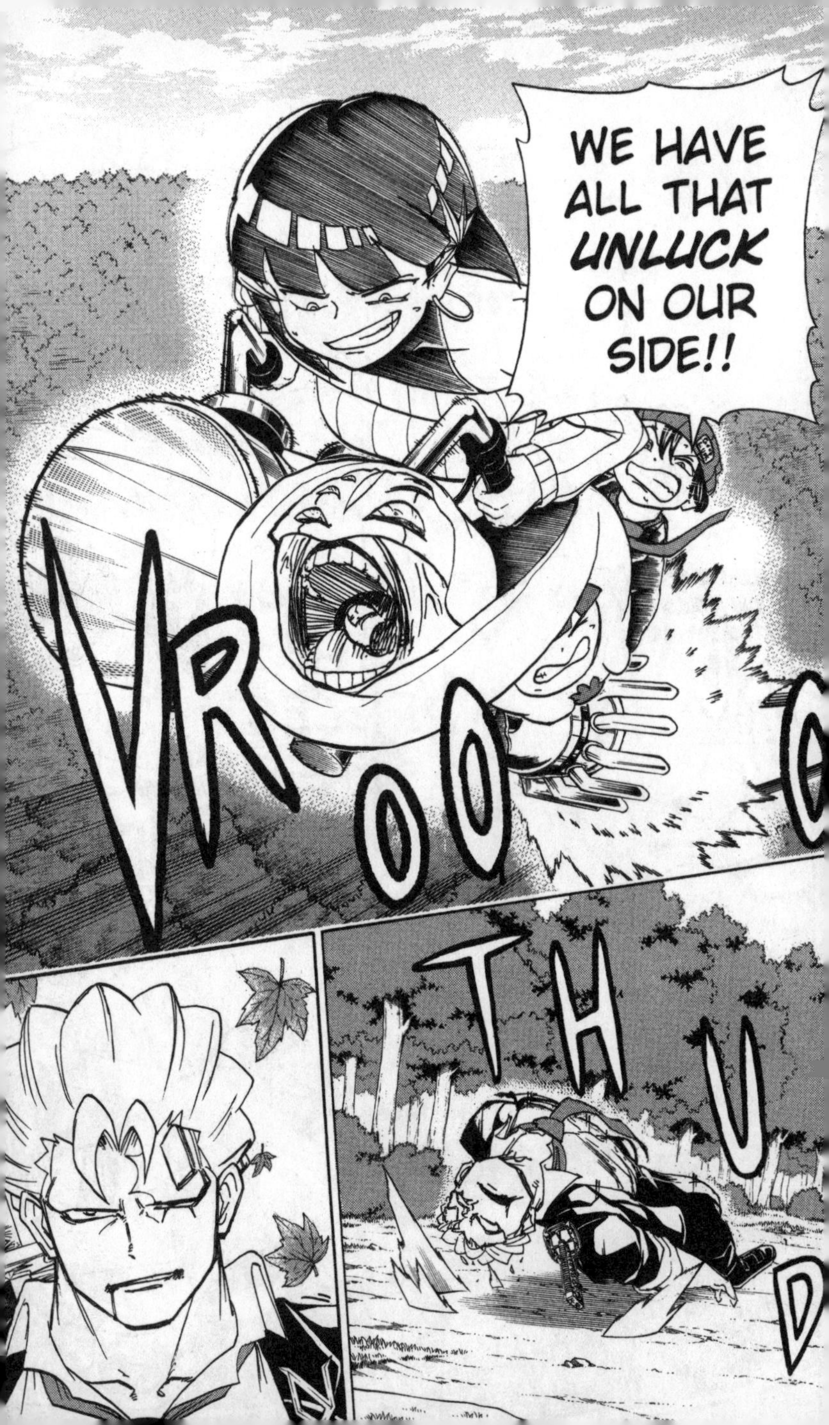
WE HAVE ALL THAT UNLUCK ON OUR SIDE!!
VROOOO
THUD

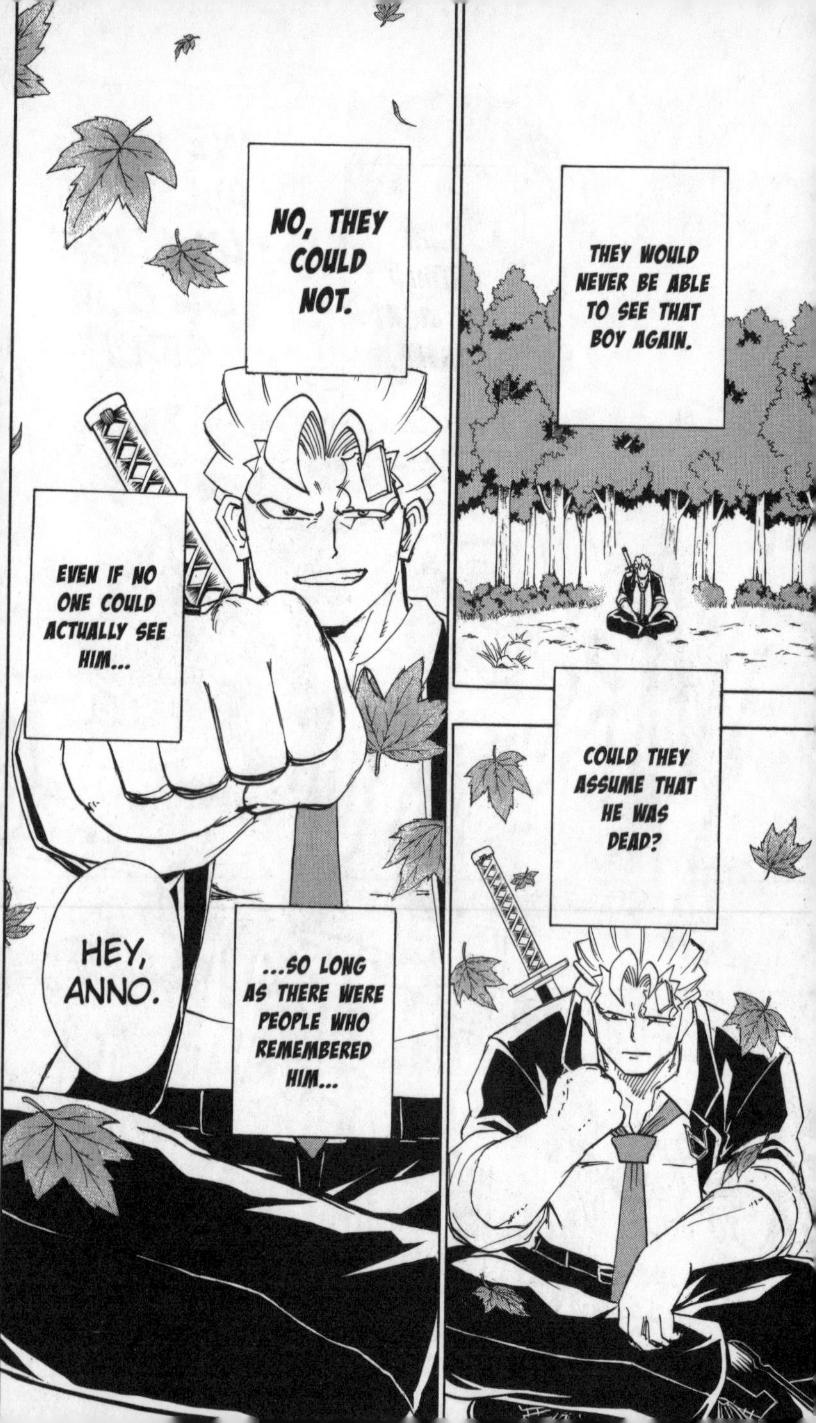
THEY WOULD NEVER BE ABLE TO SEE THAT BOY AGAIN.
COULD THEY ASSUME THAT HE WAS DEAD?
NO, THEY COULD NOT.
EVEN IF NO ONE COULD ACTUALLY SEE HIM...
...SO LONG AS THERE WERE PEOPLE WHO REMEMBERED HIM...
HEY, ANNO.

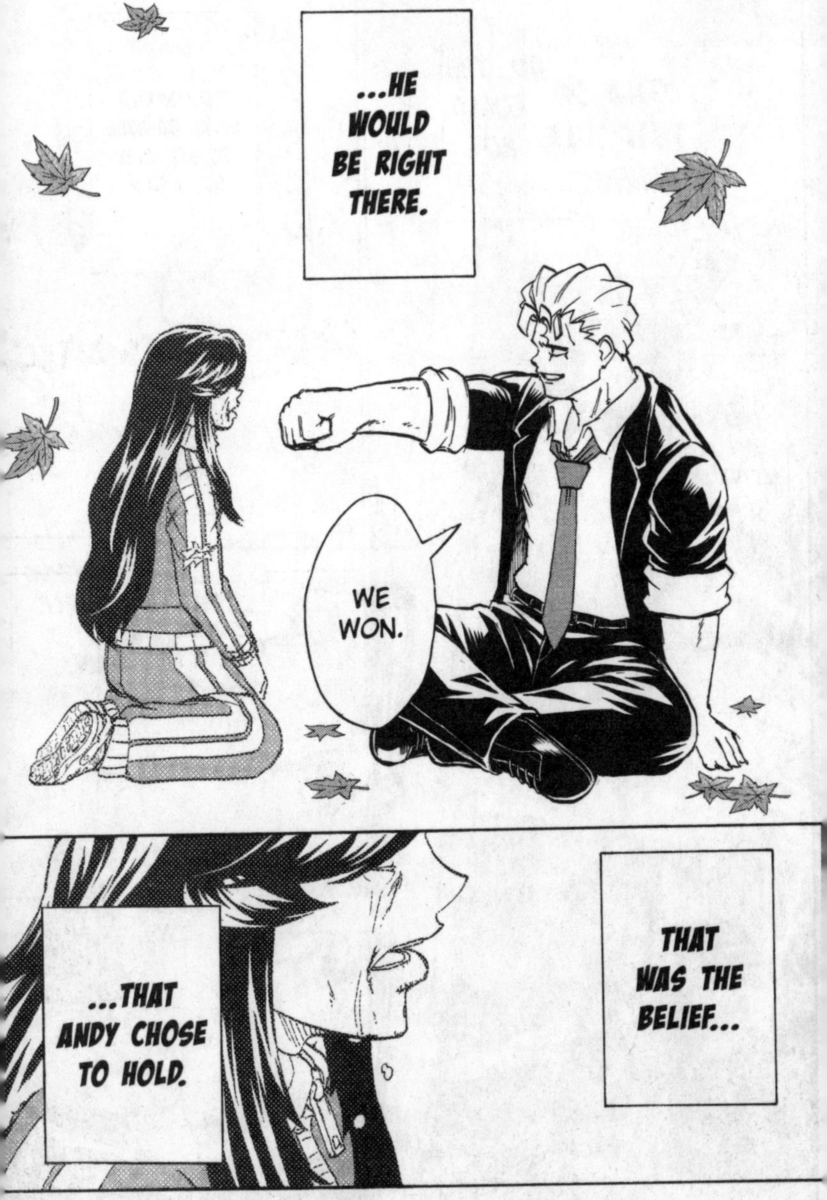
...HE WOULD BE RIGHT THERE.
WE WON.
THAT WAS THE BELIEF...
...THAT ANDY CHOSE TO HOLD.

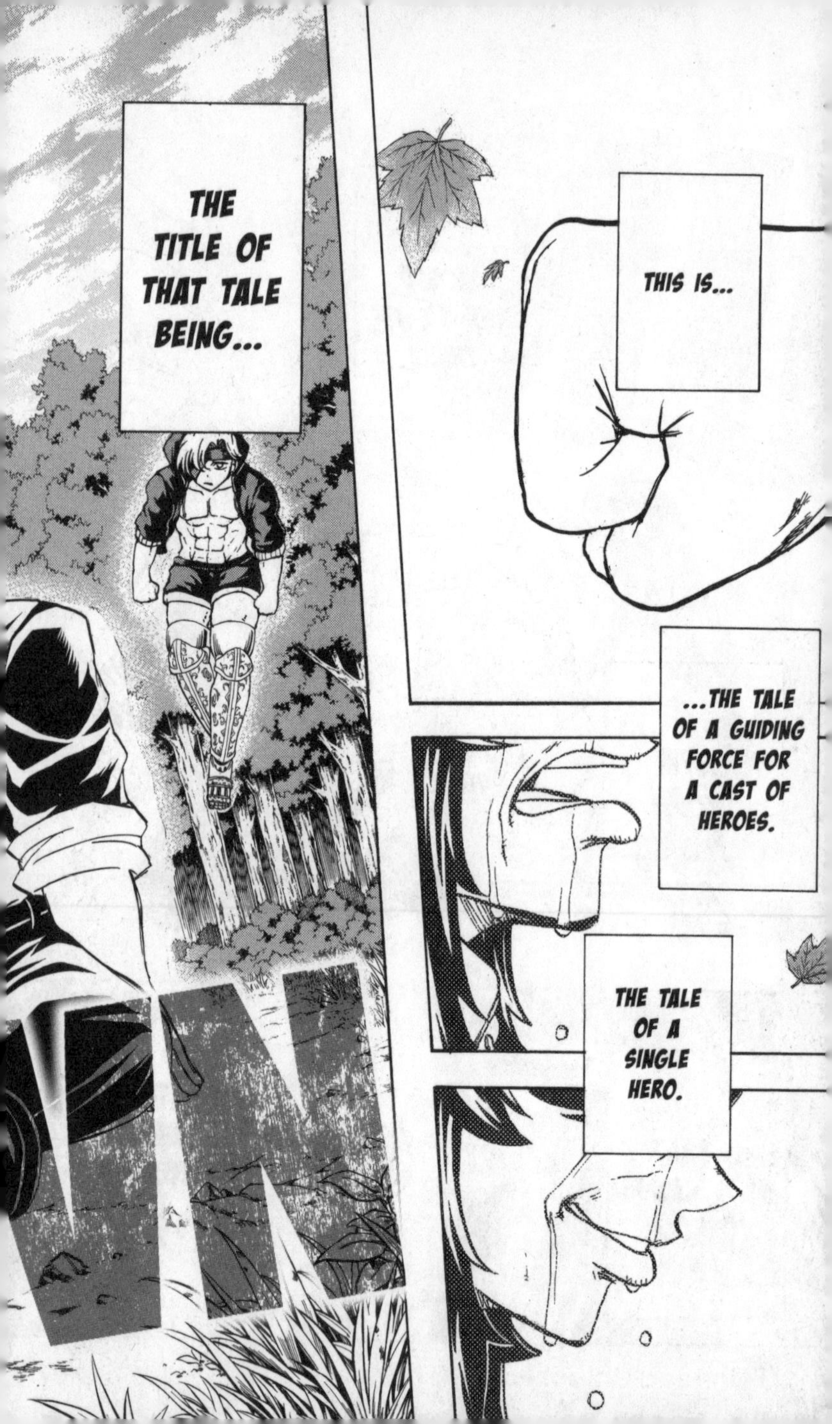
THIS IS...
...THE TALE OF A GUIDING FORCE FOR A CAST OF HEROES.
THE TALE OF A SINGLE HERO.
THE TITLE OF THAT TALE BEING...

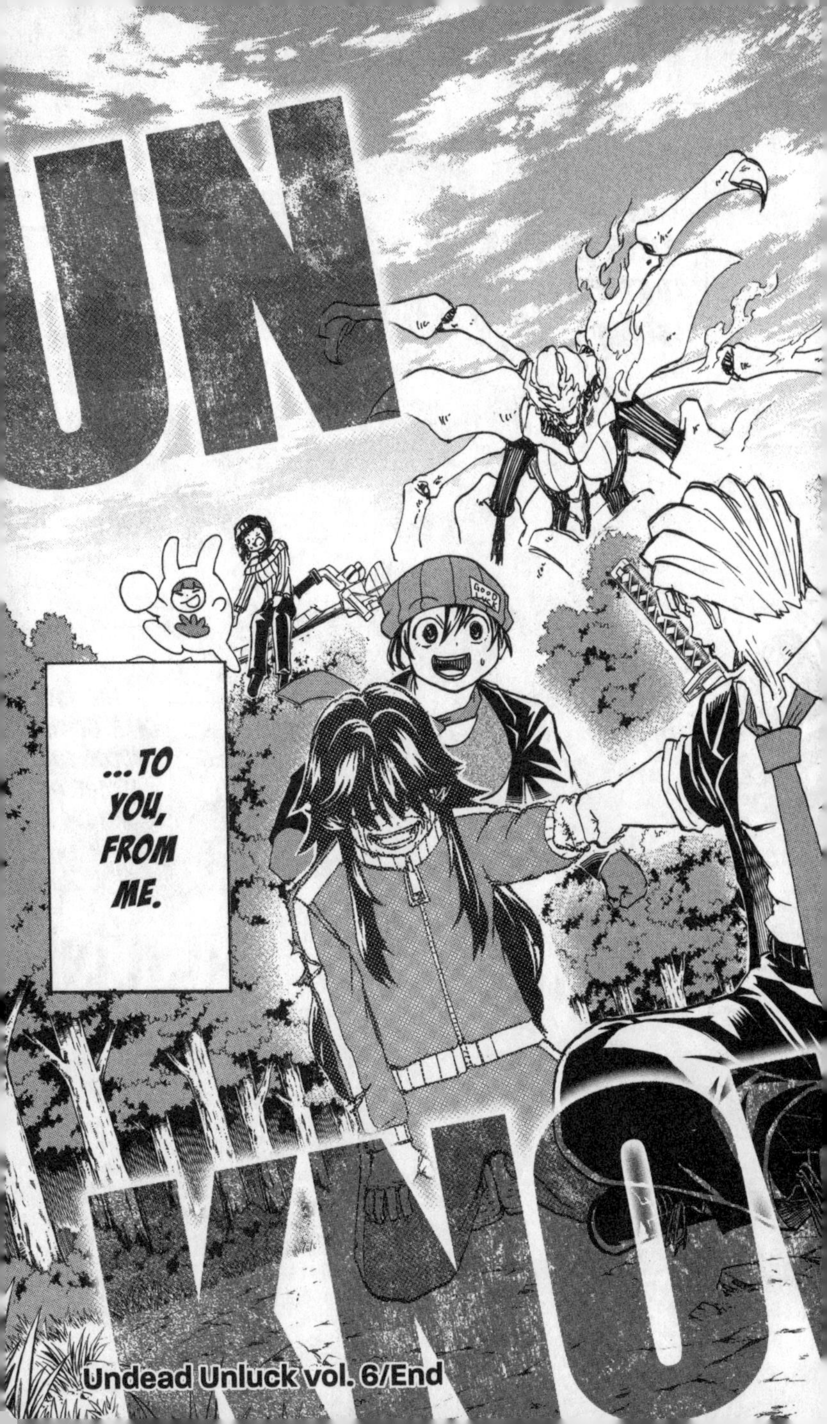
UN
...TO YOU, FROM ME.
Undead Unluck vol. 6/End

...ji Itadori is resolved to save the world from **cursed spirits** but he soon learns that the best way to do it is to slowly lose his **humanity** and become one himself!

JUJUTSU KAISEN

STORY AND ART BY
GEGE AKUTAMI

In a world where **cursed spirits** feed on unsuspecting humans, fragments of the legendary and feared demon **Ryomen Sukuna** were lost and scattered about. Should any demon consume Sukuna's body parts, the power they gain could **destroy the world** as we know it. Fortunately, there exists a mysterious school of **Jujutsu Sorcerers** who exist to protect the precarious existence of the living from the **supernatural!**

This is the LAST PAGE!

You're reading THE WRONG WAY!

UNDEAD UNLUCK reads from right to left, starting in the upper-right corner. Japanese is read from right to left, meaning that action, sound effects, and word-balloon order are completely reversed from English order.

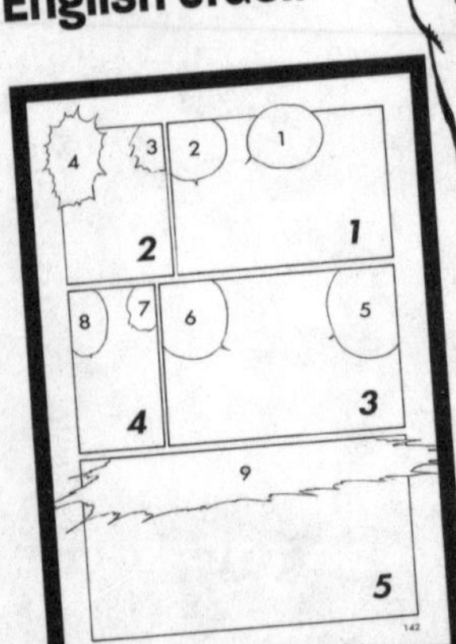

1
2
3
4
1
2
5
6
7
8
3
4
9
5
142

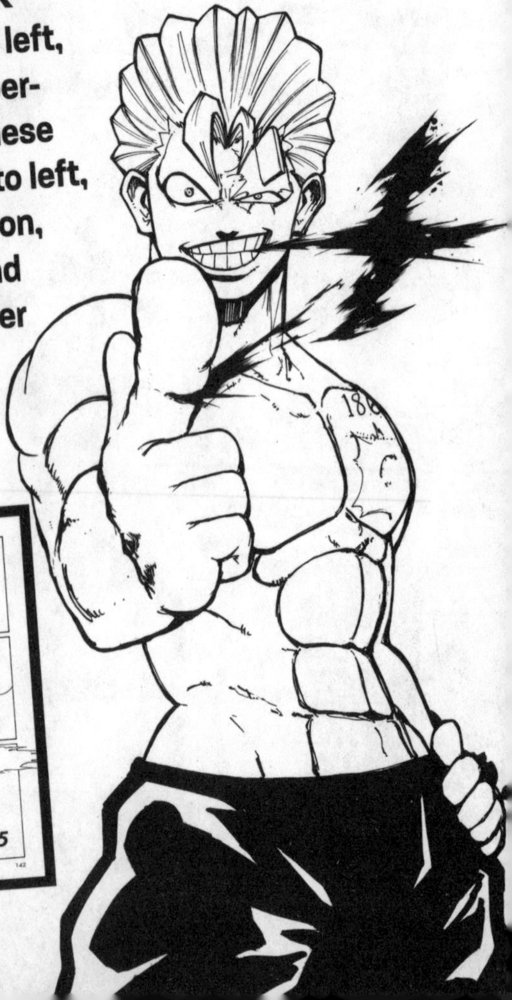